ORACLE 10g
The Database
with HTMLDB

ORACLE 10g
The Database
with HTMLDB

By
Ivan Bayross

BPB PUBLICATIONS
B-14, CONNAUGHT PLACE, NEW DELHI-1

FIRST INDIAN EDITION 2005

Distributors:

MICRO BOOK CENTRE
2, City Centre, CG Road,
Near Swastic Char Rasta,
AHMEDABAD-380009 Phone: 26421611

COMPUTER BOOK CENTRE
12, Shrungar Shopping Centre, M.G. Road,
BANGALORE-560001 Phone: 5587923, 5584641

MICRO BOOKS
Shanti Niketan Building, 8, Camac Street,
KOLKATTA-700017 Phone: 22826518, 22826519

BUSINESS PROMOTION BUREAU
8/1, Ritchie Street, Mount Road,
CHENNAI-600002 Phone: 28410796, 28550491

DECCAN AGENCIES
4-3-329, Bank Street,
HYDERABAD-500195 Phone: 24756400, 24756967

MICRO MEDIA
Shop No. 5, Mahendra Chambers, 150 D.N. Road,
Next to Capital Cinema V.T. (C.S.T.) Station,
MUMBAI-400001 Ph.: 22078296, 22078297

BPB PUBLICATIONS
B-14, Connaught Place, **NEW DELHI-110001**
Phone: 23325760, 23723393, 23737742

INFO TECH
G-2, Sidhartha Building, 96 Nehru Place,
NEW DELHI-110019
Phone: 26438245, 26415092, 26234208

INFO TECH
Shop No. 2, F-38, South Extension Part-1
NEW DELHI-110049
Phone: 24691288, 24641941

BPB BOOK CENTRE
376, Old Lajpat Rai Market,
DELHI-110006 PHONE: 23861747

NOTE: THE CD-ROM INCLUDED WITH THE BOOK HAS NO COMMERCIAL VALUE AND CANNOT BE SOLD SEPARATELY.

Price : Rs. 240/-

ISBN 81-8333-044-4

Published by Manish Jain for BPB Publications, B-14, Connaught Place, New Delhi-110 001 and Printed by him at Pressworks, New Delhi.

Foreword

The Oracle Database Server is the world's largest selling RDBMS product. It is estimated that sales of Oracle database products account for around 80% of the RDBMSystems sold worldwide. These products are constantly undergoing change and evolving. Their cost of ownership is being brought down and their functionality ever expands. The current, version, of this product is Oracle 10g.

The natural language of this RDBMS product is ANSI SQL and PL/SQL, which is a superset of ANSI SQL.

This book has been written to address the needs of programmers who wish to have a ready reference book, with real life examples, which covers SQL and PL/SQL the core language of Oracle 10g including all its latest enhancements.

I've tried to use my extensive application development experience in Oracle to produce this book that should cover most of the areas that seem to puzzle programmers from time to time in their application development career.

I've chosen several key areas in commercial application development and addressed issues in these areas that most commercial application developers require. Concepts are built using simple language, examples have easily understood logic. Once grasped, this skill will allow commercial application developers to program in ANSI SQL and PL/SQL very quickly.

Additionally, there is a section devoted to creating Forms, Reports and Charts using the HTMLDB development framework introduced in Oracle 10g. HTMLDB allows creating database-centric web applications with just a few clicks. This section is very simply laid out. It has all the information required to create the framework in which forms, reports and charts can run. The greatest advantage of this is that all a client computer requires is a Web Browser to run an HTMLDB Application comprising of Forms, Reports and Charts. This section has been written to address the needs of programmers who wish to have a ready reference book, with real life examples, covering Master forms, Master/Detail forms, Reports and Charts built using HTMLDB to run on the Internet.

All commercial application areas have not been covered, indeed if I tried to do this I would probably fail because I myself have not yet experienced all aspects of commercial application development even though I've spent more than 30 years working in this domain. I think it's this very fact that keeps me working in this domain i.e. there's always some new business process to figure out and code for.

This foreword will not be complete without my thanking the many people who encouraged me and put up with the many revisions and updations of the manuscript with patience and tolerance.

My sincere **THANKS** go to:

- My publisher Mr. Manish Jain. He has brought enormous changes in my life. This is a debt of gratitude I will never be able to pay in full.

- Mr. Hansel Colaco who is in charge of quality control. Who personally took care that everything in the manuscript was rigidly bound to the specifications of our quality manual. You've done a really fine job.

- Mrs. Vaishali Shah who personally, laid out the manuscripts logic flow, tested the logic flow, grabbed the screens and structured much of the material. Vaishali without your tender, loving, care this manuscript would never have come together as it did. Your attention to detail was superb, you've done a really terrific job.

- Mr. Sharanam Shah the Tech lead on this project, your attention to detail in ANSI SQL syntax and its binding to HTML Forms, based commercial applications, is excellent, you've done a splendid job.

- The many SQL programmers who read this material, without you all I would not be an author. I welcome both your brickbats and bouquets. You can contact me via BpB, New Delhi else you could check out my web site appropriately named ivanbayross.com.

- Finally, my wife Cynthia who has always encouraged me whenever I thought that I'd never get a manuscript ready for publishing. You have always helped to keep my feet firmly on the ground, in you I am truly blessed.

Ivan N. Bayross

TABLE OF CONTENS

1. UNDERSTANDING THE FRAMEWORK

Programmers the world over are always looking for stable, tried and trusted, programming environments, that run on a standard O/s, network, framework to craft commercial applications with. A stable, tried and tested, programming environment that works well with an O/s, is runnable on a network, always goes a long way in ensuring an application that is scalable and secure.

These kind of stable, scaleable, environments are often called production environments. This means good quality, production level, code can be developed using such an environment.

Another vital ingredient of any commercial application today, is a **DataBase Management System** (i.e. DBMS). A DBMS is always used to store valid business data for future reference so that business managers can be empowered to make informed business decisions.

The Internet is the largest, heterogeneous, stable, network in existence today. Hence, it makes the most sense to craft commercial applications that can run successfully on the Internet.

This will permit any business entity to have worldwide reach in capturing, validating and storing its business data, irrespective of which part of the world the business model is being run in and which part of the world is being used to control and monitor the business processes of the business entity.

To recap, programmers the world over are really looking for the best programming environment, O/s, and DBMS from which to craft Internet enabled, commercial applications, to make use of the worlds biggest and most stable network.

Oracle Database and HTMLDB on M.S. Windows XP are two critical ingredients that permit Internet based, commercial applications, to be crafted, that run smoothly and successfully.

There cannot be a better choice of **R**elational-DBMS (i.e. RDBMS) than Oracle. This is an RDBMS perfectly suited for a commercial application developer's needs. This is an RDBMS that has stood the test of time and has matured into production strength, product over the years. It is robust, secure, scalable relatively easy to install and maintain on M.S. Windows and several other O/s as well.

Oracle HTML DB is a new feature of the Oracle Database 10g. It provides a declarative development framework for creating database-centric Web applications. Development is done using an online service. Deployment is done by simply downloading a run-time module and the application, then running it within the enterprise.

It combines rapid web application development with the power of the Oracle database. Its easy to use, browser based, application builder, enables developers and non-programmers to develop and deploy database driven web applications with minimal effort.

Oracle HTML DB will help consolidate the management and security of data currently scattered throughout the organization, in spreadsheets and personal databases. At the same time, access to information will be improved by making the data available to anyone with a web browser and appropriate authorization. M.S. Windows XP is a client O/s, that is standard, stable, scaleable, secure, multi user and multi tasking.

The above-mentioned framework can thus help build complete industrial strength, commercial applications.

To conclude the following framework will be setup:
❑ **M.S. Windows XP** as the **Operating System**
❑ **Oracle 10g Database** as the **RDBMS**
❑ **HTMLDB** as the web based programming environment

The framework in this material is deployed on the following two Servers:
❑ Orchid (192.168.0.2) – The **Application** Server (Using Oracle HTTP service and HTMLDB Engine)
❑ Lily (192.168.0.101) – The **Database** Server (Using Oracle Database 10g)

This simply means **two computers** are involved:
❑ **An Application Server** – HTMLDB and the Oracle HTTP Service will be installed on the computer named **Orchid**
❑ **Database Server** – Oracle Database 10g will be installed on the computer named **Lily**

Diagram 1.1 and diagram 1.2 depicts the physical framework that is going to be built.

Node Type	Windows Application Server
Host Name	Orchid
IP	192.168.0.2
Processor	Pentium IV 1.8 Ghz
RAM	512
O/S	M.S. Windows XP With SP2
Version	
HTMLDB	10g (Release 10.1.0.2.0)
HTTP Server	Apache Standalone (Release 9.0.4.0.0)

Node Type	Windows Database Server
Host Name	Lily
IP	192.168.0.101
Processor	AMD Athlon 2.8 Ghz
RAM	512
O/S	M.S. Windows XP With SP2
Version	
Database	10g (Release 10.1.0.2.0)

Diagram 1.1

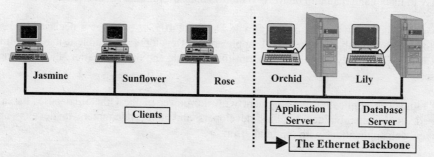

Diagram 1.2: The Complete Framework.

The Ethernet backbone could be cable, fiber optic, wireless, infrared, with hub, without hub, with Switch, without Switch and so on depending on whether the network topology is **bus** or **star**.

In this type of architecture the **clients** and **server/s** are **always connected** to one another when switched on and active.

In this framework, the applications created will be served by the Application Server (i.e. Orchid). The client machines (i.e. Jasmine, Sunflower and Rose) will be served using the Oracle HTTP service available on the Application Server (i.e. Orchid). The client machines using a client-based application called a **Web browser**, (i.e. *Internet Explorer, Netscape Communicator, Opera are examples*) can communicate with the Application Server (i.e. Orchid). The Data will be stored and accessed by the Application Server before serving it to the clients from the Database Server (i.e. Lily).

It is the **HTMLDB Engine** and the **Oracle HTTP Server** that setup a link between the clients and the database server thus allowing the communication to take place. The most common protocol (*language of communication*) used to set up this link is HTTP. The two applications **i.e.** Web browsers at the clients end and Web server software resident on the Application server communicate using a **Request / Response** paradigm. What this really means is that when a Web browser (i.e. the client machine) wishes to communicate with the Web server software it broadcasts such a request blindly to **port 7777** on which the HTMLDB Engine listens by default. The broadcast will contain the **ip** address of the Web server with which the Web browser wishes to communicate. All Web servers hear the broadcast but only the Web server whose **ip** is contained within the broadcast, replies.

Once the Web server replies it immediately terminates the link setup between the Web browser and itself. In fact the Web server immediately forgets which Web browser contacted it, hence the term **Reply/Response communication paradigm**.

This really means that there is no permanent link setup between the client and server computers. Any link setup is valid **only for the duration** of the Request and Reply paradigm. Primarily this is done to decongest network bandwidth and permit the millions of Web Browsers and Web servers to communicate freely and effectively on the Internet.

As can be seen, this really is a huge change from a standard wired Ethernet backbone used for commercial applications.

HOW THE FRAMEWORK WORKS

The basic Client / Server framework on the Internet is as shown in diagram 1.3.

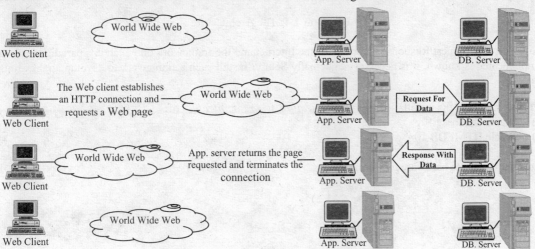

Diagram 1.3: The Request/Response Paradigm.

Apache is the web server software available on the **Application server** responsible for responding to requests received from client browsers for information. **Oracle** is the **database** in which such information is stored. **HTMLDB** is the **middleware**, programming environment of choice that can:
1. Respond to such information requests being processed by Apache, the Oracle HTTP Server
2. Access the Oracle database tables where the information requested is stored
3. Return the information requested to the client browser via Apache HTTP server
Thus servicing the client's request for information.

All this is because a HTTP server (*Apache*) **cannot communicate** directly with a database management system (*Oracle*) hence the HTMLDB Engine plays the role of mediator.

Decomposing The Server Side Architecture

Diagram 1.4 decomposes the Web server side framework that works together in harmony to respond to a client browser's request for information.

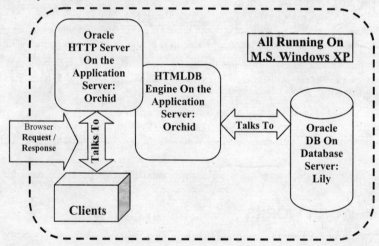

Diagram 1.4: The Architecture

Now that the Request/Response paradigm of the Internet and the framework on which this paradigm can be implemented is known, it is necessary to actually Setup / Install such a framework to develop applications on.

This will involve the installation (*and configuration, where applicable*) of:
❑   Oracle Database 10g
❑   Oracle HTMLDB 10g

On an appropriate hardware platform.

2. SETTING UP ORACLE DATABASE 10g

INSTALLING THE ORACLE 10g DATABASE SERVER

Oracle 10g Database, from Oracle Corporation, is an enhanced version of the Oracle 9i Database Server.

The installation of Oracle 10g Database Server is carried out via a CD-ROM. The installation process of Oracle 10g Database Server **depends** on the Operating System. Being a server based application, the setup tool that comes with Oracle 10g can automatically detect whether the operating system is Windows NT/XP or Windows 9x/ME. If the operating system belongs to the Windows 9x family the installation is terminated. For a Windows NT base operating system it commences with installing for **Oracle 10g Database**.

DOWNLOADING THE PRODUCT

Oracle Database 10g is available for download from the Oracle website **http://otn.oracle.com/software/products/database/oracle10g/index.html**. (Refer diagram 2.1)

 Note

> All software downloads from the oracle website are free and each comes with a development license that allows you to use full versions of the products only while developing and prototyping your applications. You can buy Oracle products with full-use licenses at any time from the online Oracle Store or from your Oracle sales representative.

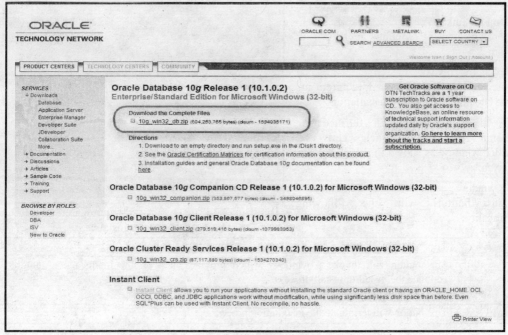

Diagram 2.1: Downloading Oracle 10g Database CD

INSTALLATION OF ORACLE DATABASE 10G ON WINDOWS

Insert the **CD-ROM** of the Oracle 10g Database on Windows into the CD-ROM drive on a Windows Server machine. The CD-ROM will auto run to display the window, as shown in diagram 2.2.

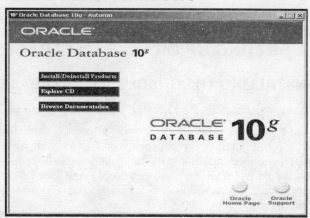

 Note

If the CD-ROM does not **autorun**, navigate to the **autorun** directory under the CD-ROM's root and double click on **autorun.exe**.

Diagram 2.2: Autorun window of Oracle 10g Database Server.

This window contains links described below:

Install/Deinstall Products	This link invokes the Oracle Database 10g installation kit.
Explore CD	This link will open the Windows Explorer to view the contents of the CD-ROM.
Browse Documentation	This link will open an Internet Browser (generally I.E.), which displays information about Oracle Database 10g installation and product tips which are in HTML format.
Oracle Home Page	This link will open an Internet Browser and attempt to connect to **www.oracle.com**.
Oracle Support	This link will open an Internet Browser and attempt to connect to **www.oracle.com/supports**.

Table 1.1

Click on the link **Install/Deinstall Products** to get a DOS console window as shown in diagram 2.3.

This window invokes the Oracle Universal Installer, and verifies the system requirements for the Oracle Database 10g installation.

When all requirements are fulfilled the Welcome screen for **Oracle Universal Installer** window as shown in diagram 2.4 is displayed.

This window as shown in diagram 2.4 contains buttons with the following functionality:

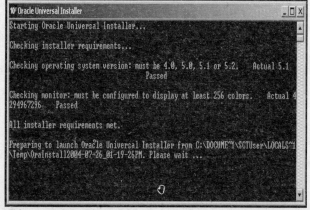

Diagram 2.3: The DOS based window initializing Oracle Universal Installer

Browse...	This button will invoke a dialog box with a directory listing.
Help	This button will invoke a window, which provides help on the inputs/action required to continue the install/uninstall process.
Next	This button will proceed to the next step in the installation process.
Cancel	This button will terminate the installation process.

Table 1.2

This screen allows two types of installation processes:

❑ Basic Installation
❑ Advanced Installation

When the **Basic Installation** option is selected, the screen accepts information related Oracle Home i.e. the destination, the Global Database Name and a common password for users such as SYS, SYSTEM, SYSMAN, and DBSNMP.

The **Destination** path i.e. Oracle Home Location can be changed as desired.

The **Advanced Installation** option can be used to give different passwords for different user accounts.

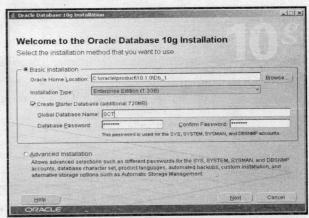

Diagram 2.4: The Welcome screen.

 Note

While creating this material the **Global Database name** was set to **SCT**.

After specifying the **Global Database Name**, click [Next] to continue.

A progress bar is displayed as shown in diagram 2.5.1. This progress bar depicts the loading progress of the installation process.

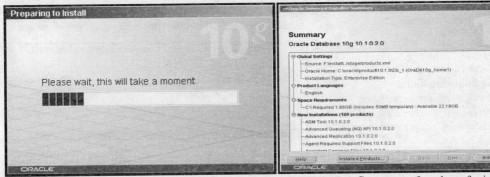

Diagram 2.5.1: Progress bar for the loading process.   **Diagram 2.6:** Summary of products for installation.

 Note

If Windows XP has Service Pack 2 installed then just after the loading process as seen in diagram 2.5.1 completes, a message box prompting a Windows Security Alert pops up. Refer diagram 2.5.2. This is because the Windows Firewall is active and is preventing a java based program from running. Since this alert has popped up while installing Oracle 10g, the java program can be unblocked. Click Unblock to proceed with the Oracle 10g installation.

Diagram 2.5.2: Windows Security Alert (SP2 Only).

After the loading process completes, a screen as shown in diagram 2.6 summarizes the settings for the installation that is going to be carried out now.

Click **Install** to start the actual transfer of files to their destination on the computer's HDD.

This window as shown in diagram 2.6 contains buttons with the following functionality:

Help	This button will invoke a window, which provides help on the inputs/action required to continue the install/uninstall process.
Installed Products...	This button will display a dialog box, which lists Oracle products installed on the machine previously.
Install	This button will start the actual transfer of files to their destination on the computer's HDD.
Cancel	This button will terminate the installation process.

The Installation starts as seen in diagram 2.7 indicating the progress of the installation.

This screen provides a **Stop installation...** button to terminate the file transfer during installation. Refer diagram 2.7.

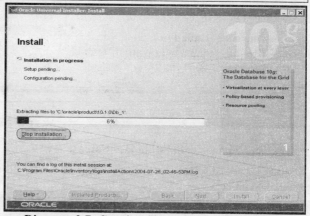

After the copying of files to their destination is complete, the installation process automatically proceeds to configuration of all installed tools. Refer diagram 2.8.

Diagram 2.7: Copying files to the destination path.

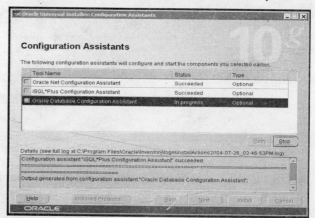

The auto-configuration process will configure the following tools:
- ❑ Oracle Net Configuration Assistant
- ❑ iSQL*Plus Configuration Assistant
- ❑ Oracle Database Configuration Assistant

A Windows Security Alert will pop up (Refer diagram 2.5.2) just before the Oracle **Database Configuration Assistant** begins. *This is only applicable for Windows XP Service Pack 2.*

Diagram 2.8: Auto-configuration for Oracle 10g tools.

While the **Oracle Database Configuration Assistant** is being configured a dialog box as shown in diagram 2.9.1 appears. This dialog box indicates the progress of the database creation.

This process is responsible for the actual database creation.

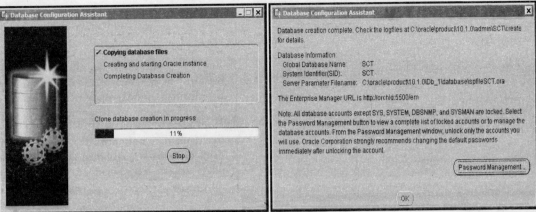

Diagram 2.9.1: Creation of Database.   **Diagram 2.9.2:** Completion of database configuration.

Once complete, a screen displaying a summary and an option to start the Password Management tool appears as seen in diagram 2.9.2.

Click the **Password Management** button present on the lower right corner and unlock the **SCOTT** user account by removing the tick mark as shown in diagram 2.9.3.

*This is because the examples in this material will be generated using the **SCOTT schema**.*

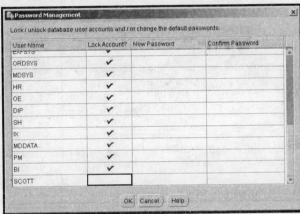

Diagram 2.9.3: Unlocking SCOTT user account via the Password Management Tool.

Click **OK** and this will take back to the screen as seen in diagram 2.9.2. Now click **OK** and a screen as shown in diagram 2.9.4 appears. Click **Next**.

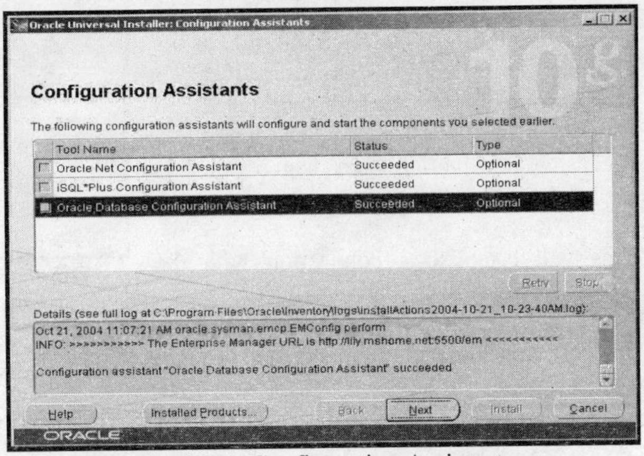

Diagram 2.9.4: Configuration Assistant screen

That's the end of a successful installation. A message for the same appears as shown in diagram 2.10.1.

This window informs the following:
- The **place** where the database has been installed
  URLs For The Following:
- Ultra Search
  http://ORCHID:5620/ultrasearch
- Ultra Search Administration Tool
  http://ORCHID:5620/ultrasearch/admin
- iSQL*Plus
  http://ORCHID:5560/isqlplus
- Enterprise Manager Database Control
  http://ORCHID:5500/em

These are some of the **GUI tools** provided by Oracle 10g. The URLs need to be noted down for using them later.

Click [Exit]. This will display a confirmation dialog box to exit the installation tool, as shown in diagram 2.10.2. Click [Yes] to end the installation.

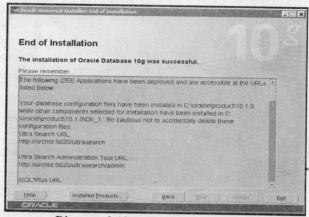

Diagram 2.10.1: Installation complete.

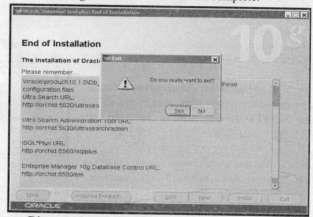

Diagram 2.10.2: Confirmation to Exit the installer.

After exiting from the Oracle Database 10g installation a window as shown in the diagram 2.11.1 automatically appears in the default Web browser.

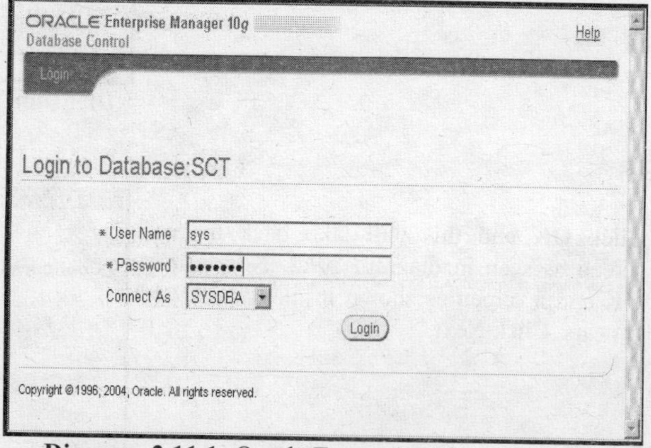

This is the Oracle Enterprise Manager, which will allow configuring service names, listeners, users and so on. Login using **SYS** as the **User Name**, provide the **Password** specified earlier and select **SYSDBA** in the **Connect As** dropdown List-box, screens as seen in diagram 2.11.2 and diagram 2.11.3 appears. In the first screen: The Oracle 10g Licensing Information, (i.e. diagram 2.11.2) click **I Agree**.

This will establish a connection with the Oracle Database 10g.

For now close the enterprise manager window.

Diagram 2.11.1: Oracle Enterprise Manager Login.

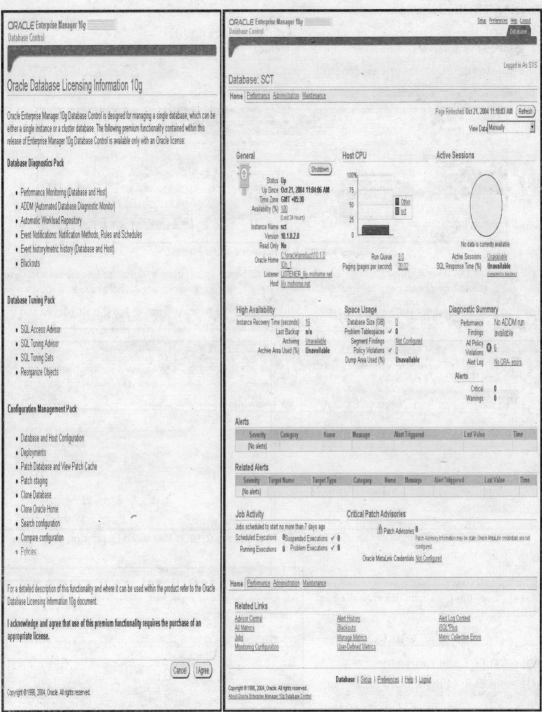

Diagram 2.11.2: Oracle Enterprise
Manager Licensing Information

Diagram 2.11.3: Oracle Enterprise Manager

Testing The Installation

Invoke SQL Plus, the interactive tool of Oracle as: (Refer diagram 2.12.1)

Start→Programs→Oracle – OracleDB10g_home1→Application Development→SQL Plus

This will start the SQL Plus tool as seen in diagram 2.12.2

The tool prompts for a user name, password and the connection string.

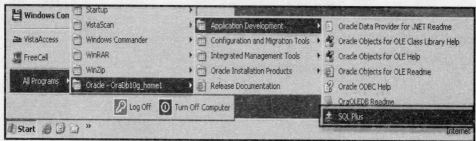

Diagram 2.12.1: Invoking SQL Plus.

Enter **scott** as the **user name** and **tiger** as the **password**. Since an attempt to login to Oracle on the same machine is made there is no need to enter the connection string. (Refer diagram 2.12.2)

The first time the user **scott** logs in, a message indicating that the password has expired is displayed and the system prompts for the old and new password as shown in diagram 2.12.3.

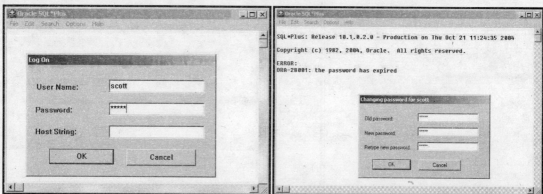

Diagram 2.12.2: Logging in as user scott.   **Diagram 2.12.3:** Password Expiration of the user scott.

Enter the old password as **tiger** and the new password as **tiger** as well. (Refer diagram 2.12.3)

Fire an SQL query at the SQL prompt as:

SQL> SELECT * FROM TAB;

SQL> SELECT * FROM DEPT;

The output appears on the screen indicating the successful installation of Oracle Database 10g. (Refer diagram 2.12.4)

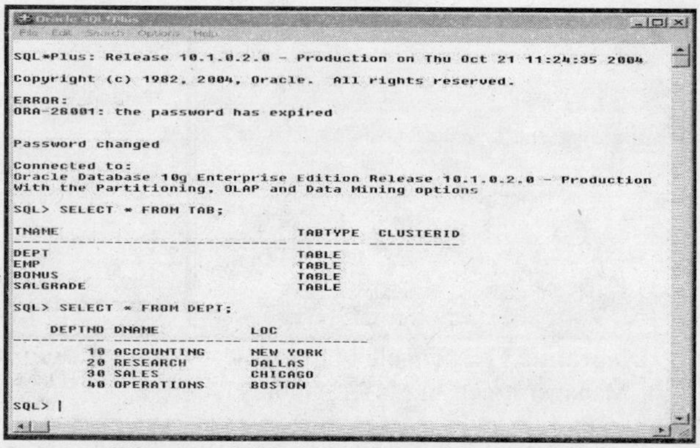

Diagram 2.12.4: Querying the database.

INSTALLATION OF ORACLE 10g ON A CLIENT MACHINE

Insert **CD-ROM** for the Oracle 10g Client into the CD-ROM drive on a Windows based machine. The CD-ROM will auto run to display the Autorun window as shown in diagram 2.13.1.

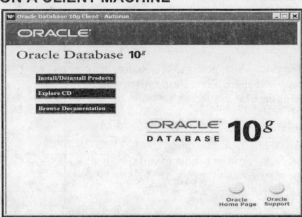

Note

> If the CD-ROM does not **autorun**, navigate to the **autorun** directory under the CD-ROM's root and double click on **autorun.exe**.

Diagram 2.13.1: The Welcome screen.

Click on the link [Install/Deinstall Products] to get a DOS console window as shown in diagram 2.13.2.

This window invokes the Oracle Universal Installer and verifies the system requirements for the Oracle 10g Client installation.

When all requirements are fulfilled the Oracle 10g Splash screen is displayed for a brief moment. Refer diagram 2.13.3.

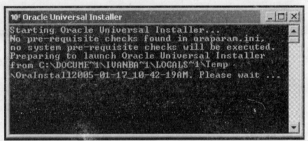

Diagram 2.13.2: The DOS based window initializing Oracle Universal Installer

Diagram 2.13.3: The Splash Screen.

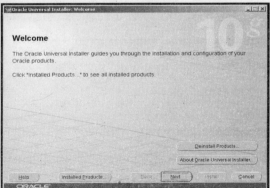

Diagram 2.14: The Welcome screen.

While the splash screen is being displayed, the Oracle 10g installation kit is invoked in memory. On completion, the Welcome screen for **Oracle Universal Installer** window as shown in diagram 2.14 is displayed.

The next screen accepts information related to the location of the source and destination of files transferred during installation. Refer diagram 2.15.

The path, which points to the Source, can be kept unchanged. The **Destination** path can be changed as desired.

After browsing to the appropriate directory for **Destination** files, click [Next]. A products list from **products.xml** specified in the **Source** field will now load into the Client machine.

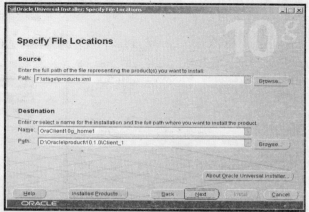

Diagram 2.15: Select the File Locations

Note

During the loading process, the installation kit will identify the Operating System running on the computer.

The next screen, as shown in diagram 2.16.1, prompts the type of installation based on the following options:

- InstantClient (83MB): Installs the instant Client software
- Administrator (460MB): Installs management tools with communication tools
- Runtime (218MB): Installs communication tools
- Custom: Allows manual selection of products and services to be installed

Select the **Administrator** option and click [Next] to continue.

The installation will start loading the initial tools and utilities required to proceed. The progress bar at the top right corner of the screen indicates this. Refer diagram 2.16.2.

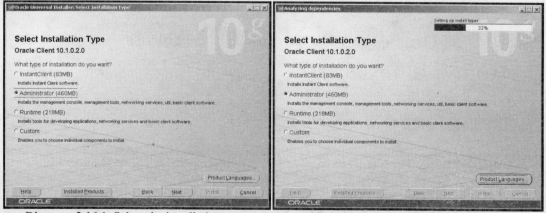

Diagram 2.16.1: Select the installation type.   **Diagram 2.16.2:** Loading initial tools.

After the loading of the required tools completes, a summary screen will appear as shown in diagram 2.17. This screen displays a list of products and settings that have been selected for installation.

Click **Install** to start the actual transfer of files to their destination on the computer's HDD.

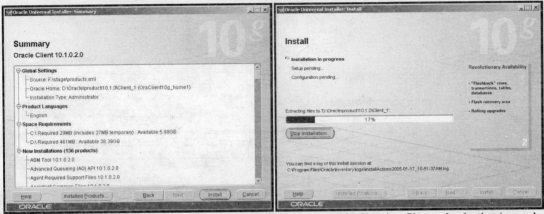

Diagram 2.17: Summary of products for installation. **Diagram 2.18:** Copying files to the destination path.

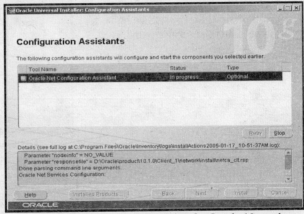

The next screen indicates the progress of the installation. This screen only provides a **Stop installation...** button to terminate the file transfer during installation. Refer diagram 2.18.

After the copying of files to their destination is complete, the installation process will automatically proceed to configuration of all installed tools. Refer diagram 2.19.

Diagram 2.19: Auto-configuration for Oracle 10g tools.

*If the configuration process hangs or does not respond while configuring the Oracle Net Configuration Assistant then click **STOP** and then **RETRY** to restart the configuration. Otherwise the Net Configuration Assistant can also be invoked later on using Start → All Programs → Oracle - OraClient10g home1 → Configuration and Migration Tools → Net Configuration Assistant.*

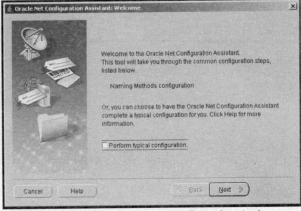

During the configuration process, the **Oracle Net Configuration Assistant** wizard appears as shown in the diagram 2.20.1. The wizard starts with the configuration of **Naming Methods**. Click **Next**.

Diagram 2.20.1: Oracle Net Configuration Assistant.

The window dealing with Naming Method Configuration appears as shown in the diagram 2.20.2. It shows the recommended naming methods prescribed for the client machine.

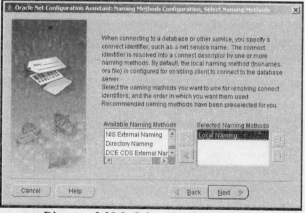

Click [Next] to get a screen as shown in diagram 2.20.3.

Diagram 2.20.2: Select Naming Methods.

This screen prompts for the service name for the database. Enter the service name as **SCT** and click [Next] to get the screen as shown in the diagram 2.20.4.

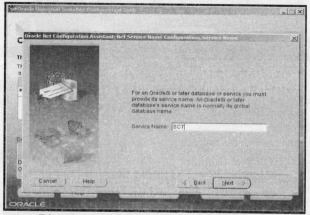

Diagram 2.20.3: Prompt for a Service Name.

Select an appropriate network protocol from the options provided, to allow communication with the database server over the network.

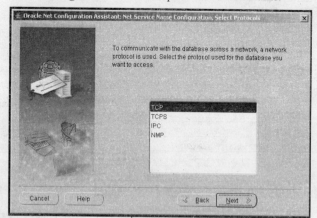

Diagram 2.20.4: Select the network protocol.

Click [Next ⟩] to get a screen as shown in diagram 2.20.5. This screen accepts information related to the computer hosting the database server.

Enter the IP address belonging to the computer hosting the database server in the **HostName** field. Also specify the **PortNumber** at which the database server will respond.

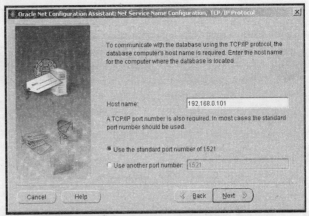

Diagram 2.20.5: Provide the IP or Host Name.

Tip

The **HostName** field could also hold a string. This is possible by binding the string with the **ip** address of the computer hosting the database server by making appropriate entries in the host file on the client computer, **found** **at** **C:\WINDOWS\SYSTEM32\DRIV ERS\ETC\HOSTS.**

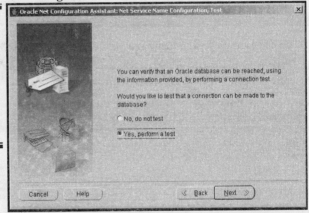

Diagram 2.20.6: Performing a Connection Test.

Click [Next ⟩]. A screen as shown in diagram 2.20.6 appears. This provides an option to test the connection between the Oracle client and the database residing on the server.

Select the option **Yes, perform a test** and click [Next] to continue.

The next screen displays the result of the test. If the connection is successful, the screen will appear as shown in diagram 2.20.7.1.

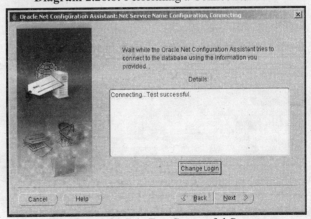

Diagram 2.20.7.1: Test Successful Screen.

Caution

Usually the default login used in the attempt to connect to the database server is **system**. As the passwords were reset / changed during the Oracle Installation, the connection may not succeed as shown in the diagram 2.20.7.2.

To overcome this problem use the user name as **scott** and password as **tiger** which is the default user always provided with the oracle installation.

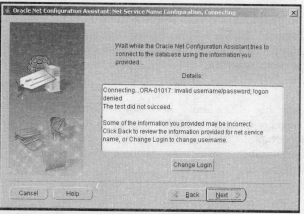

Diagram 2.20.7.2: Connection Failed.

To change the login name, click on `Change Login` to get a dialog box as shown in diagram 2.20.7.3. Enter the **Username** as **scott** and its **Password** as **tiger**. Click `OK` to retest the connection.

After passing an appropriate login id and password to the Oracle Database Server click `Next` to get a screen as shown in diagram 2.20.8.

This screen accepts a net service name. Provide an appropriate name and click

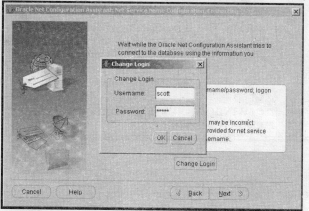

Diagram 2.20.7.3: Changing the login information.

`Next` to get a screen as shown in diagram 2.20.9. *This name will now be used to connect to the database server via the SQL *PLUS client using the connection string as SCT.*

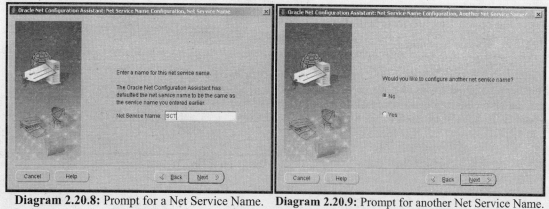

Diagram 2.20.8: Prompt for a Net Service Name.   **Diagram 2.20.9:** Prompt for another Net Service Name.

This screen provides an option to create another Oracle Net Connection. Select the option **No.** Click `Next`.

A screen indicating that the **Net Service Name** configuration is completed will appear as shown in diagram 2.20.10.

Click ⬜ Next ⬜ to get a screen indicating that the Naming Methods Configuration is complete as shown in the diagram 2.20.11.

Click ⬜ Next ⬜ to get a screen indicating that the **Oracle Net Configuration** is completed as shown in diagram 2.20.12.

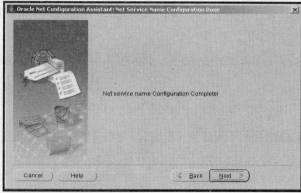

Diagram 2.20.10: Net service name configuration complete.

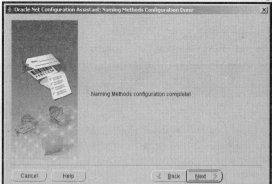

Diagram 2.20.11: Naming Methods Configuration complete.

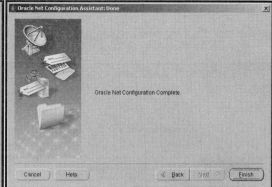

Diagram 2.20.12: Oracle Net Configuration complete.

After the configuration of Oracle 10g tools is successfully completed, the **End of Installation** screen as shown in diagram 2.21.1 appears.

Click ⬜ Exit ⬜.

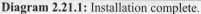

Diagram 2.21.1: Installation complete.

Diagram 2.21.2: Confirmation to Exit the installer.

This will confirm exiting the installation tool, as shown in diagram 2.21.2. Click on Yes to end the installation.

After exiting the installation of Oracle 10g, the **Oracle Enterprise Manager** window appears.

This is the Oracle Enterprise Manager, which will allow configuring service names, listeners, users and so on. For now this window can simply be closed.

CONNECTING A CLIENT TO THE ORACLE SERVER

Once an Oracle client has a Net Service Name pointing to a database server, it is possible for the Oracle client to access resources stored on the database server. Access to any resource will be based on a login ID and password.

To access the resources of the database server follow the steps mentioned below.

Invoke SQL Plus, the interactive tool of Oracle as: (Refer diagram 2.22.1.1)
   Start → All Programs → Oracle – OraClient10g_home1 → Application Development → SQL Plus

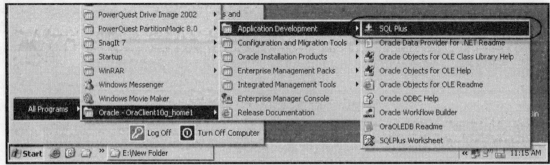

Diagram 2.22.1.1: Invoking SQL Plus when installed with the Administrator option.

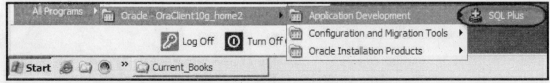

Diagram 2.22.1.2: Invoking SQL Plus when installed with the Runtime option.

This will start the SQL Plus tool as seen in diagram 2.22.2

The tool prompts for a user name, password and the connection string.

Enter **scott** as the **user name** and **tiger** as the **password** and **SCT** as the connection string. Since an attempt to login to the Oracle Database on a remote machine is made there is a need to enter the connection string (which was created while installing Oracle 10g Client as seen in Diagram 2.20.8). (Refer diagram 2.12.2)

This connection string contains information about the Oracle Database Server, its location i.e. the IP Address via which a connection can be made.

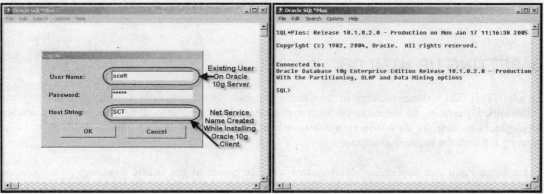

Diagram 2.22.2: Logging in as user scott.   **Diagram 2.22.3:** A valid Oracle login.

If the values entered in the **Log On** dialog box are valid, then the SQL *Plus window appears as shown in diagram 2.22.3.

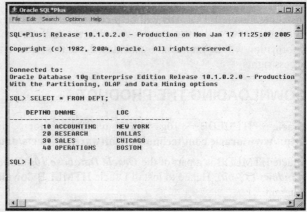

Fire an SQL query at the SQL prompt as:

SQL> SELECT * FROM DEPT;

The output appears on the screen indicating a successful connection to the remote Oracle Database from a client machine. (Refer diagram 2.22.4)

Diagram 2.22.4: Querying the database.

3. SETTING UP HTMLDB

Oracle HTML DB is a new feature of the Oracle Database 10g. It provides a declarative development framework for creating database-centric Web applications. Development is done using an online service. Deployment is done by downloading a run-time module and the application via the Internet and then running it within the business enterprise.

It combines rapid web application development with the power of the Oracle database. Its easy to use browser based application builder enables developers and non-programmers to develop and deploy database driven, web applications in very little time.

Installing Oracle HTML DB will help consolidate the management and security of data currently scattered throughout the organization in spreadsheets and personal databases. At the same time, access to information will be improved by making the data available to anyone with a Web browser and appropriate access rights.

DOWNLOADING THE PRODUCT

Oracle HTMLDB 10g is available for download from the Oracle website **http://www.oracle.com/technology/software/products/database/oracle10g/htdocs/winsoft.html**.

Oracle HTMLDB is a part of the ***Oracle Database 10g Companion CD Release 1 (10.1.0.2) for Microsoft Windows (32-bit)***. Hence to install Oracle HTMLDB download the **10g_win32_companion.zip** file. Refer diagram 3.1.

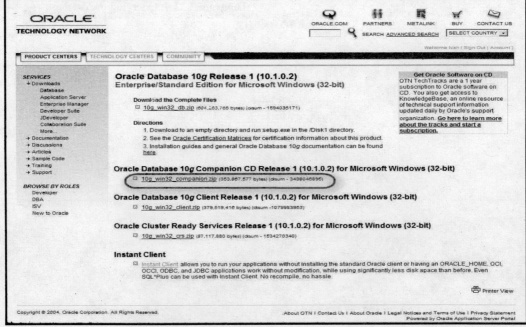

Diagram 3.1: Downloading Oracle 10g Companion CD

Note

All software downloads from the Oracle website are free, and each comes with a development license that allows the use of full versions of the products **only** while developing and prototyping applications. Oracle products with full-use licenses can be bought at any time from the online Oracle Store or from any Oracle sales representative.

Once downloaded burn the contents of the zip file on to a CDROM.

BEGINNING THE INSTALLATION

The installation of Oracle 10g HTMLDB is carried out via the CD-ROM. The installation process **depends** on the **Operating System**. The setup tool that comes with Oracle 10g can automatically detect whether the operating system is Windows NT/XP or Windows 9x/ME. If the operating system belongs to the Windows 9x family the installation is terminated. For a Windows NT based operating system the installation of **Oracle 10g HTMLDB** commences.

Insert the Oracle 10g Companion **CD-ROM** into the CD-ROM drive on a Windows Server machine. The CD-ROM will auto run to display the window, as shown in diagram 3.2.

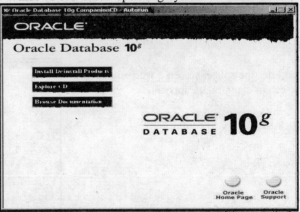

Note

If the CD-ROM does not **autorun**, navigate to the **autorun** directory under the CD-ROM's root and double click on **autorun.exe**.

Diagram 3.2: Autorun window of Oracle Database 10g Companion CDROM.

This window contains links described below:

Install/Deinstall Products	This link invokes the Oracle Database 10G installation kit.
Explore CD	This link will open Windows Explorer to view the contents of the CD-ROM.
Browse Documentation	This link will open an Internet Browser (generally **I.E.**), which displays information about Oracle Database 10G installation and product tips which are in HTML format.
Oracle Home Page	This link will open an Internet Browser and attempt to connect to **www.oracle.com**.
Oracle Support	This link will open an Internet Browser and attempt to connect to **www.oracle.com/support**.

Table 3.1

Click on the link [Install/Deinstall Products] to get a DOS console window as shown in diagram **3.3**.

This window invokes the Oracle Universal Installer, which verifies the system requirements for Oracle 10g Companion Disk installation.

When all requirements are fulfilled the Welcome screen for **Oracle Universal Installer** window as shown in diagram 3.4 is displayed.

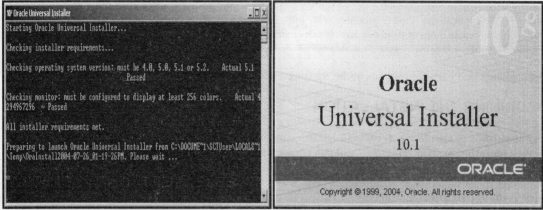

Diagram 3.3: The DOS based window initializing Oracle Universal Installer

Diagram 3.4: The Oracle Universal Installer

Just after the splash screen a welcome screen as seen in diagram 3.5 appears.

Click Next to continue.

The screen as shown in diagram 3.6 is displayed which contains the following buttons:

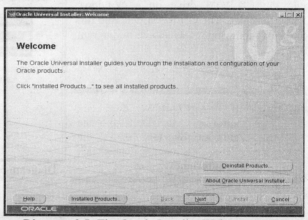

Diagram 3.5: The Oracle Installer Welcome screen

Browse...	This button will invoke a dialog box with a directory listing.
Help	This button will invoke a window, which provides help on the inputs/action required to continue the install/uninstall process.
Next	This button will proceed to the next step in the installation process.
Cancel	This button will terminate the installation process.

Table 3.2

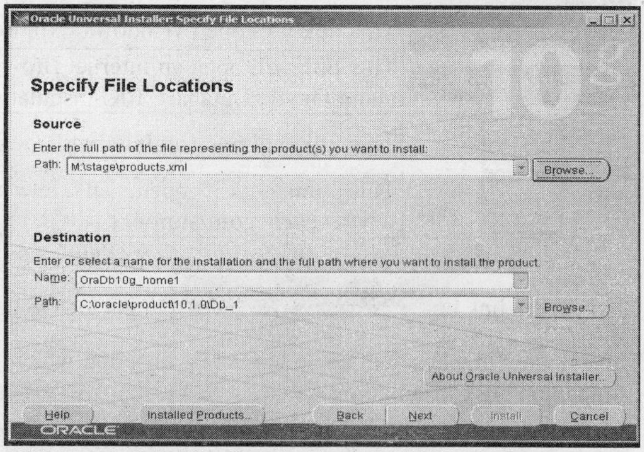

Diagram 3.6: The Oracle Specify File Locations screen

This screen accepts the source, installation name and the destination.

By default Oracle Installer displays the last destination path used in any previous installations. HTMLDB can only be installed in a different Oracle Home and thus a different destination has to be selected.

Change the **Destination Name** to OraDb10g_home2 and the **Destination Path** to <Path>\Db_2. Leave the source path unchanged.

Click Next to continue.

Diagram 3.7: Select A Product To Install screen

A screen as shown in diagram 3.7 appears. This screen prompts for a product selection. Select the second option i.e. **Oracle Database 10g Companion Products 10.1.0.2.0.** Click Next to continue.

A screen as shown in diagram 3.8 appears.

This screen will prompt for the product's component selection. Select both the components as seen in diagram 3.8. Click Next to continue.

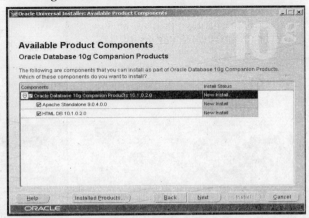

Diagram 3.8: Available Product Components screen

The installer will now prompt for some HTMLDB configuration information. (Refer diagram 3.9)

Enter the information as:

HostName: 192.168.0.101 (IP address of the machine hosting Oracle Database 10g)

For machines having more than one network adapter, specify the IP address of the adapter which is active (ENABLED) and in use.

Port: 1521 (Default). Leave this unchanged.

Database Service Name: SCT (The Oracle SID given while installing Oracle Database 10g)

SYS Password / HTML DB Password: *******
(User Choice)

TABLESPACE Name: SYSAUX (Default). Leave this unchanged.

Click Next to get a summary of the installation as seen in diagram 3.10

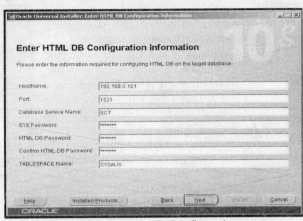

Diagram 3.9: HTML DB Configuration screen

To start the actual installation click **Install**.

The installation process will start and is indicated via a progress bar as seen in diagram 3.11.1.

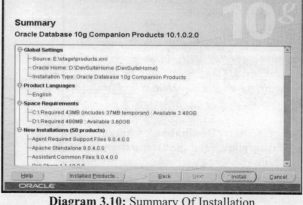

Diagram 3.10: Summary Of Installation

Just after the installation process reaches 100% the configuration process begins as seen in diagram 3.12.1 and diagram 3.12.2.

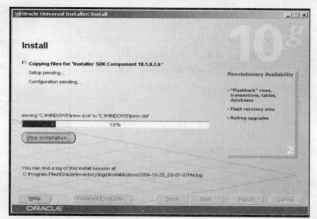

Diagram 3.11.1: Installation in progress

If Windows XP has Service Pack 2 installed then just after the loading process as seen in diagram 3.11.1 completes, a message box prompting a Windows Security Alert pops up. Refer diagram 3.11.2. This is because the Windows Firewall is active and is preventing a java based program from running. Since this alert has popped up while installing Oracle 10g, the java program can be unblocked. Click **Unblock** to proceed with the Oracle 10g installation.

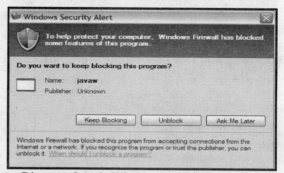

Diagram 3.11.2: Windows Security Alert (SP2 Only).

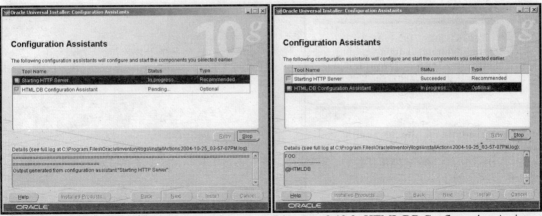

Diagram 3.12.1: Staring HTTP Server In Progress   **Diagram 3.12.2:** HTML DB Configuration Assistant
In Progress

The HTMLDB Configuration Assistant usually takes a lot of time while the configuration process. Please be patient.

Once the configuration process completes, an End Of Installation screen as seen in diagram 3.13 appears. *Note down the URL shown in diagram 3.13.* Click **Exit** to quit the Installer. (Refer diagram 3.14)

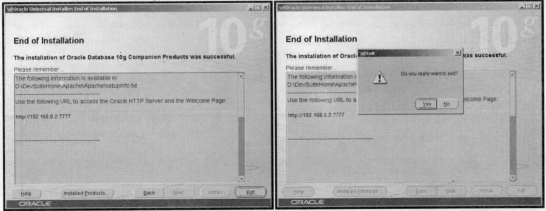

Diagram 3.13: End Of Installation screen   **Diagram 3.14:** Quit Installation

TESTING THE INSTALLATION

Point the default web browser (e.g. Internet Explorer) to the following url:

**http://<IP_ADDRESS>:7777/pls/html
db /htmldb_admin**

The **hostname** will be IP address of the machine hosting the Oracle 10g HTML DB in this case being 192.168.0.2 and hence the URL will be **http://192.168.0.2:7777/pls /htmldb/htmldb_admin** (Refer diagram 3.15). This is because the Oracle 10g HTML DB is installed on the machine having an IP address 192.168.0.2.

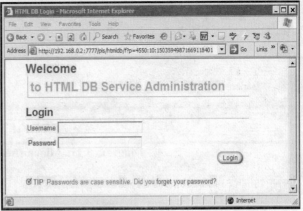

Diagram 3.15: Welcome screen of HTML DB Service

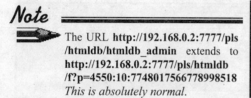

The URL **http://192.168.0.2:7777/pls /htmldb/htmldb_admin** extends to **http://192.168.0.2:7777/pls/htmldb /f?p=4550:10:7748017566778998518** *This is absolutely normal.*

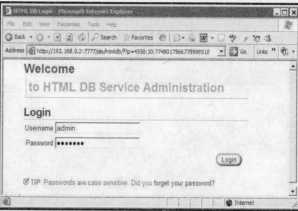

Login using **admin** as the **username** and **password** as the one specified while the installing the Oracle 10g HTML DB (Refer diagram 3.9 for the password entered).

The Administration Home page appears as seen in diagram 3.17.

Diagram 3.16: Logging In

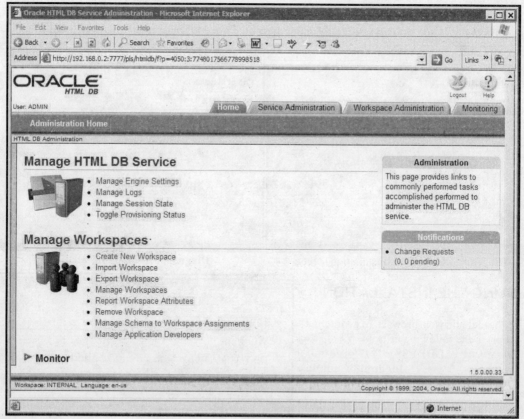

Diagram 3.17: Administration Home Page

This completes the testing and installation of Oracle 10g HTML DB.

4. OVERVIEW OF ORACLE DATABASE 10g

INTRODUCTION

Oracle Corporation has been openly and strongly advocating their next release of the Oracle database, (i.e. Oracle 10g). Understanding how the database has changed and the host (or not) of new attributes it brings to the application development space will help businesses decide to upgrade or not.

ORACLE 10g OVERVIEW

The main thrust of the new features and enhancements for Oracle 10g are geared towards grid computing which is an extension of the clustering features (Real Application Clusters) introduced in Oracle 9i.

What Exactly Is Grid Computing?

In the 1980s companies like Digital Equipment Corp, developed clustering technology which allowed two or more computers to appear as if they were just one to the end-user, thereby enabling load-balancing and hot standby.

Oracle (from release 9i) absorbed this technology into their database software so that users of their databases could benefit from its load-balancing and hot-standby capabilities without having to worry about installing additional clustering software or manually switching users from one database instance to another should a failure occur. Equally importantly, without the application having to be cluster-aware.

That was one stepping stone in the evolutionary process, but recently companies like Sun Microsystems have been extending the concept of clusters to be able to include different types (makes) of computers running different operating systems in a **pool** of computing resources that can be made available as and when required to meet peak demands and then released back into the pool when no longer needed.

Oracle 10g is a database engine that is able to dynamically requisition resources from the pool (i.e. the resource grid) to meet levels of peak demand. Additionally, the pool can be heterogeneous (i.e. different types of hardware and/or operating systems).

The motivation for the development of grid computing is to reduce the need to have dedicated resources sized for peak capacity. Research has shown that the average CPU usage is only 15-20% and storage usage is only 50% of peak capacity. Having dedicated resources for each major application also means that there can be a large number of systems to maintain. The solution to this is to create a pool of low-cost servers + storage that can be allocated to applications to meet peak loads.

Other enhancements for Oracle 10g are aimed at reducing costs and improving the quality of service by making the database easier to deploy and manage, including **backup**, **recovery** and **data warehousing** enhancements.

Ease Of Management

As with Oracle 9i, another major focus area of this release has been to reduce costs and increase database up-time by making the database easier to manage. One way of doing this is to automate tasks that previously had to be done manually by the DBA. To achieve this Oracle 10g, has introduced a new Automated Storage Management (ASM) sub-system.

This feature removes the need to have a file system or a volume manager for managing database files and eliminates the complexity of balancing data across disks and controllers manually. Instead, the ASM stripes data across the disks automatically, thereby maximizing throughput and minimizing the risk of data loss. The ASM also maintains the data striping as disks are added/removed and re-balances the i/o load dynamically.

Oracle 10g has also been given a self-management infrastructure which captures information about the running of the database and stores it in the Automatic Workload Repository. This information is used by tools such as the new Automatic Database Diagnostic Monitor (ADDM), which analyses data such as the top SQL statements and passes this onto the SQL Tuning Advisor, which provides recommendations for improving performance. These recommendations can be implemented transparently to the application making it a useful feature for 3rd-party applications.

Other major enhancements in this area include:
❑ Enhancing Enterprise Manager to be able to manage the whole grid and the complete stack of resources
❑ Simplifying installation and configuration by reducing the number of initialization parameters - for example there are now just two memory size parameters, one each for the SGA and the PGA.

Availability

Real Application Clusters have been enhanced to provide Automatic Service Provisioning - servers are automatically allocated to work loads and clients are automatically assigned to the server with the least load. Also on failure of a server, the surviving servers are automatically re-allocated to work loads.

Other enhancements in this area include:
❑ Flashback available at the row, transaction, table or database level
❑ Recovery area on disk that is maintained automatically by the database and contains only those blocks changed since the last backup - thereby enabling faster recovery from media failure
❑ Data guard (standby database) has been enhanced to enable compression and encryption of log traffic from the master database to the standby system
❑ Tables can now be re-defined without invalidating stored procedures
❑ Support for rolling upgrades of the hardware, operating system and the database to reduce planned down time.

Data Warehousing

Improvements in this area include increasing the size limits of the database to support ultra-large databases totaling millions of terabytes (exabytes) with ultra-large files of terabytes in size. The 4GB restriction on LOBs has been raised to 128 terabytes.

Improvements to Real Application Clusters (RAC) enable resources to be allocated automatically. That means operational data can be used immediately without the need to copy it to another database.

Enhancements to OLAP analytics, a data-mining GUI and a new SQL model allow query results to be treated as sets of multi-dimensional arrays on which complex inter-dependent operations - such as forecasting - can be run without the need to extract data to spreadsheets or perform complex joins and unions on the data.

A new changed data capture facility based on Oracle Streams provides low or zero latency trickle feeds that combined with integrated extraction, transformation and loading (etl) enable real-time warehousing.

Summary

As they did with Oracle 9i, Oracle have made many enhancements to support their largest customers in terms of database size limits and they have continued to remove complexity from the database to make the database easier to manage and thereby reduce the total cost of ownership (TCO), thereby keeping everyone happy and enhancing the competitiveness of Oracle compared to Microsoft, in particular, and IBM.

With spending on technology beginning to increase slightly when compared to the past few years, more companies will start to consider upgrading to Oracle 10g, but there may not be many companies using the grid technology if its licensing proves to be complex.

5. INTERACTIVE SQL PART - I

TABLE FUNDAMENTALS

A **table** is database object that holds user data. The simplest analogy is to think of a table as a spreadsheet. The cells of the spreadsheet equate to the columns of a table having a specific **data type** associated with them. If the spreadsheet cell has a number data type associated with it, then storing letters (**i.e.** characters) in the same cell is **not allowed**. The same logic is applied to a table's column. Each column of the table will have a specific data type bound to it. Oracle ensures that only data, which is identical to the data type of the column, will be stored within the column.

Oracle Data Types

Basic Data Types

Data types come in several forms and sizes, allowing the programmer to create tables perfectly suited to the scope of a project. The decisions made in choosing proper data types greatly influence the performance of a database, so it is wise to have a detailed understanding of these concepts.

Oracle is capable of dealing with many data types that even a novice programmer has probably already been exposed to. Some of the more common data types in use include: (Refer to table 5.1)

Data Type	Description
CHAR(size [BYTE | CHAR])	This data type is used to store character strings values of fixed length. The size in brackets determines the number of characters the cell can hold. The maximum number of characters (i.e. the size) this data type can hold is 255 characters. The data held is right-padded with spaces to whatever length specified.
VARCHAR2(size [BYTE | CHAR])	Variable-length character string having maximum length size bytes or characters. Maximum size is 4000 bytes or characters, and minimum is 1 byte or 1 character. You must specify size for VARCHAR2. BYTE indicates that the column will have byte length semantics; CHAR indicates that the column will have character semantics.
NVARCHAR2 (size)	Variable-length character string having maximum length size characters. Maximum size is determined by the national character set definition, with an upper limit of 4000 bytes. A size must be specified with NVARCHAR2.
NUMBER(p, s)	Number having precision p and scale s. The precision p can range from 1 to 38. The scale s can range from -84 to 127. Valid values are 0 and positive or negative numbers with magnitude 1.0E-130 to 9.9...E125.
LONG	Character data of variable length up to 2 gigabytes, or 2^{31} -1 bytes.
DATE	Valid date range from January 1, 4712 BC to December 31, 9999 AD. The standard format is DD-MON-YY as in 01-JAN-00.
BINARY_ FLOAT	32-bit floating point number. This datatype requires 5 bytes, including the length byte.
BINARY_ DOUBLE	64-bit floating point number. This datatype requires 9 bytes, including the length byte.

Table 5.1

Data Type	Description
TIMESTAMP (fractional_ seconds_precision)	Year, month and day values of date, as well as hour, minute and second values of time, where fractional_seconds_precision is the number of digits in the fractional part of the SECOND datetime field. Accepted values of fractional_seconds_precision are 0 to 9. The default is 6.
TIMESTAMP (fractional_ seconds_precision) WITH TIME ZONE	All values of TIMESTAMP as well as time zone displacement value, where fractional_seconds_precision is the number of digits in the fractional part of the SECOND datetime field. Accepted values are 0 to 9. The default is 6.
TIMESTAMP (fractional_ seconds_precision) WITH LOCAL TIME ZONE	All values of TIMESTAMP WITH TIME ZONE, with the following exceptions: ❑ Data is normalized to the database time zone when it is stored in the database. ❑ When the data is retrieved, users see the data in the session time zone.
INTERVAL YEAR (year_ precision) TO MONTH	Stores a period of time in years and months, where year_precision is the number of digits in the YEAR datetime field. Accepted values are 0 to 9. The default is 2.
INTERVAL DAY (day_precision) TO SECOND (fractional_seconds _precision)	Stores a period of time in days, hours, minutes, and seconds, where ❑ day_precision is the maximum number of digits in the DAY datetime field. Accepted values are 0 to 9. The default is 2. ❑ fractional_seconds_precision is the number of digits in the fractional part of the SECOND field. Accepted values are 0 to 9. The default is 6.
RAW(size)	Raw binary data of length size bytes. Maximum size is 2000 bytes. Specifying the size for a RAW value is must.
LONG RAW	Raw binary data of variable length up to 2 gigabytes.
ROWID	Base 64 string representing the unique address of a row in its table. This datatype is primarily for values returned by the ROWID pseudo-column.
UROWID [(size)]	Base 64 string representing the logical address of a row of an index-organized table. The optional size is the size of a column of type UROWID. The maximum size and default is 4000 bytes.
CHAR(size [BYTE | CHAR])	Fixed-length character data of length size bytes. Maximum size is 2000 bytes or characters. Default and minimum size is 1 byte. BYTE and CHAR have the same semantics as for VARCHAR2.
NCHAR(size)	Fixed-length character data of length size characters. Maximum size is determined by the national character set definition, with an upper limit of 2000 bytes. Default and minimum size is 1 character.
CLOB	A character large object containing single-byte or multibyte characters. Both fixed-width and variable-width character sets are supported, both using the database character set. Maximum size is (4 gigabytes - 1) * (database block size).
NCLOB	A character large object containing Unicode characters. Both fixed-width and variable-width character sets are supported, both using the database national character set. Maximum size is (4 gigabytes - 1) * (database block size). Stores national character set data.
BLOB	A binary large object. Maximum size is (4 gigabytes - 1) * (database block size).
BFILE	Contains a locator to a large binary file stored outside the database. Enables byte stream I/O access to external LOBs residing on the database server. Maximum size is 4 gigabytes.

Table 5.1 (Continued)

Prior using a table to store user data it needs to be created. Table creation is done using Create Table syntax. When Oracle creates a table in response to a create table command, it stores the table structure information within its Data Dictionary.

Firming Upon A Model

Learning various commands and techniques is easier if the examples used follow a real-life scenario. To facilitate the same, the examples will be based on a simple Car Rental System. The basic Entity Relationship model for the Car Rental will be as shown in diagram 5.1.

Diagram 5.1 provides a visual representation of the **E**ntity **R**elationships between the tables used to store business process data of the car rental system.

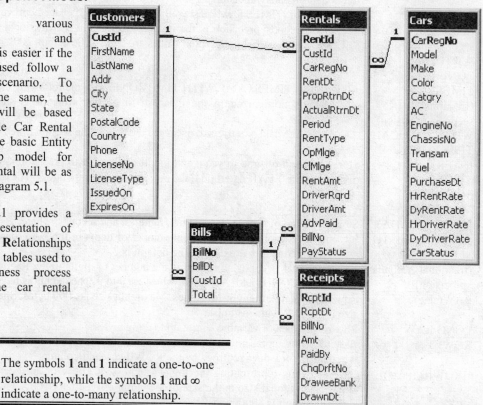

Note

The symbols **1** and **1** indicate a one-to-one relationship, while the symbols **1** and ∞ indicate a one-to-many relationship.

Diagram 5.1

Normalized tables design together with a detailed description of each table structure used in the proposed computerized system now follow:

Table Name : **Cars**
Primary Key : Cars.CarRegNo
Foreign Key : - -

Column Definition:

Column Name	Data Type	Width	Allow Null	Default
CarRegNo	VarChar2	20	No	
Model	VarChar2	25	No	
Make	VarChar2	25	No	
Color	VarChar2	10	No	
Catgry	VarChar2	1	No	
AC	VarChar2	1	No	
EngineNo	VarChar2	25	No	
ChassisNo	VarChar2	25	No	

Column Definition: (Continued)

Column Name	Data Type	Width	Allow Null	Default
TransAM	VarChar2	1	No	M
Fuel	VarChar2	1	No	D
PurchaseDt	Date		No	
HrRentRate	Decimal	6,2	No	
DyRentRate	Decimal	6,2	No	
HrDriverRate	Decimal	6,2	No	
DyDriverRate	Decimal	6,2	No	
CarStatus	VarChar2	1	No	

Table Column Description:

Column Name	Description
CarRegNo	Car's identity number (**Primary Key**)
Model	Car's model name
Make	Company / Type of the car
Color	Color of the car
Catgry	The kind of vehicle flag; L-Luxury, V-Van, J-Jeep, S-Small Car
AC	Flag Y for vehicles with A/c, N for vehicles without A/c
EngineNo	The Engine Number of the car
ChassisNo	The Chassis Number of the car
TransAM	Transmission A-Automatic, M-Manual
Fuel	Fuel used C-CNG, D-Diesel, P-Petrol, L-LPG
PurchaseDt	Car's purchase date
HrRentRate	Rate for renting the car on per hour basis
DyRentRate	Rate for renting the car on per day basis
HrDriverRate	Driver service chargers on per hour basis
DyDriverRate	Driver service chargers on per day basis
CarStatus	A – Car available and R – Car rented

Explanation:

This table holds detailed information about each car available for hire with the car rental company.

Table Name 　　: **Customers**
Primary Key 　　: **Customers.CustId**
Foreign Key 　　: - -

Column Definition:

Column Name	Data Type	Width	Allow Null	Default
CustId	Number	5	No	
FirstName	VarChar2	20	No	
LastName	VarChar2	20	Yes	
Addr	VarChar2	250	Yes	
City	VarChar2	15	Yes	
State	VarChar2	15	Yes	
PostalCode	VarChar2	15	Yes	
Country	VarChar2	15	Yes	
Phone	VarChar2	30	Yes	
LicenseNo	VarChar2	20	No	
LicenseType	VarChar2	50	No	
IssuedOn	Date		No	
ExpiresOn	Date		No	

Table Description:

Column Name	Description
CustId	Customer's identity number (**Primary Key**)
FirstName	Customer's first name
LastName	Customer's last name
Addr	Customer's residential address
City	City of residence
State	State of residence
PostalCode	Residential postal code
Country	Residential country of residence
Phone	Customer's telephone number(s)
LicenseNo	Customer's Driving License number
LicenseType	Customer's Driving License category
IssuedOn	The Date on which the License was issued
ExpiresOn	The Date on which the License expires.

Explanation:

This table holds the contact and personal information of each customer who has hired a car from the car rental company.

Table Name   : **Bills**
Primary Key   : Bills.**BillNo**
Foreign Key   : Bills.CustId

Column Definition:

Column Name	Data Type	Width	Allow Null	Default
BillNo	Number	5	No	
BillDt	Date		No	
CustId	Number	5	No	
Total	Decimal	8,2	No	

Table Description:

Column Name	Description
BillId	Bill identity number (**Primary Key**)
BillDt	Bill date
CustId	(Posted from Customers.CustId)
Total	Total amount charged in the bill.

Explanation:

This table holds identification for bills presented to the customer.

Table Name   : **Rentals**
Primary Key   : Rentals.**RentId**
Foreign Key   : Rentals.CustId, Rentals.CarRegNo, Rentals.BillNo

Column Definition:

Column Name	Data Type	Width	Allow Null	Default
RentId	Number	5	No	
CustId	Number	5	No	
CarRegNo	VarChar2	20	No	
RentDt	Date		No	
PropRtrnDt	Date		No	

Column Definition: (Continued)

Column Name	Data Type	Width	Allow Null	Default
ActualRtrnDt	Date		Yes	
RentType	VarChar2	1	No	
Period	Number	3	Yes	
OpMlge	Number	8	Yes	
ClMlge	Number	8	Yes	
RentAmt	Decimal	8,2	No	
DriverRqrd	VarChar2	1	No	
DriverAmt	Decimal	8,2	Yes	
AdvPaid	Decimal	8,2	Yes	
BillNo	Number	5	No	
PayStatus	VarChar2	1	Yes	

Table Description:

Column Name	Description
RentId	Rent identity number (**Primary Key**)
CustId	(Posted from Customers.CustId)
CarRegNo	(Posted from Cars.CarRegNo)
RentDt	Date when the car is rented
PropRtrnDt	Date when the car will be returned
ActualRtrnDt	Date when the car actually returns
RentType	(H - Hourly Rent D - Daily Rent)
Period	Time for which the car is rented (in hours or days only)
OpMlge	Mileage reading at the time of renting the car
ClMlge	Mileage reading after the returning the car
RentAmt	Programmatically calculated amount for renting the car
DriverRqrd	Whether a driver is required along with the car
DriverAmt	Programmatically calculated amount for the driver's fee
AdvPaid	Advance amount received from the customer
BillNo	Identity number for the corresponding invoice / bill.
PayStatus	(P – Paid, N – Not Paid)

Explanation:
This table holds details of each car rental transaction between a customer and the car rental company.

Table Name : Receipts
Primary Key : Receipts.RcptId
Foreign Key : Receipts.BillNo

Column Definition:

Column Name	Data Type	Width	Allow Null	Default
RcptId	Number	5	No	
RcptDt	Date		No	
BillNo	Number	5	No	
Amt	Decimal	8,2	No	
PaidBy	VarChar2	1	No	
ChqDrftNo	VarChar2	9	Yes	
DraweeBank	VarChar2	30	Yes	
DrawnDt	Date		Yes	

Table Description:

Column Name	Description
RcptId	Receipt identity number (**Primary Key**)
RcptDt	Receipt's date
BillNo	(Posted from Bills.BillNo)
Amt	Total amount received
PaidBy	(C – Cash, R – Credit Card, B – Cheque, D – Draft)
ChqDrftNo	Cheque number
DraweeBank	Amount received as advance
DrawnDt	Date on which the cheque or the DD is drawn

Explanation:
This table holds details of receipts issued to customers for the payment received against car rental bills.

The CREATE TABLE Command

The **CREATE TABLE** command defines each column of the table uniquely. Each column has a minimum of three attributes, a name, datatype and size (**i.e.** column width). Each table column definition is a single clause in the create table syntax. Each table column definition is separated from the other by a comma. Finally, the SQL statement is terminated with a semi colon.

Rules For Creating Tables
1. A table name can have maximum of 30 characters
2. Alphabets from A-Z, a-z and numbers from 0-9 are allowed
3. A table name should begin with an alphabet
4. The use of the special character like _ is allowed and also recommended. (Special characters like $, # are allowed **only in Oracle**).
5. SQL reserved words **not** allowed. For Example: create, select and so on.

Syntax:
```
CREATE TABLE [Schema.]<TableName>
    (<ColumnName1> <DataType>(<size>), <ColumnName2> <DataType>(<Size>));
```

Note

Each column must have a datatype. The column should either be defined as null or not null and if this value is left blank, the database assumes "null" as the default.

A Brief Checklist When Creating Tables
The following provides a small checklist for the issues that need to be considered before creating a table:
- What are the attributes of the rows to be stored?
- What are the data types of the attributes?
- varchar2 be used instead of char?
- Which columns should be used to build the primary key?
- Which columns should not allow null values? Which columns do / do not, allow duplicates?
- Are there default values for certain columns that **also** allow null values?

Example 1:
Create the **BILLS** table belonging to the **Car Rental System**.

CREATE TABLE Bills(BillNo Number(5), BillDt Date, CustId Number(5), Total Number(8,2)**);**

Output:
```
Table created.
```

Note

All table columns belong to a **single record**. Therefore all the table column definitions are enclosed within parenthesis.

Inserting Data Into Tables

Once a table is created, the most natural thing to do is load this table with data to be manipulated later.

When inserting a single row of data into the table, the insert operation:
❑ Creates a new row (empty) in the database table
❑ Loads the values passed (by the SQL insert) into the empty columns specified

Syntax:
```
INSERT INTO <TableName> (<ColumnName1>[, ...])
    VALUES (<Expression1>[, <Expression2>]);
```

Example 2:
Insert the following values into the BILLS table:

Table Name: BILLS

BillNo	BillDt	CustId	Total	BillNo	BillDt	CustId	Total
1	10-Jun-2000	1	129060.00	2	27-Jul-2000	2	19424.00
3	12-Aug-2000	3	4788.00	4	31 Aug 2000	4	44880.00
5	03-Nov-2000	1	78122.00	6	30-Nov-2000	2	62656.00

INSERT INTO Bills (BillNo, BillDt, CustId, Total) **VALUES**(1, '10-Jun-2000', 1, 129060.00);
INSERT INTO Bills (BillNo, BillDt, CustId, Total) **VALUES** (2, '27-Jul-2000', 2, 19424.00);
INSERT INTO Bills (BillNo, BillDt, CustId, Total) **VALUES** (3, '12-Aug-2000', 3, 4788.00);
INSERT INTO Bills (BillNo, BillDt, CustId, Total) **VALUES** (4, '31-Aug-2000', 4, 44880.00);
INSERT INTO Bills (BillNo, BillDt, CustId, Total) **VALUES** (5, '03-Nov-2000', 1, 78122.00);
INSERT INTO Bills (BillNo, BillDt, CustId, Total) **VALUES** (6, '30-Nov-2000', 2, 62656.00);

Output for <u>each</u> of the above INSERT INTO statements:
```
1 row created.
```

Note

The SOL statements for creating and inserting records in the Car Rental System are available under *Book_CDROM:/Chap05_Codes/Chap05_TblStr.txt* file on the accompanying Book CD-ROM. *To continue with the following examples these records have to be fired in SQL *Plus using the copy paste technique.*

Tip

Character expressions placed within the **INSERT INTO** statement must be enclosed in **single quotes** (').

In the **INSERT INTO** SQL sentence, table columns and values have a one to one relationship, (**i.e.** the first value described is inserted into the first column, while the second value described is inserted into the second column and so on).

Hence, in an **INSERT INTO** SQL sentence if there are exactly the same numbers of values as there are columns and the values are sequenced exactly in accordance with the data type of the table columns, there is **no need** to indicate the column names.

However, if there are less values being described than there are columns in the table, then it is **mandatory** to indicate **both** the table **column name** and its corresponding **value** in the **INSERT INTO** SQL sentence.

In the absence of mapping a table column name to a value in the **INSERT INTO** SQL sentence; the Oracle engine will not know which columns to insert the data into. This will generally cause a loss of data integrity. Then the data held within the table will be largely useless.

VIEWING DATA IN THE TABLES

Once data has been inserted into a table, the next most logical operation would be to view what has been inserted. The **SELECT** SQL verb is used to achieve this. The SELECT command is used to retrieve rows selected from one or more tables.

All Rows And All Columns

In order to view global table data the **syntax** is:
```
SELECT <ColumnName_1> TO <ColumnName_N> FROM TableName;
```

Note

Here, **ColumnName_1 to ColumnName_N** represents table column names.

Syntax:
```
SELECT * FROM <TableName>;
```

Example 3:
Show the Id number, first name and last name for all Customers of the Car Rental business. A partial extract of the **Customers** table is as shown below:
Table Name: Customers

CustId	FirstName	LastName	Phone	CustId	FirstName	LastName	Phone
1	Rahul Mohan	Sharma	28765654	2	John Simon	Brownie	23657868
3	Jennifer	Smith	23756775	4	Wilson	Fernandes	24443760
5	Raju	Prasad	42739894	6	Parvez	Khan	
7	Mosie	Shah	76756537	8	Preity	Sen	
9	Ashwini	Joshi	24403031	10	Alex Joseph	D'Mello	23445576

SELECT CustId, FirstName, LastName **FROM** Customers;

Output:
```
     CUSTID FIRSTNAME                 LASTNAME
---------- --------------------     --------------------
         1 Rahul Mohan               Sharma
         2 John Simon                Brownie
         3 Jennifer                  Smith
         4 Wilson                    Fernandes
         5 Raju                      Prasad
         6 Parvez                    Khan
         7 Mosie                     Shah
         8 Preity                    Sen
         9 Ashwini                   Joshi
        10 Alex Joseph               D'Mello
```

10 rows selected.

Example 4:
Show all details held in the BILLS table. A partial extract of the **Bills** table is as shown below:

Table Name: Bills

BillNo	BillDt	CustId	Total	BillNo	BillDt	CustId	Total
1	10-Jun-2000	1	129060.00	2	27-Jul-2000	2	19424.00
3	12-Aug-2000	3	4788.00	4	31-Aug-2000	4	44880.00
5	03-Nov-2000	1	78122.00	6	30-Nov-2000	2	62656.00

SELECT * FROM Bills;

Output:
```
    BILLNO BILLDT          CUSTID      TOTAL
---------- ---------   ----------  ----------
         1 10-JUN-00            1      129060
         2 27-JUL-00            2       19424
         3 12-AUG-00            3        4788
         4 31-AUG-00            4       44880
         5 03-NOV-00            1       78122
         6 30-NOV-00            2       62656
```
. . .

40 rows selected.

Tip

When data from all rows and columns from the table are to be viewed the syntax of the SELECT statement will be: **SELECT * FROM <TableName>;**

Oracle allows the use of the Meta character asterisk (*), this is expanded by Oracle to mean all rows and all columns in the table.

The Oracle Server parses and compiles the SQL query, executes it and retrieves data from all rows/columns from the table.

Filtering Table Data

While viewing data from a table it is rare that **all the data** from the table will be required **each time**. Hence, SQL provides a method of filtering table data that is not required.

The ways of filtering table data are:
- Selected columns and all rows
- Selected rows and all columns
- Selected columns and selected rows

Selected Columns And All Rows

The retrieval of specific columns from a table can be done as shown below:

Syntax:
```
SELECT <ColumnName1>, <ColumnName2> FROM <TableName>;
```

Example 5:
Show the first name and the last name of the customer's of the car rental business. A partial extract of the **Customers** table is as shown below:

Table Name: Customers

CustId	FirstName	LastName	Phone	CustId	FirstName	LastName	Phone
1	Rahul Mohan	Sharma	28765654	2	John Simon	Brownie	23657868
3	Jennifer	Smith	23756775	4	Wilson	Fernandes	24443760
5	Raju	Prasad	42739894	6	Parvez	Khan	
7	Mosie	Shah	76756537	8	Preity	Sen	
9	Ashwini	Joshi	24403031	10	Alex Joseph	D'Mello	23445576

SELECT FirstName, LastName **FROM** Customers;

Output:
```
FIRSTNAME               LASTNAME
--------------------    --------------------
Rahul Mohan             Sharma
John Simon              Brownie
Jennifer                Smith
Wilson                  Fernandes
Raju                    Prasad
Parvez                  Khan
Mosie                   Shah
Preity                  Sen
Ashwini                 Joshi
Alex Joseph             D'Mello

10 rows selected.
```

Selected Rows And All Columns

If information of a particular client is to be retrieved from a table, its retrieval must be based on a **specific condition**.

The SELECT statement used until now displayed all rows. This is because there was no condition set that informed Oracle about how to choose a specific set of rows (**or** a specific row) from any table. Oracle provides the option of using a **WHERE Clause** in an SQL query to apply a filter on the rows retrieved.

When a where clause is added to the SQL query, the Oracle engine compares each record in the table with the condition specified in the where clause. The Oracle engine displays only those records that satisfy the specified condition.

Syntax:

SELECT * FROM <TableName> WHERE <Condition>;

Here, <Condition> is always quantified as <ColumnName = Value>

Example 6:
Display the information of bills drawn after June 2003. A partial extract of the **Bills** table is as shown below:

Table Name: Bills

BillNo	BillDt	CustId	Total	BillNo	BillDt	CustId	Total
35	20-Jan-2003	2	103937.50	36	30-Jan-2003	5	95680.00
37	09-Apr-2003	1	111198.00	38	03-Jun-2003	3	131850.00
39	29-Jul-2003	5	120000.00	40	31-Jul-2003	9	94350.00

SELECT * FROM Bills **WHERE** BillDt > '30-Jun-2003';

Output:

```
    BILLNO BILLDT        CUSTID      TOTAL
---------- ---------- ---------- ----------
        39 29-JUL-03          5     120000
        40 31-JUL-03          9      94350
```

 Note

 When specifying a condition in the **where clause** all standard operators such as logical, arithmetic, predicates and so on, can be used.

Selected Columns And Selected Rows

To view a specific set of rows and columns from a table the syntax will be as follows:

Syntax:

SELECT <ColumnName1>, <ColumnName2> FROM <TableName>
    WHERE <Condition>;

Example 7:
Display the customer's license details for those residents in the city of Mumbai. A partial extract of the **Customers** table is as shown below:

Table Name: Customers

CustId	LicenseNo	LicenseType	IssuedOn	ExpiresOn
1	B-14879	LMV and Motor Cycle	25-Apr-1995	24-Apr-2015
2	UB-40201	LMV	15-Oct-1999	14-Oct-2019
3	UB-43564	LMV	30-Jan-1997	29-Jan-2017
4	B-1034	HMV	30-Nov-2000	29-Nov-2003
5	C-2345	HMV	17-Feb-2001	16-Feb-2004
6	UC-23923	LMV and Motor Cycle	05-Jun-2000	04-Jun-2020

Table Name: Customers (Continued)

CustId	LicenseNo	LicenseType	IssuedOn	ExpiresOn
7	UZ-3498	HMV	20-Nov-2001	19-Nov-2004
8	D-1089	LMV	05-May-1989	04-May-2009
9	B-10163	LMV	12-Jul-1995	12-Jul-2015
10	B-20345	HMV	24-Jan-2001	23-Jan-2004

SELECT CustId, LicenseNo, LicenseType, IssuedOn, ExpiresOn **FROM** Customers
WHERE City = 'Mumbai';

Output:
```
CUSTID LICENSENO  LICENSETYPE                               ISSUEDON  EXPIRESON
------ ---------- ----------------------------------------  --------- ---------
     1 B-14879    LMV and Motor Cycle                       25-APR-95 24-APR-15
     4 B-1034     HMV                                       30-NOV-00 29-NOV-03
     8 D-1089     LMV                                       05-MAY-89 04-MAY-09
     9 B-10163    LMV                                       12-JUL-95 12-JUL-15
```

ELIMINATING DUPLICATE ROWS WHEN USING A SELECT STATEMENT

A table could hold duplicate rows. In such a case, to view only unique rows the distinct clause can be used.

The DISTINCT clause allows removing duplicates from the result set. The DISTINCT clause can only be used with select statements.

The **DISTINCT** clause scans through the values of the column/s specified and displays only unique values from amongst them.

Syntax:
```
SELECT DISTINCT <ColumnName1>, <ColumnName2> FROM <TableName>;
```

The **SELECT DISTINCT** * SQL syntax scans through **entire rows** and eliminates rows that have exactly the same contents in each column.

Syntax:
```
SELECT DISTINCT * FROM <TableName>;
```

Example 8:
Show different cities of customer's residence belonging to the car rental business by eliminating the repeated city names

SELECT DISTINCT City **FROM** Customers;

Output:
```
CITY
---------------
Chennai
Dubai
Fujaira
Mumbai
New York
Panji

6 rows selected.
```

Example 9:

Show only unique bills information.

The partial extract of the **Bills** table is as shown below:

Table Name: Bills

BillNo	BillDt	CustId	Total
1	10-Jun-2000	1	129060.00
3	12-Aug-2000	3	4788.00
5	03-Nov-2000	1	78122.00

BillNo	BillDt	CustId	Total
2	27-Jul-2000	2	19424.00
4	31-Aug-2000	4	44880.00
6	30-Nov-2000	2	62656.00

First insert one more record (To create duplicates rows) in the table **Bills** so as to see the output for this example.

INSERT INTO Bills (BillNo, BillDt, CustId, Total) **VALUES**(5, '03-Nov-2000', 1, 78122.00);

SELECT DISTINCT * FROM Bills;

The following output shows the entry for Bill number 5 only once even though entered twice in the table.

Output:

```
    BILLNO BILLDT        CUSTID       TOTAL
---------- ---------  ----------  ----------
         1 10-JUN-00           1      129060
         2 27-JUL-00           2       19424
         3 12-AUG-00           3        4788
         4 31-AUG-00           4       44880
         5 03-NOV-00           1       78122
         6 30-NOV-00           2       62656
. . .

40 rows selected.
```

SORTING DATA IN A TABLE

Oracle allows data from a table to be viewed in a sorted order. The rows retrieved from the table will be sorted in either **ascending** or **descending** order depending on the condition specified in the **SELECT** sentence. The syntax for viewing data in a sorted order is as follows:

Syntax:

```
SELECT * FROM <TableName>
    ORDER BY <ColumnName1>, <ColumnName2> <[Sort Order]>;
```

The ORDER BY clause sorts the result set based on the columns specified. The ORDER BY clause can only be used in SELECT statements.

Example 10:

Show the customer details after ascending data in accordance to the first name of the customer. A partial extract of the **Customers** table is as shown below:

Table Name: Customers

CustId	FirstName	LastName	Phone
1	Rahul Mohan	Sharma	28765654
3	Jennifer	Smith	23756775
5	Raju	Prasad	42739894
7	Mosie	Shah	76756537
9	Ashwini	Joshi	24403031

CustId	FirstName	LastName	Phone
2	John Simon	Brownie	23657868
4	Wilson	Fernandes	24443760
6	Parvez	Khan	
8	Preity	Sen	
10	Alex Joseph	D'Mello	23445576

SELECT FirstName, LastName **FROM** Customers **ORDER BY** FirstName;

Output:
```
FIRSTNAME                LASTNAME
------------------       --------------------
Alex Joseph              D'Mello
Ashwini                  Joshi
Jennifer                 Smith
John Simon               Brownie
Mosie                    Shah
Parvez                   Khan
Preity                   Sen
Rahul Mohan              Sharma
Raju                     Prasad
Wilson                   Fernandes

10 rows selected.
```

Tip

> For viewing data in descending sorted order the word **DESC** must be mentioned **after** the column name and before the semi colon in the **order by** clause. In case there is no mention of the sort order, the Oracle engine sorts in **ascending order by default**.

Example 11:
Show the customer details in accordance to the first name of the customer in descending order.

SELECT FirstName, LastName **FROM** Customers **ORDER BY** FirstName **DESC**;

Output:
```
FIRSTNAME                LASTNAME
--------------------     --------------------
Wilson                   Fernandes
Raju                     Prasad
Rahul Mohan              Sharma
Preity                   Sen
Parvez                   Khan
Mosie                    Shah
John Simon               Brownie
Jennifer                 Smith
Ashwini                  Joshi
Alex Joseph              D'Mello

10 rows selected.
```

CREATING A TABLE FROM A TABLE

Syntax:
```
CREATE TABLE <TableName> (<ColumnName>, < ColumnName>)
    AS SELECT <ColumnName>, <ColumnName> FROM <TableName>
```

Example 12:
Create a table named **Business** having three fields i.e. BillNo, CustId and Total from the source table named **Bills** and rename the field Total to Charges.

CREATE TABLE Business (BillNo, CustId, Charges) **AS SELECT** BillNo, CustId, Total **FROM** Bills;

Output:
```
Table created.
```

> If the Source Table **Bills** was populated with records then the target table **Business** will also be populated with the same.

The **Source** table is the table identified in the **SELECT** section of this SQL sentence. The **Target** table is one identified in the **CREATE** section of this SQL sentence. This SQL sentence populates the Target table with data from the Source table.

To create a Target table without the records from the source table (i.e. create the structure only), the select statement must have a **WHERE clause**. The **WHERE clause** must specify a condition that **cannot** be satisfied.

This means the **SELECT** statement in the CREATE TABLE definition **will not retrieve** any rows from the source table, it will just retrieve the table structure thus the target table will be created empty.

Example 13:
Drop the table Business if it already exists. Create a table named **Business** having three fields i.e. BillNo, CustId and Total from the source table named Bills and rename the field Total to Charges. The table Business should not be populated with any records.

DROP TABLE Business;

CREATE TABLE Business (BillNo, CustId, Charges) **AS SELECT** BillNo, CustId, Total **FROM** Bills
    WHERE 1=2;

Output:
```
Table created.
```

INSERTING DATA INTO A TABLE FROM ANOTHER TABLE

In addition to inserting data one row at a time into a table, it is quite possible to populate a table with data that already exists in another table. The syntax for doing so is as follows:

Syntax:
```
INSERT INTO <TableName>
    SELECT <ColumnName 1>, <ColumnName N> FROM <TableName>;
```

Example 14:
Insert data in the table **Business** using the table **Bills** as a source of data.

INSERT INTO Business **SELECT** BillNo, CustId, Total **FROM** Bills;

Output:
```
40 rows created.
```

Insertion Of A Data Set Into A Table From Another Table

Syntax:
```
INSERT INTO <TableName> SELECT <ColumnName 1>, <ColumnName N>
    FROM <TableName> WHERE <Condition>;
```

Example 15:
Populate the **Business** table with only those bills dated earlier than November 2000 using the data from the **Bills** table.

INSERT INTO Business **SELECT** BillNo, CustId, Total **FROM** Bills **WHERE** BillDt < '01-Nov-2000';

Output:
```
4 rows created.
```

DELETE OPERATIONS

The DELETE command deletes rows from the table that satisfies the condition provided by its where clause, **and** returns the number of records deleted.

If a DELETE statement without a WHERE clause is issued then, all rows are deleted.

The verb **DELETE** in SQL is used to remove either:
❑ All the rows from a table
OR
❑ A set of rows from a table

Removal Of All Rows

Syntax:
```
DELETE FROM <TableName>;
```

Example 16:
Empty the Customers table

DELETE FROM Customers;

Output:
```
16 rows deleted.
```

Removal Of Specific Row(s)

Syntax:
```
DELETE FROM <TableName> WHERE <Condition>;
```

Example 17:
Remove only those bills dated earlier than August 2000 from the **Bills** table.

DELETE FROM Bills **WHERE** BillDt < '01-Aug-2000';

Output:
```
2 rows deleted.
```

Removal Of Specific Row(s) Based On The Data Held By The Other Table

Sometimes it is desired to delete records in one table based on values in another table. Since it is not possible to list more than one table in the FROM clause while performing a delete, the EXISTS clause can be used.

Example 18:
Remove the rental details of the customer named **Raju**.

DELETE FROM Rentals **WHERE EXISTS(SELECT** FirstName **FROM** Customers
    WHERE Customers.CustId = Rentals.CustId **AND** Customers.FirstName = 'Raju');

Output:
```
7 rows deleted.
```

Explanation:
The above SQL sentence will delete all those records from the **Rentals** table where the CustId field holds a value that matches the CustId field of the **Customers** table. This is done using a sub-query which is responsible to extract the CustId of the customer named 'Raju' using the **WHERE** clause.

UPDATING THE CONTENTS OF A TABLE

The **UPDATE** command is used to change or modify data values in a table.

The verb update in SQL is used to either update:
❑   All the rows from a table
OR
❑   A set of rows from a table

Updating All Rows

The **UPDATE** statement updates columns in the existing table's rows with new values. The **SET** clause indicates which column data should be modified and the new values that they should hold. The **WHERE** clause, if given, specifies which rows should be updated. Otherwise, **all** table rows are updated.

Syntax:
```
UPDATE <TableName>
    SET <ColumnName1>=<Expression1>, <ColumnName2>=<Expression2>;
```

Example 19:
Update the customer's address details by changing its city name to Bombay

UPDATE Customers **SET** City = 'Bombay';

Output:
```
10 rows updated.
```

Updating Records Conditionally

Syntax:
```
UPDATE <TableName>
    SET <ColumnName1> = <Expression1>, <ColumnName2> = <Expression2>
        WHERE <Condition>;
```

Example 20:
Update the customer's address details by changing the state named 'New York' to 'Old York'.

UPDATE Customers **SET** State='Old York' **WHERE** State='New York';

Output:
```
2 rows updated.
```

MODIFYING THE STRUCTURE OF TABLES

The structure of a table can be modified by using the **ALTER TABLE** command. **ALTER TABLE** allows **changing the structure of an existing table**. With **ALTER TABLE** it is possible to **add** or **delete** columns, **create** or **destroy** indexes, **change the data type** of existing columns, or **rename columns** or the **table** itself.

ALTER TABLE works by making a temporary copy of the original table. The alteration is performed on the copy, then the original table is deleted and the new one is renamed. While **ALTER TABLE** is executing, the original table is still readable by users of Oracle.

Updates and **writes** to the table are **stalled** until the new table is ready and then are automatically redirected to the new table **without any failed updates**.

Note

To use **ALTER TABLE**, the **ALTER, INSERT** and **CREATE** privileges for the table are required.

Adding New Columns

Syntax:
```
ALTER TABLE <TableName>
    ADD(<NewColumnName> <Datatype> (<Size>),
        <NewColumnName> <Datatype> (<Size>)...);
```

Example 21:
Enter a new field called BillDt in the table **Business**.

ALTER TABLE Business **ADD** (BillDt Date);

Output:
```
Table altered.
```

Dropping A Column From A Table

Syntax:
```
ALTER TABLE <TableName> DROP COLUMN <ColumnName>;
```

Example 22:
Drop the column BillDt from the **Business** table.

ALTER TABLE Business **DROP COLUMN** BillDt;

Output:
```
Table altered.
```

Modifying Existing Columns

Syntax:
```
ALTER TABLE <TableName>
      MODIFY (<ColumnName> <NewDatatype>(<NewSize>));
```

Example 23:
Alter the **Customers** table to allow the FirstName field to hold maximum of 30 characters.

ALTER TABLE Customers **MODIFY** (FirstName VarChar2(30));

Output:
```
Table altered.
```

Restrictions on the ALTER TABLE

The following tasks **cannot** be performed when using the **ALTER TABLE** clause:
- Change the name of the table
- Change the name of the column
- Decrease the size of a column if table data exists

RENAMING TABLES

Oracle allows renaming of tables. The rename operation is done **atomically**, which means that **no other thread** can access any of the tables while the rename process is running.

Note

To rename a table the ALTER and DROP privileges on the original table, and the CREATE and INSERT privileges on the new table are required.

The syntax to rename a table is described as:

Syntax:
```
RENAME <TableName> TO <NewTableName>
```

Example 24:
Change the name of **Business** table to **Income** table

RENAME Business **TO** Income;

Output:
```
Table renamed.
```

TRUNCATING TABLES

TRUNCATE TABLE empties a table completely. Logically, this is equivalent to a **DELETE** statement that deletes all rows, but there are practical differences under some circumstances.

TRUNCATE TABLE differs from **DELETE** in the following ways:
- Truncate operations drop and re-create the table, which is much faster than deleting rows one by one
- Truncate operations are not transaction-safe (i.e. an error will occur if an active transaction or an active table lock exists)
- The number of deleted rows are not returned

Syntax:
```
TRUNCATE TABLE <TableName>;
```

Example 25:
Truncate the table Customers

TRUNCATE TABLE Customers;

Output:
```
Table truncated.
```

DESTROYING TABLES

Sometimes tables within a particular database become obsolete and need to be discarded. In such situation using the DROP TABLE statement with the table name can destroy a specific table.

Syntax:
```
DROP TABLE <TableName>;
```

Caution

 If a table is dropped all records held within it are lost and cannot be recovered.

Example 26:
Remove the table Bills along with the data held.

DROP TABLE Bills;

Output:
```
Table dropped.
```

CREATING SYNONYMS

A **synonym** is an **alternative name** for objects such as tables, views, sequences, stored procedures and other database objects.

Syntax:
```
CREATE [OR REPLACE]  [PUBLIC] SYNONYM [SCHEMA .]
      SYNONYM_NAME FOR [SCHEMA .] OBJECT_NAME [@ DBLINK];
```

In the syntax,
- The **OR REPLACE** phrase allows recreating the synonym (if it already exists) without having to issue a DROP synonym command.
- The **PUBLIC** phrase means that the synonym is a public synonym and is accessible to all users Remember though that the user must first have the appropriate object privileges to use the synonym
- The **SCHEMA** phrase points to an appropriate schema. If this phrase is omitted, Oracle assumes that a reference is made to the user's own schema

❑ The **OBJECT_NAME** phrase is the name of the object for which you are creating the synonym. It can be one of the following:

- Table
- Package
- View
- Materialized View
- Sequence
- Java Class Schema Object
- Stored Procedure
- User-Defined Object
- Function
- Synonym

Example 27:
Create a synonym for a table named **Rentals** held by the user SCOTT.

To create a **PUBLIC** synonym log in as the **System DBA** using the **SYS** user.

CONNECT SYS/<password>@SCT as **SYSDBA;**

Output:
```
Connected.
```

CREATE PUBLIC SYNONYM Transactions **FOR** SCOTT.Rentals;

Output:
```
Synonym created.
```

Explanation:
Now, users of other schemas can reference the table RENTALS, now referred to as TRANSACTIONS **without** having to prefix the table name with the schema named SCOTT. For example a user named SHARANAM logs in via SQL *Plus and needs to access the Rentals (i.e. Transactions) table owned by the user name SCOTT. This can simply be done using:

SELECT * FROM **TRANSACTIONS**;

Dropping Synonyms

Syntax:
> DROP [PUBLIC] SYNONYM [SCHEMA.]SYNONYM_NAME [FORCE];

In the syntax,
❑ The **PUBLIC** phrase allows dropping a public synonym. If public is specified, then there is no need to specify a schema.
❑ The **FORCE** phrase will force Oracle to drop the synonym even if it has dependencies. It is probably not a good idea to use the force phrase as it can cause dependent Oracle objects to become invalid.

Example 28:
Drop the public synonym named **Transactions**

To drop a **PUBLIC** synonym log in as the **System DBA** using the **SYS** user.

CONNECT SYS/<password>@SCT as **SYSDBA;**

Output:
```
Connected.
```

DROP PUBLIC SYNONYM Transactions;

Output:
```
Synonym dropped.
```

Login as SCOTT to go through the following examples using:
CONNECT SCOTT/tiger@SCT;

Output:
```
Connected.
```

EXAMINING OBJECTS CREATED BY A USER

To Find Out Table/s Created By A User

The command shown below is used to determine the tables to which a user has access. The tables created under the **currently selected** tablespace are displayed.

Example 29:

SELECT * FROM TAB;

Output:

```
TNAME                              TABTYPE  CLUSTERID
-----------------------------      -------  ----------
DEPT                               TABLE
EMP                                TABLE
BONUS                              TABLE
SALGRADE                           TABLE
CUSTOMERS                          TABLE
BIN$CmpDTqKgTUa2eLbPG+zlQQ==$0     TABLE
BIN$TMz2weqyQ569EmzCq1yvgw==$0     TABLE
BIN$iBF7Q15eR8WPn5dukFd4ow==$0     TABLE
BIN$5Bq2WFBUTd0yhcpTqv03Yw==$0     TABLE
BIN$WsY6ANQZRwSmfYyObOaMzg==$0     TABLE
CARS                               TABLE
RENTALS                            TABLE
RECEIPTS                           TABLE
INCOME                             TABLE

14 rows selected.
```

Note

In the output seen above there are also a few tables such as BIN$... created by Oracle 10g. These tables are usually created to support the flashback feature of Oracle 10g. This will be discussed later.

Displaying A Table's Structure

To display information about the columns defined in a table use the following syntax

Syntax:
   DESCRIBE <TableName>;

This command displays the column names, the data types and the special attributes connected to the table.

Example 30:
Show the table structure of table **Bills**

DESCRIBE Bills;

Output:

```
Name                              Null?     Type
---------------------------------- --------  ---------------------------
BILLNO                                       NUMBER(5)
BILLDT                                       DATE
CUSTID                                       NUMBER(5)
TOTAL                                        NUMBER(8,2)
```

DATA CONSTRAINTS

All businesses of the world run on business data being gathered, stored and analyzed. Business managers determine a set of business rules that must be applied to their data prior to it being stored in the database/table to ensure its integrity.

For instance, no employee in the sales department can have a salary of less than Rs.1000/-.

Such rules have to be enforced on data stored. Only data, which satisfies the conditions set, should be stored for future analysis. If the data gathered fails to satisfy the conditions set, it must be rejected. This ensures that the data stored in a table will be valid and thus have integrity.

Business rules that are applied to data are completely **System dependent**. The rules applied to data gathered and processed by a **Savings Bank System** will be very different, to the business rules applied to data gathered and processed by an **Inventory System**, which in turn will be very different, to the business rules applied to data gathered and processed by a **Personnel Management System**.

Business rules, which are enforced on data being stored in a table, are called **Constraints**. Constraints, **super control** the data being entered into a table for permanent storage.

To understand the concept of data constraints, several tables will be created and different types of constraints will be applied to table columns **or** the table itself. The set of tables are described below. Appropriate examples of data constraints are bound to these tables.

Applying Data Constraints

Oracle permits data constraints to be attached to table columns via SQL syntax that checks data for integrity prior storage. Once data constraints are part of a table column construct, the Oracle database engine checks the data being entered into a table column against the data constraints. If the data passes this check, it is stored in the table column, else the data is rejected. Even if a single column of the record being entered into the table fails a constraint, the **entire record is rejected and not stored in the table**.

Both the **Create Table** and **Alter Table** SQL verbs can be used to write SQL sentences that attach constraints (i.e. Business / System rules) to a table column.

Caution

 Until now tables created in this material have **not** had any data constraints attached to their table columns. Hence the tables have **not** been given any instructions to filter what is being stored in the table. This situation **can** and **does**, result in erroneous data being stored in the table.

Once a constraint is attached to a table column, any SQL **INSERT** or **UPDATE** statement automatically causes these constraints to be applied to data prior it is being inserted into the table column for storage.

Note

 Oracle also permits applying data constraints at **Table level**. More on table level constraints later in this material.

TYPES OF DATA CONSTRAINTS

There are two types of data constraints that can be applied to data being inserted into an Oracle table. One type of constraint is called an **I/O** constraint (**i**nput / **o**utput). This data constraint determines the speed at which data can be inserted or extracted from an Oracle table. The other type of constraint is called a **business rule** constraint.

I/O Constraints

The input/output data constraints are further divided into **two** distinctly different constraints.

The PRIMARY KEY Constraint

A primary key is one or more column(s) in a table used to uniquely identify **each row** in the table. None of the fields that are part of the primary key can contain a null value. A table can have only one primary key. A **primary key column** in a table has special attributes:

❑ It defines the column, as a mandatory column (**i.e.** the column cannot be left blank). As its NOT NULL attribute is active
❑ The data across the column MUST be UNIQUE

A single column primary key is called a **Simple** key. A multicolumn primary key is called a **Composite** primary key. The only function of a primary key in a table is to **uniquely identify a row**. When a record cannot be uniquely identified using a value in a simple key, a composite key must be defined. A primary key can be defined in either a **CREATE TABLE** statement or an **ALTER TABLE** statement.

For example, a **SALES_ORDER_DETAILS** table will hold multiple records that are sales orders. Each such sales order will have multiple products that have been ordered. Standard business rules do not allow multiple entries for the same product. However, multiple orders will definitely have multiple entries of the same product.

Under these circumstances, the only way to uniquely identify a row in the **SALES_ORDER_DETAILS** table is via a composite primary key, consisting of **ORDER_NO** and **PRODUCT_NO**. Thus the combination of order number and product number will uniquely identify a row.

Features of Primary key
1. Primary key is a column or a set of columns that uniquely identifies a row. Its main purpose is the **Record Uniqueness**
2. Primary key will not allow duplicate values
3. Primary key will also not allow null values
4. Primary key is not compulsory but it is recommended
5. Primary key helps to identify one record from another record and also helps in relating tables with one another
6. Primary key cannot be LONG or LONG RAW data type
7. Only one Primary key is allowed per table
8. Unique Index is created automatically if there is a Primary key
9. One table can combine upto 16 columns in a Composite Primary key

PRIMARY KEY Constraint Defined At Column Level

Syntax:
    <ColumnName> <Datatype>(<Size>) PRIMARY KEY

Example 1:
Drop the **Bills** table, if it already exists. Create a table **Bills** such that the contents of the column **BillNo** is unique and not null.

DROP TABLE Bills**;**
CREATE TABLE Bills **(**BillNo Number(5) **PRIMARY KEY**, BillDt Date, CustId Number(5),
    Total Decimal(8,2)**);**

Output:
```
Table created.
```

For testing purpose, execute the following **INSERT INTO** statement:
INSERT INTO Bills (BillNo, BillDt, CustId, Total) **VALUES(**1, '10-Jun-2000', 1, 129060.00**);**

Output:
```
1 row created.
```

To verify whether the Primary Key Constraint is functional, reissue the same **INSERT INTO** statement.
The result is the following error:

Output:
```
INSERT INTO Bills (BillNo, BillDt, CustId, Total) VALUES(1, '10-Jun-2000',
1, 129060.00)
*
ERROR at line 1:
ORA-00001: unique constraint (SCOTT.SYS_C005427) violated
```

PRIMARY KEY Constraint Defined At Table Level

Syntax:
```
PRIMARY KEY (<ColumnName>, <ColumnName>)
```

Example 2:
Drop the **Bills** table, if it already exists. Create a table **Bills** where there is a composite primary key mapped
to the columns **BillNo** and **CustId**.
Since this constraint spans across columns, **it must be described at table level**.

DROP TABLE Bills;
CREATE TABLE Bills (BillNo Number(5), BillDt Date, CustId Number(5), Total Decimal(8,2),
    PRIMARY KEY(BillNo, CustId));

Output:
```
Table created.
```

For testing purpose, execute the following **INSERT INTO** statement:
INSERT INTO Bills (BillNo, BillDt, CustId, Total) **VALUES(**1, '10-Jun-2000', 1, 129060.00**);**

Output:
```
1 row created.
```

To verify whether the Composite Primary Key Constraint is functional, reissue the same **INSERT INTO**
statement. The result is the following error:

Output:
```
INSERT INTO Bills (BillNo, BillDt, CustId, Total) VALUES(1, '10-Jun-2000',
1, 129060.00)
*
ERROR at line 1:
ORA-00001: unique constraint (SCOTT.SYS_C005428) violated
```

Now, simply modify the INSERT INTO statement as shown below, to allow the record to pass the
composite primary key constraint:
INSERT INTO Bills (BillNo, BillDt, CustId, Total) **VALUES(**1, '10-Jun-2000', **2**, 129060.00**);**

Output:
```
1 row created.
```

The Foreign Key (Self Reference) Constraint

Foreign keys represent relationships between tables. A foreign key is a column (or a group of columns) whose values are derived from the **primary key** or **unique key** of some other table.

The table in which the foreign key is defined is called a **Foreign table** or **Detail table**. The table that defines the **primary** or **unique** key and is referenced by the **foreign key** is called the **Primary table** or **Master table**. A Foreign key can be defined in either a CREATE TABLE statement or an ALTER TABLE statement

The master table can be referenced in the foreign key definition by using the clause **REFERENCES TableName.ColumnName** when defining the foreign key, column attributes, in the detail table.

Features of Foreign Keys
1. Foreign key is a column(s) that references a column(s) of a table and it can be the same table also
2. Parent that is being referenced has to be unique or Primary key
3. Child may have duplicates and nulls but unless it is specified
4. Foreign key constraint can be specified on child but not on parent
5. Parent record can be deleted provided no child record exist
6. Master table cannot be updated if child record exist

This constraint establishes a relationship between records (i.e. column data) across a Master and a Detail table. This relationship ensures:

❑ Records cannot be **inserted** into a **detail table** if corresponding records in the master table do not exist
❑ Records of the **master table** cannot be **deleted** if corresponding records in the detail table actually exist

Insert Or Update Operation In The Foreign Key Table

The existence of a foreign key implies that the table with the foreign key is **related** to the master table from which the foreign key is derived. A foreign key must have a corresponding primary key or unique key value in the master table.

For example a personnel information system includes two tables (i.e. department and employee). An employee cannot belong to a department that does not exist. Thus the department number specified in the employee table must be present in the department table.

Delete Operation On The Primary Key Table

Oracle **displays an error message** when a record in the master table is deleted and corresponding records exists in a detail table and **prevents the delete operation** from going through.

Note

The default behavior of the foreign key can be changed, by using the **ON DELETE CASCADE** option. When the **ON DELETE CASCADE** option is specified in the foreign key definition, if a record is deleted in the master table, all corresponding records in the detail table along with the record in the master table will be deleted.

Principles of **Foreign Key/References** constraint:
❑ Rejects an **INSERT** or **UPDATE** of a value, if a corresponding value does not currently exist in the master key table
❑ If the **ON DELETE CASCADE** option is set, a **DELETE** operation in the master table will trigger a **DELETE** operation for corresponding records **in all** detail tables
❑ If the **ON DELETE SET NULL** option is set, a **DELETE** operation in the master table will set the value held by the foreign key of the detail tables to null

- ❑ **Rejects** a **DELETE** from the Master table if **corresponding records** in the DETAIL table **exist**
- ❑ Must reference a **PRIMARY KEY** or **UNIQUE** column(s) in primary table
- ❑ Requires that the **FOREIGN KEY** column(s) and the **CONSTRAINT** column(s) have **matching** data types
- ❑ . Can reference the same table named in the **CREATE TABLE** statement

FOREIGN KEY Constraint Defined At The Column Level

Syntax:

> **<ColumnName> <DataType>(<Size>) REFERENCES <TableName> [(<ColumnName>)]**
>   **[ON DELETE CASCADE]**

> Example 3 and Example 4 use CustId as the Foreign Key in the Bills table. For these examples to go through the Customers table needs to be recreated with CustId as a Primary Key. This can be done as follows:
> **DROP TABLE** Customers;
> **CREATE TABLE** Customers (CustId Number(5) **PRIMARY KEY**,
>   FirstName VarChar2(20), LastName VarChar2(20), Addr VarChar2(250),
>   City VarChar2(15), State VarChar2(15), PostalCode VarChar2(15),
>   Country VarChar2(15), Phone VarChar2(30), LicenseNo VarChar2(20),
>   LicenseType VarChar2(50), IssuedOn Date, ExpiresOn Date);

Example 3:
Drop the table **Bills**, if it already exists. Create a table **Bills**, with its primary as **BillNo**, referencing the foreign key **CustId** in the **Customers** table.

DROP TABLE Bills;
CREATE TABLE Bills (BillNo Number(5) **PRIMARY KEY**, BillDt Date,
    CustId Number(5) **REFERENCES** Customers, Total Decimal(8,2));

Output:
```
Table created.
```

The **REFERENCES** key word points to the table **Customers**. *The table **Customers** must have the column **CustId** as its primary key column.* Since no column is specified in the foreign key definition, Oracle applies an automatic (default) link to the primary key column i.e. **CustId** of the table **Customers**.

The foreign key definition is specified as:
    CustId Number(5) **REFERENCES** Customers

FOREIGN KEY Constraint Defined At The Table Level

Syntax:

> **FOREIGN KEY (<ColumnName> [,<ColumnName>])**
>   **REFERENCES <TableName> [(<ColumnName>,<ColumnName>)**

Example 4:
Drop the table **Bills**, if it already exists. Create a table **Bills** with **CustId** as foreign key referencing column **CustId** in the **Customers** table

DROP TABLE Bills;
CREATE TABLE Bills (BillNo Number(5), BillDt Date, CustId Number(5), Total Decimal(8,2),
    FOREIGN KEY(CustId) **REFERENCES** Customers(CustId));

Output:
```
Table created.
```

FOREIGN KEY Constraint Defined With ON DELETE CASCADE

Example 5:
Drop the tables **Bills** and **Customers**, if they already exist. Create a table **Customers** with the field **CustId** as its primary key.

Create a table **Bills** with its foreign key as **CustId** with the ON DELETE CASCADE option. The foreign key is **CustId** and is available as a primary key column named **CustId** in the **Customers** table.

Insert some records into both the tables.

DROP TABLE Bills;
DROP TABLE Customers;
CREATE TABLE Customers (CustId Number(5) **PRIMARY KEY**, FirstName VarChar2(20),
    LastName VarChar2(20), Addr VarChar2(250), City VarChar2(15), State VarChar2(15),
    PostalCode VarChar2(15), Country VarChar2(15), Phone VarChar2(30),
    LicenseNo VarChar2(20), LicenseType VarChar2(50), IssuedOn Date, ExpiresOn Date);

Output:
```
Table created.
```

CREATE TABLE Bills (BillNo Number(5), BillDt Date, CustId Number(5), Total Decimal(8,2),
    FOREIGN KEY(CustId) **REFERENCES** Customers(CustId)
        ON DELETE CASCADE);

Output:
```
Table created.
```

Now delete a record from the Customers table as:

DELETE FROM Customers **WHERE** CustId = 1;

Output:
```
1 row deleted.
```

Query the table Bills for records:

SELECT * FROM Bills;

Notice the deletion of the records in the **Bills** table belonging to customers with **CustId** 1.

Explanation:
In this example, a primary key is created in the **Customers** table. i.e. **CustID** field. Then, a foreign key is created in the **Bills** table that references the Customers table based on the contents of the **CustId** field.

Because of the **CASCADE DELETE** option, when a record in the **Customers** table is deleted, all records in the **Bills** table will also be deleted that have the same **CustId** value.

FOREIGN KEY Constraint Defined With ON DELETE SET NULL:

A FOREIGN key with a **SET NULL ON DELETE** means that if a record in the parent table is deleted, then the corresponding records in the child table will have the foreign key fields set to **null**. The records in the child table **will not** be deleted.

A FOREIGN key with a **SET NULL ON DELETE** can be defined in either a CREATE TABLE statement or an ALTER TABLE statement.

Example 6:
Drop the tables **Bills** and **Customers**, if it already exists. Create a table **Customers** with the field **CustId** as its primary key.

Create a table **Bills** with its foreign key as **CustId** with the ON DELETE SET NULL option. The foreign key is **CustId** and is available as a primary key column named **CustId** in the **Customers** table.

Insert some records into both the tables.

DROP TABLE Bills;
DROP TABLE Customers;
CREATE TABLE Customers (CustId Number(5) **PRIMARY KEY**, FirstName VarChar2(20),
    LastName VarChar2(20), Addr VarChar2(250), City VarChar2(15), State VarChar2(15),
    PostalCode VarChar2(15), Country VarChar2(15), Phone VarChar2(30),
    LicenseNo VarChar2(20), LicenseType VarChar2(50), IssuedOn Date, ExpiresOn Date);

Output:
```
Table created.
```

CREATE TABLE Bills (BillNo Number(5), BillDt Date, CustId Number(5), Total Decimal(8,2),
    FOREIGN KEY(CustId) REFERENCES Customers(CustId)
        ON DELETE SET NULL);

Output:
```
Table created.
```

Now delete a record from the **Customers** table as:

DELETE FROM Customers **WHERE** CustId = 1;

Output:
```
1 row deleted.
```

Query the table **Bills** for records:

SELECT * FROM Bills;

Notice that value held in the **CustId** field of the **Bills** table is set to null, for those records belonging to customers with **CustId** 1.

Explanation:
In this example, a primary key is created in the **Customers** table. i.e. **CustId** field. Then, a foreign key is created in the **Bills** table that references the **Customers** table based on the **CustId** field.

Because of the **CASCADE SET NULL**, when a record in the **Customers** table is deleted, all corresponding records in the **Bills** table will have the **CustId** values set to **null**.

Assigning User Defined Names To Constraints

When constraints are defined, Oracle assigns a **unique name** to each constraint. The convention used by Oracle is
    SYS_Cn
where **n** is a **numeric value** that makes the constraint name **unique**.

Constraints can be given a unique user-defined name along with the constraint definition. A constraint can then, be dropped by referring to the constraint by its name. Under these circumstances a user-defined constraint name becomes very convenient.

User named constraints simplifies the task of dropping constraints. A constraint can be given a user-defined name by preceding the constraint definition with the reserved word **CONSTRAINT** and a **user-defined name**.

Syntax:
  CONSTRAINT <Constraint Name> <Constraint Definition>

Example 7:
Drop the **Customers** table, if it already exists. Create a table **Customers** with a primary key constraint on the column **CustId** and also define its constraint name.

DROP TABLE Customers;
CREATE TABLE Customers (
    CustId Number(5) **CONSTRAINT** PK_Customers_CustId **PRIMARY KEY**,
    FirstName VarChar2(20), LastName VarChar2(20), Addr VarChar2(250), City VarChar2(15),
    State VarChar2(15), PostalCode VarChar2(15), Country VarChar2(15), Phone VarChar2(30),
    LicenseNo VarChar2(20), LicenseType VarChar2(50), IssuedOn Date, ExpiresOn Date);

Output:
```
Table created.
```

Example 8:
Drop the table **Rentals**, if it already exists. Create a table **Rentals** with its foreign key as **CarRegNo**. *The foreign key is **CarRegNo** and **should be** available as a primary key in the **Cars** table.* Also define the name of the foreign key.

DROP TABLE Rentals;
CREATE TABLE Rentals (RentId Number(5), CustId Number(5), CarRegNo VarChar2(20),
    RentDt Date, PropRtrnDt Date, ActualRtrnDt Date, RentType VarChar2(1), Period Number(3),
    OpMlge Decimal(8), ClMlge Decimal(8), RentAmt Decimal(8,2), DriverRqrd VarChar(1),
    DriverAmt Decimal(8,2), AdvPaid Decimal(8,2), BillNo Number(5), PayStatus VarChar2(1),
    CONSTRAINT FK_Rental_CarRegNo **FOREIGN KEY**(CarRegNo) **REFERENCES** Cars);

Output:
```
Table created.
```

The Unique Key Constraint

The **Unique** column constraint **permits multiple entries** of NULL into the column. These NULL values are clubbed at the top of the column in the order in which they were entered into the table. This is **the essential difference** between the Primary Key and the Unique constraints when applied to table column(s).

Key point about Unique Constraint:
1. Unique key will not allow duplicate values
2. Unique index is created automatically
3. A table can have more than one Unique key which is not possible in Primary key
4. Unique key can combine upto 16 columns in a Composite Unique key
5. Unique key can not be LONG or LONG RAW data type

UNIQUE Constraint Defined At The Column Level

Syntax:

     <ColumnName> <Datatype>(<Size>) UNIQUE

Example 9:
Drop the **Cars** table, if it already exists. Create a table **Cars** such that the contents of the column **CarRegNo** are unique across the entire column.

DROP TABLE Cars;
CREATE TABLE Cars **(**
     CarRegNo VarChar2(20) **UNIQUE**, Model VarChar2(25), Make VarChar2(25), Color VarChar2(10),
     Catgry VarChar2(1), AC VarChar2(1), EngineNo VarChar2(25), ChassisNo VarChar2(25),
     TransAM VarChar2(1), Fuel VarChar2(1), PurchaseDt Date, HrRentRate Decimal(6,2),
     DyRentRate Decimal(6,2), HrDriverRate Decimal(6,2), DyDriverRate Decimal(6,2),
     CarStatus VarChar2(1)**);**

Output:
```
Table created.
```

For testing the Unique constraint execute the following INSERT INTO statements:

INSERT INTO Cars **(**CarRegNo, Model, Make, Color, Catgry, AC, EngineNo, ChassisNo, TransAM, Fuel,
           PurchaseDt, HrRentRate, DyRentRate, HrDriverRate, DyDriverRate, CarStatus**)**
     VALUES('MH-01-B-2083', 'Esteem', 'Maruti', 'Grey', 'L', 'Y', 'ME-03042000-A34', 'B7-82347939-
         E90', 'M', 'P', '03-Apr-2000', 190.00, 4180.00, 30.00, 600.00, 'A'**);**
INSERT INTO Cars **(**CarRegNo, Model, Make, Color, Catgry, AC, EngineNo, ChassisNo, TransAM, Fuel,
           PurchaseDt, HrRentRate, DyRentRate, HrDriverRate, DyDriverRate, CarStatus**)**
     VALUES('MH-01-B-2083', 'Sumo', 'Tata', 'White', 'J', 'N', 'SU-30112000-T12', 'U4-93497878-H93',
         'M', 'D', '30-Nov-2000', 180.00, 3960.00, 30.00, 600.00, 'A'**);**
INSERT INTO Cars **(**CarRegNo, Model, Make, Color, Catgry, AC, EngineNo, ChassisNo, TransAM, Fuel,
           PurchaseDt, HrRentRate, DyRentRate, HrDriverRate, DyDriverRate, CarStatus**)**
     VALUES('MH-02-C-5876', 'Omni', 'Maruti', 'White', 'V', 'N', 'MO-15082000-B34', 'H9-83548647-
         G85', 'M', 'P', '15-Aug-2000', 170.00, 3740.00, 27.50, 550.00, 'A'**);**

Output:
The first INSERT INTO statement will execute without any errors as show below:
```
1 row created.
```

When the second INSERT INTO statement is executed an errors occurs as show below:
```
INSERT INTO Cars (CarRegNo, Model, Make, Color, Catgry, AC, EngineNo,
ChassisNo, TransAM, Fuel, Purc
*
ERROR at line 1:
ORA-00001: unique constraint (SCOTT.SYS_C005446) violated
```

The third INSERT INTO statement rectifies this and the result is as show below:
```
1 row created.
```

When a SELECT statement is executed on the Cars table the records retrieved are:

SELECT CarRegNo, Model, Make, Color **FROM** Cars;

Output:

CARREGNO	MODEL	MAKE	COLOR
MH-01-B-2083	Esteem	Maruti	Grey
MH-02-C-5876	Omni	Maruti	White

UNIQUE Constraint Defined At The Table Level

Syntax:

    CREATE TABLE TableName
        (<ColumnName1> <Datatype>(<Size>), <ColumnName2> <Datatype>(<Size>),
            UNIQUE (<ColumnName1>, <ColumnName2>));

Example 10:
Drop the **Cars** table, if it already exists. Create a table **Cars** such that the contents of the column **CarRegNo** are unique across the entire column.

DROP TABLE Cars;
CREATE TABLE Cars (
    CarRegNo VarChar2(20), Model VarChar2(25), Make VarChar2(25), Color VarChar2(10),
    Catgry VarChar2(1), AC VarChar2(1), EngineNo VarChar2(25), ChassisNo VarChar2(25),
    TransAM VarChar2(1), Fuel VarChar2(1), PurchaseDt Date, HrRentRate Decimal(6,2),
    DyRentRate Decimal(6,2), HrDriverRate Decimal(6,2), DyDriverRate Decimal(6,2),
    CarStatus VarChar2(1), **UNIQUE(CarRegNo)**);

Output:
Table created.

In the case of the table level unique constraints, the result for the following INSERT INTO statement will remain the same as explained earlier.

INSERT INTO Cars (CarRegNo, Model, Make, Color, Catgry, AC, EngineNo, ChassisNo, TransAM, Fuel,
            PurchaseDt, HrRentRate, DyRentRate, HrDriverRate, DyDriverRate, CarStatus)
        VALUES('MH-01-B-2083', 'Esteem', 'Maruti', 'Grey', 'L', 'Y', 'ME-03042000-A34', 'B7-82347939-
            E90', 'M', 'P', '03-Apr-2000', 190.00, 4180.00, 30.00, 600.00, 'A');
INSERT INTO Cars (CarRegNo, Model, Make, Color, Catgry, AC, EngineNo, ChassisNo, TransAM, Fuel,
            PurchaseDt, HrRentRate, DyRentRate, HrDriverRate, DyDriverRate, CarStatus)
        VALUES('MH-01-B-2083', 'Sumo', 'Tata', 'White', 'J', 'N', 'SU-30112000-T12', 'U4-93497878-H93',
            'M', 'D', '30-Nov-2000', 180.00, 3960.00, 30.00, 600.00, 'A');
INSERT INTO Cars (CarRegNo, Model, Make, Color, Catgry, AC, EngineNo, ChassisNo, TransAM, Fuel,
            PurchaseDt, HrRentRate, DyRentRate, HrDriverRate, DyDriverRate, CarStatus)
        VALUES('MH-02-C-5876', 'Omni', 'Maruti', 'White', 'V', 'N', 'MO-15082000-B34', 'H9-83548647-
            G85', 'M', 'P', '15-Aug-2000', 170.00, 3740.00, 27.50, 550.00, 'A');

Business Rule Constraints

Oracle allows the application of **business rules** to table columns. Business managers determine business rules, they vary from system to system as mentioned earlier. These rules are applied to data, **prior** the data is being inserted into table columns. This ensures that the data (**records**) in the table have integrity.

For example, the rule that no employee in the company shall get a salary less than Rs.1000/- is a business rule. This means that no cell in the **salary** column of the employee table should hold a **value** less than 1000. If an attempt is made, to insert a value less than 1000 into the salary column, the database engine rejects the entire record automatically.

Business rules can be implemented in Oracle by using **CHECK** constraints. Check Constraints can be bound to a **column** or a **table** using the **CREATE TABLE** or **ALTER TABLE** command.

Business rule validation checks are performed when any table **write** operation is carried out. Any insert or update statement causes the relevant Check constraint to be evaluated. The Check constraint must be satisfied for the write operation to succeed. Thus **Check constraints** ensure the integrity of the data in tables.

Conceptually, data constraints are connected to a column, by the Oracle engine, as **flags**. Whenever, an attempt is made to load the column with data, the Oracle engine observes the flag and recognizes the presence of a constraint. The Oracle engine then retrieves the Check constraint definition and then applies the Check constraint definition, to the data being loaded into the table column. If the data being entered into a column fails any of the data constraint checks, the **entire** record is rejected. The Oracle engine will then flash an appropriate **error message** to the console where the insert statement originated.

Oracle allows programmers to define constraints at**:**
❑   Column Level
❑   Table Level

Column Level Constraints

If data constraints are defined as an attribute of a column definition when creating or altering a table structure, they are **column level constraints**.

Caution

Column level constraints are applied to the **current column**. The current   column is the column that immediately **precedes** the constraint (**i.e.** they are local to a specific column).   A column level constraint **cannot** be applied if the data constraint spans **across multiple columns** in a table.

Table Level Constraints

If data constraints are defined **after defining all table column attributes** when creating or altering a table structure, it is a **table level constraint**.

Note

A table level constraint **must** be applied if the data constraint **spans across multiple columns** in a table.

Constraints are stored as a part of the global table definition by the Oracle engine in its **system tables**. The SQL syntax used to attach the constraint will change depending upon whether it is a column level or table level constraint.

NULL Value Concepts

Often there may be records in a table that do not have values for every field. This could be because the information is not available at the time of data entry or because the field is not applicable in every case. If the column was created as **NULLABLE**, Oracle will place a NULL value in the column in the **absence** of a user-defined value.

A NULL value is **different from** a blank or a zero. A **NULL value** can be inserted into **columns** of **any data type**.

Principles Of NULL Values

❑ Setting a NULL value is appropriate when the actual value is unknown, or when a value would not be meaningful

❑ A NULL value is **not equivalent** to a value of **zero** if the data type is **number** and is not equivalent to **spaces** if the data type is **character**

❑ A NULL value will evaluate to NULL in any expression (**e.g.** NULL multiplied by 10 is NULL)

❑ NULL value can be inserted into columns of **any data type**

❑ If the column has a NULL value, Oracle ignores any UNIQUE, FOREIGN KEY, CHECK constraints that may be attached to the column

Difference Between An Empty String And A NULL Value

Oracle has changed its rules about empty strings and null values in newer versions of Oracle. Now, an empty string is treated as a null value in Oracle.

To understand this, go through the following example:

Example 11:
Drop the table **Bills**, if it already exists. Create a table **Bills** with its primary as **BillNo**.

DROP TABLE Bills;
CREATE TABLE Bills (BillNo Number(5) **PRIMARY KEY**, BillDt Date,
    CustId Number(5), Total Decimal(8,2));

Insert two records into the Bills table.

INSERT INTO Bills (BillNo, BillDt, CustId, Total) **VALUES**(1, **null**, 1, 129060.00);

Output:
```
1 row created.
```

INSERT INTO Bills (BillNo, BillDt, CustId, Total) **VALUES**(2, '', 1, 129060.00);

Output:
```
1 row created.
```

The first statement inserts a record with a BillDt that is null, while the second statement inserts a record with an empty string as a Bill Date.

Now, retrieve all rows with a BillDt that is an empty string value as follows:

SELECT * FROM Bills **WHERE** BillDt = '';

When this statement is executed, it is expected to retrieve the row that was inserted above. But instead, this statement will not retrieve any records at all.

Now, try retrieving all rows where the Bill Date contains a null value:

SELECT * FROM Bills **WHERE** BillDt **IS NULL**;

When this statement is executed, both rows are retrieved. This is because Oracle has now changed its rules so that empty strings behave as null values.

It is also important to note that the null value is unique. Usual operands such as =, <, > and so on cannot be used on a null value. Instead, the IS NULL and IS NOT NULL conditions have to be used.

NOT NULL Constraint Defined At The Column Level

In addition to Primary key and Foreign Key, Oracle has **NOT NULL** as column constraint. The **NOT NULL** column constraint ensures that a table column cannot be left empty.

When a column is defined as **NOT NULL**, it becomes a **mandatory** column. Hence, a value must be entered into the column if the record is to be stored in the table, else the record is rejected and not stored.

Syntax:

    <ColumnName> <Datatype>(<Size>) NOT NULL

Example 12:
Drop the table **Bills**, if it already exists and then create it again making the Date of Bill field -NOT NULL.

DROP TABLE Bills;
CREATE TABLE Bills (BillNo Number(5), BillDt Date **NOT NULL**, CustId Number(5),
    Total Decimal(8,2));

Output:
```
Table created.
```

Note

> The **NOT NULL** constraint can only be applied at column level.

Execute the following INSERT INTO statements to verify whether mandatory field constraints are applied:

INSERT INTO Bills (BillNo, BillDt, CustId, Total) **VALUES(1, null, 1, 129060.00);**

Output:
```
INSERT INTO Bills (BillNo, BillDt, CustId, Total) VALUES(1, null, 1,
129060.00)

ERROR at line 1:
ORA-01400: cannot insert NULL into ("SCOTT"."BILLS"."BILLDT")
```

The above **error** message confirms that the mandatory field constraints are applied successfully.

Caution

> The **NOT NULL** constraint can only be applied at column level. Although **NOT NULL** can be applied as a **CHECK** constraint, Oracle Corp recommends that this should **not be done**.

The CHECK Constraint

Business Rule validations can be applied to a table column by using the **CHECK** constraint. **CHECK** constraints must be specified as a logical expression that evaluates either to **TRUE** or **FALSE**.

Note

> A **CHECK** constraint takes substantially longer to execute as compared to NOT NULL, PRIMARY KEY, FOREIGN KEY or UNIQUE. Thus CHECK constraints must be avoided if the constraint can be defined using the Not Null, Primary key or Foreign key constraint.

CHECK constraint defined at the column level:

Syntax:

    `<ColumnName> <Datatype>(<Size>) CHECK (<Logical Expression>)`

Example 13:
Drop the table **Customers**, if already exists. Create a table **Customers** with the following check constraints:
❏   Data values being inserted into the column **FirstName** and **LastName** should be in **upper case** only

DROP TABLE Customers;
CREATE TABLE Customers (CustId Number(5),
    FirstName VarChar2(20) **CHECK** (FirstName = UPPER(FirstName)),
    LastName VarChar2(20) **CHECK** (LastName = UPPER(LastName)),
    Addr VarChar2(250), City VarChar2(15), State VarChar2(15), PostalCode VarChar2(15),
    Country VarChar2(15), Phone VarChar2(30), LicenseNo VarChar2(20), LicenseType VarChar2(50),
    IssuedOn Date, ExpiresOn Date);

Output:
```
Table created.
```

CHECK Constraint Defined At The Table Level:

Syntax:

    `CHECK (<Logical Expression>)`

Example 14:
Drop the table **Customers**, if already exists. Create a table **Customers** with the following check constraints:
❏   Data values being inserted into the column **FirstName and LastName** should be in **upper case** only

DROP TABLE Customers;
CREATE TABLE Customers (CustId Number(5), FirstName VarChar2(20), LastName VarChar2(20),
    Addr VarChar2(250), City VarChar2(15), State VarChar2(15), PostalCode VarChar2(15),
    Country VarChar2(15), Phone VarChar2(30), LicenseNo VarChar2(20), LicenseType VarChar2(50),
    IssuedOn Date, ExpiresOn Date,
    CHECK (FirstName = UPPER(FirstName)), **CHECK** (LastName = UPPER(LastName)));

Output:
```
Table created.
```

Execute the following INSERT INTO statements to verify whether check constraints are applied:

INSERT INTO Customers (CustId, FirstName, LastName, Addr, City, State, PostalCode, Country, Phone,
        LicenseNo, LicenseType, IssuedOn, ExpiresOn)
    VALUES(2, 'John Simon', 'Brownie', '123/A, North Links', 'New York', 'New York', 'NY-200546', 'U.
        S. A.', '23657868', 'UB-40201', 'LMV', '15-Oct-1999', '14-Oct-2019');

Output:
```
INSERT INTO Customers (CustId, FirstName, LastName, Addr, City, State,
PostalCode, Country, Phone, L
*
ERROR at line 1:
ORA-02290: check constraint (SCOTT.SYS_C005454) violated
```

The above **error** messages confirm that the check constraints defined are applied successfully.

When using **CHECK** constraints, consider the ANSI / ISO standard, which states that a CHECK constraint is violated only if the condition evaluates to **False**. A check constraint is not violated if the condition evaluates to **True**.

Note

If the expression in a check constraint does not return a **true / false**, the value is **Indeterminate** or **Unknown.** Unknown values do not violate a check constraint condition. For example, consider the following CHECK constraint for Total column in the Bills table:
    CHECK (Total > 0)

At first glance, this rule may be interpreted as "do not allow a row in the **Bills** table unless the **Total** is **greater than** 0". However, note that if a row is inserted with a **null Total**, the row **does not violate** the CHECK constraint because the entire check condition is evaluated as **unknown**.

In this particular case, prevent such violations by placing the **not null** integrity constraint along with the check constraint on **Total** column of the table **Bills**.

Restrictions On CHECK Constraints

A **CHECK** integrity constraint requires that a condition be **true** or **unknown** for the row to be processed. If an SQL statement causes the condition to evaluate to **false**, an appropriate error message is displayed and processing stops.

A **CHECK** constraint has the following limitations:
- The condition must be a **Boolean** expression that can be evaluated using the values in the row being inserted or updated.
- The condition cannot contain **subqueries** or **sequences**.
- The condition cannot include the SYSDATE, UID, USER or USERENV SQL functions.

DEFINING DIFFERENT CONSTRAINTS ON A TABLE

Example 15:
Drop the table **Bills**, if already exists. Create **Bills** table where:
- The **BillNo** is a primary key to this table
- The **CustId** is the foreign key referencing the table **Customers**
- The fields **BillDt** and **Total** cannot have a NULL value
- **Total** column should be greater than 0

DROP TABLE Bills;
CREATE TABLE Bills (BillNo Number(5), BillDt Date **NOT NULL**, CustId Number(5),
    Total Decimal(8,2) **NOT NULL**,
    CONSTRAINT PK_Bills_BillNo **PRIMARY KEY**(BillNo),
    CONSTRAINT FK_Bills_CustId **FOREIGN KEY**(CustId) **REFERENCES** Customers(CustId),
    CHECK(Total > 0)
);

Output:
```
Table created.
```

THE USER_CONSTRAINTS TABLE

A table can be created with multiple constraints attached to its columns. If a user wishes to see the table structure along with its constraints, Oracle provides the **DESCRIBE <TableName>** command.

This command displays only the column names, data type, size and the NOT NULL constraint. The information about the other constraints that may be attached to the table columns such as the PRIMARY KEY, FOREIGN KEY, and so on, is not available using the DESCRIBE verb.

Oracle stores such information in a table called **USER_CONSTRAINTS**. Querying **USER_CONSTRAINTS** provides information bound to the names of all the constraints on the table. **USER_CONSTRAINTS** comprises of multiple columns, some of which are described below:

USER_CONSTRAINTS Table:

Column Name	Description
OWNER	The owner of the constraint.
CONSTRAINT_NAME	The name of the constraint
TABLE_NAME	The name of the table associated with the constraint
CONSTRAINT_TYPE	The type of constraint: **P**: Primary Key Constraint **R**: Foreign Key Constraint **U**: Unique Constraint **C**: Check Constraint
SEARCH_CONDITION	The search condition used (for CHECK Constraints)
R_OWNER	The owner of the table referenced by the FOREIGN KEY constraints
R_CONSTRAINT_NAME	The name of the constraint referenced by a FOREIGN KEY constraint.

Example 16:
View the constraints of the table Bills

SELECT OWNER, CONSTRAINT_NAME, CONSTRAINT_TYPE **FROM USER_CONSTRAINTS**
    WHERE TABLE_NAME = 'BILLS';

Output:
```
OWNER         CONSTRAINT_NAME                   C
-----------   -----------------------------     -
SCOTT         SYS_C005708                       C
SCOTT         SYS_C005709                       C
SCOTT         SYS_C005710                       C
SCOTT         PK_BILLS_BILLNO1                  P
SCOTT         FK_BILLS_CUSTID1                  R
```

DEFINING INTEGRITY CONSTRAINTS VIA THE ALTER TABLE COMMAND

Integrity constraints can be defined using the **constraint** clause, in the **ALTER TABLE** command.

Oracle **will not allow** constraints defined using the **ALTER TABLE**, to be applied to the table if data previously placed in the table **violates such constraints**.

If a Primary key constraint was being applied to a table in retrospect and the column has duplicate values in it, the Primary key constraint **will not** be set to that column.

The following examples show the definitions of several integrity constraints:

Example 17:
Alter the table **Receipts** by adding a primary key on the column **RcptId**.

ALTER TABLE Receipts **ADD PRIMARY KEY** (RcptId);

Output:
```
Table altered.
```

Example 18:
Add FOREIGN KEY constraint on the column **BillNo** belonging to the table **Receipts**, which references the table **Bills**. Modify column **RcptDt** to include the **NOT NULL** constraint

ALTER TABLE Receipts
    ADD CONSTRAINT FK_Receipts_BillNo **FOREIGN KEY**(BillNo) **REFERENCES** Bills
        MODIFY(RcptDt **NOT NULL**);

Output:
```
Table altered.
```

DROPPING INTEGRITY CONSTRAINTS VIA THE ALTER TABLE COMMAND

Integrity constraint can be dropped if the rule that it enforces is no longer **true** or if the constraint is no longer **needed**. Drop the constraint using the **ALTER TABLE** command with the **DROP** clause. The following examples illustrate the dropping of integrity constraints:

Example 19:
Drop the PRIMARY KEY constraint from **Receipts**.

ALTER TABLE Receipts **DROP PRIMARY KEY;**

Output:
```
Table altered.
```

Example 20:
Drop FOREIGN KEY constraint on column BillNo from the table Receipts

ALTER TABLE Receipts **DROP CONSTRAINT** FK_Receipts_BillNo;

Output:
```
Table altered.
```

Note

Dropping UNIQUE and PRIMARY KEY constraints **also drops all** associated indexes.

DEFAULT VALUE CONCEPTS

At the time of table creation a **default value** can be assigned to a column. When a record is loaded into the table, and the column is left empty, the Oracle engine will automatically load this column with the default value specified. The data type of the default value should match the data type of the column. The **DEFAULT** clause can be used to specify a default value for a column.

Syntax:
```
<ColumnName> <Datatype>(<Size>) DEFAULT <Value>;
```

Example 21:

Create Cars table where the column FUEL is a VarChar2 and by default it should hold the value **D**. The other column TransAM is a VarChar2 and by default it should hold the value **M**.

CREATE TABLE Cars (CarRegNo VarChar2(20),   Model VarChar2(25), Make VarChar2(25),
Color VarChar2(10), Catgry VarChar2(1), AC VarChar2(1), EngineNo VarChar2(25),
ChassisNo VarChar2(25), TransAM VarChar2(1) **DEFAULT** 'M', Fuel VarChar2(1) **DEFAULT** 'D',
PurchaseDt Date, HrRentRate Decimal(6,2), DyRentRate Decimal(6,2), HrDriverRate Decimal(6,2),
DyDriverRate Decimal(6,2), CarStatus VarChar2(1))**;**

Output:
```
Table created.
```

Note

- ❑ The data type of the default value should match the data type of the column
- ❑ Character and date values will be specified in single quotes
- ❑ If a column level constraint is defined on the column with a default value, the default value clause must precede the constraint definition

Thus the syntax will be:

<ColumnName> <Datatype>(<Size>) DEFAULT <Value> <constraint definition>

SELF REVIEW QUESTIONS

FILL IN THE BLANKS

1. A _____ is a database object that holds user data.

2. Table creation is done using the _____ syntax.

3. Character expressions placed within the insert into statement must be enclosed in _____ quotes.

4. Oracle provides the option of using a _____ _____ in an SQL query to apply a filter on the rows retrieved.

5. The _____ _____ SQL syntax scans through the values of the column/s specified and displays only unique values from amongst them.

6. The SQL sentence populates the _____ table with data from the _____ table.

7. The name of the column cannot be changed using the _____ _____ clause.

8. The _____ command is used to change or modify data values in a table.

9. All table columns belong to a _____ _____.

10. Business rules, which are enforced on data being stored in a table, are called _____.

11. If the column was created as _____ Oracle will place a NULL value in the column in the absence of a user-defined value.

12. When a column is defined as not null, then that column becomes a _____ column.

13. The _____ constraint can only be applied at column level.

14. A _____ value can be inserted into the columns of any data type.

15. A single column primary key is called a _____ key.

16. The data held across the primary key column must be _____.

17. _____ keys represent relationships between tables.

18. The table in which the foreign key is defined is called a Foreign table or _____ table.

19. The default behavior of the foreign key can be changed by using the _____ option.

20. _____ constraints must be specified as a logical expression that evaluates either to TRUE or FALSE.

21. In a CHECK constraint the condition must be a _____ expression that can be evaluated using the values in the row being inserted or updated.

22. _____ constraints can be defined using the constraint clause, in the ALTER TABLE command.

23. Dropping UNIQUE and PRIMARY KEY constraints also drops all associated _____.

TRUE OR FALSE

24. If a spreadsheet has a number data type associated with, then it can store characters as well.

25. Each table column definition is separated from the other by a colon.

26. All table columns belong to a single record.

27. In the insert into SQL sentence table columns and values have a one to many relationship.

28. The SELECT DISTINCT SQL syntax scans through entire rows, and eliminates rows that have exactly the same contents in each column.

29. When specifying a condition in the where clause only logical standard operators can be used.

30. Oracle allows data from a table to be viewed in a sorted order.

31. In order to view the data in descending sorted order the word 'desc' must be mentioned after the column name and before the semi colon in the order by clause.

32. The MODIFY command is used to change or modify data values in a table.

33. The name of the table cannot be changed using the ALTER TABLE clause.

34. Business rules that have to be applied to data are completely System dependent.

35. Constraints super control the data being entered into a table for temporary storage.

36. A NULL value is equivalent to a value of zero.

37. Setting a NULL value is appropriate when the actual value is unknown.

38. A table cannot contain multiple unique keys.

39. Oracle ignores any UNIQUE, FOREIGN KEY, CHECK constraints on a NULL value.

40. A primary key column in a table is an optional column.

41. Standard business rules do not allow multiple entries for the same product.

42. The master table can be referenced in the foreign key definition by using the clause REFERENCES tablename.columnname when defining the foreign key.

43. A CHECK constraint consists of subqueries and sequences.

44. The USER_CONSTRAINTS command displays only the column names, data type, size and the NOT NULL constraint.

45. Drop the constraint using the DROP TABLE command with the DELETE clause.

46. At the time of table creation a default value can be assigned to a column.

47. If a column level constraint is defined on the column with a default value, the default value clause must precede the constraint definition.

HANDS ON EXERCISES

1. **Create the tables described below:**

Table Name: **CLIENT_MASTER**
Description: Used to store client information.

Column Name	Data Type	Size	Default	Attributes
CLIENTNO	Varchar2	6		Primary Key / first letter must start with 'C'
NAME	Varchar2	20		Not Null
ADDRESS1	Varchar2	30		
ADDRESS2	Varchar2	30		
CITY	Varchar2	15		
PINCODE	Number	8		
STATE	Varchar2	15		
BALDUE	Number	10,2		

Table Name: **PRODUCT_MASTER**
Description: Used to store product information.

Column Name	Data Type	Size	Default	Attributes
PRODUCTNO	Varchar2	6		Primary Key / first letter must start with 'P'
DESCRIPTION	Varchar2	15		Not Null
PROFITPERCENT	Number	4,2		Not Null
UNITMEASURE	Varchar2	10		Not Null
QTYONHAND	Number	8		Not Null
REORDERLVL	Number	8		Not Null
SELLPRICE	Number	8,2		Not Null, Cannot be 0
COSTPRICE	Number	8,2		Not Null, Cannot be 0

Table Name: **SALESMAN_MASTER**
Description: Used to store salesman information working for the company.

Column Name	Data Type	Size	Default	Attributes
SALESMANNO	Varchar2	6		Primary Key / first letter must start with 'S'
SALESMANNAME	Varchar2	20		Not Null
ADDRESS1	Varchar2	30		Not Null
ADDRESS2	Varchar2	30		
CITY	Varchar2	20		
PINCODE	Number	8		
STATE	Varchar2	20		

Table describes for the SALESMAN_MASTER table (Continued)

Column Name	Data Type	Size	Default	Attributes
SALAMT	Number	8,2		Not Null, Cannot be 0
TGTTOGET	Number	6,2		Not Null, Cannot be 0
YTDSALES	Number	6,2		Not Null
REMARKS	Varchar2	60		

Table Name: SALES_ORDER

Description: Used to store client's orders.

Column Name	Data Type	Size	Default	Attributes
ORDERNO	Varchar2	6		Primary Key / first letter must start with 'O'
CLIENTNO	Varchar2	6		Foreign Key references ClientNo of Client_Master table
ORDERDATE	Date			Not Null
DELYADDR	Varchar2	25		
SALESMANNO	Varchar2	6		Foreign Key references SalesmanNo of Salesman_Master table
DELYTYPE	Char	1	F	Delivery: part (P) / full (F)
BILLYN	Char	1		
DELYDATE	Date			Cannot be less than Order_Date
ORDERSTATUS	Varchar2	10		Values ('In Process', 'Fulfilled', 'BackOrder', 'Cancelled')

Table Name: SALES_ORDER_DETAILS

Description: Used to store client's orders with details of each product ordered.

Column Name	Data Type	Size	Default	Attributes
ORDERNO	Varchar2	6		Foreign Key references OrderNo of Sales_Order table
PRODUCTNO	Varchar2	6		Foreign Key references ProductNo of Product_Master table
QTYORDERED	Number	8		
QTYDISP	Number	8		
PRODUCTRATE	Number	10,2		

2. **Insert the following data into their respective tables:**

a)   Data for **CLIENT_MASTER** table:

ClientNo	Name	City	Pincode	State	BalDue
C00001	Ivan Bayross	Mumbai	400054	Maharashtra	15000
C00002	Mamta Muzumdar	Madras	780001	Tamil Nadu	0
C00003	Chhaya Bankar	Mumbai	400057	Maharashtra	5000
C00004	Ashwini Joshi	Bangalore	560001	Karnataka	0
C00005	Hansel Colaco	Mumbai	400060	Maharashtra	2000
C00006	Deepak Sharma	Mangalore	560050	Karnataka	0

b)   Data for **PRODUCT_MASTER** table:

ProductNo	Description	Profit Percent	Unit Measure	QtyOn Hand	ReorderLvl	SellPrice	CostPrice
P00001	T-Shirts	5	Piece	200	50	350	250
P0345	Shirts	6	Piece	150	50	500	350
P06734	Cotton Jeans	5	Piece	100	20	600	450
P07865	Jeans	5	Piece	100	20	750	500
P07868	Trousers	2	Piece	150	50	850	550
P07885	Pull Overs	2.5	Piece	80	30	700	450
P07965	Denim Shirts	4	Piece	100	40	350	250
P07975	Lycra Tops	5	Piece	70	30	300	175
P08865	Skirts	5	Piece	75	30	450	300

c)   Data for **SALESMAN_MASTER** table:

SalesmanNo	Name	Address1	Address2	City	PinCode	State
S00001	Aman	A/14	Worli	Mumbai	400002	Maharashtra
S00002	Omkar	65	Nariman	Mumbai	400001	Maharashtra
S00003	Raj	P-7	Bandra	Mumbai	400032	Maharashtra
S00004	Ashish	A/5	Juhu	Mumbai	400044	Maharashtra

SalesmanNo	SalAmt	TgtToGet	YtdSales	Remarks
S00001	3000	100	50	Good
S00002	3000	200	100	Good
S00003	3000	200	100	Good
S00004	3500	200	150	Good

d)   Data for Sales_Order table:

OrderNo	ClientNo	OrderDate	SalesmanNo	DelyType	BillYN	DelyDate	OrderStatus
O19001	C00001	12-June-04	S00001	F	N	20-July-02	In Process
O19002	C00002	25-June-04	S00002	P	N	27-June-02	Cancelled
O46865	C00003	18-Feb-04	S00003	F	Y	20-Feb-02	Fulfilled
O19003	C00001	03-Apr-04	S00001	F	Y	07-Apr-02	Fulfilled
O46866	C00004	20-May-04	S00002	P	N	22-May-02	Cancelled
O19008	C00005	24-May-04	S00004	F	N	26-July-02	In Process

e)   Data for Sales_Order_Details table:

OrderNo	ProductNo	QtyOrdered	QtyDisp	ProductRate
O19001	P00001	4	4	525
O19001	P07965	2	1	8400
O19001	P07885	2	1	5250
O19002	P00001	10	0	525
O46865	P07868	3	3	3150
O46865	P07885	3	1	5250
O46865	P00001	10	10	525
O46865	P0345	4	4	1050
O19003	P03453	2	2	1050
O19003	P06734	1	1	12000
O46866	P07965	1	0	8400
O46866	P07975	1	0	1050
O19008	P00001	10	5	525
O19008	P07975	5	3	1050

3.   Exercise on retrieving records from a table
a.   Find out the names of all the clients.
b.   Retrieve the entire contents of the Client_Master table.
c.   Retrieve the list of names, city and the sate of all the clients.
d.   List the various products available from the Product_Master table.
e.   List all the clients who are located in Mumbai.
f.   Find the names of salesmen who have a salary equal to Rs.3000.

4.   Exercise on updating records in a table
a.   Change the city of ClientNo 'C00005' to 'Bangalore'.
b.   Change the BalDue of ClientNo 'C00001' to Rs. 1000.
c.   Change the cost price of 'Trousers' to Rs. 950.00.
d.   Change the city of the salesman to Pune.

5. Exercise on deleting records in a table
a. Delete all salesmen from the Salesman_Master whose salaries are equal to Rs. 3500.
b. Delete all products from Product_Master where the quantity on hand is equal to 100.
c. Delete from Client_Master where the column state holds the value 'Tamil Nadu'.

6. Exercise on altering the table structure
a. Add a column called 'Telephone' of data type 'number' and size ='10' to the Client_Master table.
b. Change the size of SellPrice column in Product_Master to 10,2.

7. Exercise on deleting the table structure along with the data
a. Destroy the table Client_Master along with its data.

8. Exercise on renaming the table
a. Change the name of the Salesman_Master table to sman_mast.

6. INTERACTIVE SQL PART - II

COMPUTATIONS DONE ON TABLE DATA

None of the techniques used till now allows display of data from a table **after some arithmetic** has been done with it.

Computations may include displaying an employee's name and the employee's salary from the Employee_Master table along with the **annual salary** of the employee (**i.e.** Salary*12). The arithmetic (Salary * 12) is an example of table data arithmetic.

Arithmetic and logical operators give a new dimension to SQL sentences.

Arithmetic Operators

Oracle allows arithmetic operators to be used while viewing records from a table or while performing Data Manipulation operations such as Insert, Update and Delete. These are:

+	Addition	*	Multiplication
-	Subtraction	**	Exponentiation
/	Division	( )	Enclosed operation

Example 1:
List those Rental Transactions where cars have been hired by customers and returned after the due date. Also calculate the **period of delay in returning** the vehicles.

Synopsis:

Tables:	Rentals
Columns:	RentId, CustId, CarRegNo, PropRtrnDt, ActualRtrnDt
Technique:	**Functions: ROUND(); Operators: -, ||; Clauses: WHERE**

Solution:
SELECT RentId, CustId, CarRegNo, ROUND((ActualRtrnDt - PropRtrnDt), 2) || ' days'
    FROM Rentals **WHERE** PropRtrnDt < ActualRtrnDt;

Output:
```
RENTID CUSTID CARREGNO       ROUND ((ACTUALRTRNDT-PROPRTRNDT), 2) ||'DAYS'
------ ------ ------------   -----------------------------------------------
     2      2 MH-01-B-2083   4.08 days
     3      3 MH-01-B-2083   2.13 days
 . . .
    38      3 MH-13-P-3249   9.5 days
22 rows selected.
```

Explanation:
Here, **ROUND ((ActualRtrnDt - PropRtrnDt), 2)** is **not** a column in the table **Rentals**. However, the arithmetic specified is done on the contents of the columns **ActualRtrnDt** and **PropRtrnDt** of the table **Rentals** and displayed in the output of the query.

By default, the Oracle engine will use the column names of the table **Rentals** as column headers when displaying column output on the VDU screen.

Since there are no columns with the arithmetic expression applied on the table **Rentals**, the Oracle engine performs the required arithmetic and uses the **formula** as the **default** column header when displaying output as seen above.

Renaming Columns Used With Expression Lists

Rename the default output column names with an **alias**, when required.

Syntax:
```
SELECT <ColumnName> <AliasName>, <ColumnName> <AliasName>
    FROM <TableName>;
```

Example 2:
List those Rental Transactions where cars have been hired by customers and returned after the due date. Also calculate the **period of delay in returning** the vehicles. Use an **ALIAS** to rename the calculated column to **Delay Period**.

Synopsis:

Tables:	Rentals
Columns:	RentId, CustId, CarRegNo, PropRtrnDt, ActualRtrnDt
Technique:	**Functions:** ROUND(); **Operators:** - (Subtraction); **Clauses:** WHERE; **Others:** ALIAS, ‖ (Concatenate)

Solution:
```
SELECT RentId, CustId, CarRegNo, ROUND((ActualRtrnDt - PropRtrnDt), 2) ‖ ' days' "Delay Period"
    FROM Rentals WHERE PropRtrnDt < ActualRtrnDt;
```

Output:
```
RENTID CUSTID CARREGNO       Delay Period
------ ------ ------------   ------------
     2      2 MH-01-B-2083   4.08 days
     3      3 MH-01-B-2083   2.13 days
. . .
    38      3 MH-13-P-3249   9.5 days

22 rows selected.
```

Explanation:
Here, **ROUND ((ActualRtrnDt - PropRtrnDt), 2)** is renamed to ALIAS **"Delay Period"**.

Logical Operators

The logical operators that can be used in SQL sentences are:

The AND Operator

The AND operator allows creating an SQL statement based on two or more conditions being met. It can be used in any valid SQL statement such as select, insert, update or delete. The AND operator requires that **each condition must be met** for the record to be included in the result set.

The Oracle engine will process all rows in a table and display the result only when **all** of the conditions specified using the **AND** operator are satisfied.

Example 3:
Display all payments received in the first quarter of the financial year 2002-2003.

Synopsis:

Tables:	Receipts
Columns:	All Columns
Technique:	**Functions:** TO_DATE(); **Operators:** AND; **Clauses:** WHERE

Solution:
SELECT * FROM Receipts WHERE RcptDt >= **TO_DATE**('01/04/2002', 'DD/MM/YYYY')
     AND RcptDt <= **TO_DATE**('30/06/2002', 'DD/MM/YYYY');

Output:
```
   RCPTID RCPTDT       BILLNO         AMT P CHQDRFTNO DRAWEEBANK      DRAWNDT
---------- ---------  --------- ---------- - --------- --------------- ---------
       52 27-APR-02        27      32725 B 100215    Bank Of India   23-APR-02
       53 02-MAY-02        26      72210 R
       54 15-MAY-02        28      15400 C
       55 17-JUN-02        29      17100 R
       56 25-JUN-02        27     104665 B 782004    Bank Of India   23-JUN-02
       57 30-JUN-02        28      55425 C
6 rows selected.
```

Explanation:
Here, the AND operator is used to compare the value held in the date field i.e. **RCPTDT** with two constants i.e. **01/01/2003** and **31/03/2003**. Only those transactions carried that satisfy this comparison are shown.

The OR Operator

The OR condition allows creating an SQL statement where records are returned when **any one** of the conditions are met. It can be used in any valid SQL statement such as select, insert, update or delete. The OR condition requires that any of the conditions must be met for the record to be included in the result set.

The Oracle engine will process all rows in a table and display the result only when **any of** the conditions specified using the **OR** operator is satisfied.

Example 4:
Display customers residing in either Mumbai or New Delhi.

Synopsis:

Tables:	Customers
Columns:	CustId, FirstName, LastName
Technique:	**Operators:** OR; **Clauses:** WHERE; **Others:** || (Concatenate)

Solution:
SELECT CustId, FirstName \|\| ' ' \|\| LastName "Customers" **FROM** Customers
        WHERE City = 'Mumbai' **OR** City = 'New Delhi';

Output:
```
   CUSTID Customers
---------- -----------------------------------------
        1 Rahul Mohan Sharma
        4 Wilson Fernandes
        8 Preity Sen
        9 Ashwini Joshi
```

Explanation:
Here, the **OR** operator is used to compare the value held in the **City** field. This condition will only be satisfied if the value held in the City field is **Mumbai** or **New Delhi**.

Combining The AND And OR Operator

The **AND** and **OR** conditions can be combined in a single SQL statement. It can be used in any valid SQL statement such as select, insert, update or delete.

When combining these conditions, it is important to use brackets so that the database knows the order in which to evaluate each condition.

The Oracle engine will process all rows in a table and display the result only when **all** of the conditions specified using the **AND** operator are satisfied and when **any of** the conditions specified using the **OR** operator are satisfied.

Example 5:
Display all customers whose **last name** begin with the alphabet 'S' and are not from **INDIA** <u>or</u> all Indian customers who's **driving License expires by the end of 2003.**

Synopsis:

Tables:	Customers
Columns:	CustId, FirstName, LastName, Country, ExpiresOn
Technique:	**Functions:** UPPER(); **Operators:** LIKE, AND, OR; **Clauses:** WHERE; **Others:** || (Concatenate)

Solution:
SELECT CustId, FirstName || ' ' || LastName "Customers", Country, ExpiresOn **FROM** Customers
    WHERE (LastName **LIKE** 'S%' **AND NOT UPPER**(Country)='INDIA') **OR**
      (**UPPER**(Country)='INDIA' **AND** ExpiresOn <= **TO_DATE**('31/12/2003', 'DD/MM/YYYY'));

Output:
```
CUSTID Customers                    COUNTRY      EXPIRESON
---------- ----------------------- -----------  ---------
        3 Jennifer Smith           U. S. A.     29-JAN-17
        4 Wilson Fernandes         INDIA        29-NOV-03
        7 Mosie Shah               U. A. E.     19-NOV-04
```

Explanation:
The above SQL query returns all those records:
1. Where the value held in the field **Country** is not **INDIA**
    AND
    The first character in the **LastName** field is 'S'
OR
2. Where The value held in the field **Country** is **INDIA**
    AND
    The value calculated by the expression **i.e.** Driving License's Expiry Date is less than **31/12/2003**
The brackets determine what order the **AND** / **OR** conditions are evaluated in.

The NOT Operator

The Oracle engine will process all rows in a table and display only those records that **do not** satisfy the condition specified.

Example 6:
List the description of all cars **but not** those, which have been purchased in the years 2000 and 2002.

Synopsis:

Tables:	Cars
Columns:	CarRegNo, Model, Make, Color, PurchaseDt
Technique:	**Functions:** TO_CHAR(); **Operators:** NOT, OR; **Clauses:** WHERE

Solution:
SELECT CarRegNo, Model, Make, Color **FROM** Cars
    WHERE NOT (**TO_CHAR**(PurchaseDt, 'YYYY') = '2000'
      OR TO_CHAR(PurchaseDt, 'YYYY') = '2002');

Output:

CARREGNO	MODEL	MAKE	COLOR
MH-04-Y-4849	Safari	Tata	Dark Green
MH-12-A-8758	800	Maruti	Light Blue
MH-03-X-0987	Indica	Tata	Black
MH-14-Y-4039	Indica V2	Tata	Black

Explanation:
The above query **will not** display rows where the year value of the field **PurchaseDt** is either **2000** or **2002**. Hence, all those records, which satisfy the condition specified using **the NOT operator, will not be shown**.

Range Searching

In order to select data that is within a range of values, the **BETWEEN** operator is used. The **BETWEEN** operator allows the selection of rows that contain values within a specified lower and upper limit. The **range** specified after the word **BETWEEN** is **inclusive**.

The lower value must be specified first. The two values in between the range must be linked with the keyword **AND**. The **BETWEEN** operator can be used with both character and numeric data types. However, the data types cannot be mixed (**i.e.** the lower value, of a range of values from a character column and the higher value from a numeric column).

Example 7:
List payments made in months of October, November and December in the year 2002.

Synopsis:

Tables:	Receipts
Columns:	RcptId, RcptDt, BillNo, Amt
Technique:	**Functions:** TO_CHAR(); **Operators:** AND, BETWEEN; **Clauses:** WHERE

Solution:
SELECT RcptId, RcptDt, BillNo, Amt **FROM** Receipts **WHERE TO_CHAR**(RcptDt, 'YYYY') = '2002'
    AND TO_CHAR(RcptDT, 'MM') **BETWEEN** 10 **AND** 12;

Equivalent to:
SELECT RcptId, RcptDt, BillNo, Amt **FROM** Receipts **WHERE TO_CHAR**(RcptDt, 'YYYY') = '2002'
    AND TO_CHAR(RcptDT, 'MM') >= 10 **AND TO_CHAR**(RcptDT, 'MM') <= 12;

Output:

RCPTID	RCPTDT	BILLNO	AMT
63	31-OCT-02	33	20812.5
64	28-NOV-02	33	62437.5

Explanation:
The first query will retrieve all those records from the **Receipts** table where the value held in the **RcptDt** field is October '02, November '02 or December '02 (all three values inclusive). This is done using TO_CHAR() function which extracts the month and year values from the **RcptDt** field. This is then compared using the **BETWEEN** operator.

The second query gives the same output using the AND operator.

Pattern Matching

The use of the LIKE predicate

The comparison operators discussed so far have compared one value, exactly to one other value. Such precision may not always be desired or necessary. For this purpose Oracle provides the **LIKE** predicate.

The **LIKE** predicate allows comparison of one string value with another string value, which is **not identical** in all aspects. This is achieved by using wildcard characters. Two wildcard characters that are available are:

For character data types:
- ❑ % allows finding a match for any string of any length (including zero length)
- ❑ _ allows finding a match for any single character

Example 8:
List the customers whose names have the second character as **a** or **s**.

Synopsis:

Tables:	Customers
Columns:	CustId, FirstName, LastName
Technique:	**Operators: LIKE; Clauses:** WHERE

Solution:
SELECT CustId, FirstName, LastName **FROM** Customers
     WHERE FirstName **LIKE** '_a%' **OR** FirstName **LIKE** '_s%';

Output:
```
    CUSTID FIRSTNAME              LASTNAME
---------- --------------------   --------------------
         1 Rahul Mohan            Sharma
         5 Raju                   Prasad
         6 Parvez                 Khan
         9 Ashwini                Joshi
```

Explanation:
In the above example, all those records where the value held in the field **FirstName** contains the second character as **a** or **s** are displayed. The _a and _s (i.e. underscore a and underscore s) indicates that only one character can **precede** the character a or s. The **%** indicates that any number of characters can **follow** the letters **a** or **s**.

The IN and NOT IN predicates:

The arithmetic operator (**=**) compares a single value to another single value. In case a value needs to be compared to a list of values then the **IN** predicate is used. The IN predicate helps reduce the need to use multiple OR conditions

Example 9:
List the driving license number of the customers named Raju, Mosie and Preity.

Synopsis:

Tables:	Customers
Columns:	CustId, FirstName, LastName, LicenseNo
Technique:	**Operators: IN, Clauses:** WHERE

Solution:
SELECT CustId, FirstName, LastName, LicenseNo **FROM** Customers
     WHERE FirstName **IN(**'Raju', 'Mosie', 'Preity'**);**

Output:

```
   CUSTID FIRSTNAME          LASTNAME             LICENSENO
---------- ------------------ -------------------- --------------------
        5 Raju               Prasad               C-2345
        7 Mosie              Shah                 UZ-3498
        8 Preity             Sen                  D-1089
```

Explanation:

The above example, displays all those records where the **FirstName** field holds any one of the three specified values.

Note

The **NOT IN** predicate is the opposite of the **IN** predicate. This will select all the rows where values **do not** match the values in the list.

The Oracle Table - DUAL

DUAL is a table owned by **SYS**. SYS owns the data dictionary and DUAL is part of the data dictionary. DUAL is a small Oracle worktable, which consists of only one row and one column and contains the value **x** in that column. Besides arithmetic calculations, it also supports **date** retrieval and it's formatting.

Often a simple calculation needs to be done, for example, 2*2. The only SQL verb to cause an output to be written to a VDU screen is **SELECT**. However, a SELECT must have a table name in its FROM clause, otherwise the SELECT **fails**.

When an arithmetic exercise is to be performed such as 2*2 or 4/2 and so on (only **numeric literals** being used), and there is no table being referenced the SELECT must fail.

To facilitate such calculations via a SELECT, Oracle provides a **dummy** table called **DUAL**, against which SELECT statements that are required to manipulate numeric literals can be fired and appropriate output obtained.

The structure of the dual table if viewed is as follows:
DESC DUAL;

Output:
```
Name                   Null?    Type
------------------     -------- ----------------
DUMMY                           VARCHAR2(1)
```

If the dual table is queried for records the output is as follows:
SELECT * FROM DUAL;

Output:
```
D
-
X
```

Example 10:
SELECT 2*2 FROM DUAL;

Output:
```
     2*2
---------
       4
```

SYSDATE

SYSDATE is a **pseudo** column that contains the current date and time. It requires no arguments when used with the table DUAL. It returns the current date.

Example 11:
SELECT SYSDATE FROM DUAL;

Output:
```
SYSDATE
---------
21-JAN-05
```

ORACLE FUNCTIONS

Oracle Functions serve the purpose of manipulating data items and returning a result. Functions are also capable of accepting user-supplied variables or constants and working on them. Such variables or constants are called **arguments**. Any number of arguments (**or** no arguments at all) can be passed to a function in the following format:

Function_Name(argument1, argument2,..)

Oracle Functions can be clubbed together depending upon whether they operate on a single row or a group of rows retrieved from a table. Accordingly, functions can be classified as follows:

Group Functions (Aggregate Functions)

Functions that act on a **set of values** are called **Group Functions**. For example, **SUM** is a Group function, which calculates the total set of numbers. A group function returns a single result row for a group of queried rows.

Scalar Functions (Single Row Functions)

Functions that act on **only one value** at a time are called **Scalar Functions**. For example, **LENGTH** is a Scalar function, which calculates the length of one particular string value. A single row function returns one result for every row of a queried table or view.

Single row functions can be further grouped together by the data type of their arguments and return values. For example, **LENGTH** relates to the **String** Data type. Functions can be classified corresponding to different data types as:

String Functions: For **String** Data type
Numeric Functions: For **Number** Data type
Conversion Functions: For **Conversion** of one Data type to another.
Date Functions: For **Date** Data type

Aggregate Functions

AVG: Returns an average value of '**n**', **ignoring** null values in a column.

Syntax:
```
AVG ([<DISTINCT>|<ALL>] <n>)
```
Example:
SELECT AVG(HrRentRate) "Average Hourly Rent" FROM Cars;

Output:
```
Average Hourly Rent
-------------------
            187
```

Note

In the above SELECT statement, the **AVG** function is used to calculate the average hourly rent of all cars. The selected column is renamed as **Average Hourly Rent** in the output.

MIN: Returns a minimum value of **expr**.

Syntax:

    MIN([<DISTINCT>|<ALL>] <expr>)

Example:
SELECT MIN(HrRentRate) "Minimum Hourly Rent" **FROM** Cars;

Output:
```
Minimum Hourly Rent
-------------------
                145
```

COUNT(expr): Returns the number of rows where **expr** is not null.

Syntax:

    COUNT([<DISTINCT>|<ALL>] <expr>)

Example:
SELECT COUNT(CustId) "No. Of Customers" **FROM** Customers;

Output:
```
No. Of Customers
----------------
              10
```

COUNT(*): Returns the number of rows in the table, including duplicates and those with nulls.

Syntax:

    COUNT(*)

Example:
SELECT COUNT(*) "No. Of Customers" **FROM** Customers;

Output:
```
No. Of Customers
----------------
              10
```

MAX: Returns the maximum value of **expr**.

Syntax:

    MAX([<DISTINCT>|<ALL>] <expr>)

Example:
SELECT MAX(HrRentRate) "Maximum Hourly Rent" **FROM** Cars;

Output:
```
Maximum Hourly Rent
-------------------
                250
```

SUM: Returns the sum of the values of **'n'**.

Syntax:
    SUM([<DISTINCT>|<ALL>] <n>)

Example:
SELECT SUM(HrRentRate) "Total Hourly Rent" **FROM** Cars;

Output:
```
Total Hourly Rent
-----------------
             1870
```

Numeric Functions

ABS: Returns the absolute value of **'n'**.

Syntax:
    ABS(n)

Example:
SELECT ABS(-15) "Absolute" **FROM DUAL;**

Output:
```
Absolute
--------
      15
```

POWER: Returns **m** raised to the nth power. **n** must be an integer, else an error is returned.

Syntax:
    POWER(m,n)

Example:
SELECT POWER(3,2) "Raised" **FROM DUAL;**

Output:
```
Raised
------
     9
```

ROUND: Returns **n**, rounded to **m** places to the right of a decimal point. If **m** is omitted, **n** is rounded to **0** places. **m** can be negative to round off digits to the left of the decimal point. **m** must be an integer.

Syntax:
    ROUND(n[,m])

Example:
SELECT ROUND(15.19,1) "Round" **FROM DUAL;**

Output:
```
Round
-----
 15.2
```

SQRT: Returns square root of **n**. If **n<0**, NULL. SQRT returns a **real** result.

Syntax:
    SQRT(n)

Example:
SELECT SQRT(25) "Square Root" **FROM DUAL;**

Output:
```
Square Root
-----------
          5
```

EXP: Returns **e** raised to the **nth** power, where **e = 2.71828183**.

Syntax:
   EXP(n)

Example:
SELECT EXP(5) "Exponent" **FROM DUAL;**

Output:
```
  Exponent
-----------
148.413159
```

EXTRACT: Returns a value extracted from a date or an interval value. A DATE can be used only to extract YEAR, MONTH and DAY, while a timestamp with a time zone datatype can be used only to extract TIMEZONE_HOUR and TIMEZONE_MINUTE.

Syntax:
   EXTRACT({year | month | day | hour | minute | second | timezone_hour |
             timezone_minute | timezone_region | timezone_abbr}
        FROM { date_value | interval_value })

Example:
SELECT EXTRACT(YEAR FROM DATE '2005-07-12') "Year",
    EXTRACT(MONTH FROM SYSDATE) "Month" **FROM DUAL;**

Output:
```
 Year  Month
----- ------
 2005      1
```

GREATEST: Returns the greatest value in a list of expressions.

Syntax:
   GREATEST(expr1, expr2, ... expr_n)
where, **expr1, expr2, ... expr_n** are expressions that are evaluated by the greatest function.

Example:
SELECT GREATEST(4, 5, 17) "Num", **GREATEST**('4', '5', '17') "Text" **FROM DUAL;**

Output:
```
 Num  Text
---- -----
  17     5
```

LEAST: Returns the least value in a list of expressions.

Syntax:
    LEAST(expr1, expr2, ... expr_n)
where, **expr1**, **expr2**, ... **expr_n** are expressions that are evaluated by the least function.

Example:
SELECT LEAST(4, 5, 17) "Num", **LEAST**('4', '5', '17') "Text" **FROM DUAL;**

Output:
```
Num  Text
----  -----
  4     17
```

> In the **GREATEST()** and **LEAST()** functions if the datatypes of the expressions are different, all expressions will be converted to the datatype of the first expression in the list. If the comparison is based on a character comparison, one character is considered greater than another if it has a higher character set value in the ASCII chart.

MOD: Returns the remainder of a first number, divided by second number, passed as parameter. If the second number is zero, the result is **the same** as the first number.

Syntax:
    MOD(m, n)

Example:
SELECT MOD(15, 7) "Mod1", **MOD**(15.7, 7) "Mod2" **FROM DUAL;**

Output:
```
Mod1  Mod2
-----  -----
   1    1.7
```

TRUNC: Returns a number truncated to a certain number of decimal places. The decimal place value must be an integer. If this parameter is omitted, the TRUNC function will truncate the number to **0** decimal places.

Syntax:
    TRUNC(number, [decimal_places])

Example:
SELECT TRUNC(125.815, 1) "Trunc1", **TRUNC**(125.815, -2) "Trunc2" **FROM DUAL;**

Output:
```
Trunc1  Trunc2
-------  -------
 125.8     100
```

FLOOR: Returns the largest integer value that is equal to or less than a number.

Syntax:
    FLOOR(n)

Example:
SELECT FLOOR(24.8) "Flr1", **FLOOR**(13.15) "Flr2" **FROM DUAL;**

Output:
```
 Flr1  Flr2
----- -----
   24    13
```

CEIL: Returns the smallest integer value that is greater than or equal to a number.

Syntax:
> *CEIL(n)*

Example:
SELECT CEIL(24.8) "Ceil1",**CEIL**(13.15) "Ceil2" **FROM DUAL;**

Output:
```
Ceil1 Ceil2
----- -----
   25    14
```

Note

Several other Numeric functions are available in Oracle. These include the following:

- ❏ **ACOS(), ASIN(), ATAN(), ATAN2(),**
- ❏ **COS(), COSH(), SIN(), SINH(), TAN(), TANH(),**
- ❏ **COVAR_POP(), COVAR_SAMP(), VAR_POP(), VAR_SAMP(),**
- ❏ **CORR(), SIGN()**

String Functions

LOWER: Returns char, with all letters in lowercase.

Syntax:
> **LOWER(char)**

Example:
SELECT LOWER('SHARANAM SHAH') "Lower" **FROM DUAL;**

Output:
```
Lower
-------------
sharanam shah
```

INITCAP: Returns a string with the first letter of each word in **upper case**.

Syntax:
> **INITCAP(char)**

Example:
SELECT INITCAP('IVAN BAYROSS') "Title Case" **FROM DUAL;**

Output:
```
Title Case
------------
Ivan Bayross
```

UPPER: Returns char, with all letters forced to uppercase.

Syntax:

UPPER (char)

Example:
SELECT UPPER('vAiShalI ShaH') "Capitalised" **FROM DUAL;**

Output:
```
Capitalised
-------------
VAISHALI SHAH
```

SUBSTR: Returns a portion of characters, beginning at character **m** and going upto character **n**. If **n** is omitted, the result returned is upto the last character in the string. The first position of char is **1**.

Syntax:

SUBSTR(<string>, <start_position>, [<length>])

where, **string** is the source string.
start_position is the position for extraction. The first position in the string is always 1.
length is the number of characters to extract.

Example:
SELECT SUBSTR('SECURE',3,4) "Substring" **FROM DUAL;**

Output:
```
Subs
----
CURE
```

ASCII: Returns the NUMBER code that represents the specified character. If more than one character is entered, the function will return the value for the first character and ignore all of the characters after the first.

Syntax:

ASCII(<single_character>)

where, **single_character** is the specified character to retrieve the NUMBER code for.

Example:
SELECT ASCII('a') "ASCII1", **ASCII**('A') "ASCII2" **FROM DUAL;**

Output:
```
ASCII1 ASCII2
------ ------
    97     65
```

COMPOSE: Returns a Unicode string. It can be a **char**, **varchar2**, **nchar**, **nvarchar2**, **clob** or **nclob**.

Syntax:

COMPOSE(<single>)

Below is a listing of **unistring** values that can be combined with other characters in the compose function.

Unistring Value	Resulting character
UNISTR('\0300')	grave accent (`)
UNISTR('\0301')	acute accent (´)
UNISTR('\0302')	circumflex (^)
UNISTR('\0303')	tilde (~)
UNISTR('\0308')	umlaut (¨)

Example:
SELECT 'ol' || COMPOSE('e' || UNISTR('\0301')) "Composed" FROM DUAL;

Output:
```
Composed
--------
olé          (Notice the acute accent (´) is attached with the letter e)
```

DECOMPOSE: Accepts a Unicode string and returns a normal string.

Syntax:
> **DECOMPOSE(<single>)**

Example:
SELECT DECOMPOSE('ol' || COMPOSE('e' || UNISTR('\0301'))) FROM DUAL;

Output:
```
Decomposed
----------
ole´         (Notice the acute accent (´) appears after the letter e)
```

INSTR: Returns the location of a substring in a string.

Syntax:
> **INSTR(<string1>, <string2>, [<start_position>], [<nth_appearance>])**

where, **string1** is the string to search for
string2 is the substring to search for in string1
start_position is the position in **string1** where the search will start. If omitted, it defaults to 1. The first position in the string is 1. If the **start_position** is negative, the function counts back **start_position** number of characters from the end of **string1** and then searches towards the beginning of **string1**.
nth_appearance is the **nth** appearance of **string2**. If omiited, it defaults to 1.

Example:
SELECT INSTR('SCT on the net', 't') "Instr1", INSTR('SCT on the net', 't', 1, 2) "Instr2"
> **FROM DUAL;**

Output:
```
 Instr1  Instr2
 ------- -------
      8      14
```

TRANSLATE: Replaces a sequence of characters in a string with another set of characters. However, it replaces a single character at a time. For example, it will replace the 1st character in the string_to_replace with the 1st character in the replacement_string. Then it will replace the 2nd character in the string_to_replace with the 2nd character in the replacement_string and so on.

Syntax:
> **TRANSLATE(<string1>, <string_to_replace>, <replacement_string>)**

where, **string1** is the string in which the replacement will take place
string_to_replace is the string that will be searched for in string1
replacement_string is the string that will be used as the replacement string in string1
All characters in the **string_to_replace** will be replaced with corresponding characters in **replacement_string**.

Example:
SELECT TRANSLATE('1sct523', '123', '7a9') "Change" FROM DUAL;

Output:
```
Change
-------
7sct5a9
```

LENGTH: Returns the length of a word.

Syntax:
LENGTH(word)

Example:
SELECT LENGTH('SHARANAM') "Length" FROM DUAL;

Output:
```
Length
------
     8
```

LTRIM: Removes characters from the left of char with initial characters removed upto the first character not in set.

Syntax:
LTRIM(char[,set])

Example:
SELECT LTRIM('NISHA','N') "LTRIM" FROM DUAL;

Output:
```
LTRIM
-----
ISHA
```

RTRIM: Returns char, with final characters removed after the last character not in the set. **'set'** is optional, it defaults to spaces.

Syntax:
RTRIM (char,[set])

Example:
SELECT RTRIM('SUNILA','A') "RTRIM" FROM DUAL;

Output:
```
RTRIM
-----
SUNIL
```

TRIM: Removes all specified characters either from the beginning or the ending of a string.

Syntax:
TRIM([leading | trailing | both [<trim_character> FROM]] <string1>)

where, **leading** - remove **trim_string** from the front of **string1**.
trailing - remove **trim_string** from the end of **string1**.
both - remove **trim_string** from the front and end of **string1**.
If none of the above option is chosen, the **TRIM** function will remove **trim_string** from both the front and end of **string1**.
trim_character is the character that will be removed from string1. If this parameter is omitted, the trim function will remove all leading and trailing spaces from string1.
string1 is the string to trim.

Example 1:
SELECT TRIM(' Hansel ') "Trim both sides" **FROM DUAL;**

Output:
```
Trim b
------
Hansel
```

Example 2:
SELECT TRIM(LEADING 'x' **FROM** 'xxxHanselxxx') "Remove prefixes" **FROM DUAL;**

Output:
```
Remove pr
---------
Hanselxxx
```

Example 3:
SELECT TRIM(BOTH 'x' **FROM** 'xxxHanselxxx') "Remove prefixes N suffixes" **FROM DUAL;**

Output:
```
Remove
------
Hansel
```

Example 4:
SELECT TRIM(BOTH '1' **FROM** '123Hansel12111') "Remove string" **FROM DUAL;**

Output:
```
Remove str
----------
23Hansel12
```

LPAD: Returns **char1**, left-padded to length **n** with the sequence of characters specified in **char2**. If **char2** is not specified Oracle uses blanks by default.

Syntax:
> **LPAD(char1,n [,char2])**

Example:
SELECT LPAD('Page 1',10,'*') "LPAD" **FROM DUAL;**

Output:
```
LPAD
----------
****Page 1
```

RPAD: Returns **char1**, right-padded to length **n** with the characters specified in **char2**. If **char2** is not specified, Oracle uses blanks by default.

Syntax:
> **RPAD(char1,n[,char2])**

Example:
SELECT RPAD(FirstName,10,'x') "RPAD Example" **FROM** Customers **WHERE** FirstName = 'Raju';

Output:
```
RPAD Examp
----------
Rajuxxxxxx
```

VSIZE: Returns the number of bytes in the internal representation of an expression.

Syntax:

   VSIZE(<expression>)

Example:
SELECT VSIZE('SCT on the net') "Size" **FROM DUAL;**

Output:
```
     Size
----------
       14
```

Conversion Functions

TO_NUMBER: Converts **char**, a **CHARACTER** value expressing a number, to a NUMBER datatype.

Syntax:

   TO_NUMBER(char)

Example:
UPDATE Cars **SET** DyRentRate = DyRentRate + **TO_NUMBER(SUBSTR('$100',2,3));**

Output:
```
10 rows updated.
```

Note

Here, the value 100 will be added to every daily rent rate in the **Cars** table.

TO_CHAR (number conversion): Converts a value of a **NUMBER** datatype to a **character** datatype, using the optional format string. TO_CHAR() accepts a number (**n**) and a numeric format (**fmt**) in which the number has to appear. If **fmt** is omitted, **n** is converted to a char value exactly long enough to hold all significant digits.

Syntax:

   TO_CHAR (n[,fmt])

Example:
SELECT TO_CHAR(17145, '$099,999') "Char" **FROM DUAL;**

Output:
```
Char
--------
$017,145
```

TO_CHAR (date conversion): Converts a value of a **DATE** datatype to **CHAR** value. TO_CHAR() accepts a date, as well as the format (**fmt**) in which the date has to appear. **fmt** must be a date format. If **fmt** is omitted, the **date** is converted to a character value using the default date format, **i.e.** "DD-MON-YY".

Syntax:

   TO_CHAR(date[,fmt])

Example:
SELECT TO_CHAR(RcptDt, 'Month DD, YYYY') "New Date Format" **FROM** Receipts
   WHERE RcptId = 1;

Output:
```
New Data Format
---------------
May  15, 2000
```

DATE CONVERSION FUNCTIONS

The DATE data type, which is used to store date and time information has special properties associated with it. It stores information about century, year, month, day, hour, minute and second for **each** date value.

The value in the column of a DATE data type **is always** stored in a specific **default** format. This default format is 'DD-MON-YY HH:MI:SS'. Hence, when a date has to be inserted in a date field, its value has to be specified in the same format. Additionally, values of DATE columns are always displayed in the **default** format when **retrieved** from the table.

If data from a date column has to be viewed in any other format other than the default format, Oracle provides the **TO_DATE** function that can be used to specify the required format.

The same function can also be used for storing a date into a DATE field in a particular format (other than default). This can be done by specifying the date value, **along with the format** in which it is to be stored. The TO_DATE() function also allows part insertion of a DATE value into a column, for example, only the day and month portion of the date value.

To enter the time portion of a date, the TO_DATE function must be used with a **format mask** indicating the time portion.

TO_DATE: Converts a character field to a date field.

Syntax:
```
    TO_DATE(char [, fmt])
```

Example:
INSERT INTO Rentals(RentId, CustId, CarRegNo, RentDt) **VALUES**(41, 10, 'MH-14-Y-4039',
    TO_DATE('25-JAN-2005 10:55 A.M.', 'DD-MON-YY HH:MI A.M.'));

Output:
```
1 row created.
```

DATE FUNCTIONS

To manipulate and extract values from the date column of a table Oracle provides date functions. Some are discussed below:

ADD_MONTHS: Returns a date after adding the number of months specified in the function.

Syntax:
```
    ADD_MONTHS(d,n)
```

Example:
SELECT ADD_MONTHS(SYSDATE, 4) "Add Months" FROM DUAL;

Output:
```
Add Months
----------
16-MAY-05
```

LAST_DAY: Returns the last date of the month specified with the function.

Syntax:
```
    LAST_DAY(d)
```

Example:
SELECT SYSDATE, LAST_DAY(SYSDATE) "LastDay" FROM DUAL;

Output:
```
SYSDATE    LastDay
--------- ---------
21-JAN-05 31-JAN-05
```

MONTHS_BETWEEN: Returns the number of months between **d1** and **d2**.

Syntax:
```
MONTHS_BETWEEN(d1, d2)
```

Example:
SELECT MONTHS_BETWEEN('02-MAY-92', '02-JAN-92') "Months" FROM DUAL;

Output:
```
Months
------
     4
```

NEXT_DAY: Returns the date of the first weekday described as **char** that is after the date specified in **date**. **NOTE:- char** must be a day of the week.

Syntax:
```
NEXT_DAY(date, char)
```

Example:
SELECT NEXT_DAY('06-JULY-04', 'Saturday') "NEXT DAY" FROM DUAL;

Output:
```
NEXT DAY
---------
10-JUL-04
```

ROUND: Returns a date rounded to a specific unit of measure. If the second parameter is omitted, the **ROUND** function will round the date to the nearest day.

Syntax:
```
ROUND(date, [format])
```

Below are the valid format parameters:

Unit	Format parameters	Rounding Rule
Year	SYYYY, YYYY, YEAR, SYEAR, YYY, YY, Y	Rounds up on July 1st
ISO Year	IYYY, IY, I	
Quarter	Q	Rounds up on the 16th day of the second month of the quarter
Month	MONTH, MON, MM, RM	Rounds up on the 16th day of the month
Week	WW	Same day of the week as the first day of the year
IW	IW	Same day of the week as the first day of the ISO year
W	W	Same day of the week as the first day of the month
Day	DDD, DD, J	
Hour	HH, HH12, HH24	
Start day of the week	DAY, DY, D	
Minute	MI	

Example:
SELECT ROUND(TO_DATE('01-DEC-04'), 'YYYY') "Year" **FROM DUAL;**

Output:
```
Year
---------
01-JAN-05
```

NEW_TIME: Returns the date after converting it from **time zone1** to a date in **time zone2**.

Syntax:
> **NEW_TIME(date, zone1, zone2)**

Value	Description	Value	Description
AST	Atlantic Standard Time	ADT	Atlantic Daylight Time
BST	Bering Standard Time	BDT	Bering Daylight Time
CST	Central Standard Time	CDT	Central Daylight Time
EST	Eastern Standard Time	EDT	Eastern Daylight Time
GMT	Greenwich Mean Time	HST	Alaska-Hawaii Standard Time
HDT	Alaska-Hawaii Daylight Time	MST	Mountain Standard Time
MDT	Mountain Daylight Time	NST	Newfoundland Standard Time
PST	Pacific Standard Time	PDT	Pacific Daylight Time
YST	Yukon Standard Time	YDT	Yukon Daylight Time

Example:
The following example converts an Atlantic Standard Time into a Mountain Standard Time:
SELECT NEW_TIME(TO_DATE('2004/07/01 01:45', 'yyyy/mm/dd HH24:MI'), 'AST', 'MST') "MST"
> **FROM DUAL;**

Output:
```
MST
---------
30-JUN-04
```

Note

Several other Date function are available in Oracle. These include the following:
❑   **DbTimeZone(), SessionTimeZone(), SysTimestamp(), Tz_Offset()**

The above Oracle date functions are **just a few** selected from the **many date** functions that are built into Oracle. These Oracle functions are commonly used in commercial application development.

MANIPULATING DATES IN SQL USING DATE()

A column of data type **Date** is always displayed in a default format, which is **'DD-MON-YY'**. If this default format is not used when entering data into a column of the **date** data type, Oracle **rejects the data** and returns an error message.

If a **date** has to be retrieved or inserted into a table in a format **other than** the default one, Oracle provides the **TO_CHAR** and **TO_DATE** functions to do this.

TO_CHAR

The TO_CHAR function facilitates the retrieval of data in a format different from the default format. It can also extract a part of the date, i.e. the date, month or the year from the date value and use it for sorting or grouping of data according to the date, month or year.

Syntax:
    TO_CHAR(<date value> [,<fmt>])

where **date value** stands for the date and **fmt** is the specified format in which date is to be displayed.

Example 1:
SELECT TO_CHAR(SYSDATE, 'DD-MM-YY') FROM DUAL;

Output:
```
TO_CHAR(
--------
21-01-05
```

TO DATE

TO_DATE converts a **char** value into a **date** value. It allows a user to insert date into a date column in any required format, by specifying the **character** value of the date to be inserted and its format.

Syntax:
    TO_DATE(<char value>[,<fmt>])

where **char value** stands for the value to be inserted in the date column and **fmt** is a date format in which the 'char value' is specified.

Example 2:
SELECT TO_DATE ('21/01/05', 'DD/MM/YY') FROM DUAL;

Output:
```
TO_DATE('
---------
21-JAN-05
```

Example 3:
List the payment received for the year 2000 in order of the months. The dates when payment received should be displayed in **'DD/MM/YY'** format.

Synopsis:

Tables:	Receipts
Columns:	RcptId, RcptDt, BillNo, Amt
Technique:	**Functions: TO_CHAR(); Clauses:** WHERE, ORDER BY

Solution:
SELECT RcptId, **TO_CHAR**(RcptDt, 'DD/MM/YY') "Receipt Date", BillNo, Amt **FROM** Receipts
    WHERE TO_CHAR(RcptDt, 'YYYY') = '2000' **ORDER BY TO_CHAR**(RcptDt, 'MM');

Output:
```
   RCPTID Receipt       BILLNO         AMT
---------- --------   ---------- ----------
        1 15/05/00          1        32265
        2 12/06/00          1        96795
        3 21/07/00          2         3190
        4 27/07/00          2        16234
        5 10/08/00          3          330
        6 20/08/00          4        11220
        7 02/09/00          3         4458
        8 04/09/00          4        33660
        9 14/10/00          5      18232.5
       10 08/11/00          5      59889.5
       11 15/11/00          6        15015
```

Output: (Continued)
```
     RCPTID Receipt     BILLNO        AMT
     ---------- --------  ----------  ----------
         12 05/12/00          7     6343.75
         13 11/12/00         10       29700
         14 16/12/00          9       43030
         15 24/12/00          9       11950
         16 27/12/00          8     6328.13
16 rows selected.
```

Explanation:
Here the value held in the **RcptDt** field is formatted using the **TO_CHAR()** function to display the date in the **DD/MM/YY** format. The ordering of the output data set is based on the "**MONTH**" segment of the data in the column **RcptDt**. This is done using the **TO_CHAR()** function, in the order by clause, extracting only the "**MONTH**" segment of the **RcptDt** to sort on.

Example 4:
Insert the following data in the table **Rentals**, where the **time component** has to be stored along with the date in the column **RentDt**.

RentId	CustId	CarRegNo	RentDt
42	8	MH-13-P-3249	16/Jan/2005 12:23:00

INSERT INTO Rentals(RentId, CustId, CarRegNo, RentDt)
    VALUES(42, 8, 'MH-13-P-3249', **TO_DATE**('16/Jan/2005 12:23:00', 'DD/MON/YY hh:mi:ss'));

Output:
```
1 row created.
```

Special Date Formats Using TO_CHAR function

Sometimes, the date value is required to be displayed in special formats, for example, instead of 01-JAN-05, displays the date as 01st of January, 2005. For this, Oracle provides **special attributes**, which can be used in the format specified with the **TO_CHAR** and **TO_DATE** functions. The significance and use of these characters are explained in the examples below.

All three examples below are based on the **Receipts** table

The query is as follows:
SELECT RcptId, RcptDt, BillNo, Amt **FROM** Receipts **WHERE** RcptId > 60;

Output:
```
     RCPTID RCPTDT       BILLNO        AMT
     ---------- --------- ----------  -----------
         61 23-AUG-02         31       83250
         62 17-AUG-02         30       61875
         63 31-OCT-02         33     20812.5
         64 28-NOV-02         33     62437.5
```

Variations in this output can be achieved as follows:
❑ **Use of TH in the TO_CHAR() function:**
DDTH places TH, RD, ND for the date (DD), for example, 2ND, 3RD, 08TH etc

SELECT RcptId, **TO_CHAR**(RcptDt, 'DDTH-MON-YY') "Rcptdt_DDTH", BillNo, Amt
    FROM Receipts **WHERE** RcptId > 60;

Output:

```
    RCPTID Rcptdt_DDTH      BILLNO        AMT
---------- ------------ ---------- ----------
        61 23RD-AUG-02          31      83250
        62 17TH-AUG-02          30      61875
        63 31ST-OCT-02          33    20812.5
        64 28TH-NOV-02          33    62437.5
```

❑ Use of SP in the TO_CHAR() function

DDSP indicates that the date (DD) must be displayed by spelling the date such as ONE, TWELVE etc.

SELECT RcptId, **TO_CHAR(**RcptDt, **'DDSP')** "Rcptdt_DDSP", BillNo, Amt
   FROM Receipts **WHERE** RcptId > **60;**

Output:

```
    RCPTID Rcptdt_DDSP      BILLNO        AMT
---------- ------------ ---------- ----------
        61 TWENTY-THREE         31      83250
        62 SEVENTEEN            30      61875
        63 THIRTY-ONE           33    20812.5
        64 TWENTY-EIGHT         33    62437.5
```

❑ Use of 'SPTH' in the to_char function

SPTH displays the date (DD) with **th** added to the spelling fourteen**th**, twel**fth**.

SELECT RcptId, **TO_CHAR(**RcptDt, **'DDSPTH')** "Rcptdt_DDSPTH", BillNo, Amt
   FROM Receipts **WHERE** RcptId > **60;**

Output:

```
    RCPTID Rcptdt_DDSPTH    BILLNO        AMT
---------- ------------- ---------- ----------
        61 TWENTY-THIRD         31      83250
        62 SEVENTEENTH          30      61875
        63 THIRTY-FIRST         33    20812.5
        64 TWENTY-EIGHTH        33    62437.5
```

MISCELLANEOUS FUNCTIONS

UID: This function returns an integer value corresponding to the UserID of the user currently logged in.

Syntax:
   UID [INTO <variable>]
where, **variable** will now contain the id number for the user's session.

Example:
SELECT UID FROM DUAL;

Output:
```
UID
----
 57
```

USER: This function returns the **user name** of the user who has logged in. The value returned is in varchar2 data type.

Syntax:
   USER

Example:
SELECT USER FROM DUAL;

Output:
```
USER
-----
SCOTT
```

SYS_CONTEXT: Can be used to retrieve information about Oracle's environment.

Syntax:

SYS_CONTEXT (<namespace>, <parameter>, [<length>])

where, **namespace** is an Oracle namespace that has already been created. If the **namespace** of **USERENV** is used, attributes describing the current Oracle session can be returned.
parameter is a valid attribute that has been set using the DBMS_SESSION.set_context procedure.
length is the length of the return value in bytes. If this parameter is omitted or if an invalid entry is provided, the **SYS_CONTEXT** function will default to **256 bytes**.

The valid parameters for the namespace called **USERENV** are as follows:

Parameter	Explanation	Return Length
AUDITED_CURSORID	Returns the cursor ID of the SQL that triggered the audit	N/A
AUTHENTICATION_DATA	Authentication data	256
AUTHENTICATION_TYPE	Describes how the user was authenticated. Can be one of the following values: Database, OS, Network or Proxy	30
BG_JOB_ID	If the session was established by an Oracle background process, this parameter will return the Job ID. Otherwise, it will return NULL.	30
CLIENT_IDENTIFIER	Returns the client identifier (global context)	64
CLIENT_INFO	User session information	64
CURRENT_SCHEMA	Returns the default schema used in the current schema	30
CURRENT_SQL	Returns the SQL that triggered the audit event	64
CURRENT_USER	Name of the current user	30
CURRENT_USERID	Userid of the current user	30
DB_NAME	Name of the database from the DB_NAME initialization parameter	30
ENTRYID	Available auditing entry identifier	30
EXTERNAL_NAME	External of the database user	256
HOST	Name of the host machine from which the client has connected	54
CURRENT_SCHEMAID	Returns the identifier of the default schema used in the current schema	30
DB_DOMAIN	Domain of the database from the DB_DOMAIN initialization parameter	256
FG_JOB_ID	If the session was established by a client foreground process, this parameter will return the Job ID. Otherwise, it will return NULL.	30
GLOBAL_CONTEXT_MEMORY	The number used in the System Global Area by the globally accessed context	N/A
INSTANCE	The identifier number of the current instance	30
IP_ADDRESS	IP address of the machine from which the client has connected	30
ISDBA	Returns TRUE if the user has DBA privileges. Otherwise, it will return FALSE.	30
LANG	The ISO abbreviate for the language	62
LANGUAGE	The language, territory and character of the session. In the following format: language_territory.characterset	52
NETWORK_PROTOCOL	Network protocol used	256

Parameter	Explanation	Return Length
NLS_CALENDAR	The calendar of the current session	62
NLS_CURRENCY	The currency of the current session	62
NLS_DATE_FORMAT	The date format for the current session	62
NLS_DATE_LANGUAGE	The language used for dates	62
NLS_SORT	BINARY or the linguistic sort basis	62
NLS_TERRITORY	The territory of the current session	62
OS_USER	The OS username for the user logged in	30
PROXY_USER	The name of the user who opened the current session on behalf of SESSION_USER	30
PROXY_USERID	The identifier of the user who opened the current session on behalf of SESSION_USER	30
SESSION_USER	The database user name of the user logged in	30
SESSION_USERID	The database identifier of the user logged in	30
SESSIONID	The identifier of the auditing session	30
TERMINAL	The OS identifier of the current session	10

Example:
SELECT SYS_CONTEXT('USERENV', 'NLS_DATE_FORMAT') "SysContext" **FROM DUAL;**

Output:
```
SysContext
----------
DD-MON-RR
```

USERENV: Can be used to retrieve information about the current Oracle session. Although this function still exists in Oracle for backwards compatibility, it is recommended that the **SYS_CONTEXT** function is used instead.

Syntax:
    USERENV(<parameter>)

where, **parameter** is the value to return from the current Oracle session.

The possible values are:

Parameter	Explanation
CLIENT_INFO	Returns user session information stored using the DBMS_APPLICATION_INFO package
ENTRYID	Available auditing entry identifier
INSTANCE	The identifier number of the current instance
ISDBA	Returns TRUE if the user has DBA privileges. Otherwise, it will return FALSE.
LANG	The ISO abbreviate for the language
LANGUAGE	The language, territory and character of the session. In the following format: language_territory.characterset
SESSIONID	The identifier of the auditing session
TERMINAL	The OS identifier of the current session

Example:
SELECT USERENV('LANGUAGE') **FROM DUAL;**

Output:
```
USERENV('LANGUAGE')
---------------------------
AMERICAN_AMERICA.WE8MSWIN1252
```

COALESCE: Returns the first non-null expression in the list. If all expressions evaluate to null, then the **coalesce** function will return null.

Syntax:

    COALESCE(<expr1>, <expr2>, ... <expr_n>)

Example:
SELECT CustId, **COALESCE**(Phone, 'Postal Code = '|| PostalCode) **Contact FROM** Customers;

The above coalesce statement is equivalent to the following IF-THEN-ELSE statement:
IF Phone **IS NOT NULL THEN**
    Contact := Phone;
ELSIF PostalCode **IS NOT NULL THEN**
    Contact := Postal Code = PostalCode;
ELSE
    Contact := **NULL**;
END IF;

Output:
```
    CUSTID CONTACT
---------- ------------------------------
         1 28765654
         2 23657868
         3 23756775
         4 24443760
         5 42739894
         6 Postal Code = UAE-93240
         7 76756537
         8 Postal Code = 400067
         9 24403031
        10 23445576

10 rows selected.
```

Explanation:
In the above example, Oracle will display the contact number i.e. the value held in the field **Phone** if **Phone** field holds a value. If it does not hold a value, then Oracle will move on to the next column in the **COALESCE** function and display the value held in the next column i.e. **PostalCode** if it holds a value.

In case the second column also does not hold a value, then Oracle will display null as an output.

GROUPING DATA FROM TABLES IN SQL

The Concept Of Grouping

Till now, all SQL **SELECT** statements have:
❑ Retrieved all the rows from tables
❑ Retrieved selected rows from tables with the use of a **WHERE** clause, which returns only those rows that meet the conditions specified
❑ Retrieved unique rows from the table, with the use of **DISTINCT** clause
❑ Retrieved rows in the sorted order **i.e.** ascending or descending order, as specified, with the use of **ORDER BY** clause.

Other than the above clauses, there are two other clauses, which facilitate selective retrieval of rows. These are the **GROUP BY** and **HAVING** clauses. These are parallel to the **order by** and **where** clause, except that they act on record sets and **not on** individual records.

GROUP BY Clause

The **GROUP BY** clause is another section of the **select** statement. This optional clause tells Oracle to group rows based on distinct values that exist for **specified columns**. The GROUP BY clause creates a data set, containing several sets of records **grouped together** based on a condition.

Syntax:
```
SELECT <ColumnName1>, <ColumnName2>, <ColumnNameN>,
    AGGREGATE_FUNCTION (<Expression>)
    FROM TableName WHERE <Condition>
        GROUP BY <ColumnName1>, <ColumnName2>, <ColumnNameN>;
```

Example 1:
Find out how many times each cars has been hired.

Synopsis:

Tables:	Rentals
Columns:	CarRegNo, RentId
Technique:	**Functions:** COUNT(); **Clauses:** GROUP BY; **Others:** Alias

Solution:
```
SELECT CarRegno "Car No.", COUNT(RentId) "No. Of Rentals"
    FROM Rentals GROUP BY CarRegNo;
```

Output:
```
Car No.                  No. Of Rentals
--------------------     --------------
MH-01-B-2083                   7
MH-02-C-5876                   6
MH-02-Z-3840                   7
MH-03-F-3499                   2
MH-03-X-0987                   2
MH-04-Y-4849                   2
MH-12-A-8758                   2
MH-13-P-3249                   5
MH-14-Y-4039                   3
MMZ-888                        5

10 rows selected.
```

Explanation:
In the above example, the data that has to be retrieved is available in the **Rentals** table. Since the **number of rentals** per car is required, the records need to be **grouped** on the basis of field **CarRegNo** and then the **COUNT()** function must be applied to the field **RentId** which calculates the number of rentals on a per car basis.

HAVING Clause

The **HAVING** clause can be used in conjunction with the **GROUP BY** clause. **HAVING** imposes a condition on the **GROUP BY** clause, which further filters the groups created by the **GROUP BY** clause. Each column specification specified in the HAVING clause must occur within a statistical function or must occur in the list of columns named in the GROUP BY clause.

Example 2:
Find out the customers having rented a car more than five times.

Synopsis:

Tables:	Rentals
Columns:	CustId, RentId, PayStatus
Technique:	**Functions:** COUNT(); **Operators:** > (Greater Than); **Clauses:** GROUP BY ... HAVING; **Others:** Alias

Solution:

SELECT CustId, **COUNT**(RentId) "No. Of Rentals" **FROM** Rentals
    WHERE PayStatus ='P' **GROUP BY** CustId **HAVING COUNT**(RentId)>5;

Output:
```
    CUSTID No. Of Rentals
---------- --------------
         1              7
         5              7
```

Explanation:

In the above example, the data that has to be retrieved is available in the **Rentals** table. The **Count()** function is applied to the field **RentId**. This filtered information is then **grouped** on the basis of Customer Id (i.e. the **CustId** field). Since only those customers who have hired a vehicle more than five times are to be retrieved, the **HAVING** clause is used to finally filter the data to retain only those records where the value calculated using the **COUNT()** function is **greater than 5**.

Rules For **Group By ... Having** Clause

❑ Columns listed in the select statement have to be listed in the GROUP BY clause
❑ Columns listed in the GROUP BY clause need not be listed in the SELECT statement
❑ Only group functions can be used in the HAVING clause
❑ The group functions listed in the having clause need not be listed in the SELECT statement

Determining Whether Values Are Unique

The **HAVING** clause can be used to find unique values in situations to which DISTINCT does not apply.

The **DISTINCT** clause eliminates duplicates, but does not show which values actually were duplicated in the original data. The **HAVING** clause can identify which values were unique or non-unique.

Example 3:

List customers, who have hired car only once. (Unique Entries Only)

Synopsis:

Tables:	Rentals
Columns:	Custid, Rentid
Technique:	**Functions:** COUNT(), **Clauses:** GROUP BY ... HAVING, **Others:** Alias

Solution:

SELECT CUSTID, **COUNT**(RENTID) "No. Of Rentals"
    FROM RENTALS **GROUP BY** CUSTID **HAVING COUNT**(RENTID) = 1;

Output:
```
    CUSTID No. Of Rentals
---------- --------------
        11              1
```

Explanation:

In the above example, the data that has to be retrieved is available in the RENTALS table. This table holds data related to the rental transactions. The **Count()** function is applied to the field **RENTID** which will hold the number of times a car is hired by a particular customer. This information is then **grouped** on the basis of Customer Number (i.e. the **CUSTID** field). Since only those customers who have hired a car **once** are to be retrieved, the **HAVING** clause is used to finally filter the data to retain only those records where the value calculated using the **COUNT()** function is **equal to 1**.

Example 7:

List the customers associated with **more** than one rental transaction. (Non-Unique Entries)

Synopsis:

Tables:	Rentals
Columns:	Custid, Rentid
Technique:	**Functions:** COUNT(), **Clauses:** GROUP BY ... HAVING, **Others:** Alias

Solution:

SELECT CUSTID, **COUNT**(RENTID) "No. Of Rentals"
    FROM RENTALS **GROUP BY** CUSTID **HAVING COUNT**(RENTID) > 1;

Output:

```
    CUSTID No. Of Rentals
----------- --------------
          1              7
          2              5
          3              5
          4              2
          5              7
          6              2
          7              2
          8              4
          9              2
         10              6

10 rows selected.
```

Explanation:

In the above example, the data that has to be retrieved is available in the RENTALS table.

This table holds data related to the rental transactions. The **COUNT()** function is applied to the field **RENTID** which will hold the number of times the car is hired by a particular customer. This information is then **grouped** on the basis of Customer Number (i.e. the **CUSTID** field). Since only those customers who have hired a car more than once are to be retrieved, the **HAVING** clause is used to finally filter the data to retain only those records where the value calculated using the **COUNT()** function is **greater than 1**.

Group By Using The ROLLUP Operator

The ROLLUP operator is used to calculate aggregates and super aggregates for expressions within a GROUP BY statement. Report writers usually use this operator to extract statistics and/or summaries from a result set.

Example 8:

Create a report on the customers involved in the rentals transactions, providing the **amount paid as advance as well as balance payment** on a per transaction and further on per customer basis providing an aggregate of transactions with each and all the customers.

Synopsis:

Tables:	Rentals
Columns:	RentId, CustId, RentAmt, DriverAmt, AdvPaid
Technique:	**Functions:** SUM(); **Operators:** +, ROLLUP(), **Clauses:** GROUP BY; **Others:** Alias

Solution:
SELECT CustId, RentId, SUM(AdvPaid) "Advance",
    SUM((RentAmt + DriverAmt – AdvPaid**))** "Balance Payment" **FROM** Rentals
       GROUP BY ROLLUP (CustId, RentId**);**

Output:

CUSTID	RENTID	Advance	Balance Payment	CUSTID	RENTID	Advance	Balance Payment
1	1	32265	96795	5	33	20812.5	62437.5
1	5	18232.5	54697.5	5	36	22000	66000
1	9	11950	35850	5	39	0	120000
1	16	19380	58140	**5**		**138181.88**	**534545.62**
1	23	19635	58905	6	11	20570	61710
1	31	27750	83250	6	29	17100	51300
1	37	0	98955	**6**		**37670**	**113010**
1		**129212.5**	**486592.5**	7	12	7250	21750
2	2	3190	9570	7	28	15400	46200
2	6	15015	45045	**7**		**22650**	**67950**
2	17	16730	50190	8	13	18240	54720
2	21	28215	84645	8	25	41800	125400
2	34	0	96250	8	30	20625	61875
2		**63150**	**285700**	**8**		**80665**	**241995**
3	3	330	990	9	18	15500	46500
3	7	6343.75	19031.25	9	40	0	94350
3	14	19380	58140	**9**		**15500**	**140850**
3	24	22990	68970	10	19	27487.5	82462.5
3	38	0	111000	10	22	20790	62370
3		**49043.75**	**258131.25**	10	26	22990	68970
4	4	11220	33660	10	32	0	118800
4	8	29700	89100	10	35	20812.5	62437.5
4		**40920**	**122760**	**10**		**92080**	**395040**
5	10	6328.13	18984.37	11	41	0	94350
5	15	28403.75	85211.25	**11**		**0**	**94350**
5	20	27912.5	83737.5			*669073.13*	*2740924.37*
5	27	32725	98175				

53 rows selected.

Explanation:
In the above example, the data that has to be retrieved is available in the **Rentals** table. This table holds data related to rental transactions associated with each customer. The **SUM()** function is applied on the field **AdvPaid** and the calculated value of difference between the total cost of rental (i.e. sum of **RentAmt** and **DriverAmt**) and the advance paid, (i.e. **AdvPaid**). This thus provides the sum of advance payment and the due amount. This information is then **grouped** on the basis of **CustId** and **RentId** using the **ROLLUP** operator.

The **ROLLUP** operator is used to display the advance payments and the due amount per rental transaction (i.e. per RentId) and per customer (i.e. per CustId).

The ROLLUP operator first calculates the standard aggregate values for the groups specified in the group by clause (**SUM** of **AdvPaid** AND (**RentAmt** PLUS **DriverAmt** LESS **AdvPaid**) for each rental transaction (i.e. per **RentId**) then creates higher level subtotals, moving from right to left through the list of grouping columns (i.e. per **CustId**).

Group By Using The CUBE Operator

The **CUBE** operator can be applied to all aggregates functions like **AVG()**, **SUM()**, **MAX()**, **MIN()** and **COUNT()** within a **GROUP BY** statement. This operator is usually used by, report writers to extract cross-tabular reports from a result set. CUBE produces subtotals for all possible combinations of groupings specified in the **GROUP BY** clause along with a grand total as against the ROLLUP operator which produces only a fraction of possible subtotal combinations.

Example 9:
Find out the advance received for rentals on per customer along with a grand total.

Synopsis:

Tables:	Rentals
Columns:	CustId, RentId, AdvPaid
Technique:	**Functions:** SUM(); **Operators:** CUBE(); **Clauses:** GROUP BY

Solution:
SELECT CustId, RentId, SUM(AdvPaid) **FROM** Rentals **GROUP BY CUBE** (CustId, RentId);

Output:

CUSTID	RENTID	SUM(ADVPAID)
		669073.13
	1	32265
	2	3190
	3	330
	4	11220
	5	18232.5
	6	15015
	7	6343.75
	8	29700
	9	11950
	10	6328.13
	11	20570
	12	7250
	13	18240
	14	19380
	15	28403.75
	16	19380
	17	16730
	18	15500
	19	27487.5
	20	27912.5
	21	28215
	22	20790
	23	19635
	24	22990
	25	41800
	26	22990
	27	32725
	28	15400
	29	17100
	30	20625
	31	27750
	32	0
	33	20812.5
	34	0
	35	20812.5
	36	22000
	37	0
	38	0
	39	0
	40	0
	41	0
1		**129212.5**
1	1	32265
1	5	18232.5
1	9	11950
1	16	19380
1	23	19635
1	31	27750
1	37	0
2		**63150**
2	2	3190
2	6	15015
2	17	16730
2	21	28215
2	34	0
3		**49043.75**
3	3	330
3	7	6343.75
3	14	19380
3	24	22990
3	38	0
4		**40920**
4	4	11220
4	8	29700

Output: (Continued)

CUSTID	RENTID	SUM(ADVPAID)
5		**138181.88**
5	10	6328.13
5	15	28403.75
5	20	27912.5
5	27	32725
5	33	20812.5
5	36	22000
5	39	0
6		**37670**
6	11	20570
6	29	17100
7		**22650**
7	12	7250
7	28	15400
8		**80665**
8	13	18240
8	25	41800
8	30	20625
9		**15500**
9	18	15500
9	40	0
10		**92080**
10	19	27487.5
10	22	20790
10	26	22990
10	32	0
10	35	20812.5
11		**0**
11	41	0

94 rows selected.

Explanation:

In the above example, the data that has to be retrieved is available in the **Rentals** table. The **SUM()** function is applied to the field **AdvPaid** which will hold the sum of advance paid per customer. This information is then **grouped** on the basis of **CustId** and **RentId** using the **CUBE** operator.

The advance payment of every transaction that occurs with a customer is displayed using the group by clause. The **CUBE** operator is used to display the **Advance Payment per transaction**, the **total Advance Payment** by a customer for the transactions undertaken, the total **Advance Payment** per transaction irrespective of the customer and the total **Advance Payment** for all the transactions irrespective of the customers involved.

The **CUBE** operator first calculates the standard aggregate values for the groups specified in the group by clause (Sum of **ADVPAID** for each rental transaction) then creates higher level subtotals, moving from right to left through the list of grouping columns (Sum of **ADVPAID** for each Customer). Additionally the **CUBE** operator displays the total **ADVPAID** per Customer irrespective of rental transactions and the total **ADVPAID** of all the rental transactions irrespective of the customers.

SUBQUERIES

A **subquery** is a form of an SQL statement that appears inside another SQL statement. It is also termed as **nested query**. The statement containing a subquery is called a **parent** statement. The parent statement uses the rows (i.e. the result set) returned by the subquery.

It can be used for the following:
- To insert records in a target table
- To create tables and insert records in the table created
- To update records in a target table
- To create views
- To provide values for **conditions** in WHERE, HAVING, IN and so on used with SELECT, UPDATE and DELETE statements

Example 10:
Retrieve the rental transaction details of a customer named 'Ashwini Joshi '.

Synopsis:

Tables:	Customers, Rentals
Columns:	Customers: CustId, FirstName, LastName
	Rentals: CustId, CarRegNo, RentDt, ActualRtrnDt, PayStatus
Technique:	**Sub-Queries; Operators:** IN; **Clauses:** WHERE

Solution:
SELECT CustId "Cust. No.", CarRegNo, RentDt, ActualRtrnDt, PayStatus
    FROM RENTALS **WHERE CustId IN(SELECT** CustId **FROM** Customers
        WHERE FirstName = 'Ashwini' AND LastName = 'Joshi');

Output:
```
Cust. No. CARREGNO              RENTDT    ACTUALRTR P
--------- -------------------- --------- --------- -
        9 MH-13-P-3249          15-JUL-03 31-JUL-03 P
        9 MH-04-Y-4849          30-JUN-01 09-JUL-01 P
```

Explanation:
In the above example, the data that has to be retrieved is available in the **RENTALS** table, which holds the transactions associated with the customer named '**Ashwini Joshi**'. This table holds all the rental transaction details identified by the customer number i.e. **CUSTID**. However, the **RENTALS** table does not contain the field, which holds the customer's name, which is required to make a comparison.

The Customers Name is available in the **CUSTOMERS** table where each customer is identified by a unique number (i.e. **CUSTID**). So it is required to access the table **CUSTOMERS** and retrieve the **CUSTID** by supplying the Customer's Name based on which a comparison can be made with the **CUSTID** field held in the table **RENTALS**.

Using the **CUSTID** retrieved from the **CUSTOMERS** table, it is now possible to retrieve the rental transaction details from the **RENTALS** table by finding a matching value in the **CUSTID** field in that table.

This type of processing can be done elegantly using a subquery.

In the above solution the sub-query is as follows:
SELECT CustId **FROM** Customers
        WHERE FirstName = 'Ashwini' AND LastName = 'Joshi';

The target table will be as follows:
Output:
```
    CUSTID
----------
        9
```

The outer sub-query output will simplify the solution as shown below:
SELECT CustId "Cust. No.", CarRegNo, RentDt, ActualRtrnDt, PayStatus
    FROM RENTALS **WHERE CustId IN(9);**

When the above SQL query is executed the resulting output is equivalent to the desired output of the SQL query using two levels of Sub-queries.

Example 11:
Find the customers who have been rented a Black colored car.

Synopsis:

Tables:	Customers, Rentals, Cars
Columns:	Customers: CustId, FirstName, LastName RENTALS: CustId Cars: Color
Technique:	**Sub-Queries, Operators:** IN, **Clauses:** WHERE, **Other:** Concat (‖)

Solution:
SELECT (FirstName ‖ ' ' ‖ LastName) "Customer" **FROM** Customers
    WHERE CustId **IN(SELECT** CustId **FROM** Rentals **WHERE** CarRegNo **IN(SELECT** CarRegNo
        FROM Cars **WHERE** Color = 'Black'));

Output:
```
Customer
--------------------
Preity Sen
Alex Joseph D'Mello
Raju Prasad
```

Explanation:
In the above example, the data that has to be retrieved is available in the **Customers**, which holds the Customer details. The **Customers** table will only provide all the customer names but to retrieve only those customers who have been rented Black colored car, **two** more tables will be involved that is **Rentals** which holds the **CarRegNo** and **Cars** table which holds the **Color**. Via the CustId field of the Customers table it is possible to reach the CustId field of the Rentals table and via the CarRegNo field of the Cars tables it is possible to reach the CarRegNo field of the Cars table. Once the Cars table is reached, the Color field of that table can be used to extract the value held for a comparison.

To understand the solution the query mentioned above needs to be simplified. The inner most sub-queries should be handled first and then proceeded outwards.

The **first step** is to identify the Cars via its CarRegNo field which are red colored. This is done by extracting the value held in the **Color** field of the Cars table (i.e. **CARS**). The SQL query for this will be as follows:
    SELECT CarRegNo **FROM** Cars **WHERE** Color = 'Black';

The target table will be as follows:
Output:
```
CARREGNO
---------------
MH-03-X-0987
MH-14-Y-4039
```

The resulting output simplifies the solution as shown below:
    SELECT (FirstName ‖ ' ' ‖ LastName) "Customer" **FROM** Customers
        WHERE CustId **IN(SELECT** CustId **FROM** Rentals **WHERE** CarRegNo
        IN('MH-03-X-0987', 'MH-14-Y-4039'));

The **second step** is to identify the customers who have been rented the Black Car. To do this the customer numbers (i.e. **CustId**) have to be retrieved from the Rentals table (i.e. **RENTALS**). The SQL query for this will be as follows:
    SELECT CustId **FROM** Rentals **WHERE** CarRegNo **IN(**'MH-03-X-0987', 'MH-14-Y-4039');

The target table will be as follows:
Output:
```
   CUSTID
----------
        8
       10
        5
        5
```

The outer sub-query output will simplify the solution as shown below:
SELECT (FirstName || ' ' || LastName) "Customer" **FROM** Customers
      WHERE CustId **IN**(8,10,5,5)**;**

When the above SQL query is executed the resulting output is equivalent to the desired output of the SQL query using two levels of Sub-queries.

Using Sub-query In The FROM Clause

A subquery can be used in the **FROM** clause of the **SELECT** statement. The concept of using a subquery in the **FROM** clause of the **SELECT** statement is called an **inline view**. A subquery in the **FROM** clause of the **SELECT** statement defines a **data source** from that particular **Select** statement.

Example 12:
List the Mileage against each rental transaction, the customer associated with the rental transaction and the average Mileage of that customer, having Mileage per rental transaction more than the average Mileage of that customer.

Synopsis:

Tables:	Rentals
Columns:	RentId, OpMlge, ClMlge, CustId
Technique:	**Sub-Queries, Join, Functions:** AVG(), **Clauses:** WHERE, GROUP BY

Solution:
SELECT A.RentId, A.ClMlge-A.OpMlge, A.CustId, **B.**AvgMlge
    FROM Rentals **A,** (**SELECT** *CustId,* **AVG**(*ClMlge-OpMlge*) *AvgMlge*
        FROM *Rentals* **GROUP BY** *CustId*) **B**
           WHERE A.CustId = **B.**CustId **AND** (A.ClMlge-A.OpMlge) > **B.**AvgMlge**;**

Output:
```
   RENTID A.CLMLGE-A.OPMLGE     CUSTID    AVGMLGE
---------- -----------------  ---------- ----------
        3              1006        3         923
        5              1435        1 1217.71429
        8              2765        4      1719.5
       11              1888        6      1871.5
       15              2475        5 1252.71429
       16              1334        1 1217.71429
       19              1849       10      1340.8
       20              1873        5 1252.71429
       21              1205        2       809.4
       23              1452        1 1217.71429
       24              1300        3         923
       25              2380        8 1473.66667
```

Output: (Continued)

RENTID	A.CLMLGE-A.OPMLGE	CUSTID	AVGMLGE
27	1402	5	1252.71429
28	1690	7	1000
32	1715	10	1340.8
34	1140	2	809.4
37	1545	1	1217.71429
38	1255	3	923
40	1752	9	1242.5

19 rows selected.

Explanation:

In the above example, the data that has to be retrieved is available in the **RENTALS** table, which holds the transaction details associated with the customers. The output requirements are the **Rent Identity**, the **Mileage** of that transaction, the **Customer Identity** associated with that rental transaction (i.e. **Rent Identity**) and the **Average Mileage** of that Customer. The first three requirements can be retrieved from the **Rentals** table.

The Average Mileage on a per customer basis requires use of another select query and a group by clause. This means a sub query can be used, but in this case, the sub query will return a value, which will be a part of the output. Since this query is going to act as a source of data it is placed in the **FROM** clause of the outer query and given an alias **B**. Finally to produce the output a join is used to get the data on the basis of the outer query i.e. (**A.**CustId = **B.** CustId) followed by a **WHERE** clause which actually filters the data before producing the output.

To understand the solution the query mentioned above needs to be simplified. The inner most sub-queries should be handled first and then continued outwards.

The **first step** is to identify the Customers and their average Mileage. This is done by, extracting the value held by the **CustId** field from the **Rentals** table. The SQL query for this will be as follows:

   SELECT CustId, **AVG(**ClMlge-OpMlge**)** AvgMlge **FROM** Rentals **GROUP BY** CustId;

The target table will be as follows:

Output:

CUSTID	AVGMLGE
1	1217.71429
2	809.4
3	923
4	1719.5
5	1252.71429
6	1871.5
7	1000
8	1473.66667
9	1242.5
10	1340.8

10 rows selected.

The **second step** is to associate the data returned by the inner query with the outer. This is done by binding the Sub-query with the **FROM** clause and using join. The output shown above is treated as an individual (temporary) table. This new table is referred as **B**, the alias name specified in the main **SELECT** statement.

The **third step** is to filter the data to output only those records where the mileage per rental transaction is more then the average mileage of the customer associated with that rental transaction. This is done using a **WHERE** clause (i.e. **(A.ClMlge-A.OpMlge) > B.AvgMlge**)

Finally, the **SELECT** statement is executed as a JOIN i.e. (**WHERE A.CustId = B.CustId**). This is explained in greater depth later in this chapter.

Using Correlated Sub-queries

A sub-query becomes correlated when the subquery references a column from a table in the parent query. A correlated subquery is evaluated once for each row processed by the parent statement, which can be any of select, delete or update.

A correlated subquery is one way of reading every row in a table and comparing values in each row against related data. It is used whenever a subquery must return a different result for each candidate row considered by the parent query.

Example 13:
List the Mileage against each rental transaction, the customer associated with the rental transaction and the average Mileage of that customer, having Mileage per rental transaction more than the average Mileage of that customer.

Synopsis:

Tables:	Rentals
Columns:	RentId, ClMlge, OpMlge, CustId
Technique:	**Sub-Queries, Join, Functions:** AVG(), **Clauses:** WHERE

Solution:
SELECT RentId, ClMlge-OpMlge, CustId **FROM** Rentals **A**
    WHERE ClMlge-OpMlge > (**SELECT AVG**(ClMlge-OpMlge) **FROM** Rentals
        WHERE CustId = A.CustId);

Output:

```
   RENTID CLMLGE-OPMLGE      CUSTID
---------- -------------  ----------
        3          1006           3
        5          1435           1
        8          2765           4
       11          1888           6
       15          2475           5
       16          1334           1
       19          1849          10
       20          1873           5
       21          1205           2
       23          1452           1
       24          1300           3
       25          2380           8
       27          1402           5
       28          1690           7
       32          1715          10
       34          1140           2
       37          1545           1
       38          1255           3
       40          1752           9

19 rows selected.
```

Explanation:

In the above example, the data that has to be retrieved is available in the **RENTALS** table, which holds the transaction details associated with the customers. The output requirements are the **Rent Identity**, the **Mileage** of that transaction, the **Customer Identity** associated with that rental transaction (i.e. **Rent Identity**) and the **Average Mileage** of that Customer. These requirements can be retrieved from the Rentals table. However the average mileage on a per customer basis requires use of another select query.

This means a correlated sub query can be used. The correlated sub-query specifically computes the average mileage of each customer. Since both the queries (i.e. Outer and the Inner) use **Rentals** table an alias is allotted to the table in the outer query. It is because of this **alias** the inner query is able to distinguish the inner column from the outer column.

Using Multi Column Subquery

Example 14:
Find out all the customers having same last names and reside in the same city.

Synopsis:

Tables:	Customers
Columns:	FirstName, LastName, City, CustId
Technique:	**Sub_Queries, Operators:** IN, **Clauses:** WHERE

Solution:

To obtain a sensible output from the above SQL query, it is required that the Customers table should contain appropriate information. The following INSERT INTO statement is executed via the SQL *PLUS console window:

INSERT INTO Customers VALUES(12, 'Anil', 'Sharma', 'A/14, Greedy Colony', 'Mumbai', 'Maharasthra', '400101', 'INDIA', '28365154', 'B-12829', 'Motor Cycle', '21-Apr-1998', '14-Apr-2018');
COMMIT;

SELECT A.FirstName, A.LastName, City **FROM** Customers **A**
    WHERE (A.LastName, A.City**) IN(SELECT B**.LastName, B.City
        FROM Customers **B** WHERE A.CustId <> B.CustId);

Output:
```
FIRSTNAME                LASTNAME                CITY
-------------------      --------------------    ----------------
Anil                     Sharma                  Mumbai
Rahul Mohan              Sharma                  Mumbai
```

Explanation:

In the above example, each row of the outer query is compared with the values from the inner query (Multi Row and Multi Column). This means that the values held in the **LastName** and **City** fields from the outer query are compared with the values held in the **LastName** and **City** fields retrieved by the inner query.

Using Sub-query in CASE Expressions

Example 15:
List the Bill details such as Bill No., bill date, bill amount, the customer identity and the payment status whether the payment is received or pending.

Synopsis:

Tables:	Bills, Receipts
Columns:	Bills: BillNo, CustId, BillDt, Total
	Receipts: BillNo
Technique:	**Sub_Queries, Operators:** IN, **Clauses:** CASE WHEN ... THEN

Solution:
SELECT BillNo, CustId, BillDt, (**CASE WHEN** BillNo **IN(SELECT** BillNo **FROM** Receipts)
    THEN 'Payment Received' **ELSE** 'Pending' END) "Payment Status", Total **FROM** Bills;

Output:
```
   BILLNO     CUSTID  BILLDT     Payment Status        TOTAL
---------- ---------- ---------- ----------------- ----------
        1          1 10-JUN-00  Payment Received      129060
        2          2 27-JUL-00  Payment Received       19424
        3          3 12-AUG-00  Payment Received        4788
. . .
       31          1 05-AUG-02  Payment Received      111000
       32         10 13-NOV-02  Pending               118800
       33          5 14-NOV-02  Payment Received       83250
       34         10 06-JAN-03  Pending                83250
       35          2 20-JAN-03  Pending              103937.5
. . .
       40          9 31-JUL-03  Pending                94350

40 rows selected.
```

Explanation:
In the above example, the inner query will return a value (i.e. if a record exists in the **Receipts** table then the payment is received or else the payment is pending). Based on the value returned, the outer query will display the Payment Status as either Payment Received or Pending.

Using Subquery In An ORDER BY clause

Example 16:
List the Rental transaction details in the order of the Bill Date.

Synopsis:

Tables:	Rentals, Bills
Columns:	Rentals: RentId, RentDt, ClMlge, OpMlge, CustId, CarRegNo
	Bills: BillNo, BillDt
Technique:	**Sub_Queries, Clauses:** ORDER BY **Others:** Alias, Concat (||)

Solution:
SELECT RentId, RentDt, ClMlge-OpMlge, CustId, CarRegNo **FROM** Rentals **A**
    WHERE RentDt > '31-Dec-2002'
        ORDER BY (**SELECT** BillDt **FROM** Bills **B WHERE** A.BillNo = **B.BillNo);**

Output:
```
   RENTID RENTDT     CLMLGE-OPMLGE     CUSTID CARREGNO
---------- ---------- ------------- ---------- --------------------
       36 07-JAN-03           914          5 MH-14-Y-4039
       37 03-MAR-03          1545          1 MH-12-A-8758
       38 05-MAY-03          1255          3 MH-13-P-3249
       40 15-JUL-03          1752          9 MH-13-P-3249
       39 06-JUL-03           967          5 MH-14-Y-4039
```

Output: (Continued)

```
    RENTID RENTDT     CLMLGE-OPMLGE      CUSTID CARREGNO
---------- ---------  -------------   ---------- --------------------
        41 25-JAN-05                          10 MH-14-Y-4039
        42 16-JAN-05                           8 MH-13-P-3249
```

7 rows selected.

Explanation:
In the above example, the output needs to be ordered on the basis of Bill Date. The Data required is available in the **Rentals** table. Since the output needs to be ordered on the basis of Bill Date, which is available in the **Bills** table, there is a need of a separate query, which can return the appropriate Bill Date from the **Bills** table based on the Bill No. Based on the values returned from the inner query the output produced by the outer query will be ordered. This is done, by placing the inner query, in the **ORDER BY** clause and further correlating it with the outer query on the basis of the **BillNo** being **the common field** in the tables **Rentals** and **Bills**.

Using EXISTS / NOT EXISTS Operator

The **EXISTS** operator is usually used with correlated subqueries. This operator enables to test whether a value retrieved by the outer query exists in the results set of the values retrieved by the inner query. If the subquery returns at least one row, the operator returns **TRUE**. If the value does not exist, it returns **FALSE**.

The **EXISTS** operator ensures that the search in the inner query terminates when at least one match is found.

Similarly, the **NOT EXISTS** operator enables to test whether a value retrieved by the outer query is not a part of the result set of the values retrieved by the inner query.

Example 17:
List customers who have hired a car more than 5 times.

Synopsis:

Tables:	Customers, Rentals
Columns:	Customers: CustId, FirstName, LastName
	Rentals: CustId
Technique:	**Operators:** EXISTS(), **Clauses:** WHERE

Solution:
SELECT CustId, FirstName, LastName **FROM** Customers **A**
    WHERE EXISTS(SELECT COUNT(CustId) **FROM** Rentals
        WHERE CustId = **A.CustId GROUP BY 1 HAVING** COUNT(CustId)>5**);**

Output:

```
    CUSTID FIRSTNAME            LASTNAME
---------- -------------------- --------------------
         1 Rahul Mohan          Sharma
         5 Raju                 Prasad
        10 Alex Joseph          D'Mello
```

Explanation:
In the above example, the inner query is correlated with the outer query via the **CustId** field. As soon as the search in the inner query retrieves the desired match, i.e. **CustId = A.CustId** and **COUNT(CustId)>5** the search is terminated. This means that the inner query stops it's processing and the outer query then produces the output.

Example 18:
List those cars, which have not been rented yet.

Synopsis:

Tables:	Cars, Rentals
Columns:	Cars: CarRegNo, Make, Model
	Rentals: CarRegNo
Technique:	**Operators:** NOT, EXISTS(), **Clauses:** WHERE **Others:** Alias

Solution:
SELECT CarRegNo, Make, Model **FROM** Cars **A WHERE NOT EXISTS(SELECT** 'SCT'
    FROM Rentals **WHERE** CarRegNo = **A.**CarRegNo**);**

Output:
```
CARREGNO                MAKE                            MODEL
-------------------- ------------------------ ----------------
MH-00-A-23              Maruti                          Esteem
```

Explanation:
In the above example, the inner query is correlated with the outer query via the **CarRegNo** field. Since the **NOT EXISTS** operator is used, if the inner query retrieves no rows at all i.e. the condition **CarRegNo = A.CarRegNo** fails, the outer query produces the output. This means after the inner query stops it's processing, the outer query sends the output based on the operator used. In the case of the inner query there is no need to return a specific value, hence a constant **'SCT'** is used instead. This is useful in terms of performance as it will be faster to select a constant than a column.

JOINS

Joining Multiple Tables (Equi Joins)

Sometimes it is necessary to work with multiple tables as though they were a single entity. Then a single SQL sentence can manipulate data from all the tables. **Joins** are used to achieve this. Tables are joined on columns that have the same **data type** and **width** in the tables.

Tables in a database can be related to each other with keys. A primary key is a column with a unique value for each row. The purpose is to bind data together, across tables, without repeating all of the data in every table.

The JOIN operator specifies how to relate tables in the query.
Types of JOIN:
❑   INNER
❑   OUTER (LEFT, RIGHT, FULL)
❑   CROSS

INNER JOIN: Inner joins are also known as **Equi Joins**. They are the most common joins used in SQL*Plus. They are know as equi joins because the where statement generally compares two columns from two tables with the equivalence operator =. This type of join is by far the most commonly used. In fact, many systems use this type as the default join. This type of join can be used in situations where selecting only those rows that have values in common in the columns specified in the ON clause, is required. In short, the INNER JOIN returns all rows from both tables where there is a match

OUTER JOIN: Outer joins are similar to inner joins, but give a bit more flexibility when selecting data from related tables. This type of join can be used in situations where it is desired, to select all rows from the table on the left (or right, or both) regardless of whether the other table has values in common and (usually) enter NULL where data is missing.

CROSS JOIN: A cross join returns what's known as a Cartesian product. This means that the join combines every row from the left table with every row in the right table. As can be imagined, sometimes this join produces a mess, but under the right circumstances, it can be very useful. This type of join can be used in situations where it is desired, to select all possible combinations of rows and columns from both tables. This kind of join is usually not preferred as it may run for a very long time and produce a huge result set that may not be useful.

Syntax:
ANSI-style
SELECT <ColumnName1>, <ColumnName2>, <ColumnName N> FROM <TableName1>
   INNER JOIN <TableName2>
      ON <TableName1>.<ColumnName1>=<TableName2>.<ColumnName2>
         WHERE <Condition>
           ORDER BY <ColumnName1>, <ColumnName2>, <ColumnNameN>

Theta-style
SELECT <ColumnName1>, <ColumnName2>, <ColumnName N>
   FROM <TableName1>,<TableName2>
   WHERE <TableName1>.<ColumnName1> = <TableName2>.<ColumnName2>
      AND <Condition>
        ORDER BY <ColumnName1>, <ColumnName2>, <ColumnNameN>

In the above syntax:
- **ColumnName1** in **TableName1** is usually that table's **Primary Key**
- **ColumnName2** in **TableName2** is a **Foreign Key** in that table
- **ColumnName1** and **ColumnName2** must have the **same Data Type** and for certain data types, the same size

Inner Join

Example 19:
List the customer details along with rental transactions.

Synopsis:

Tables:	Customers, Rentals
Columns:	Customers: CustId, FirstName, LastName
	Rentals: RentId, RentDt, OpMlge, ClMlge, CustId
Technique:	**Join:** INNER JOIN ... ON, SIMPLE, **Clauses:** WHERE, **Others:** Concat (‖)

Solution 1 (Ansi-style):
SELECT A.CustId, (A.FirstName ‖ ' ' ‖ A.LastName) "Name", B.RentId,
   B.RentDt, B.ClMlge-B.OpMlge "Mileage" **FROM Customers A**
      INNER JOIN Rentals B ON B.CustId = A.CustId;

Solution 2 (Theta-style):
SELECT A.CustId, (A.FirstName ‖ ' ' ‖ A.LastName) "Name", B.RentId, B.RentDt,
   B.ClMlge-B.OpMlge "Mileage" **FROM** Customers **A**, Rentals **B WHERE** B.CustId = A.CustId;

Output:

```
   CUSTID Name                              RENTID RENTDT      Mileage
---------- -------------------------------- ---------- --------- ----------
       10 Alex Joseph D'Mello                   41 25-JAN-05
        8 Preity Sen                            42 16-JAN-05
        1 Rahul Mohan Sharma                     1 15-MAY-00        1206
        2 John Simon Brownie                     2 21-JUL-00         447

        3 Jennifer Smith                        38 05-MAY-03        1255
        5 Raju Prasad                           39 06-JUL-03         967
        9 Ashwini Joshi                         40 15-JUL-03        1752
```

42 rows selected.

Explanation:
In the above example, in the **Customers** table, the **CustId** column is the **primary key**, meaning that no two rows can have the same **CustId**. The **CustId** distinguishes two persons even if they have the same name. The data required in this example is available in two tables i.e. **Customers** and **Rentals**. This is because rental details are going to be a part of the output but are not available in the **Customers** table.

Notice that:
- The **CustId** column is the primary key of the **Customers** table
- The **RentId** column is the primary key of the **Rentals** table
- The **CustId** column in the **Customers** table is used to refer to the customers in the **Rentals** table without using their names

On the basis of the reference available in the **Customers** table i.e. the **CustId** field its possible to link to the **Rentals** table and fetch the desired Rental details for display. This is easily possible with the use of inner join based on the condition (**B**.CustId = **A**.CustId).

Note

> If the column names on which the **join** is to be specified are the same in each table reference the columns using **TableName.ColumnName**.

Example 20:
List the cars along with their rental transactions.

Synopsis:

Tables:	Cars, Rentals
Columns:	Cars: CarRegNo, Model, Make, Color
	Rentals: RentId, RentDt, CustId, RentAmt
Technique:	**Join:** INNER JOIN ... ON, SIMPLE; **Clauses:** WHERE; **Others:** Concat (‖)

Solution 1 (Ansi-style):
SELECT **A**.CarRegNo, **A**.Model, **A**.Make, **A**.Color, **B**.RentId, **B**.RentDt, **B**.CustId, **B**.RentAmt
          FROM **Cars A** INNER JOIN **Rentals B** ON **A**.CarRegNo = **B**.CarRegNo;

Solution 2 (Theta-style):
SELECT **A**.CarRegNo, **A**.Model, **A**.Make, **A**.Color, **B**.RentId, **B**.RentDt, **B**.CustId, **B**.RentAmt
     FROM **Cars A, Rentals B** WHERE **A**.CarRegNo = **B**.CarRegNo;

Output:

```
CARREGNO        MODEL        MAKE    COLOR   RENTID RENTDT      CUSTID RENTAMT
-------------   -----------  ------  ------  ------ ----------  ------ -------
MH-14-Y-4039    Indica V2    Tata    Black       41 25-JAN-05      10
MH-13-P-3249    Qualis       Toyota  White       42 16-JAN-05       8
MH-01-B-2083    Esteem       Maruti  Grey         1 15-MAY-00       1  112860
MH-01-B-2083    Esteem       Maruti  Grey         2 21-JUL-00       2   11020
. . .
MH-13-P-3249    Qualis       Toyota  White       38 05-MAY-03       3   99000
MH-14-Y-4039    Indica V2    Tata    Black       39 06-JUL-03       5  105600
MH-13-P-3249    Qualis       Toyota  White       40 15-JUL-03       9   84150

42 rows selected.
```

Explanation:

In the above example, the data required is available in two tables i.e. Cars and Rentals. Both the tables are linked via a common field. This is because the data is spread across the tables based on a normalization schema.

Notice that:
❑ The **CarRegNo** column is the primary key of the **Cars** table
❑ The **Rentals** is a table that holds the rental transactions with the customers via cars.
   In **Rentals** table:
   o **RentId** column is the primary key of that table.
   o **CarRegNo** column is used to refer to the cars in the **Cars** table

To retrieve the data required, both the tables have to be linked on the basis of a common column using joins as follows:
❑ **A.**CarRegNo = **B.**CarRegNo
This means the CarRegNo field of Cars table is joined with CarRegNo field of the Rentals table

Now since both the tables are linked using a join, data can be retrieved as if they are all in one table using the alias as:
A.CarRegNo, **A.**Model, **A.**Make, **A.**Color, **B.**RentId, **B.**RentDt, **B.**CustId, **B.**RentAmt

Outer Join

Example 21:
List the bill details along with the receipts (if any) Using Left Outer Join.

Synopsis:

Tables:	Bills, Receipts
Columns:	Bills: BillNo, BillDt, CustId, Total
	Receipts: RcptId, RcptDt, Amt
Technique:	**Join:** LEFT JOIN ... ON, **Clauses:** WHERE

Solution 1 (Ansi-style):
SELECT A. BillNo, **A.**BillDt, **A.**CustId, **A.**Total, **B.**RcptId, **B.**RcptDt, **B.**Amt
   FROM Bills **A LEFT JOIN** Receipts **B ON A.**BillNo = **B.**BillNo;

Solution 2 (Theta-style):
SELECT A. BillNo, **A.**BillDt, **A.**CustId, **A.**Total, **B.**RcptId, **B.**RcptDt, **B.**Amt
   FROM Bills **A**, Receipts **B WHERE A.**BillNo = **B.**BillNo **(+);**

Output:

BILLNO	BILLDT	CUSTID	TOTAL	RCPTID	RCPTDT	AMT
1	10-JUN-00	1	129060	1	15-MAY-00	32265
1	10-JUN-00	1	129060	2	12-JUN-00	96795
. . .						
33	14-NOV-02	5	83250	63	31-OCT-02	20812.5
33	14-NOV-02	5	83250	64	28-NOV-02	62437.5
37	09-APR-03	1	111198	71	22-APR-03	111198
36	30-JAN-03	5	95680	67	07-JAN-03	22000
32	13-NOV-02	10	118800	65	27-NOV-02	118800
. . .						
35	20-JAN-03	2	103937.5	70	13-FEB-03	62437.5

72 rows selected.

Explanation:
In the above example, the data required is all the bill details along with their receipts details **if any**. This means all the bill details have to be listed even though their corresponding receipts information is not present. The data is available in two tables i.e. Bills and Receipts.

In such a situation, the **LEFT JOIN** can be used which returns all the rows from the first table (i.e. Bills), even if there are no matches in the second table (Receipts). This means, if there are Bills entered in **Bills table** that do not have any receipts in **Receipts** table, those rows will also be listed. Notice the keyword **LEFT JOIN** in the first solution (Ansi-style) and the **(+)** in the second solution (Theta-style). This indicates that all rows from the first table i.e. Bills will be displayed even though there exists no matching rows in the second table i.e. Receipts.

Notice that:
- The **BillNo** column is the primary key of the **Bills** table
- The **Receipts** is a table that holds the receipts for the payments received
  In **Receipts** table:
  - **BillNo** column is used to refer to the Bills in the Bills table via the BillNo column.

To retrieve the data required, both the tables have to be linked on the basis of common columns using joins as follows:
- **A.**BillNo = **B.**BillNo

This means the BillNo field of Bills table is joined with BillNo field of the Receipts table

Example 22:
List the bill details along with the receipts (if any) Using Right Outer Join.

Synopsis:

Tables:	Bills, Receipts
Columns:	Bills: BillNo, BillDt, CustId, Total
	Receipts: RcptId, RcptDt, Amt
Technique:	**Join:** RIGHT JOIN ... ON, **Clauses:** WHERE

Solution 1 (Ansi-style):
SELECT A. BillNo, **A.**BillDt, **A.**CustId, **A.**Total, **B.**RcptId, **B.**RcptDt, **B.**Amt
    FROM Receipts **B RIGHT JOIN** Bills **A ON B.**BillNo = **A.**BillNo;

Solution 2 (Theta-style):
SELECT A.BillNo, A.BillDt, A.CustId, A.Total, B.RcptId, B.RcptDt, B.Amt
    FROM Receipts **B**, Bills **A WHERE** B.BillNo(+) = A.BillNo;

Output:

```
BILLNO BILLDT        CUSTID       TOTAL RCPTID RCPTDT         AMT
------ ---------     ------  ---------- ------ ---------  ----------
     1 10-JUN-00          1      129060      1 15-MAY-00       32265
     1 10-JUN-00          1      129060      2 12-JUN-00       96795
. . .
    33 14-NOV-02          5       83250     63 31-OCT-02     20812.5
    33 14-NOV-02          5       83250     64 28-NOV-02     62437.5
    37 09-APR-03          1      111198     71 22-APR-03      111198
    36 30-JAN-03          5       95680     67 07-JAN-03       22000
    32 13-NOV-02         10      118800     65 27-NOV-02      118800
. . .
    35 20-JAN-03          2    103937.5     70 13-FEB-03     62437.5

72 rows selected.
```

Explanation:
In the above example, the data required is all the bill details along with their receipts details **if any**. But in this case **RIGHT JOIN** is being used. This means all the Bill details have to be listed even though their corresponding Receipts are not present. The data is available in two tables i.e. Bills and Receipts.

Since the **RIGHT JOIN** returns all the rows from the second table even if there are no matches in the first table, the first table in the **FROM** clause will have to be **Receipts** and the second table **Bills**. This means, if there are Bills that do not have any receipts, those rows will also be listed. Notice the keyword **RIGHT JOIN** in the first solution (Ansi-style) and the **(+)** in the second solution (Theta-style). This indicates that all rows from the second table i.e. Bills will be displayed even though there exists no matching rows in the first table i.e. Receipts.

Notice that:
❑ The **BillNo** column is the primary key of the **Bills** table
❑ The **Receipts** is a table that holds the receipts for the payments received
    In **Receipts** table:
    ○ **BillNo** column is used to refer to the Bills in the Bills table via the BillNo column.

To retrieve the data required, both the tables have to be linked on the basis of common columns using joins as follows:
❑ A.BillNo = B.BillNo
This means the BillNo field of Bills table is joined with BillNo field of the Receipts table

Cross Join

Suppose it is desired to combine each car's hourly rental rate with a Car Rental Slab table so as to analyze each car at different minimum and maximum hourly periods along with discount wherever applicable. This is elegantly done using a cross join.

Example 23:
Create a report using **cross join** that will display the rental amounts for pre-defined Rental Slabs, based on the Minimum and Maximum hourly periods. *Ensure that the table RentalsSlab is created and populated with some records.*

Synopsis:

Tables:	Cars, RentalsSlab
Columns:	Cars: Model, CarRegNo, HrRentRate
	RentalsSlab: MinHr, MaxHr, Discount
Technique:	**Join:** CROSS JOIN, **Operators:** (*), (/)

Prior executing the SQL statement the RentalsSlab table has to be created and filled in with some sample data.

CREATE TABLE RentalsSlab (SlabId **NUMBER(2),** MinHr **NUMBER(5),**
    MaxHr **NUMBER(5),** Discount **NUMBER(5,2));**

Insert Statements for the table RentalsSlab:
INSERT INTO RentalsSlab **VALUES**(1, 1, 6, 1**);**
INSERT INTO RentalsSlab **VALUES**(2, 7, 12, 2**);**
INSERT INTO RentalsSlab **VALUES**(3, 13, 18, 3**);**
INSERT INTO RentalsSlab **VALUES**(4, 19, 24, 4**);**

Solution:
SELECT TRIM(C.Model || ' – ' || **C.**CarRegNo) "CARS", **C.**HrRentRate, **S.**MinHr, **S.**MaxHr, **S.**Discount,
    ROUND((C. HrRentRate * **S.**MinHr) * ((100 - **S.**Discount) / 100)) "Min. Amt.",
    ROUND((C. HrRentRate * **S.**MaxHr) * ((100 - **S.**Discount) / 100)) "Max. Amt."
    FROM Cars **C CROSS JOIN** RentalsSlab **S;**

Output:

CARS	HRRENTRATE	MINHR	MAXHR	DISCOUNT	Min. Amt.	Max. Amt.
Esteem - MH-01-B-2083	190	1	6	1	188	1129
Omni - MH-02-C-5876	170	1	6	1	168	1010
Premium - MMZ-888	145	1	6	1	144	861
Sumo - MH-02-Z-3840	180	1	6	1	178	1069
Safari - MH-04-Y-4849	250	1	6	1	248	1485
800 - MH-12-A-8758	145	1	6	1	144	861
Indica - MH-03-X-0987	190	1	6	1	188	1129
Santro - MH-03-F-3499	175	1	6	1	173	1040
Qualis - MH-13-P-3249	225	1	6	1	223	1337
Indica V2 - MH-14-Y-4039	200	1	6	1	198	1188
Esteem - MH-01-B-2083	190	7	12	2	1303	2234
Omni - MH-02-C-5876	170	7	12	2	1166	1999
Premium - MMZ-888	145	7	12	2	995	1705
Sumo - MH-02-Z-3840	180	7	12	2	1235	2117
Safari - MH-04-Y-4849	250	7	12	2	1715	2940
800 - MH-12-A-8758	145	7	12	2	995	1705
Indica - MH-03-X-0987	190	7	12	2	1303	2234
Santro - MH-03-F-3499	175	7	12	2	1201	2058
Qualis - MH-13-P-3249	225	7	12	2	1544	2646
Indica V2 - MH-14-Y-4039	200	7	12	2	1372	2352
Esteem - MH-01-B-2083	190	13	18	3	2396	3317
Omni - MH-02-C-5876	170	13	18	3	2144	2968
Premium - MMZ-888	145	13	18	3	1828	2532
Sumo - MH-02-Z-3840	180	13	18	3	2270	3143
Safari - MH-04-Y-4849	250	13	18	3	3153	4365
800 - MH-12-A-8758	145	13	18	3	1828	2532
Indica - MH-03-X-0987	190	13	18	3	2396	3317
Santro - MH-03-F-3499	175	13	18	3	2207	3056

Output: (Continued)

CARS	HRRENTRATE	MINHR	MAXHR	DISCOUNT	Min. Amt	Max. Amt.
Qualis - MH-13-P-3249	225	13	18	3	2837	3929
Indica V2 - MH-14-Y-4039	200	13	18	3	2522	3492
Esteem - MH-01-B-2083	190	19	24	4	3466	4378
Omni - MH-02-C-5876	170	19	24	4	3101	3917
Premium - MMZ-888	145	19	24	4	2645	3341
Sumo - MH-02-Z-3840	180	19	24	4	3283	4147
Safari - MH-04-Y-4849	250	19	24	4	4560	5760
800 - MH-12-A-8758	145	19	24	4	2645	3341
Indica - MH-03-X-0987	190	19	24	4	3466	4378
Santro - MH-03-F-3499	175	19	24	4	3192	4032
Qualis - MH-13-P-3249	225	19	24	4	4104	5184
Indica V2 - MH-14-Y-4039	200	19	24	4	3648	4608

40 rows selected.

Explanation:

In the above example, the data required is available in two tables i.e. Cars and RentalsSlab. In the table Cars, there exists, Car Models and their Hourly Rental Rates. In the second table RentalsSlab, there exists a list of Rentals slabs comprising of minimum and maximum hourly periods and the applicable discounts for those periods.

The output is required in the form of a report, which will display calculation based on the RentalsSlab table for each row held in the Cars. In such a situation, a CROSS JOIN can be used which will combine each record from the left table with that of the right table. In this example a cross join will combine each Car Model with its hourly rental rate from the Cars table with each rental slab i.e. each record in the RentalsSlab table after applying some calculations. Using Cross Join, a matrix between the tables named Cars table and the RentalsSlab table can be created.

The above SELECT statement creates a record for each car model and its hourly rental rate with the calculated discounted amount based on the minimum and maximum hourly periods. The results are known as a Cartesian product, which combines every record in the left table i.e. Cars with every record in the right table i.e. RentalsSlab.

Oracle versions **prior to 9i** don't support an explicit cross join, but the same results can be obtained by using the following statement:

SELECT TRIM(C. Model || ' – ' || **C.**CarRegNo**) "CARS", C.**HrRentRate, **S.**MinHr, **S.**MaxHr, **S.**Discount,
    ROUND((C. HrRentRate * **S.**MinHr**) * ((**100 - **S.**Discount**) / **100**)) "Min. Amt.",**
    ROUND((C. HrRentRate * **S.**MaxHr**) * ((**100 - **S.**Discount**) / **100**)) "Max. Amt."**
    FROM Cars **C,** RentalsSlab **S;**

Guidelines for Creating Joins

❑ When writing a select statement that joins tables, precede the column name with the table name for clarity

❑ If the same column name appears in more than one table, the column name must be prefixed with the table name

❑ The WHERE clause, is the most critical clause in a join select statement. Always make sure to include the WHERE clause

Joining A Table To Itself (Self Joins)

In some situations, it is necessary to join a table to itself, as though joining two separate tables. This is referred to as a **self-join**. In a self-join, two rows from the same table combine to form a result row.

To join a table to itself, **two** copies of the very same table have to be opened in memory. Hence in the **FROM** clause, the table name needs to be mentioned twice. Since the table names are the same, the second table will overwrite the first table and in effect, result in only one table being in memory. This is because a table name is translated into a specific memory location. To avoid this, each table is opened using an alias. Now these table aliases will cause two identical tables to be opened in different memory locations. This will result in two identical tables to be physically present in the computer's memory.

Using the table alias names these two identical tables can be joined.

FROM <TableName> [<Alias1>], <TableName> [<Alias2>] ....

Example 24:
Retrieve the names of the employees and the names of their respective managers from the employee table. *This table is pre-created and pre-populated in the SCOTT schema.*

Synopsis:

Tables:	Emp
Columns:	Ename
Technique:	**Joins:** SELF, **Clauses**: WHERE **Others:** Alias

Solution:
SELECT E.ENAME "Employee", M.ENAME "Manager" **FROM** Emp E, Emp M
    WHERE E.MGR = **M**.EMPNO;

Note

In this query, the **Emp** table is treated as two separate tables named **E** and **M**, using the table **alias** feature of SQL.

Output:
```
Employee    Manager
----------  ---------
SCOTT       JONES
FORD        JONES
ALLEN       BLAKE
WARD        BLAKE
JAMES       BLAKE
TURNER      BLAKE
MARTIN      BLAKE
MILLER      CLARK
ADAMS       SCOTT
JONES       KING
CLARK       KING
BLAKE       KING
SMITH       FORD

13 rows selected.
```

Explanation:
In the above example, the data required are all the employees and the names of their respective managers to whom they report. This data is available in the table **Emp**. The **Emp** table holds the employee number, their names and the manager numbers who in turn are employees in the same table.

The table Emp holds the following data:

```
EMPNO  ENAME              MGR
-----  ----------       ----------
 7369  SMITH              7902
 7499  ALLEN              7698
 7521  WARD               7698
 7566  JONES              7839
 7654  MARTIN             7698
 7698  BLAKE              7839
 7782  CLARK              7839
 7788  SCOTT              7566
 7839  KING
 7844  TURNER             7698
 7876  ADAMS              7788
 7900  JAMES              7698
 7902  FORD               7566
 7934  MILLER             7782
```

As can be seen from the data above employee named **Smith** having employee number **7369** reports to a manager (employee) named **Ford** having employee number **7902**.

This means:
- The **EmpNo** column is the primary key of the **Emp** table
- The **Mgr** column is used to refer to the Employee details in the same table i.e. **Emp** via the **EmpNo** column

This simply means that **Mgr** is a foreign key mapping to the EmpNo which is the primary key of the table.

From the data available in the **Emp** table seen above, it is possible to extract the manager number to which the employee reports, but in order to extract the manager name i.e. the employee's name (since the manager is also an employee) a reference to the same table **Emp** has to be made. This can be done using a SELF JOIN i.e. making a copy of the same table **Emp** and then referring to the columns to get the employee name against the manager number.

To form a copy of the same table alias have to be used in the FROM clause as:
　　FROM Emp **E**, Emp **M**
Here the **E** is the **first copy** of the table **Emp** and **M** is the **second copy** of the table **Emp**.

To retrieve the data required, both the copies of the same tables have to be linked on the basis of common columns using joins as follows:
- **E.Mgr = M.EmpNo**
　　This means the Mgr field of **Emp** table (First Copy: **E**) is joined with EmpNo field of the **Emp** (Second Copy: **M**) table

USING THE UNION, INTERSECT AND MINUS CLAUSE

To understand these concepts a table named Suppliers will be created and populated as shown below.

The CREATE statement for the Suppliers table will be as follows:
　　CREATE TABLE Suppliers (SuplrId **Number(5)**, FirstName **VarChar2(20)**,
　　　　LastName **VarChar2(20)**, City **VarChar2(15)**, Phone **VarChar2(30)**);

The INSERT INTO statements for the Suppliers table will be as follows:
    INSERT INTO Suppliers VALUES(1, 'Rahul Mohan', 'Sharma', 'Mumbai', '28765654');
    INSERT INTO Suppliers VALUES(2, 'Sharanam', 'Shah', 'Mumbai', '24303760');
    INSERT INTO Suppliers VALUES(3, 'Wilson', 'Fernandes', 'Mumbai', '24443760');
    INSERT INTO Suppliers VALUES(4, 'Hansel', 'Dias', 'Goa', '75643760');
    INSERT INTO Suppliers VALUES(5, 'Raju', 'Prasad', 'Chennai', '42739894');

Union Clause

Multiple queries can be put together and their output can be combined using the **union** clause. The **Union** clause merges the output of two or more queries into a single set of rows and columns.

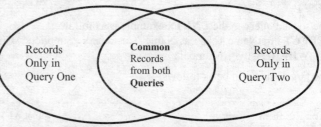

Diagram 6.1: Output of the Union Clause.

 Note

The output of both the queries will be as displayed above. The final output of the union clause will be: **Output** = Records from query one + records from query two +
    A single set of records, common in both queries.

While working with the UNION clause the following pointers should be considered:
- The number of columns and the data types of the columns being selected must be identical in all the **SELECT** statement used in the query. The names of the columns need not be identical.
- **UNION** operates over all of the columns being selected.
- **NULL** values are not ignored during duplicate checking.
- The **IN** operator has a higher precedence than the **UNION** operator.
- By default, the output is sorted in ascending order of the first column of the **SELECT** clause.

Example 25:
Retrieve the names of all the customers and suppliers residing in the city of **Mumbai**. Ensure that duplicates are eliminated.

Synopsis:

Tables:	Customers, Suppliers
Columns:	Customers: FirstName, LastName, City
	Suppliers: FirstName, LastName, City
Technique:	**Operators:** ‖; **Clauses:** WHERE, UNION; **Others:** Alias

Solution:
SELECT FirstName ‖ ' ' ‖ LastName "Customers / Suppliers", City **FROM** Customers
    WHERE City = 'Mumbai'
UNION
SELECT FirstName ‖ ' ' ‖ LastName "Customers / Suppliers", City **FROM** Suppliers
    WHERE City = 'Mumbai';

Explanation:
Oracle executes the queries as follows:

The first query in the **UNION** example is as follows:
SELECT FirstName ‖ ' ' ‖ LastName "Customers / Suppliers", City **FROM** Customers
    WHERE City = 'Mumbai';

The target table will be as follows:
```
Customers / Suppliers                          CITY
------------------------------------------     ---------------
Anil Sharma                                    Mumbai
Rahul Mohan Sharma                             Mumbai
Wilson Fernandes                               Mumbai
Preity Sen                                     Mumbai
Ashwini Joshi                                  Mumbai
```

The second query in the **UNION** example is as follows:
SELECT FirstName || ' ' || LastName "Customers / Suppliers", City **FROM** Suppliers
     WHERE City = 'Mumbai';

The target table will be as follows:
```
Customers / Suppliers                          CITY
------------------------------------------     ---------------
Rahul Mohan Sharma                             Mumbai
Sharanam Shah                                  Mumbai
Wilson Fernandes                               Mumbai
```

The **UNION** clause picks up the common records as well as the individual records in both queries. Thus, the output after applying the **UNION** clause will be:
Output:
```
Customers / Suppliers                          CITY
------------------------------------------     ---------------
Anil Sharma                                    Mumbai
Ashwini Joshi                                  Mumbai
Preity Sen                                     Mumbai
Rahul Mohan Sharma                             Mumbai
Sharanam Shah                                  Mumbai
Wilson Fernandes                               Mumbai
```
6 rows selected.

The Restrictions on using a union are as follows:
❑ Number of columns in all the queries should be the same
❑ The data type of the columns in each query must be same
❑ Unions cannot be used in subqueries
❑ Aggregate functions cannot be used with union clause

The alias assigned to the first query will be applied in the final output even though an alias has been assigned to the second query it is not applicable.

Intersect Clause

Multiple queries can be put together and their output combined using the intersect clause. The **Intersect** clause outputs only rows produced by **both** the queries intersected **i.e.** the output in an Intersect clause will include only those rows that are retrieved common to both the queries.

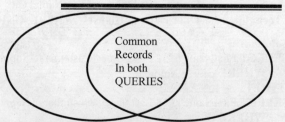

Diagram 6.2: Output of the Intersect clause.

The output of both the queries will be as displayed above. The final output of the Intersect clause will be: **Output** = A single set of records which are common in both queries.

While working with the INTERSECT clause the following pointers should be considered:
☐   The number of columns and the data types of the columns being selected by the **SELECT** statement in the queries must be identical in all the **SELECT** statements used in the query. The names of the columns need not be identical.
☐   Reversing the order of the intersected tables does not alter the result.
☐   **INTERSECT** does not ignore **NULL** values.

Example 26:
Retrieve the customers who are suppliers as well as resident in the city of **Mumbai**.

Synopsis:

Tables:	Customers, Suppliers
Columns:	Customers: FirstName, LastName, City Suppliers: FirstName, LastName, City
Technique:	**Operators: ||; Clauses: WHERE, INTERSECT; Others:** Alias

Solution:
SELECT FirstName || ' ' || LastName "Customers / Suppliers", City **FROM** Customers
    WHERE City = 'Mumbai'
INTERSECT
SELECT FirstName || ' ' || LastName "Customers / Suppliers", City
    FROM Suppliers **WHERE** City = 'Mumbai';

Explanation:
Oracle executes the queries as follows:

The first query in the **INTERSECT** example is as follows:
SELECT FirstName || ' ' || LastName "Customers / Suppliers", City **FROM** Customers
    WHERE City = 'Mumbai';

The target table will be as follows:
```
Customers / Suppliers                    CITY
---------------------------------------- ---------------
Anil Sharma                              Mumbai
Rahul Mohan Sharma                       Mumbai
Wilson Fernandes                         Mumbai
Preity Sen                               Mumbai
Ashwini Joshi                            Mumbai
```

The second query in the **INTERSECT** example is as follows:
SELECT FirstName || ' ' || LastName "Customers / Suppliers", City **FROM** Suppliers
    WHERE City = 'Mumbai';

The target table will be as follows:
```
Customers / Suppliers                    CITY
---------------------------------------- ---------------
Rahul Mohan Sharma                       Mumbai
Sharanam Shah                            Mumbai
Wilson Fernandes                         Mumbai
```

The **INTERSECT** clause picks up records that are common in both queries. Thus, the output after applying the INTERSECT clause will be as shown in the output.

Output:
```
Customers / Suppliers                    CITY
---------------------------------------- ---------------
Rahul Mohan Sharma                       Mumbai
Wilson Fernandes                         Mumbai
```

Minus Clause

Multiple queries can be put together and their output combined using the minus clause. The **Minus** clause outputs the rows produced by the first query, after **filtering** the rows retrieved by the second query.

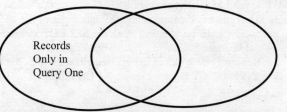

Records
Only in
Query One

Diagram 6.3: Output of the Minus clause.

Note

The output of both the queries will be as displayed above. The final output of the minus clause will be: **Output** = Records only in query one

While working with the MINUS clause the following pointers should be considered:
❑   The number of columns and the data types of the columns being selected by the **SELECT** statement in the queries must be identical in all the **SELECT** statements used in the query. The names of the columns need not be identical.
❑   All the columns in the **WHERE** clause must be in the **SELECT** clause for the **MINUS** operator to work.

Example 27:
Retrieve the customers who are not suppliers but resident in the city of **Mumbai**.

Synopsis:

Tables:	Customers, Suppliers
Columns:	Customers: FirstName, LastName, City
	Suppliers: FirstName, LastName, City
Technique:	**Operators:** ‖; **Clauses:** WHERE, MINUS; **Others:** Alias

Solution:
SELECT FirstName ‖ ' ' ‖ LastName "Customers / Suppliers", City **FROM** Customers
    WHERE City = 'Mumbai'
MINUS
SELECT FirstName ‖ ' ' ‖ LastName "Customers / Suppliers", City **FROM** Suppliers
    WHERE City = 'Mumbai';

Explanation:
Oracle executes the queries as follows:

The first query in the **MINUS** example is as follows:
SELECT FirstName ‖ ' ' ‖ LastName "Customers / Suppliers", City **FROM** Customers
    WHERE City = 'Mumbai';

The target table will be as follows:
```
Customers / Suppliers                      CITY
---------------------------------------- ---------------
Anil Sharma                                Mumbai
Rahul Mohan Sharma                         Mumbai
Wilson Fernandes                           Mumbai
Preity Sen                                 Mumbai
Ashwini Joshi                              Mumbai
```

The second query in the **MINUS** example is as follows:
SELECT FirstName || ' ' || LastName "Customers / Suppliers", City **FROM** Suppliers
    WHERE City = 'Mumbai';

The target table will be as follows:
```
Customers / Suppliers                    CITY
-----------------------------------------  ---------------
Rahul Mohan Sharma                       Mumbai
Sharanam Shah                            Mumbai
Wilson Fernandes                         Mumbai
```

The **MINUS** clause picks up records in the first query after filtering the records retrieved by the second query. Thus, the output after applying the MINUS clause will be as shown below.

Output:
```
Customers / Suppliers                    CITY
-----------------------------------------  ---------------
Anil Sharma                              Mumbai
Ashwini Joshi                            Mumbai
Preity Sen                               Mumbai
```

SELF REVIEW QUESTIONS

FILL IN THE BLANKS

1. The Oracle engine will process all rows in a table and display the result only when any of the conditions specified using the _____ operator are satisfied.

2. The _____ predicate allows for a comparison of one string value with another string value, which is not identical.

3. For character datatypes the _____ sign matches any string.

4. _____ is a small Oracle worktable, which consists of only one row and one column, and contains the value x in that column.

5. Functions that act on a set of values are called as _____ _____.

6. Variables or constants accepting by functions are called _____.

7. The _____ function returns a string with the first letter of each word in upper case.

8. The _____ function removes characters from the left of char with initial characters removed upto the first character not in set.

9. _____ returns the string passed as a parameter after right padding it to a specified length.

10. The _____ function converts char, a CHARACTER value expressing a number, to a NUMBER datatype.

11. The _____ function converts a value of a DATE datatype to CHAR value.

12. The _____ function returns number of months between two dates.

13. The _____ function returns an integer value corresponding to the UserID of the user currently logged in.

14. The _____ clause is another section of the select statement.

15. The _____ clause imposes a condition on the GROUP BY clause

16. A _____ is a form of an SQL statement that appears inside another SQL statement.

17. A subquery is also termed as _____ query.

18. The concept of joining multiple tables is called _____.

19. The _____ clause merges the output of two or more queries into a single set of rows and columns.

20. Multiple queries can be put together and their output combined using the _____ clause.

TRUE OR FALSE

21. The Oracle engine will process all rows in a table and display the result only when none of the conditions specified using the NOT operator are satisfied.

22. In order to select data that is within a range of values, the IN BETWEEN operator is used.

23. For character datatypes the percent sign matches any single character.

24. COUNT(expr) function returns the number of rows where expr is not null.

25. ROOT function returns square root of a numeric value.

26. The second parameter in the ROUND function specifies the number of digits after the decimal point.

27. The LOWER function returns char, with all letters in lowercase.

28. The UPPER function returns a string with the first letter of each word in upper case.

29. The LENGTH function returns the length of a word.

30. The LTRIM returns char, with final characters removed after the last character not in the set. 'set' is optional, it defaults to spaces.

31. LPAD returns the string passed as a parameter after left padding it to a specified length.

32. The TO_CHAR (date conversion) converts a value of a NUMBER datatype to a character datatype, using the optional format string.

33. The DATE data type is used to store date and time information.

34. The TO_DATE() function also disallows part insertion of a DATE value into a column.

35. The ADD_MONTHS function returns date after adding the number of months specified in the function.

36. The TO-DATE function allows a user to insert date into a date column in any required format, by specifying the character value of the date to be inserted and its format.

37. The HAVING CLAUSE is an optional clause which tells Oracle to group rows based on distinct values that exist for specified columns.

38. The statement containing a subquery is called a parent statement.

39. Joining a table to itself is called Equi join.

40. If a select statement is defined as a subquery, the innermost select statement gets executed first.

41. In the union clause multiple queries can be put together but their outputs cannot be combined.

42. Unions can be used in subqueries.

43. The Intersect clause outputs only rows produced by both the queries intersected.

44. The Minus clause outputs the rows produced by the first query, before filtering the rows retrieved by the second query.

HANDS ON EXERCISES

Using the tables created previously generate the SQL statements for the operations mentioned below.

1. **Perform the following computations on table data:**
a. List the names of all clients having 'a' as the second letter in their names.
b. List the clients who stay in a city whose First letter is 'M'.
c. List all clients who stay in 'Bangalore' or 'Mangalore'
d. List all clients whose BalDue is greater than value 10000.
e. List all information from the Sales_Order table for orders placed in the month of June.
f. List the order information for ClientNo 'C00001' and 'C00002'.
g. List products whose selling price is greater than 500 and less than or equal to 750.
h. List products whose selling price is more than 500. Calculate a new selling price as, original selling price * .15. Rename the new column in the output of the above query as new_price.
i. List the names, city and state of clients who are not in the state of 'Maharashtra'.
j. Count the total number of orders.
k. Calculate the average price of all the products.
l. Determine the maximum and minimum product prices. Rename the output as max_price and min_price respectively.
m. Count the number of products having price less than or equal to 500.
n. List all the products whose QtyOnHand is less than reorder level.

2. **Exercise on Date Manipulation:**
a. List the order number and day on which clients placed their order.
b. List the month (in alphabets) and date when the orders must be delivered.
c. List the OrderDate in the format 'DD-Month-YY'. e.g. 12-February-02.
d. List the date, 15 days after today's date.

3. **Exercises on using Having and Group By Clauses:**
a. Print the description and total qty sold for each product.
b. Find the value of each product sold.
c. Calculate the average qty sold for each client that has a maximum order value of 15000.00.
d. Find out the total of all the billed orders for the month of June.

4. **Exercises on Joins and Correlation:**
a. Find out the products, which have been sold to 'Ivan Bayross'.
b. Find out the products and their quantities that will have to be delivered in the current month.
c. List the ProductNo and description of constantly sold (i.e. rapidly moving) products.
d. Find the names of clients who have purchased 'Trousers'.
e. List the products and orders from customers who have ordered less than 5 units of 'Pull Overs'.
f. Find the products and their quantities for the orders placed by 'Ivan Bayross' and 'Mamta Muzumdar'.
g. Find the products and their quantities for the orders placed by ClientNo 'C00001' and 'C00002'.

5. **Exercise on Sub-queries:**
a. Find the ProductNo and description of non-moving products i.e. products not being sold.
b. List the customer Name, Address1, Address2, City and PinCode for the client who has placed order no 'O19001'.
c. List the client names that have placed orders before the month of May'02.
d. List if the product 'Lycra Top' has been ordered by any client and print the Client_no, Name to whom it was sold.
e. List the names of clients who have placed orders worth Rs. 10000 or more.

7. INTERACTIVE SQL PART III
CODE A MATRIX REPORT IN SQL

Example:

Create a matrix report that displays the Car Model, Car Registration Number and the number of times the car has been rented.

Solution:

```
SELECT  * FROM  (SELECT B.CarRegNo "Car",
      DECODE(B.Model, '800', (SELECT COUNT(CustId) FROM Rentals R
            WHERE R.CarRegNo = (SELECT CarRegNo
                  FROM Cars WHERE Cars.Model = B.Model))) "800",
      DECODE(B.Model, 'Santro', (SELECT COUNT(CustId) FROM Rentals R
            WHERE R.CarRegNo = (SELECT CarRegNo
                  FROM Cars WHERE Cars.Model = B.Model))) "Santro",
      DECODE(B.Model, 'Indica', (SELECT COUNT(CustId) FROM Rentals R
            WHERE R.CarRegNo = (SELECT CarRegNo
                  FROM Cars WHERE Cars.Model = B.Model))) "Indica",
      DECODE(B.Model, 'Indica V2', (SELECT COUNT(CustId) FROM Rentals R
            WHERE R.CarRegNo = (SELECT CarRegNo
                  FROM Cars WHERE Cars.Model = B.Model))) " Indica2",
      DECODE(B.Model, 'Premium', (SELECT COUNT(CustId) FROM Rentals R
            WHERE R.CarRegNo = (SELECT CarRegNo
                  FROM Cars WHERE Cars.Model = B.Model))) "Premium",
      DECODE(B.Model, 'Omni', (SELECT COUNT(CustId) FROM Rentals R
            WHERE R.CarRegNo = (SELECT CarRegNo
                  FROM Cars WHERE Cars.Model = B.Model))) "Omni",
      DECODE(B.Model, 'Sumo', (SELECT COUNT(CustId) FROM Rentals R
            WHERE R.CarRegNo = (SELECT CarRegNo
                  FROM Cars WHERE Cars.Model = B.Model))) "Sumo",
      DECODE(B.Model, 'Qualis', (SELECT COUNT(CustId) FROM Rentals R
            WHERE R.CarRegNo = (SELECT CarRegNo
                  FROM Cars WHERE Cars.Model = B.Model))) "Qualis",
      DECODE(B.Model, 'Safari', (SELECT COUNT(CustId) FROM Rentals R
            WHERE R.CarRegNo = (SELECT CarRegNo
                  FROM Cars WHERE Cars.Model = B.Model))) "Safari",
      DECODE(B.Model, 'Esteem', (SELECT COUNT(CustId) FROM Rentals R
            WHERE R.CarRegNo = (SELECT CarRegNo
                  FROM Cars WHERE Cars.Model = B.Model))) "Esteem"
      FROM Rentals A, Cars B
            WHERE A.CarRegNo = B.CarRegNo
      GROUP BY B.CarRegNo, B.Model);
```

Output:

Car	800	Santro	Indica	Indica2	Premium	Omni	Sumo	Qualis	Safari	Esteem
MMZ-888					5					
MH-01-B-2083										7
MH-02-C-5876						6				
MH-02-Z-3840							7			
MH-03-F-3499		2								
MH-03-X-0987			2							
MH-04-Y-4849									2	
MH-12-A-8758	2									
MH-13-P-3249								6		
MH-14-Y-4039			3							

```
10 rows selected.
```

In the above example, **DECODE** is used which is responsible to actually create a matrix output. This means that wherever the **Model** column returns a value other than **800** (the same applies to all the other model in the query, i.e. Santro, Indica, Esteem and so on) a blank value is displayed. This makes it possible to create a matrix report.

DECODE is a handy value-substitution mechanism that returns plain-English equivalents for a coded field. One of its advantages is speed. It is much faster to query using the DECODE keyword than to perform a join to a lookup table, especially when using large tables.

DUMP/ EXAMINE THE EXACT CONTENT OF A DATABASE COLUMN

Example:
Extract the column details of the column FirstName from the Customers table.

Solution:
SELECT DUMP(FirstName) **FROM** Customers;

Output:
```
DUMP(FIRSTNAME)
----------------------------------------------------------
Typ=1 Len=4: 65,110,105,108
Typ=1 Len=11: 82,97,104,117,108,32,77,111,104,97,110
Typ=1 Len=10: 74,111,104,110,32,83,105,109,111,110
Typ=1 Len=8: 74,101,110,110,105,102,101,114
Typ=1 Len=6: 87,105,108,115,111,110
Typ=1 Len=4: 82,97,106,117
Typ=1 Len=6: 80,97,114,118,101,122
Typ=1 Len=5: 77,111,115,105,101
Typ=1 Len=6: 80,114,101,105,116,121
Typ=1 Len=7: 65,115,104,119,105,110,105
Typ=1 Len=11: 65,108,101,120,32,74,111,115,101,112,104

11 rows selected.
```

In the above example, the type is **1**, which indicates the column is VARCHAR2, the len indicates the length of the value held in the column for a particular record and values such as 65,110,105,108 indicate the ASCII code for the value held.

WAYS TO DROP A COLUMN FROM A TABLE

Prior to Oracle 8i dropping a column was **not possible** but there were **workarounds** to do this.

Example:
Drop the column LastName from the Customers table.

Solution 1:
UPDATE Customers **SET** LastName = **NULL**;

Output:
```
11 rows updated.
```

RENAME Customers **TO** CustomersBase;

Output:
```
Table renamed.
```

CREATE VIEW Customers **AS SELECT** CustId, FirstName, Addr, City, State, PostalCode, Country, Phone, LicenseNo, LicenseType, IssuedOn, ExpiresOn **FROM** Customers_Base;

Output:
```
View created.
```

In the above example, to drop the column named LastName the following steps are carried out:
1. The value held in the LastName column is set to NULL for all the records of the Customers table
2. The table named Customers is then **renamed** to CustomersBase
3. Finally a view named Customers is created which comprises of all the columns except the column LastName

The users of the table Customers, while retrieving the data, will still use Customers as the name of the table and the data will be retrieved the same way, as it was, via a table even though a view is used.

Solution 2:
CREATE TABLE CustomersNew
    AS SELECT CustId, FirstName, Addr, City, State, PostalCode, Country, Phone,
            LicenseNo, LicenseType, IssuedOn, ExpiresOn **FROM** Customers;

Output:
```
Table created.
```

DROP TABLE Customers **CASCADE CONSTRAINTS**;

Output:
```
Table dropped.
```

RENAME CustomersNew **TO** Customers;

Output:
```
Table renamed.
```

In the above example, to drop the column named LastName the following steps are carried out:
1. A **table** named CustomersNew **is created** comprising of all the columns except the column LastName
2. The table named Customers is now **dropped**
3. Finally the table just created i.e. CustomersNew **is renamed** to Customers

The table Customers is referenced by a FOREIGN KEY constraint (i.e. via its primary key CustId, it is referenced by other tables). The Oracle engine will not allow dropping the table. Using **CASCADE CONSTRAINTS** solves this problem. The **CASCADE CONSTRAINTS** option drops the FOREIGN KEY constraints of the child tables.

From Oracle8 onwards, dropping of columns can be done, by using ALTER TABLE command.

ALTER TABLE Customers **DROP COLUMN** LastName;

Output:
```
Table altered.
```
Here, the column is dropped directly using the ALTER TABLE command.

ALTER TABLE Customers **SET UNUSED COLUMN** LastName;

Output:
```
Table altered.
```

The above command can be verified as:
Log in as SYS user:
CONNECT sys/<password>@<service_name> **AS SYSDBA;**

Retrieve the unused columns:
SELECT * FROM SYS.DBA_UNUSED_COL_TABS;

Output:

OWNER	TABLE_NAME	COUNT
SCOTT	CUSTOMERS	1

Log in as SCOTT user:
CONNECT scott/tiger@<service_name>;

ALTER TABLE Customers DROP UNUSED COLUMNS;

Output:
```
Table altered.
```

Log in as SYS user:
CONNECT sys/<password>@<service_name> **AS SYSDBA;**

Retrieve the unused columns:
SELECT * FROM SYS.DBA_UNUSED_COL_TABS;

Output:

```
no rows selected
```

In this example, the column LastName is set to represent itself as an unused column. To verify the same a SELECT is fired which displays the output as shown above.

Finally, using the **ALTER TABLE command,** all those columns marked as unused are dropped and this is further verified by issuing the select command on the **SYS.DBA_UNUSED_COL_TABS table.**

WAYS TO RENAME A COLUMN IN A TABLE

Example:
Rename the column named FirstName to CustomerName from the table Customers.

Solution 1:
RENAME Customers **TO** CustomersBase;

Output:
```
Table renamed.
```

CREATE VIEW Customers **AS SELECT** CustId, FirstName "CustomerName", LastName, Addr, City, State, PostalCode, Country, Phone, LicenseNo, LicenseType, IssuedOn, ExpiresOn
      FROM CustomersBase;

Output:
```
View created.
```

In the above example,
1.   The table Customers is first renamed to CustomersBase

2. A view named Customers is created, by specifying the new column names from the table CustomerBase

Solution 2:
CREATE TABLE CustomersNew
    AS SELECT CustId, FirstName "CustomerName", LastName, Addr, City, State,
        PostalCode, Country, Phone, LicenseNo, LicenseType, IssuedOn, ExpiresOn
           FROM Customers;

Output:
```
Table created.
```

DROP TABLE Customers **CASCADE CONSTRAINTS;**

Output:
```
Table dropped.
```

RENAME CustomersNew **TO** Customers;

Output:
```
Table renamed.
```

In the above example,
1. A table named CustomersNew is created comprising of columns with new names from the old table Customers
2. The old table is then dropped
3. Finally, the newly created table is renamed to the old table name i.e. Customers

Solution 3:
ALTER TABLE Customers ADD (CustomerName VARCHAR2(25));

Output:
```
Table altered.
```

UPDATE Customers **SET** CustomerName = FirstName;

Output:
```
10 rows updated.
```

ALTER TABLE Customers **DROP COLUMN** FirstName;

Output:
```
Table altered.
```

In the above example,
1. The table customers is altered and a new column is added to represent the new name of the column to be renamed
2. The table Customers is updated by copying the data from the old column to the new column
3. Finally, the old column is dropped

VIEW EVERY NTH ROW FROM A TABLE

In Oracle, to select all even, odd, or Nth rows from a table use SQL queries like:

Example:
Solution 1: Using Sub Queries
SELECT ROWNUM **RN,** CustId, FirstName **FROM** Customers **WHERE** (ROWID, 0)
     IN (SELECT ROWID, **MOD(ROWNUM,2) FROM** Customers**);**

Output:
```
      RN     CUSTID FIRSTNAME
---------- ---------- --------------------
         1          2 John Simon
         2          4 Wilson
         3          6 Parvez
         4          8 Preity
         5         10 Alex Joseph
```

Solution 2: Using dynamic views
SELECT * FROM (SELECT ROWNUM **RN,** CustId, FirstName **FROM** Customers**) C**
     WHERE MOD(C.RN,2) = 0;

Output:
```
      RN     CUSTID FIRSTNAME
---------- ---------- --------------------
         2          2 John Simon
         4          4 Wilson
         6          6 Parvez
         8          8 Preity
        10         10 Alex Joseph
```

Solution 3: Using GROUP BY and HAVING
SELECT ROWNUM, CustId, FirstName **FROM** Customers
     GROUP BY ROWNUM, CustId, FirstName
         HAVING MOD(ROWNUM,**2) = 0 OR** ROWNUM = 2-0**;**

Output:
```
   ROWNUM    CUSTID FIRSTNAME
---------- ---------- --------------------
         2          2 John Simon
         4          4 Wilson
         6          6 Parvez
         8          8 Preity
        10         10 Alex Joseph
```

GENERATE PRIMARY KEY VALUES FOR A TABLE

Example:
Create a table Drivers with a **NOT NULL** column such as **DriverId** and a column named **NAME**. Populate these columns with some values.

Solution:
CREATE TABLE Drivers (DriverId **NUMBER,** NAME **VARCHAR2**(25));

Output:
```
Table created.
```

```
INSERT INTO Drivers VALUES(0, 'Jack');
INSERT INTO Drivers VALUES(0, 'Harry');
INSERT INTO Drivers VALUES(0, 'Tom');
INSERT INTO Drivers VALUES(0, 'Rocky');
INSERT INTO Drivers VALUES(0, 'Alex');
```

Output: (For each of the above INSERT INTO statement)
```
1 row created.
```

The data held in the table Drivers:
SELECT * FROM Drivers;

Output:
```
 DRIVERID NAME
---------- -------------------
        0 Jack
        0 Harry
        0 Tom
        0 Rocky
        0 Alex
```
Now issue the following command to generate primary key for the column DriverId:
UPDATE Drivers **SET** DriverId = ROWNUM;

Output:
```
5 rows updated.
```

The data held in the table Drivers now:
SELECT * FROM Drivers;

Output:
```
 DRIVERID NAME
---------- ----------------------
        1 Jack
        2 Harry
        3 Tom
        4 Rocky
        5 Alex
```
OR

Use a sequences generator:
CREATE SEQUENCE SEQ_DriverId **START WITH** 1 **INCREMENT BY** 1;

Output:
```
Sequence created.
```

UPDATE Drivers **SET DriverId**= SEQ_DriverId**.NEXTVAL;**

Output:
```
5 rows updated.
```

The data held in the table Drivers now:
SELECT * FROM Drivers;

Output:
```
  DRIVERID NAME
---------- --------------------
         1 Jack
         2 Harry
         3 Tom
         4 Rocky
         5 Alex
```
Finally, create a unique index on the column DriverId as:
CREATE UNIQUE INDEX idxDriverId **ON** Drivers(DriverId);

Output:
```
Index created.
```

This will now restrict the insertion of duplicate values:
INSERT INTO Drivers **VALUES(1**, 'Jack');

Output:
```
INSERT INTO Drivers VALUES(1, 'Jack')
*
ERROR at line 1:
ORA-00001: unique constraint (SCOTT.IDXDRIVERID) violated
```

ADD A DAY/HOUR/MINUTE/SECOND TO A DATE VALUE

The **SYSDATE** pseudo-column shows the current system date and time. Adding 1 to SYSDATE will advance the date by 1 day. Using fractions to add hours, minutes or seconds to the date can advance the date by hour minutes and seconds.

Example:

SELECT TO_CHAR(SYSDATE, 'DD-MON-YYYY HH:MI:SS') "Date",
    TO_CHAR(SYSDATE+1, 'DD-MON-YYYY HH:MI:SS') "By 1 Day",
    TO_CHAR(SYSDATE+1/24, 'DD-MON-YYYY HH:MI:SS') "By 1 Hour",
    TO_CHAR(SYSDATE+1/1440, 'DD-MON-YYYY HH:MI:SS') "By 1 Minute",
    TO_CHAR(SYSDATE+ 1/86400 , 'DD-MON-YYYY HH:MI:SS') "By 1 Second" **FROM** DUAL;

Output:
```
Date                 By 1 Day             By 1 Hour            By 1 Minute          By 1 Second
-------------------- -------------------- -------------------- -------------------- --------------------
28-JAN-2005 11:43:52 29-JAN-2005 11:43:52 28-JAN-2005 12:43:52 28-JAN-2005 11:44:52 28-JAN-2005 11:43:53
```

Some more forms of date additions:

Description	Code
Now	SYSDATE
Tomorow/ next day	SYSDATE + 1
Seven days from now	SYSDATE + 7
One hour from now	SYSDATE + 1/24
Three hours from now	SYSDATE + 3/24
An half hour from now	SYSDATE + 1/48
10 minutes from now	SYSDATE + 10/1440
30 seconds from now	SYSDATE + 30/86400

Description	Code
Tomorrow at 12 midnight	TRUNC(SYSDATE + 1)
Tomorrow at 8 AM	TRUNC(SYSDATE + 1) + 8/24
Next Monday at 12:00 noon	NEXT_DAY(TRUNC(SYSDATE), 'MONDAY') + 12/24
First day of the month at 12 midnight	TRUNC(LAST_DAY(SYSDATE) + 1)
The next Monday, Wednesday or Friday at 9 A.M	TRUNC(LEAST(NEXT_DAY(SYSDATE, 'MONDAY'), NEXT_DAY(SYSDATE, 'WEDNESDAY'), NEXT_DAY(SYSDATE, 'FRIDAY'))) + (9/24)

COUNT DIFFERENT DATA VALUES IN A COLUMN

Sometimes it is required to count the value held in a column that is different.

This can be done as follows:

Example:
Count the number of transactions performed per Car till date.

SELECT CarRegNo, **COUNT(*)** "TRANSACTIONS PERFORMED"
    FROM Rentals **GROUP BY** CarRegNo;

Output:
```
CARREGNO                 TRANSACTIONS PERFORMED
-------------------      ----------------------
MH-01-B-2083                               7
MH-02-C-5876                               6
MH-02-Z-3840                               7
MH-03-F-3499                               2
MH-03-X-0987                               2
MH-04-Y-4849                               2
MH-12-A-8758                               2
MH-13-P-3249                               5
MH-14-Y-4039                               2
MMZ-888                                    5

10 rows selected.
```

Example:
Create a report displaying the Car Make, the number of Luxury Cars, Vans, Jeeps, Small Cars and a total of all categories based on their Make.

SELECT Make,
    SUM(DECODE(Catgry, 'L', 1, 0)) "Luxury Cars",
    SUM(DECODE(Catgry, 'V', 1, 0)) "Vans",
    SUM(DECODE(Catgry, 'J', 1, 0)) "Jeeps",
    SUM(DECODE(Catgry, 'S', 1, 0)) "Small Cars",
    COUNT(Catgry) "TOTAL"
    FROM Cars **GROUP BY** Make;

Output:

MAKE	Luxury Cars	Vans	Jeeps	Small Cars	TOTAL
Hyundai	0	0	0	1	1
Maruti	1	1	0	1	3
Padmini	0	0	0	1	1
Tata	3	0	1	0	4
Toyota	0	0	1	0	1

RETRIEVE ONLY ROWS X TO Y FROM A TABLE

Example:
Retrieve records ranging between 4 and 7 from the Customers table

Solution 1:
SELECT * FROM (SELECT ROWNUM **RN**, FirstName **FROM** Customers
   WHERE ROWNUM < 8**) WHERE** RN **BETWEEN** 4 and 7**;**

Note that **8** is just one greater than the maximum row of the required rows. This means x= 4, y=7, so the inner value is y+1 i.e. 8).

Output:

```
      RN FIRSTNAME
---------- --------------
       4 Wilson
       5 Raju
       6 Parvez
       7 Mosie
```

Solution 2:
SELECT ROWNUM **RN**, FirstName **FROM** Customers
   GROUP BY ROWNUM, FirstName **HAVING** ROWNUM **BETWEEN** 4 **AND** 7**;**

Output:

```
      RN FIRSTNAME
---------- --------------
       4 Wilson
       5 Raju
       6 Parvez
       7 Mosie
```

Solution 3:
SELECT ROWNUM **RN**, FirstName **FROM** Customers **WHERE** ROWID **IN(**
   SELECT ROWID **FROM** Customers **WHERE** ROWNUM <= 7
   MINUS
   SELECT ROWID **FROM** Customers **WHERE** ROWNUM < 4**);**

Output:

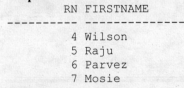

```
      RN FIRSTNAME
---------- --------------
       1 Wilson
       2 Raju
       3 Parvez
       4 Mosie
```

CHANGING THE ORACLE PASSWORD

Example:
Update the password for the Oracle user named **hansel** to **hansel123**.

Solution 1:
ALTER USER hansel **IDENTIFIED BY** hansel123;

Output:
```
User altered.
```

Oracle 8 onwards this can simply be done as:
Solution 2: To change the password for another User via the SQL*PLUS tool
Password hansel;

Output:
```
Changing password for hansel
New password: *********
Retype new password: *********
Password changed
```

Solution 3: To change the password for the Current User via the SQL*PLUS tool
Password;

Output:
```
Changing password for SCOTT
Old password: *****
New password: *****
Retype new password: *****
Password changed
```

ADDING LINE FEEDS TO SELECT STATEMENT OUTPUT

Example:
Display the Customer Details as:
Customer Name: Sharanam Chaitanya Shah   ↵
Address: Makanji Mansion   ↵
City: Mumbai   ↵

Note

> The return carriage symbol (↵) shown above is used to indicate a newline character and are not printed in the output.

Solution:
SELECT 'Customer Name: ' || FirstName || ' ' || LastName || CHR(10) ||
'Address: ' || Addr || CHR(10) || 'City: ' || City "Customer Details"
    FROM Customers;

Output:
```
Customer Details
-----------------------------------------------------
Customer Name: Rahul Mohan Sharma
Address: A/14, Sunray Colony
City:  Mumbai

Customer Name: John Simon Brownie
Address: 123/A, North Links
City:  New York

Customer Name: Jennifer Smith
Address: Baptisa Mansion, 37 West Links
City:  New York

. . .

10 rows selected.
```

TRANSLATING NUMERIC VALUES TO CHARACTER EQUIVALENTS

Example:
There are times when **amounts** in an application have to be represented by their character values. Specially while printing bank drafts the system gives the draft amount in **numbers** and **words**. In Oracle this can be simply done using the Julian Date conversion as follows:

Solution 1: FOR **UPPER-CASE** LETTERS
SELECT TO_CHAR(TO_DATE(34654,'J'),'JSP') FROM DUAL;

Output:
```
TO_CHAR(TO_DATE(34654,'J'),'JSP')
------------------------------------------
THIRTY-FOUR THOUSAND SIX HUNDRED FIFTY-FOUR
```

Solution 2: FOR **TITLE-CASE** LETTERS
SELECT TO_CHAR(TO_DATE(34654,'J'),'JsP') FROM DUAL;

Output:
```
TO_CHAR(TO_DATE(34654,'J'),'JSP')
------------------------------------------
Thirty-Four Thousand Six Hundred Fifty-Four
```

Solution 3: FOR **LOWER-CASE** LETTERS
SELECT TO_CHAR(TO_DATE(34654,'J'),'jSP') FROM DUAL;

Output:
```
TO_CHAR(TO_DATE(34654,'J'),'JSP')
------------------------------------------
thirty-four thousand six hundred fifty-four
```

Note that:
- ❑ The minimum JULIAN number allowed is 1, and, the maximum JULIAN number allowed is 5373484
- ❑ Amount larger then the maximum JULIAN number allowed cannot be converted to words
- ❑ This only works for integer amounts

❑   If rupees and paise, are also required in the output then split up the amount into it's integer and decimal parts, and handle the case of a zero amount, such as:
SELECT 'Rupees ' || **DECODE(TRUNC**(34654.23), 0, 'ZERO',
   TO_CHAR(TO_DATE(TRUNC(34654.23),'J'),'JSP'))** || ' AND ' ||
   DECODE(TRUNC(MOD(34654.23,1)*100), 0, 'ZERO',
   TO_CHAR(TO_DATE(TRUNC(MOD(34654.23,1)*100),'J'),'JSP'))** || ' Paise'
   FROM DUAL;

Output:
```
'RUPEES'||DECODE(TRUNC(34654.23),0,'ZERO',TO_CHAR(TO_DATE(TRUNC(34654.23)
--------------------------------------------------------------------------
Rupees THIRTY-FOUR THOUSAND SIX HUNDRED FIFTY-FOUR AND TWENTY-THREE Paise
```

CREATE A CSV OUTPUT

SQLPLUS can be a great tool to produce a quick report from Oracle database. As an example assume it is necessary to produce a comma separated values (CSV), output file. At first glance the user might start by appending the comma character to the database fields in the select statement.

However the solution below shows that this can be done quite easily using some of the built-in SQLPLUS commands. It also demonstrates some other commands that might be useful and can be used as a skeleton script upon which to base other reports.

Example:
Generate a report on the cars available for hiring.

Solution:

```
/* Suppress page headers, titles and all formatting */
```
SET PAGESIZE 0

```
/* Switch off the SQL text before/after any variable substitution */
```
SET VERIFY OFF

```
/* Set line size, make this as big as desired */
```
SET LINES 700

```
/* Delete any blank spaces at the end of each spooled line */
```
SET TRIMSPOOL ON

```
/* Switch off the lines number display returned by the query */
```
SET FEEDBACK OFF

```
/* Switch off SELECT output to the screen */
```
SET TERMOUT OFF

```
/* Separate each column by a comma character (ÇSV output) */
```
SET COLSEP ','

```
/* Put the SELECT output into a file*/
```
SPOOL Cars_Report.txt
SELECT CarRegNo, Model, Make, Color, EngineNo, ChassisNo
   FROM Cars;
SPOOL OFF

The output can be seen, by browsing to the bin directory available under <Drive>:\oracle\product\10.1.0\<Home_Directory>\bin. Open the file **Cars_Report.txt**

Output:

RETRIEVE RECORDS BASED ON SOUNDS

If it is desired to search all people whose name sounds like:
Neeta or Nita
Meeta or Mita
Suneel or Sunil
Pooja or Puja
Anil or Aneel
Deepa or Dipu or Dipa

This can simply be done using the Soundex function of Oracle.

Soundex returns Character String containing the phonetic representation of another string. The phonetic representation system uses a simple phonetic algorithm to reduce each name to a four character alphanumeric code. The first letter of the code corresponds to the first letter of the last name. The remainder of the code consists of three digits derived from the syllables of the word.

Rules of Soundex:
❑ Retain the first letter of the string and removes all other occurrences of the following letters: a, e, h, i, o, u, w, y
❑ Assign numbers to the remaining letters (after the first) as follows:
b, f, p, v = 1
c, g, j, k, q, s, x, z = 2
d, t = 3
l = 4
m, n = 5
r = 6
❑ If two or more letters with the same number were adjacent in the original name, or adjacent except for any intervening h and w, then omit all but the first
❑ Return the first four bytes padded with 0

Example:
To understand the use of the function follow the steps:

CREATE TABLE MyFriends (NAME VARCHAR2(15));

Output:
```
Table created.
```

INSERT INTO MyFriends **VALUES** ('Neeta');
INSERT INTO MyFriends **VALUES** ('Mita');
INSERT INTO MyFriends **VALUES** ('Dipu');
INSERT INTO MyFriends **VALUES** ('Deepu');
INSERT INTO MyFriends **VALUES** ('Dipa');
INSERT INTO MyFriends **VALUES** ('Anil');
INSERT INTO MyFriends **VALUES** ('Sunil');

Output: (For each of the above INSERT INTO statement)
```
1 row created.
```

COMMIT;

Output:
```
Commit complete.
```

SELECT * FROM MyFriends;

Output:
```
NAME
------
Neeta
Mita
Dipu
Deepu
Dipa
Anil
Sunil
```

Search for a friend whose name sounds like Nita:
SELECT * FROM MyFriends **WHERE SOUNDEX**(NAME) = SOUNDEX('Nita');

Output:
```
NAME
------
Neeta
```

Search for a friend whose name sounds like Deep:
SELECT * FROM MyFriends **WHERE SOUNDEX**(NAME) = SOUNDEX('Deep');

Output:
```
NAME
------
Dipu
Deepu
Dipa
```

To understand the working of the function issue the following:
SELECT SOUNDEX(NAME), NAME, **SOUNDEX**('DEEP') **FROM** MYFRIENDS;

Output:

```
SOUNDEX(NAME)   NAME            SOUNDEX(DEEP)
-------------   -------------   -------------
N300            Neeta           D100
M300            Mita            D100
D100            Dipu            D100
D100            Deepu           D100
D100            Dipa            D100
A540            Anil            D100
S540            Sunil           D100

7 rows selected.
```

The output shows how Oracle converts the words into numbers followed by a comparison between the two words and finally displays the output for the matching ones.

BINARY_FLOAT And BINARY_DOUBLE Data Types

One of the evolutionary changes that Oracle 10g has brought, in terms of front-end support for new language features include the BINARY_FLOAT and BINARY_DOUBLE datatypes. Both these features have an efficient and robust implementation in machine arithmetic for mathematical real numbers. A positive outcome of this implementation is the fact that algorithmic tasks that are expressed in PL/SQL using these new features can now run **much faster** than an implementation that does not have these features.

BINARY_DOUBLE is a 64-bit, double-precision floating-point number datatype. Each BINARY_DOUBLE value requires 9 bytes, including a length byte.

BINARY_FLOAT is a 32-bit, single-precision floating-point number datatype. Each BINARY_FLOAT value requires 5 bytes, including a length byte.

In a NUMBER column, floating point numbers have decimal precision. In a BINARY_FLOAT or BINARY_DOUBLE column, floating-point numbers have binary precision. The binary floating-point numbers support the special values **infinity and NaN (not a number)**.

Example 1:
The following statement creates a table named CarUsage that contains BINARY_FLOAT and BINARY_DOUBLE columns:
CREATE TABLE CarUsage (CarRegNo VARCHAR2(20) PRIMARY KEY,
     OpMlge **BINARY_FLOAT**, ClMlge **BINARY_DOUBLE**);

Example 2:
The following statements populate the table named SCT:
INSERT INTO CarUsage (CarRegNo, OpMlge, ClMlge) **VALUES('MH-02-Z-3840', 232.7f, 242.7d);**
INSERT INTO CarUsage (CarRegNo, OpMlge, ClMlge) **VALUES('MH-04-Y-4849', 452.2f, 470.9d);**

Example 3:
The following statement describes the table named CarUsage:
DESC CarUsage;

Output:

Name	Null?	Type
CARREGNO	NOT NULL	VARCHAR2(20)
OPMLGE		BINARY_FLOAT
CLMLGE		BINARY_DOUBLE

Example 4:
The following statement displays the contents of the table named CarUsage:
SELECT * FROM CarUsage;

Output:
```
CARREGNO                  OPMLGE     CLMLGE
--------------------   ----------  ----------
MH-02-Z-3840             2.327E+002 2.427E+002
MH-04-Y-4849             4.522E+002 4.709E+002
```

In addition to literal values special values can be used with the BINARY_FLOAT and BINARY_DOUBLE types. These values include:
- BINARY_FLOAT_NAN: Not a number
- BINARY_FLOAT_ INFINITY: Infinity
- BINARY_DOUBLE_NAN: Not a number
- BINARY_DOUBLE_INFINITY: Infinity

Example 5:
The following statements populate the table named CarUsage using special values:
INSERT INTO CarUsage (CarRegNo, OpMlge, ClMlge)
    VALUES('MH-12-A-8758', BINARY_FLOAT_NAN, BINARY_DOUBLE_NAN);
INSERT INTO CarUsage (CarRegNo, OpMlge, ClMlge)
    VALUES('MH-03-X-0987', BINARY_FLOAT_INFINITY, BINARY_DOUBLE_INFINITY);

Example 6:
The following statement displays the contents of the table named CarUsage (with Special values):
SELECT * FROM CarUsage;

Output:
```
CARREGNO                  OPMLGE     CLMLGE
--------------------   ----------  ----------
MH-02-Z-3840             2.327E+002 2.427E+002
MH-04-Y-4849             4.522E+002 4.709E+002
MH-12-A-8758                  Nan        Nan
MH-03-X-0987                  Inf        Inf
```

TIMESTAMP

The Oracle database has recently introduced the ability to store timestamps. The advantages of a timestamp over a DATE are:
- It can store a fractional second
- It can store zero time

The structure of information stored in the TIMESTAMP is of the format:
```
YYYY-MM-DD HH24:MI:SS.SSSSSSSSS
```
where, **YYYY** is year, **MM** is the month, **DD** is the day, **HH24** is the hour, **MI** is the minutes, **SS.SSSSSSSSS** is the seconds and its fraction

Example 1:
The following statement creates a table named CarsRegister that contains TIMESTAMP columns:
CREATE TABLE CarsRegister (CarRegNo VARCHAR2(20), InTime **TIMESTAMP,**
    OutTime **TIMESTAMP);**

Example 2:
The following statements populate the table named CarsRegister:
INSERT INTO CarsRegister (CarRegNo, InTime, OutTime)
    VALUES('MH-01-B-2083' , TIMESTAMP '2005-01-23 08:35:55.1245',
                 TIMESTAMP '2005-01-23 05:05:15.0');

INSERT INTO CarsRegister (CarRegNo, InTime, OutTime)
    VALUES('MH-02-C-5876', TIMESTAMP '2005-01-23 09:25:15.548',
                                   TIMESTAMP '2005-01-23 05:45:25.45');

Example 3:
The following statement describes the table named CarRegister:
DESC CarsRegister;

Output:
```
Name                             Null?      Type
-------------------------------- ---------- ----------------------------
CARREGNO                                    VARCHAR2(20)
INTIME                                      TIMESTAMP(6)
OUTTIME                                     TIMESTAMP(6)
```

Example 4:
The following statement displays the contents of the table named CarRegister:
SELECT * FROM CarsRegister;

Output:
```
CARREGNO      INTIME                          OUTTIME
------------- ------------------------------- -----------------------------
MH-01-B-2083  23-JAN-05 08.35.55.124500 AM    23-JAN-05 05.05.15.000000 AM
MH-02-C-5876  23-JAN-05 09.25.15.548000 AM    23-JAN-05 05.45.25.450000 AM
```

IS NAN AND IS INFINITE OPERATORS

Besides the regular operators such as LIKE, IN, IS NULL and, BETWEEN, Oracle 10g extends its list by providing two new operators to support the introduction of BINARY_FLOAT and BINARY_DOUBLE data types. These data types are capable of holding values like NaN and infinity.

The additional SQL operators are:
❑ IS NAN / IS NOT NAN: Matches the NaN special value
❑ IS INFINITE / IS NOT INFINITE: Matches infinite value

Example 1:
The following statement displays the contents of the table named SCT, after filtering it for NaN values in the OpAmt column:
SELECT * FROM SCT **WHERE** OpAmt **IS NAN**;

Output:
```
    ID     OPAMT     CLAMT
---------- --------- ----------
     3       Nan       Nan
```

Example 2:
The following statement displays the contents of the table named SCT, after filtering it for Infinite values in the ClAmt column:

SELECT * FROM SCT WHERE ClAmt IS INFINITE;

Output:

```
        ID      OPAMT     CLAMT
---------- ---------- ----------
         4        Inf       Inf
```

SIMPLIFYING JOINS WITH THE USING KEYWORD

SQL/92 allows simplifying the JOIN condition with the USING clause. However, the query should satisfy the following conditions:
- The query must use an equi-join
- The columns in the equi-join must have the same name

Example 1:
List the cars along with their rental transactions.

Synopsis:

Tables:	Cars, Rentals
Columns:	Cars: CarRegNo, Model, Make, Color
	Rentals: RentId, RentDt, CustId, RentAmt
Technique:	**Join:** INNER JOIN ... ON, SIMPLE; **Clauses:** WHERE, USING; **Others:** Concat (||)

Solution 1 (Ansi-style):
SELECT A.CarRegNo, A.Model, A.Make, A.Color, B.RentId, B.RentDt, B.CustId, B.RentAmt
        FROM Cars A INNER JOIN Rentals B ON A.CarRegNo = B.CarRegNo;

Solution 2 (Theta-style):
SELECT A.CarRegNo, A.Model, A.Make, A.Color, B.RentId, B.RentDt, B.CustId, B.RentAmt
        FROM Cars A, Rentals B WHERE A.CarRegNo = B.CarRegNo;

Solution 3 (USING clause):
SELECT CarRegNo, A.Model, A.Make, A.Color, B.RentId, B.RentDt, B.CustId, B.RentAmt
        FROM Cars A INNER JOIN Rentals B USING (CarRegNo);

Output:

```
CARREGNO        MODEL        MAKE    COLOR   RENTID RENTDT       CUSTID RENTAMT
------------- ----------- ------ ------ ------ ----------- ------ -------
MH-14-Y-4039    Indica V2    Tata    Black       41 25-JAN-05       10
MH-13-P-3249    Qualis       Toyota  White       42 16-JAN-05        8
MH-01-B-2083    Esteem       Maruti  Grey         1 15-MAY-00        1  112860
MH-01-B-2083    Esteem       Maruti  Grey         2 21-JUL-00        2   11020
. . .
MH-13-P-3249    Qualis       Toyota  White       38 05-MAY-03        3   99000
MH-14-Y-4039    Indica V2    Tata    Black       39 06-JUL-03        5  105600
MH-13-P-3249    Qualis       Toyota  White       40 15-JUL-03        9   84150

42 rows selected.
```

Explanation:
In the above example, the data required is available in two tables i.e. Cars and Rentals. Both the tables are linked via a common field. This is because the data is spread across the tables based on a normalized schema.

Notice that**:**
- The **CarRegNo** column is the primary key of the **Cars** table
- The **Rentals** is a table that holds the rental transactions with the customers via cars.
  In **Rentals** table:
  - **RentId** column is the primary key of that table.
  - **CarRegNo** column is used to refer to the cars in the **Cars** table

To retrieve the data required, both the tables have to be linked on the basis of a common column using joins with one of the following techniques shown below**:**
- **A.**CarRegNo = **B.**CarRegNo
- **USING (**CarRegNo)
This means the CarRegNo field of Cars table is joined with CarRegNo field of the Rentals table

Now since both the tables are linked using a join, data can be retrieved as if they are all in one table using the alias as:
A.CarRegNo, **A.**Model, **A.**Make, **A.**Color, **B.**RentId, **B.**RentDt, **B.**CustId, **B.**RentAmt

However, if the USING clause is specified, then the column which is used with the USING clause (i.e. CarRegNo) cannot have a qualifier (i.e. CarRegNo cannot be preceded with **A.**). Thus in this case the data can be retrieved using the alias as:
CarRegNo, **A.**Model, **A.**Make, **A.**Color, **B.**RentId, **B.**RentDt, **B.**CustId, **B.**RentAmt

Example 2:
List the car and customer details along with the associated rental transactions.

Synopsis:

Tables:	Customers, Cars, Rentals
Columns:	Customers: CustId, FirstName, LastName
	Cars: CarRegNo, Model, Make, Color
	Rentals: RentId, RentDt, CustId, RentAmt
Technique:	**Join:** INNER JOIN ... ON, SIMPLE**; Clauses:** WHERE, USING**; Others:** Concat (||)

Solution 1 (Ansi-style):
SELECT **A.**FirstName \|\| ' ' \|\| **A.**LastName "Customers", **B.**RentId, **B.**RentDt, **B.**RentAmt, **C.**CarRegNo,
        C.Model, **C.**Make, **C.**Color
    FROM **Customers A INNER JOIN Rentals B ON A.**CustId = **B.**CustId
        INNER JOIN Cars C ON B. CarRegNo = **C.**CarRegNo;

Solution 2 (Theta-style):
SELECT **A.**FirstName \|\| ' ' \|\| **A.**LastName "Customers", **B.**RentId, **B.**RentDt, **B.**RentAmt, **C.**CarRegNo,
        C.Model, **C.**Make, **C.**Color
    FROM **Customers A, Rentals B, Cars C**
        WHERE A. CustId = **B.**CustId **AND B.**CarRegNo = **C.**CarRegNo**;**

Solution 3 (USING clause):
SELECT **A.**FirstName \|\| ' ' \|\| **A.**LastName "Customers", **B.**RentId, **B.**RentDt, **B.**RentAmt, CarRegNo,
        C.Model, **C.**Make, **C.**Color
    FROM **Customers A INNER JOIN Rentals B USING (CustId)**
        INNER JOIN Cars C USING (CarRegNo);

Output:

```
Customers              RENTID RENTDT   RENTAMT CARREGNO     MODEL    MAKE    COLOR
-------------------    ------ ------   ------- ------------ -------- ------- -----
Jennifer Smith             24 23-DEC-01  91960 MH-01-B-2083 Esteem   Maruti  Grey
John Simon Brownie         21 15-OCT-01 112860 MH-01-B-2083 Esteem   Maruti  Grey
John Simon Brownie         17 02-JUN-01  58520 MH-01-B-2083 Esteem   Maruti  Grey
. . .
Raju Prasad                36 07-JAN-03  88000 MH-14-Y-4039 Indica V2 Tata   Black
Alex Joseph D'Mello        41 25-JAN-05        MH-14-Y-4039 Indica V2 Tata   Black

42 rows selected.
```

Explanation:
In the above example, the data required is available in three tables i.e. Customers, Cars and Rentals. These tables are linked via common fields. This is because the data is spread across the tables based on a normalized schema.

Notice that:
☐ The **CustId** column is the primary key of the **Customers** table
☐ The **CarRegNo** column is the primary key of the **Cars** table
☐ The **Rentals** is a table that holds the rental transactions with the customers via cars.
   In **Rentals** table:
   o **RentId** column is the primary key of that table
   o **CustId** column is used to refer to the customers in the **Customers** table
   o **CarRegNo** column is used to refer to the cars in the **Cars** table

To retrieve the data required, these tables have to be linked on the basis of a common column using joins with one of the following techniques shown below:
☐ **A.**CustId = **B.**CustId **AND B.**CarRegNo = **C.**CarRegNo
☐ **USING (**CustId**)** and **USING (**CarRegNo**)**
This means the CustId field of Customers table is joined with CustId field of the Rentals table and the CarRegNo field of Cars table is joined with CarRegNo field of the Rentals table

Now since both the tables are linked using a join, data can be retrieved as if they are all in one table using the alias as:
A.FirstName || ' ' || **A.**LastName "Customers", **B.**RentId, **B.**RentDt, **B.**RentAmt, **C.**CarRegNo, **C.**Model, **C.**Make, **C.**Color

However, if the USING clause is specified, then the column which is used with the USING clause (i.e. CarRegNo) cannot have a qualifier (i.e. CarRegNo cannot be preceded with **C.**). Thus in this case the data can be retrieved using the alias as:
A.FirstName || ' ' || **A.**LastName "Customers", **B.**RentId, **B.**RentDt, **B.**RentAmt, CarRegNo, **C.**Model, **C.**Make, **C.**Color

NEW STRING FUNCTIONS

NVL: Many a times there are records holding null values in a table. When an output of such a table is displayed it is difficult to understand the reason of null or blank values shown in the output.

The only way to overcome this problem is to replace null values with some other meaningful value while outputting the records. This can be done using the NVL function available in oracle.

Syntax:
```
NVL(<ColumnName>, <Value>)
```

It converts a NULL value into a known value. If the first parameter (i.e. the column name) holds a NULL value, the function returns the **value** specified in the second parameter. Otherwise, the **value** held by the column is returned.

Example:
SELECT FirstName || ' ' || LastName "Customers", **NVL**(Phone, 'Not Available') "Contact"
　　FROM Customers;

Output:
```
Customers                                Contact
---------------------------------------- ----------------------------
Anil Sharma                              28365154
Rahul Mohan Sharma                       28765654
John Simon Brownie                       23657868
Jennifer Smith                           23756775
Wilson Fernandes                         24443760
Raju Prasad                              42739894
Parvez Khan                              Not Available
Mosie Shah                               76756537
Preity Sen                               Not Available
Ashwini Joshi                            24403031
Alex Joseph D'Mello                      23445576

11 rows selected.
```

NVL2: Converts a NULL as well as a NOT NULL value into a desired value. If the first parameter (i.e. the column name) holds a value, the function returns the **value1** specified in the second parameter. Otherwise, the **value2** specified in the third parameter is returned.

Syntax:
　　NVL2(<ColumnName>, <Value1>, <Value2>)

Example:
SELECT FirstName || ' ' || LastName "Customers", **NVL2**(Phone, 'Available', 'Not Available') "Contact"
　　FROM Customers;

Output:
```
Customers                                Contact
---------------------------------------- -------------
Anil Sharma                              Available
Rahul Mohan Sharma                       Available
John Simon Brownie                       Available
Jennifer Smith                           Available
Wilson Fernandes                         Available
Raju Prasad                              Available
Parvez Khan                              Not Available
Mosie Shah                               Available
Preity Sen                               Not Available
Ashwini Joshi                            Available
Alex Joseph D'Mello                      Available

11 rows selected.
```

REPLACE: This function replaces a part of string with the one desired.

Syntax:
　　REPLACE(string, search_string, replace_string)

Example:
SELECT REPLACE('Sharanam is a bad boy', 'bad', 'good') "Comments" **FROM** Dual;

Output:
```
Comments
----------------------
Sharanam is a good boy
```

TRANSLATE: This function converts the occurrences of characters as desired.

Syntax:
    TRANSLATE(string, from_char, to_char)

Example:
Convert the text MESSAGE: ORACLE 10G IS GREAT into a hidden message:
SELECT TRANSLATE('MESSAGE: ORACLE 10G IS GREAT',
'ABCDEFGHIJKLMNOPQRSTUVWXYZ0123456789',
'ZYXWVUTSRQPONMLKJIHGFEDCBA9876543210') "Translated Text" **FROM** Dual;

     The above translation reverses the order of alphabets and digits (i.e. A becomes Z, B becomes Y, while 0 becomes 9 and so on).

Output:
```
Translated Text
-----------------------------
NVHHZTV: LIZXOV 89T RH TIVZG
```

NEW DATE FUNCTIONS

Using Time Intervals

Intervals are recently introduced data types that allow storing time intervals. These time intervals includes periods of time such as 2 years and 10 months, 7 hours and 3 minutes, - 4 months and 4 days, and so on.

     TIME INTERVALS are not to be confused with DATETIME or TIMESTAMPS.

The Time Interval data types are of two forms:
- ❑ **INTERVAL YEAR [(years_precision)] TO MONTH:** Stores a time interval measured in years and months. The **years_precision** variable is an optional precision for the years, which may be an integer from 0 to 9. The **year_precision** variable determines the number of digits available for storing the years in the interval. The default value for the **years_precision** is 2. An error is encountered, if attempts are made to store more year digits than the INTERVAL YEAR TO MONTH column can store.
- ❑ **INTERVAL DAY [(days_precision)] TO SECOND [(seconds_precision)]:** Stores a time interval measured in days and seconds. The **days_precision** variable is an optional precision for the days, an integer ranging from 0 to 9. Its default value is 2. Additionally, the **seconds_precision** variable is an optional precision for the fractional seconds, an integer ranging from 0 to 9. Its default value is 6.

Using The INTERVAL YEAR TO MONTH Type

Example 1:
The following statements creates a table named **CorpRental** that stores corporate information on rented cars:
CREATE TABLE CorpRental (RentId NUMBER(2) PRIMARY KEY, CarRegNo VARCHAR2(20),
    CustId NUMBER(2), ContractDt TIMESTAMP, Duration **INTERVAL YEAR(2) TO MONTH**);

The format for supplying an INTERVAL YEAR TO MONTH literal value is as follows:
   INTERVAL '[+|-] [y] [m]' [YEAR [(year_preceision)]] [TO MONTH]

where,
- the + (plus) sign or the - (minus) sign is an optional indicator that specifies whether the time interval is positive or negative (default is positive),
- **y** is the optional number of years for the interval,
- **m** is the optional number of months for the interval. **TO MONTH** is included in instances where the years and months are included in the literal,
- **years_precision** is the optional precision for the year (default is 2).

Example 2:
The following statements populate the table named **CorpRental:**
INSERT INTO CorpRental (RentId, CarRegNo, CustId, ContractDt, Duration)
    VALUES(3, 'MH-13-P-3249', 12, TIMESTAMP '2005-01-01 09:45:55.1245',
       INTERVAL '2-4' YEAR TO MONTH);
INSERT INTO CorpRental (RentId, CarRegNo, CustId, ContractDt, Duration)
    VALUES(5, 'MH-14-Y-4039', 14, TIMESTAMP '2005-01-21 19:05:00.0',
       INTERVAL '1' YEAR);

Example 3:
The following statement describes the table named **CorpRental:**
DESC CorpRental;

Output:
```
Name                           Null?    Type
---------------------------    -------- -------------------------
RENTID                         NOT NULL NUMBER(2)
CARREGNO                                VARCHAR2(20)
CUSTID                                  NUMBER(2)
CONTRACTDT                              TIMESTAMP(6)
DURATION                                INTERVAL YEAR(2) TO MONTH
```

Example 4:
The following statement displays the contents of the table named **CorpRental:**
SELECT * FROM CorpRental;

Output:
```
 RENTID CARREGNO        CUSTID CONTRACTDT                              DURATION
 ------- -------------  ------- ------------------------------------- ---------
      3 MH-13-P-3249        12 01-JAN-05 09.45.55.124500 AM          +02-04
      5 MH-14-Y-4039        14 21-JAN-05 07.05.00.000000 PM          +01-00
```

Using The INTERVAL YEAR TO MONTH Type

Example 1:
The following statements creates a table named **PvtRental** that stores private rentals information on rented cars:
CREATE TABLE PvtRental (RentId NUMBER(2) PRIMARY KEY, CarRegNo VARCHAR2(20),
    CustId NUMBER(2), ContractDt TIMESTAMP, Duration **INTERVAL DAY(2) TO SECOND(6)**);

The format for supplying an INTERVAL DAY TO SECOND literal value is as follows:
> INTERVAL '[+|-] [d] [h[:m[:s]]]' [DAY [(days_preceision)]]
> [TO HOURS | MINUTE | SECOND[(seconds_precision)]]

where,
- ❑ the + (plus) sign or the - (minus) sign is an optional indicator that specifies whether the time interval is positive or negative (default is positive),
- ❑ **d** is the optional number of days for the interval,
- ❑ **h** is the optional number of hours for the interval. The **TO HOUR** is included in instances where the days and hours are included in the literal,
- ❑ **m** is the optional number of minutes for the interval. The **TO MINUTES** is included in instances where the days and minutes are included in the literal,
- ❑ **s** is the optional number of seconds for the interval. The **TO SECOND** is included in instances where the days and seconds are included in the literal,
- ❑ **days_precision** is the optional precision for the days (default is 2),
- ❑ **seconds_precision** is the optional precision for the fractional seconds (default is 6).

Example 2:
The following statements populate the table named **PvtRental:**
INSERT INTO PvtRental (RentId, CarRegNo, CustId, ContractDt, Duration)
    VALUES(1, 'MH-03-F-3499', 8, TIMESTAMP '2005-01-05 10:00:00',
        INTERVAL '2 4:20:45.785' DAY TO SECOND);
INSERT INTO PvtRental (RentId, CarRegNo, CustId, ContractDt, Duration)
    VALUES(3, 'MH-04-Y-4849', 10, TIMESTAMP '2005-01-17 19:05:00.0',
        INTERVAL '6' HOUR);

Example 3:
The following statement describes the table named **PvtRental:**
DESC PvtRental;

Output:

```
Name                             Null?     Type
-------------------------------- --------- --------------------------
RENTID                           NOT NULL  NUMBER(2)
CARREGNO                                   VARCHAR2(20)
CUSTID                                     NUMBER(2)
CONTRACTDT                                 TIMESTAMP(6)
DURATION                                   INTERVAL DAY(2) TO SECOND(6)
```

Example 4:
The following statement displays the contents of the table named **PvtRental:**
SELECT * FROM PvtRental;

Output:
```
RENTID CARREGNO     CUSTID CONTRACTDT                    DURATION
------ ------------ ------ ----------------------------- -------------------
     1 MH-03-F-3499      8 05-JAN-05 10.00.00.000000 AM  +02 04:20:45.785000
     3 MH-04-Y-4849     10 17-JAN-05 07.05.00.000000 PM  +00 06:00:00.000000
```

Time Interval Related Functions

There are a number of functions that allows getting and processing time intervals. These functions are:

NUMTODSINTERVAL (x, interval_unit): This function converts the number **x** to an INTERVAL DAY TO SECOND with the interval for **x** supplied in **interval_unit**, which may be set to DAY, HOUR, MINUTE or SECOND.

Example:
The following statement displays the use of the **NUMTODSINTERVAL()** function:
SELECT **NUMTODSINTERVAL**(2.25, 'DAY'), **NUMTODSINTERVAL**(100.34225, 'SECOND')
      FROM DUAL;

Output:
```
NUMTODSINTERVAL(2.25,'DAY')        NUMTODSINTERVAL(100.34225,'SECOND')
---------------------------------  -----------------------------------
+000000002 06:00:00.000000000      +000000000 00:01:40.342250000
```

NUMTOYMINTERVAL (x, interval_unit): This function converts the number **x** to a YEAR TO MONTH with the interval for **x** supplied in **interval_unit**, which may be set to YEAR or MONTH.

Example:
The following statement displays the use of the **NUMTOYMINTERVAL()** function:
SELECT **NUMTOYMINTERVAL**(3.5, 'YEAR'), **NUMTOYMINTERVAL**(30.34225, 'MONTH')
      FROM DUAL;

Output:
```
NUMTOYMINTERVAL(3.5,'YEAR')   NUMTOYMINTERVAL(30.34225,'MONTH')
---------------------------   ----------------------------------
+000000003-06                 +000000002-06
```

PASSING A VALUE TO A VARIABLE IN A SCRIPT

Oracle 10g facilitate run-time passing of value(s) to variable(s) contained in SQL scripts. The variable(s) in the script are referred using a number. A script may contain multiple variables and are denoted by preceding a number with an ampersand (&). While executing the script, the values are passed immediately after naming the script file.

Example:
The following script (stored as **CarRprt.sql**) identifies the variable in the script file by using the **&1:**
SET ECHO OFF
SET VERIFY OFF
SELECT CarRegNo, Model, Make, Color **FROM** Cars **WHERE** Catgry = '**&1**';

Note

The file CarRprt.sql can be created using the ED command at the SQL prompt as:
SQL> ed CarRprt.sql

To execute the script **CarRprt.sql** enter the following command at the SQL prompt:
@CarRprt.sql L

This command will list all the luxury category cars.

Output:
```
CARREGNO        MODEL        MAKE        COLOR
--------------  -----------  ---------   ----------
MH-01-B-2083    Esteem       Maruti      Grey
MH-04-Y-4849    Safari       Tata        Dark Green
MH-03-X-0987    Indica       Tata        Black
MH-14-Y-4039    Indica V2    Tata        Black
```

@CarRprt.sql J

This command will list all the Jeep category cars.

Output:
```
CARREGNO        MODEL        MAKE        COLOR
--------------  -----------  ---------   ----------
MH-02-Z-3840    Sumo         Tata        White
MH-13-P-3249    Qualis       Toyota      White
```

AUTOMATICALLY GENERATING SQL STATEMENTS

The technique of writing SQL statements that produce other SQL statements is very useful. It can reduce on efforts put into writing SQL statements that are similar. The automatically generated SQL statements can be saved to a file and used later when required.

Example:
The following query produces a series of DROP TABLE statements that drop the tables in the **scott** schema:
SELECT 'DROP TABLE ' || table_name || ';' **FROM** user_tables;

Note

The table user_table contains the details of the tables in the user's schema. The table_name column contains names of the tables.

Output:
```
'DROPTABLE'||TABLE_NAME||';'
------------------------------------------
DROP TABLE PVTRENTAL;
DROP TABLE CROPRENTAL;
DROP TABLE SUPPLIERS;
DROP TABLE FD_AMT;
DROP TABLE FDSLAB_MSTR;
DROP TABLE RECEIPTS;
DROP TABLE RENTALS;
DROP TABLE BILLS;
DROP TABLE CUSTOMERS;
DROP TABLE CARS;
DROP TABLE SALGRADE;
DROP TABLE BONUS;
DROP TABLE EMP;
DROP TABLE DEPT;

14 rows selected.
```

HIERARCHICAL QUERIES

Quite often data that is organized into a hierarchy is required. Such data may include information like people who work in an organization, a family tree and so on. Oracle 10g facilitates arranging such information into a hierarchy.

The elements of the hierarchy also called nodes form a hierarchy tree. Trees of nodes have technical terms associated with them such as:

- **Root node:** The root is the node at the top of the tree. In the case of the **Emp** table, it will be the employee designated as the CEO or the President of the company
- **Parent node:** A parent is a node that has one or more nodes beneath it
- **Child node:** A child is a node that has one parent node above it
- **Leaf node:** A leaf is a node that has no children

Syntax:
SELECT [LEVEL], <ColumnName>, <Expression>, ... FROM <TableName>
    [WHERE <Condition>] [[START WITH <StartCondition>]
       [CONNECT BY PRIOR <PriorCondition>]];

where,

- **LEVEL** is a pseudo-column that denotes the depth of tree. It returns 1 for the root node, 2 for the child of the root and so on.
- **StartCondition** specifies where to start point for the hierarchical query. It is specified with START WITH clause.
- **PriorCondition** specifies the relationship between the parent and child rows. It is specified with the CONNECT BY PRIOR clause.

Note

    The **CONNECT BY** and **START WITH** clause is a requirement to perform hierarchical queries.

The **LEVEL** pseudo-column is an indication of how deep in the tree one is. Oracle can handle queries with a depth of up to **255** levels.

The **START WITH** clause is used to specify the start of the tree. More than one record can match the starting condition. The **CONNECT BY PRIOR** clause cannot be used to perform a join to other tables. The **CONNECT BY PRIOR** clause is rarely implemented in the other database offerings. Trying to achieve this programmatically will be difficult, as the top-level query has to be coded first, then, for each of the records, open a cursor to look for child nodes.

*One way of working around this is to use PL/SQL, open the driving cursor with the **CONNECT BY PRIOR** statement, and the select matching records from other tables on a row-by-row basis, inserting the results into a temporary table for later retrieval.*

Using The CONNECT BY And START WITH Clause

Example:
Generate a hierarchy based on the information in the **Emp** table found in the **scott** schema:
SELECT EmpNo, Mgr, EName FROM Emp
      START WITH EmpNo=7839 CONNECT BY PRIOR EmpNo = Mgr;

Output:

```
    EMPNO        MGR ENAME
---------- ---------- ----------
      7839            KING
      7566       7839 JONES
      7788       7566 SCOTT
      7876       7788 ADAMS
      7902       7566 FORD
      7369       7902 SMITH
      7698       7839 BLAKE
      7499       7698 ALLEN
      7521       7698 WARD
      7654       7698 MARTIN
      7844       7698 TURNER
      7900       7698 JAMES
      7782       7839 CLARK
      7934       7782 MILLER
```

14 rows selected.

Using The LEVEL Pseudo-Column

Example 1:
The following query uses the LEVEL pseudo-column to display the level in the tree generated with the information in the **Emp** table found in the **scott** schema:
SELECT LEVEL, EmpNo, Mgr, EName **FROM** Emp
        START WITH EmpNo=7839 **CONNECT BY** PRIOR EmpNo = Mgr **ORDER BY** LEVEL;

Output:

```
     LEVEL      EMPNO        MGR ENAME
---------- ---------- ---------- ----------
         1       7839            KING
         2       7566       7839 JONES
         2       7782       7839 CLARK
         2       7698       7839 BLAKE
         3       7788       7566 SCOTT
         3       7499       7698 ALLEN
         3       7654       7698 MARTIN
         3       7934       7782 MILLER
         3       7900       7698 JAMES
         3       7844       7698 TURNER
         3       7521       7698 WARD
         3       7902       7566 FORD
         4       7876       7788 ADAMS
         4       7369       7902 SMITH
```

14 rows selected.

Example 2:
The following query uses the COUNT() function and LEVEL to get the number of levels in the tree generated on processing the information in the **Emp** table found in the **scott** schema:
SELECT COUNT(DISTINCT LEVEL) **FROM** Emp
        START WITH EmpNo=7839 **CONNECT BY** PRIOR EmpNo = Mgr;

Output:
```
COUNT(DISTINCTLEVEL)
--------------------
                   4
```

Formatting The Result From A Hierarchical Query

The results from a hierarchical query can be formatted using LEVEL and the LPAD() function.

Example:
The following query left-pads the values with spaces in order of the LEVEL on the hierarchy generated from the **Emp** table found in the **scott** schema:
COLUMN Employee **FORMAT A25**
SELECT LEVEL, LPAD(' ', 2*LEVEL-1) || EName AS Employee **FROM** Emp
        START WITH EmpNo=7839 **CONNECT BY** PRIOR EmpNo = Mgr;

Note

The command **COLUMN** Employee **FORMAT A25** restricts the **Employee** column to a length of 25 characters.

Output:
```
     LEVEL EMPLOYEE
---------- -------------------------
         1 KING
         2   JONES
         3     SCOTT
         4       ADAMS
         3     FORD
         4       SMITH
         2   BLAKE
         3     ALLEN
         3     WARD
         3     MARTIN
         3     TURNER
         3     JAMES
         2   CLARK
         3     MILLER
```

14 rows selected.

The above example generates an Employee hierarchy. This hierarchy indicates the positions held by the employees. For Example: King is the boss of Jones, Blake and Clark. Similarly Jones is the boss of Scott and Ford. Further Adams reports to Scott and Smith reports to Ford and so on.

Starting At A Node Other Than The Root

The starting point for traversing the nodes of a tree can be changed by simply modifying the condition associated with the START WITH clause.

Note

Irrespective of the root node the LEVEL for the starting point in the hierarchical query is always set to 1.

Example:
The following query starts at employee named **JONES** while generating the hierarchical query from the
Emp table found in the **scott** schema:
COLUMN Employee **FORMAT A25**
SELECT LEVEL, LPAD(' ', 2*LEVEL-1) || EName AS Employee **FROM** Emp
　　　START WITH EName='JONES' **CONNECT BY** PRIOR EmpNo = Mgr;

Output:
```
    LEVEL EMPLOYEE
---------- -------------------------
        1 JONES
        2   SCOTT
        3     ADAMS
        2   FORD
        3     SMITH
```

Traversing Upward Through The Tree

The traversing of nodes in a tree can be reversed (i.e. from child to parent instead of parent to child). This
can be achieved by inversing the child and parent column in the **CONNECT TO PRIOR** clause.

Example:
The following query start at the employee named SMITH, who is at the lower-most level in the employee's
hierarchy tree.

COLUMN Employee **FORMAT A25**

SELECT LEVEL, LPAD(' ', 2*LEVEL-1) || EName AS Employee **FROM** Emp
　　　START WITH EmpNo= 7369 **CONNECT BY** PRIOR Mgr = EmpNo;

Output:
```
    LEVEL EMPLOYEE
---------- -------------------------
        1 SMITH
        2   FORD
        3     JONES
        4       KING
```

Eliminating Nodes And Branches From A Hierarchical Query

A particular node from a query tree can be eliminated by using a WHERE clause.

Example:
The following query eliminates the employee named JONES from the result of the hierarchical query
generated from the **Emp** table.

COLUMN Employee **FORMAT A25**

SELECT LEVEL, LPAD(' ', 2*LEVEL-1) || EName AS Employee **FROM** Emp
　　WHERE EName != 'JONES' **START WITH** EmpNo= 7839 **CONNECT BY** PRIOR EmpNo = Mgr;

Output:

```
      LEVEL EMPLOYEE
---------- -------------------------
          1  KING
          3     SCOTT
          4       ADAMS
          3     FORD
          4       SMITH
          2   BLAKE
          3     ALLEN
          3     WARD
          3     MARTIN
          3     TURNER
          3     JAMES
          2   CLARK
          3     MILLER

13 rows selected.
```

Note

> Although the entry for JONES is been excluded for the result, all subsequent child nodes have been included in the result.

RANKING FUNCTIONS INTRODUCED IN ORACLE 10g

The ranking functions can be used to calculate ranks, percentiles and n-tiles. Oracle provides various functions to process data and generate appropriate ranking based results

The keyword **OVER** is required when calling the ranking functions. The ranking is done based on values specified with the **OVER** keyword.

RANK: Returns the rank of items in a group. RANK() leaves a gap in the sequence of rankings in the event of a tie. For example, if the result of the RANK() function generates two entries for the second position then the position for the third place is skipped. The next position would therefore be the fourth place instead of third.

Syntax:
   RANK() OVER(<ColumnName>)

Example:
Rank the customers of the Car Rental business on the bases of number of rentals made by them.
SELECT CustId, **COUNT**(RentId) "Business", **RANK() OVER (ORDER BY COUNT**(RentId)) "Rank"
   FROM Rentals **GROUP BY** CustId;

Output:

```
      CUSTID  Business       Rank
---------- ----------  ----------
          4         2          1
          6         2          1
          7         2          1
          9         2          1
```

Output: (Continued)

```
    CUSTID   Business        Rank
---------- ---------- ----------
         8          3          5
         2          5          6
         3          5          6
        10          5          6
         1          7          9
         5          7          9
```

10 rows selected.

DENSE_RANK: Returns the rank of items in a group. DENSE_RANK() doesn't leave a gap in the sequence of rankings in the event of a tie.

Syntax:

> **DENSE_RANK() OVER(<ColumnName>)**

Example:

Ignore repetitive ranking, list the customers of the Car Rental business on the bases of number of rentals made by them.

SELECT CustId, **COUNT**(RentId) "Business",
>   **DENSE_RANK() OVER (ORDER BY COUNT**(RentId)) "Dense_Rank"
>   **FROM** Rentals **GROUP BY** CustId;

Output:

```
    CUSTID   Business Dense_Rank
---------- ---------- ----------
         4          2          1
         6          2          1
         7          2          1
         9          2          1
         8          3          2
         2          5          3
         3          5          3
        10          5          3
         1          7          4
         5          7          4
```

10 rows selected.

CUME_DIST: Returns the position of a specified value relative to a group of values. CUME_DIST () is short for cumulative distribution.

Syntax:

> **CUME_DIST() OVER(<ColumnName>)**

Example:

List cumulative distribution for customers of the Car Rental business based on number of rentals made by them.

SELECT CustId, **COUNT**(RentId) "Business",
>   **CUME_DIST() OVER (ORDER BY COUNT**(RentId)) "Cume_Dist"
>   **FROM** Rentals **GROUP BY** CustId **ORDER BY** CustId;

Output:

```
   CUSTID   Business   Cume_Dist
---------- ---------- ----------
        1          7           1
        2          5          .8
        3          5          .8
        4          2          .4
        5          7           1
        6          2          .4
        7          2          .4
        8          3°         .5
        9          2          .4
       10          5          .8
```

10 rows selected.

PERCENT_RANK: Returns the percent rank of a value relative to a group of values.

Syntax:

   PERCENT_RANK() OVER(<ColumnName>)

Example:
List the percentage ranking of customers based on number of rentals made by them.
SELECT CustId, **COUNT**(RentId) "Business",
   PERCENT_RANK() OVER (ORDER BY COUNT(RentId)) "Percent_Rank"
   FROM Rentals **GROUP BY** CustId **ORDER BY** CustId;

Output:

```
   CUSTID   Business Percent_Rank
---------- ---------- ------------
        1          7   .888888889
        2          5   .555555556
        3          5   .555555556
        4          2            0
        5          7   .888888889
        6          2            0
        7          2            0
        8          3   .444444444
        9          2            0
       10          5   .555555556
```

10 rows selected.

NTILE: Returns n-tiles such as tertiles, quartiles, and so on. The value passed as a parameter decides the number of groups in which the data will be divided.

Syntax:

   NTILE() OVER(<ColumnName>)

Example:
Distribute the customers of the Car Rental business into three part based on number of rentals made by them.
SELECT CustId, **COUNT**(RentId) "Business",
   NTILE(3) OVER (ORDER BY COUNT(RentId)) "NTile"
   FROM Rentals **GROUP BY** CustId **ORDER BY** CustId;

Output:

```
    CUSTID    Business        NTile
---------- ---------- ----------
         1          7          3
         2          5          2
         3          5          2
         4          2          1
         5          7          3
         6          2          1
         7          2          1
         8          3          2
         9          2          1
        10          5          3
```

10 rows selected.

ROW_NUMBER: Returns a number with each row in a group.

Syntax:

ROW_NUMBER() OVER(<ColumnName>)

Example:

Rank the customers of the Car Rental business based on number of rentals made by them. Start with customers with the least number of rentals.

SELECT CustId, **COUNT**(RentId) "Business",
    ROW_NUMBER() OVER (ORDER BY COUNT(RentId)) "Row_Number"
    FROM Rentals **GROUP BY** CustId **ORDER BY** CustId;

Output:

```
    CUSTID    Business Row_Number
---------- ---------- ----------
         1          7          9
         2          5          6
         3          5          7
         4          2          1
         5          7         10
         6          2          2
         7          2          3
         8          4          5
         9          2          4
        10          6          8
```

10 rows selected.

THE RETURNING CLAUSE

In Oracle Database 10g, the RETURNING clause can be used to return the value from an aggregate functions such as AVG(), SUM(), COUNT() and so on.

Example:

The following example performs the following tasks:
- Declares a variable named **avg_hr_rent**
- Decreases the hourly rent column of the rows in the **Cars** table and saves the average hourly rent in the **avg_hr_rent** variable using the RETURNING clause
- Rolls back the update
- Prints the value of the **avg_hr_rent** variable

Solution:
VARIABLE avg_hr_rent **NUMBER**
UPDATE Cars **SET** HrRentRate = HrRentRate * 0.90
    RETURNING AVG(HrRentRate) **INTO** :avg_hr_rent;

Output:
```
10 rows updated.
```

ROLLBACK;

Output:
```
Rollback complete.
```

PRINT avg_hr_rent

Output:
```
AVG_HR_RENT
-----------
      168.3
```

MERGING ROWS USING MERGE

Recently Oracle database introduced the MERGE statement that allows merging rows from one table into another.

Example:
Assume the table **NewCars** stores details of the changes in the cars and rates for the year 2005. It will be a need to consolidate the contents of the tables **Cars** and **NewCars**. The structure for the NewCars table will be based on the following CREATE TABLE statement:

CREATE TABLE NewCars (CarRegNo **VarChar2**(20), Model **VarChar2**(25) **NOT NULL**,
    Make **VarChar2**(25) **NOT NULL**, Color **VarChar2**(10) **NOT NULL**,
    Catgry **VarChar2**(1) **NOT NULL**, AC **VarChar2**(1) **NOT NULL**,
    EngineNo **VarChar2**(25) **NOT NULL**, ChassisNo **VarChar2**(25) **NOT NULL**,
    TransAM **VarChar2**(1) **DEFAULT** 'M', Fuel **VarChar2**(1) **DEFAULT** 'D',
    PurchaseDt **Date NOT NULL**, HrRentRate **Decimal**(6,2) **NOT NULL**,
    DyRentRate **Decimal**(6,2) **NOT NULL**, HrDriverRate **Decimal**(6,2) **NOT NULL**,
    DyDriverRate **Decimal**(6,2) **NOT NULL**, CarStatus **VarChar2**(1) **NOT NULL**,
    CONSTRAINT PK_Cars_CarRegNo **PRIMARY KEY**(CarRegNo));

The contents of the **NewCars** table will be as follows:

Table Name: NewCars

CarRegNo	Model	Make	Color	Catgry	AC	EngineNo	ChassisNo
MH-01-B-2083	Esteem	Maruti	Grey	L	Y	ME-03042000-A34	B7-82347939-E90
MH-02-Z-3840	Sumo	Tata	White	J	Y	SU-30112000-T12	U4-93497878-H93
MH-13-P-3249	Qualis	Toyota	White	J	Y	TQ-12072002-T53	V7-00873682-D87
MH-13-B-0099	**Safari**	**Tata**	**Black**	**J**	**Y**	**TS-25102003-A48**	**Z2-67600264-K02**
MH-14-Z-8530	**Qualis**	**Toyota**	**Blue**	**J**	**Y**	**TQ-03012005-T805**	**Q2-20646434-A11**

CarRegNo	TransAM	Fuel	PurchaseDt	HrRent Rate	DyRent Rate	HrDriver Rate	DyDriver Rate	CarStatus
MH-01-B-2083	M	C	03-Apr-2000	250.00	5250.00	45.00	925.00	R
MH-02-Z-3840	M	D	30-Nov-2000	370.00	7700.00	60.00	1200.00	A
MH-13-P-3249	M	C	12-Jul-2002	275.00	5775.00	50.00	1100.00	R
MH-13-B-0099	**A**	**D**	**25-Oct-2003**	**400.00**	**3850.00**	**60.00**	**1260.00**	**A**
MH-14-Z-8530	**A**	**D**	**03-Jan-2005**	**350.00**	**7500.00**	**60.00**	**1200.00**	**A**

The records can be populated into the NewCars table using the following INSERT INTO statements:

INSERT INTO NewCars VALUES('MH-01-B-2083', 'Esteem', 'Maruti', 'Grey', 'L', 'Y', 'ME-03042000-A34', 'B7-82347939-E90', 'M', 'C', '03-Apr-2000', 250.00, 5250.00, 45.00, 925.00, 'R');

INSERT INTO NewCars VALUES('MH-02-Z-3840', 'Sumo', 'Tata', 'White', 'J', 'Y', 'SU-30112000-T12', 'U4-93497878-H93', 'M', 'D', '30-Nov-2000', 370.00, 7700.00, 60.00, 1200.00, 'A');

INSERT INTO NewCars VALUES('MH-13-P-3249', 'Qualis', 'Toyota', 'White', 'J', 'Y', 'TQ-12072002-T53', 'V7-00873682-D87', 'M', 'C', '12-Jul-2002', 275.00, 5775.00, 50.00, 1100.00, 'R');

INSERT INTO NewCars VALUES('MH-13-B-0099', 'Safari', 'Tata', 'Black', 'J', 'Y', 'TS-25102003-A48', 'Z2-67600264-K02', 'A', 'D', '25-Oct-2003', 400.00, 3850.00, 60.00, 1260.00, 'A');

INSERT INTO NewCars VALUES('MH-14-Z-8530', 'Qualis', 'Toyota', 'Blue', 'J', 'Y', 'TQ-03012005-T805', 'Q2-20646434-A11', 'A', 'D', '03-Jan-2005', 350.00, 7500.00, 60.00, 1200.00, 'A');

COMMIT;

On exercising the MERGE statement the following is expected:

❑ Rows that already exists in the **Cars** table based on a comparison with the **NewCars** table using the **CarRegNo** column are updated with new values held by the **NewCars** table

❑ Rows that are not available in the **Cars** table but present in the **NewCars** table are inserted into the **Cars** table

The following statement performs the merge as defined:

MERGE INTO Cars C USING NewCars NC ON (C.CarRegNo = NC.CarRegNo)
WHEN MATCHED THEN
    UPDATE SET C.Model = NC.Model, C.Make = NC.Make, C.Color = NC.Color,
        C.Catgry = NC.Catgry, C.AC = NC.AC, C.TransAM = NC.TransAM, C.Fuel = NC.Fuel,
        C.EngineNo = NC.EngineNo, C.ChassisNo = NC.ChassisNo,
        C.HrRentRate = NC.HrRentRate, C.DyRentRate = NC.DyRentRate,
        C.HrDriverRate = NC.HrDriverRate, C.DyDriverRate = NC.DyDriverRate,
        C.PurchaseDt = NC.PurchaseDt, C.CarStatus = NC.CarStatus
WHEN NOT MATCHED THEN
    INSERT (C.CarRegNo, C.Model, C.Make, C.Color, C.Catgry, C.AC, C.EngineNo, C.ChassisNo,
        C.TransAM, C.Fuel, C.PurchaseDt, C.HrRentRate, C.DyRentRate, C.HrDriverRate,
        C.DyDriverRate, C.CarStatus)
    VALUES (NC.CarRegNo, NC.Model, NC.Make, NC.Color, NC.Catgry, NC.AC, NC.EngineNo,
        NC.ChassisNo, NC.TransAM, NC.Fuel, NC.PurchaseDt, NC.HrRentRate,
        NC.DyRentRate, NC.HrDriverRate, NC.DyDriverRate, NC.CarStatus);

Output:
```
5 rows merged.
```

The following should be remembered while using the MERGE statement:

❑ The **MERGE INTO** clause specifies the name of the table to merge the rows into

❑ The **USING ... ON** clause specifies a table join

❑ The **WHEN MATCHED THEN** clause specifies the action to take when the **USING ... ON** clause is satisfied for a row

❑ The **WHEN NOT MATCHED** clause specifies the action to lake when the **USING ... ON** clause is not satisfied for a row

QUERY FLASHBACK

A query flashback can be used to revert mistakenly committed changes and to view original records before the COMMIT was executed. If required, the results of a query flashback can be used to manually change rows back to their original values.

In addition, flashbacks can be based on a **datetime** or **system change number** (SCN). The database uses SCNs to track changes made to data, and these can be used to flash back to a particular SCN in the database.

Granting The Privilege For Using Flashbacks

Flashbacks use the PL/SQL DBMS_FLASHBACK package, for which the EXECUTE privilege is a must.

Example:
The following example connects as the **sys** user and grants the **EXECUTE** privilege on DBMS_FLASHBACK to the **scott** user:
CONNECT sys/<*password_for_sys*> **As sysdba**
GRANT EXECUTE ON SYS.DBMS_FLASHBACK **TO** scott;

Using The Time Query Flashbacks

Example:
The following example connects as scott and retrieves the CarRegNo, HrRentRate, and DyRentRate columns from the Car table:
CONNECT scott/tiger
SELECT CarRegNo, HrRentRate, DyRentRate **FROM** Cars;

Output:
```
CARREGNO              HRRENTRATE DYRENTRATE
--------------------  ---------- ----------
MH-01-B-2083                 190       4180
MH-02-C-5876                 170       3740
MMZ-888                      145       3190
MH-02-Z-3840                 180       3960
MH-04-Y-4849                 250       5500
MH-12-A-8758                 145       3190
MH-03-X-0987                 190       4180
MH-03-F-3499                 175       3850
MH-13-P-3249                 225       4950
MH-14-Y-4039                 200       4400

10 rows selected.
```

The following statement reduces the **HrRentRate** of these rows, commits the change and retrieves the rows again to get the new Hourly Rent Rate (i.e. **HrRentRate**):

UPDATE Cars **SET** HrRentRate = HrRentRate * 0.95;

Output:
```
10 rows updated.
```

COMMIT;

Output:
```
Commit complete.
```

SELECT CarRegNo, HrRentRate, DyRentRate **FROM** Cars;

Output:

CARREGNO	HRRENTRATE	DYRENTRATE
MH-01-B-2083	**180.5**	4180
MH-02-C-5876	**161.5**	3740
MMZ-888	**137.75**	3190
MH-02-Z-3840	**171**	3960
MH-04-Y-4849	**237.5**	5500
MH-12-A-8758	**137.75**	3190
MH-03-X-0987	**180.5**	4180
MH-03-F-3499	**166.25**	3850
MH-13-P-3249	**213.75**	4950
MH-14-Y-4039	**190**	4400

10 rows selected.

To understand the flaskback concept, execute the DBMS_FLASHBACK.ENABLE_AT_TIME() procedure, which enables the performance of a flashback to a particular datetime. This procedure accepts a datetime. The example passes **SYSDATE - 10 / 1440** to the procedure, which means **ten minutes back**: **EXECUTE DBMS_FLASHBACK.ENABLE_AT_TIME(SYSDATE - 10 / 1440);**

Output:
PL/SQL procedure successfully completed.

Any queries executed after the Flashback will display the rows as they were ten minutes ago. Assuming the earlier UPDATE was performed less than ten minutes ago, the following query will display the Hourly Rent Rate as they were before the **Cars** table was updated.

SELECT CarRegNo, HrRentRate, DyRentRate **FROM** Cars;

Output:

CARREGNO	HRRENTRATE	DYRENTRATE
MH-01-B-2083	**190**	4180
MH-02-C-5876	**170**	3740
MMZ-888	**145**	3190
MH-02-Z-3840	**180**	3960
MH-04-Y-4849	**250**	5500
MH-12-A-8758	**145**	3190
MH-03-X-0987	**190**	4180
MH-03-F-3499	**175**	3850
MH-13-P-3249	**225**	4950
MH-14-Y-4039	**200**	4400

10 rows selected.

To disable flashback, execute **DBMS_FLASHBACK.DISABLE()**, as shown in the following example: **EXECUTE DBMS_FLASHBACK.DISABLE();**

Output:
PL/SQL procedure successfully completed.

A flashback should be disabled before it can be enabled again.

When the queries are performed after disabling the flashback, the rows will be retrieved, as they currently exist.

Using The System Change Number Query Flashbacks

Flashbacks based on system change numbers (SCNs) can be more precise than those based on a time, because the database uses SCNs to track changes. To get the current SCN, execute the DBMS_FLASHBACK.GET_SYSTEM_CHANGE_NUMBER() function as shown below:
VARIABLE current_scn **NUMBER**
EXECUTE :current_scn := **DBMS_FLASHBACK.GET_SYSTEM_CHANGE_NUMBER();**

Output:
```
PL/SQL procedure successfully completed.
```

PRINT current_scn

Output:
```
CURRENT_SCN
-----------
    1671920
```

Example:
The following adds a row to the Customers table, commits the change and retrieves the newly inserted row:
INSERT INTO Customers **VALUES**(16, 'Jack', 'Thomas', '44/A, Juhu Scheme,', 'Mumbai', ' Maharasthra',
'400056', 'INDIA', '', 'E-50345', 'LMV', '15-Dec-2002', '14-Dec-2005');

Output:
```
1 row created.
```

COMMIT;

Output:
```
Commit complete.
```

SELECT * FROM Customers WHERE CustId=16;

Output:
```
CUSTID FIRSTNAME LASTNAME ADDR                  CITY    STATE       POSTALCODE
------ --------- -------- ------------------ ------ ----------- ----------
COUNTRY PHONE   LICENSENO LICENSETYPE ISSUEDON  EXPIRESON
------- ------- --------- ----------- --------- ---------
    16 Jack      Thomas   44/A, Juhu Scheme, Mumbai Maharasthra     400056
INDIA          E-50345   LMV             15-DEC-02 14-DEC-05
```

Finally, execute the DBMS_FLASHBACK.ENABLE_AT_SYSTEM_CHANGE_NUMBER() procedure, which enables the performance of a flashback to an SCN. This procedure accepts an SCN, and the example passes **current_scn** to the procedure:
EXECUTE DBMS_FLASHBACK.ENABLE_AT_SYSTEM_CHANGE_NUMBER(:current_scn);

Output:
```
PL/SQL procedure successfully completed.
```

Any queries executed after the Flashback will display the rows as they were at the SCN stored in **current_scn** before the **INSERT INTO** statement.

Example:
The following query will attempt to retrieve the newly inserted record for the **Customers** table.
SELECT * FROM Customers WHERE CustId=16;

Output:
```
no rows selected
```

The query does not return the record because the new row was added after the SCN was stored in the variable **current_scn**.

To disable a flashback, execute the **DBMS_FLASHBACK.DISABLE()** function, as shown in the following example:
EXECUTE DBMS_FLASHBACK.DISABLE();

Flashback Table

Consider a situation where the Cars table has been accidentally deleted.

```
SQL> DROP TABLE Cars;
Table dropped.

SQL>
```

Now, with Oracle 10g the table has been moved to the recycle bin rather than actually deleted.

To check this, issue the **SHOW RECYCLEBIN** command.

```
SQL> SHOW RECYCLEBIN;
ORIGINAL NAME RECYCLEBIN NAME                    OBJECT TYPE  DROP TIME
------------- ------------------------------     ------------ -------------------
CARS          BIN$THCd8QFQTWintWi8QaxnRg==$0 TABLE           2005-02-04:12:25:21
SQL>
```

Now, to restore the table Cars, issue the **FLASHBACK TABLE** <TABLE_NAME> **TO BEFORE DROP** command.

```
SQL> FLASHBACK TABLE Cars TO BEFORE DROP;
Flashback complete.

SQL>
```

If instead it is desired to clear the table down completely and thus release the space taken up by the table, issue the **PURGE RECYCLEBIN** command.

```
SQL> DROP TABLE CARS;
Table dropped.
```

Verify It as:

```
SQL> SHOW RECYCLEBIN;
ORIGINAL NAME   RECYCLEBIN NAME                  OBJECT TYPE   DROP TIME
-------------   ------------------------------   -----------   -------------------
CARS            BIN$WdfeZRViQy21girCyMp69w==$0 TABLE           2005-02-04:12:34:08
```

Purge The RecycleBin as:

```
SQL> PURGE RECYCLEBIN;
Recyclebin purged.
```

Verify It as:

```
SQL> SHOW RECYCLEBIN;
SQL>
```

What actually happens is that the table being dropped is actually renamed to a system defined name, starting with BIN$ rather than the table being actually dropped. The flashback table feature is intelligent enough to be able to manage multiple stored copies of the same table, if the table is dropped and recreated with a different structure. It also purges old copies of recycled tables if the database starts to run short of space.

If desired to drop the table Cars without sending it to the RecycleBin then issue **DROP TABLE <TABLE_NAME> PURGE** to drop the table and skip the RecycleBin in the first place. *This is something similar to using **SHIFT+DEL** Key Stroke to delete a file permanently in windows via the windows explorer.*

Drop the table without sending it to RecycleBin:

```
SQL> DROP TABLE Cars PURGE;
Table dropped.
```

Verify It as:

```
SQL> SHOW RECYCLEBIN;
SQL>
```

SQL MODEL CLAUSE

The SQL Model clause allows users to embed spreadsheet-like models in a SELECT statement, in a way that was previously the domain of dedicated multidimensional OLAP servers such as Oracle Express and Oracle 9i OLAP. The SQL Model clause brings an entirely new dimension to Oracle analytical queries and addresses a number of traditional shortcomings with the way SQL normally works.

The aim of the SQL Model clause is to give normal SQL statements the ability to create a multidimensional array from the results of a normal SELECT statement, carry out any number of interdependent inter-row and inter-array calculations on this array, and then update the base tables with the results of the model.

Thus in short the Model clause allows treating relational data as a multidimensional array to which spreadsheet-like calculations can be applied. The result is a query that is easier to develop, understand, and modify.

The MODEL clause defines a multidimensional array by mapping the columns of a query into three groups i.e. partitioning, dimension, and measure columns.
These elements perform the following tasks:
- Partitions define logical blocks of the result set in a way similar to the partitions of the analytical functions. MODEL rules are applied to the cells of each partition.
- Dimensions identify each measure cell within a partition. These columns identify characteristics such as date, region, and product name.

❑ Measures are analogous to the measures of a **fact** table in a **star** schema. They typically contain numeric values such as sales units or cost. Each cell is accessed within its partition by specifying its full combination of dimensions.

To create rules on these multidimensional arrays, computation rules are defined and expressed in terms of the dimension values. The rules are flexible and concise, and can use wild cards and FOR loops for maximum expressiveness. Calculations built with the MODEL clause improve on traditional spreadsheet calculations by integrating analyses into the database, improving readability with symbolic referencing, and providing scalability and much better manageability.

Example 1:

Suppose it is desired to project rental transactions per destination and model for the year 2005 based on the rental transactions of the years 2003 & 2004. A table named **CarRevenue** will be created holding the **Dest**, Model, Year and the Revenue earned in that Year.

Solution: (Table Creation)

```
CREATE TABLE CarRevenue (
    Dest VARCHAR2(20),
    Model VARCHAR2(20),
    Year NUMBER(4),
    Revenue NUMBER(8)
);
```

Solution: (Records Population)

```
INSERT INTO CarRevenue Values ('Mumbai', 'Toyato Qualis', 2003, 4500);
INSERT INTO CarRevenue Values ('Mumbai', 'Toyato Qualis', 2004, 9500);
INSERT INTO CarRevenue Values ('Shirdi', 'Toyato Qualis', 2003, 8500);
INSERT INTO CarRevenue Values ('Shirdi', 'Toyato Qualis', 2004, 12500);
INSERT INTO CarRevenue Values ('Bangalore', 'Toyato Qualis', 2003, 6500);
INSERT INTO CarRevenue Values ('Bangalore', 'Toyato Qualis', 2004, 10500);

INSERT INTO CarRevenue Values ('Mumbai', 'Tata Sumo', 2003, 4500);
INSERT INTO CarRevenue Values ('Mumbai', 'Tata Sumo', 2004, 7500);
INSERT INTO CarRevenue Values ('Shirdi', 'Tata Sumo', 2003, 6900);
INSERT INTO CarRevenue Values ('Shirdi', 'Tata Sumo', 2004, 6500);
INSERT INTO CarRevenue Values ('Bangalore', 'Tata Sumo', 2003, 6300);
INSERT INTO CarRevenue Values ('Bangalore', 'Tata Sumo', 2004, 10500);

INSERT INTO CarRevenue Values ('Mumbai', 'Tata Indica', 2003, 4500);
INSERT INTO CarRevenue Values ('Mumbai', 'Tata Indica', 2004, 5500);
INSERT INTO CarRevenue Values ('Shirdi', 'Tata Indica', 2003, 6500);
INSERT INTO CarRevenue Values ('Shirdi', 'Tata Indica', 2004, 16500);
INSERT INTO CarRevenue Values ('Bangalore', 'Tata Indica', 2003, 6500);
INSERT INTO CarRevenue Values ('Bangalore', 'Tata Indica', 2004, 12500);
```

Solution: (Revenue Projection)

```
SELECT Dest, Model, Year, Revenue FROM CarRevenue
MODEL
PARTITION BY (Dest, Model)
DIMENSION BY (Year)
MEASURES (Revenue)
RULES (
    Revenue[2005] = ROUND(Revenue[2004] * (Revenue[2004]/Revenue[2003]))
)
ORDER BY Year, Dest, Model;
```

Output:

DEST	MODEL	YEAR	REVENUE
Bangalore	Tata Indica	2003	6500
Bangalore	Tata Sumo	2003	6300
Bangalore	Toyato Qualis	2003	6500
Mumbai	Tata Indica	2003	4500
Mumbai	Tata Sumo	2003	4500
Mumbai	Toyato Qualis	2003	4500
Shirdi	Tata Indica	2003	6500
Shirdi	Tata Sumo	2003	6900
Shirdi	Toyato Qualis	2003	8500
Bangalore	Tata Indica	2004	12500
Bangalore	Tata Sumo	2004	10500
Bangalore	Toyato Qualis	2004	10500
Mumbai	Tata Indica	2004	5500
Mumbai	Tata Sumo	2004	7500
Mumbai	Toyato Qualis	2004	9500
Shirdi	Tata Indica	2004	16500
Shirdi	Tata Sumo	2004	6500
Shirdi	Toyato Qualis	2004	12500
Bangalore	**Tata Indica**	**2005**	**24038**
Bangalore	**Tata Sumo**	**2005**	**17500**
Bangalore	**Toyato Qualis**	**2005**	**16962**
Mumbai	**Tata Indica**	**2005**	**6722**
Mumbai	**Tata Sumo**	**2005**	**12500**
Mumbai	**Toyato Qualis**	**2005**	**20056**
Shirdi	**Tata Indica**	**2005**	**41885**
Shirdi	**Tata Sumo**	**2005**	**6123**
Shirdi	**Toyato Qualis**	**2005**	**18382**

27 rows selected.

Explanation:

The calculations performed in the above example are usually used when modeling sales in a spreadsheet.

To use the MODEL clause, the data has to be conceptually formed into a multidimensional array. Each result set row becomes a cell in that array.

Partition columns

Partition columns divide the result set into blocks. Rules defined in the model clause are applied independently of other partitions to each partition.

When a model is created, begin by ideating about how and whether to partition the model into separate arrays. Partitioning is optional, but it gives the database a point at which to parallelize the work, and it makes formulas much easier to write. In this example, there exists data of the revenues earned based on destination and the car model used, and each (destination and model)'s forecast together is independent of the others, so it is required to partition by destination and the model.

MODEL
PARTITION BY (Dest, Model)

Dimension columns
Dimension columns define how cells within a partition can be accessed.

This is then followed by data dimension. This means deciding which values will combine to uniquely identify a row in the array. For the revenues earned data, the data can be dimensioned by the Year column. For each destination and car model, the value held in the year column uniquely identifies a row in the array.

MODEL
PARTITION BY (Dest, Model)
DIMENSION BY (Year)

Measure columns
The columns defined as measures can be assigned new values in the rules section of the model clause.

Each cell in a model holds one or more values, but the forecasting formula requires just the revenue value, so a column has to be specified as a measure of calculation.

MODEL
PARTITION BY (Dest, Model)
DIMENSION BY (Year)
MEASURES (Revenue)

Once the measure is decided its now time to create a formulae to do the actual projections for the Year 2005. Begin by writing rules, which define the calculations that is to be performed using the measure specified. In this example to forecast the revenues that will be earned in the Year 2005 the following formulae is used:

Revenue[2005] = ROUND(Revenue[2004] * (Revenue[2004]/Revenue[2003]))

The cell reference (called **Positional Referencing**) begins with the column name specified in the MEASURES clause. Next comes a list of dimension values enclosed within square brackets (In this case only one value is used as a dimension).

Finally using cell referencing the formulae is created which accesses the value held in the Year 2004 and 2003 and after performing some calculations on it transfers it to the Year 2005. This is enclosed within RULES.

Note ══

The RULES keyword, shown in the examples at the start of the rules, is optional, but recommended for easier reading.

Example 2:
Suppose it is desired to project rental transactions per destination and model for the year 2005 based on the rental transactions of the years 2003 & 2004. (ONLY UPDATES NO NEW RECORDS)

Solution:
SELECT Dest, Model, Year, Revenue
    FROM CarRevenue
MODEL
PARTITION BY (Dest, Model)
DIMENSION BY (Year)
MEASURES (Revenue)
RULES UPDATE(
    Revenue[2005] = ROUND(Revenue[2004] * (Revenue[2004]/Revenue[2003]))
)
ORDER BY Year, Dest, Model;

Output:

DEST	MODEL	YEAR	REVENUE
Bangalore	Tata Indica	2003	6500
Bangalore	Tata Sumo	2003	6300
Bangalore	Toyato Qualis	2003	6500
Mumbai	Tata Indica	2003	4500
Mumbai	Tata Sumo	2003	4500
Mumbai	Toyato Qualis	2003	4500
Shirdi	Tata Indica	2003	6500
Shirdi	Tata Sumo	2003	6900
Shirdi	Toyato Qualis	2003	8500
Bangalore	Tata Indica	2004	12500
Bangalore	Tata Sumo	2004	10500
Bangalore	Toyato Qualis	2004	10500
Mumbai	Tata Indica	2004	5500
Mumbai	Tata Sumo	2004	7500
Mumbai	Toyato Qualis	2004	9500
Shirdi	Tata Indica	2004	16500
Shirdi	Tata Sumo	2004	6500
Shirdi	Toyato Qualis	2004	12500

18 rows selected.

Explanation:

This example is same as the example 1 but for the difference that if the data for the year 2005 doesn't exists then no new records will be inserted. Whereas if the data for the year 2005 exists then the data will be updated based on the calculations specified in the RULE.

This is done using the keyword UPDATE with RULE (i.e. **RULES UPDATE**). This indicates that the calculation will be applied only on the current available data based on the criteria specified and no new records will be inserted to show the projections.

Example 3:

Suppose it is desired to project rental transactions per destination and model for the year 2005 & 2006 and 2007 & 2008 based on the rental transactions of the years 2003 & 2004 and 2005 & 2006 respectively. Use FOR LOOP.

Solution:

SELECT Dest, Model, Year, Revenue
    FROM CarRevenue
MODEL
PARTITION BY (Dest, Model)
DIMENSION BY (Year)
MEASURES (Revenue)
RULES (
    Revenue[FOR Year IN(2005,2006)] = ROUND(Revenue[2004] * (Revenue[2004]/Revenue[2003])),
    Revenue[FOR Year IN(2007,2008)] = ROUND(Revenue[2006] * (Revenue[2006]/Revenue[2005]))
)
ORDER BY Year, Dest, Model;

Output:

DEST	MODEL	YEAR	REVENUE
Bangalore	Tata Indica	2003	6500
Bangalore	Tata Sumo	2003	6300
Bangalore	Toyato Qualis	2003	6500
Mumbai	Tata Indica	2003	4500
Mumbai	Tata Sumo	2003	4500
Mumbai	Toyato Qualis	2003	4500
Shirdi	Tata Indica	2003	6500
Shirdi	Tata Sumo	2003	6900
Shirdi	Toyato Qualis	2003	8500
Bangalore	Tata Indica	2004	12500
Bangalore	Tata Sumo	2004	10500
Bangalore	Toyato Qualis	2004	10500
Mumbai	Tata Indica	2004	5500
Mumbai	Tata Sumo	2004	7500
Mumbai	Toyato Qualis	2004	9500
Shirdi	Tata Indica	2004	16500
Shirdi	Tata Sumo	2004	6500
Shirdi	Toyato Qualis	2004	12500
Bangalore	**Tata Indica**	**2005**	**24038**
Bangalore	**Tata Sumo**	**2005**	**17500**
Bangalore	**Toyato Qualis**	**2005**	**16962**
Mumbai	**Tata Indica**	**2005**	**6722**
Mumbai	**Tata Sumo**	**2005**	**12500**
Mumbai	**Toyato Qualis**	**2005**	**20056**
Shirdi	**Tata Indica**	**2005**	**41885**
Shirdi	**Tata Sumo**	**2005**	**6123**
Shirdi	**Toyato Qualis**	**2005**	**18382**
Bangalore	**Tata Indica**	**2006**	**24038**
Bangalore	**Tata Sumo**	**2006**	**17500**
Bangalore	**Toyato Qualis**	**2006**	**16962**
Mumbai	**Tata Indica**	**2006**	**6722**
Mumbai	**Tata Sumo**	**2006**	**12500**
Mumbai	**Toyato Qualis**	**2006**	**20056**
Shirdi	**Tata Indica**	**2006**	**41885**
Shirdi	**Tata Sumo**	**2006**	**6123**
Shirdi	**Toyato Qualis**	**2006**	**18382**
Bangalore	*Tata Indica*	*2007*	*24038*
Bangalore	*Tata Sumo*	*2007*	*17500*
Bangalore	*Toyato Qualis*	*2007*	*16962*
Mumbai	*Tata Indica*	*2007*	*6722*
Mumbai	*Tata Sumo*	*2007*	*12500*
Mumbai	*Toyato Qualis*	*2007*	*20056*
Shirdi	*Tata Indica*	*2007*	*41885*
Shirdi	*Tata Sumo*	*2007*	*6123*
Shirdi	*Toyato Qualis*	*2007*	*18382*
Bangalore	*Tata Indica*	*2008*	*24038*
Bangalore	*Tata Sumo*	*2008*	*17500*
Bangalore	*Toyato Qualis*	*2008*	*16962*
Mumbai	*Tata Indica*	*2008*	*6722*
Mumbai	*Tata Sumo*	*2008*	*12500*
Mumbai	*Toyato Qualis*	*2008*	*20056*
Shirdi	*Tata Indica*	*2008*	*41885*
Shirdi	*Tata Sumo*	*2008*	*6123*
Shirdi	*Toyato Qualis*	*2008*	*18382*

54 rows selected.

Explanation:

The MODEL clause provides a FOR construct that can be used inside rules to express computations more concisely. The FOR construct is allowed on both sides of rules.

In the above example, a FOR LOOP is used to specify RULES for more than one year, thus avoids multiple entries for the same formulae.

If the above solution was written **without** the word FOR:

```
SELECT Dest, Model, Year, Revenue
    FROM CarRevenue
MODEL
PARTITION BY (Dest, Model)
DIMENSION BY (Year)
MEASURES (Revenue)
RULES (
    Revenue[Year IN(2005,2006)] = ROUND(Revenue[2004] * (Revenue[2004]/Revenue[2003])),
    Revenue[Year IN(2007,2008)] = ROUND(Revenue[2006] * (Revenue[2006]/Revenue[2005]))
)
ORDER BY Year, Dest, Model;
```

If the word **FOR** is omitted then no new rows will be added. This means that only if there exists any rows belonging to the Years 2005-2008 will be updated. In this case the output would be as seen below. As there are no rows belonging to the Years 2005-2008 only the old rows are displayed.

Output:

DEST	MODEL	YEAR	REVENUE
Bangalore	Tata Indica	2003	6500
Bangalore	Tata Sumo	2003	6300
Bangalore	Toyato Qualis	2003	6500
Mumbai	Tata Indica	2003	4500
Mumbai	Tata Sumo	2003	4500
Mumbai	Toyato Qualis	2003	4500
Shirdi	Tata Indica	2003	6500
Shirdi	Tata Sumo	2003	6900
Shirdi	Toyato Qualis	2003	8500
Bangalore	Tata Indica	2004	12500
Bangalore	Tata Sumo	2004	10500
Bangalore	Toyato Qualis	2004	10500
Mumbai	Tata Indica	2004	5500
Mumbai	Tata Sumo	2004	7500
Mumbai	Toyato Qualis	2004	9500
Shirdi	Tata Indica	2004	16500
Shirdi	Tata Sumo	2004	6500
Shirdi	Toyato Qualis	2004	12500

18 rows selected.

Note

The MODEL clause has a **limit** of 10,000 rules, and the virtual rules generated by FOR constructs are counted toward that limit. It is important to consider the total number of rules potentially generated by FOR constructs to avoid exceeding the rule limit.

Example 4:

Suppose it is desired to project rental transactions per destination and model for every alternate year ranging from 2005 to 2012 based on the rental transactions of the years 2003 & 2004. Use FOR LOOP FROM With INCREMENT.

Solution:
SELECT Dest, Model, Year, Revenue
    FROM CarRevenue
MODEL
PARTITION BY (Dest, Model)
DIMENSION BY (Year)
MEASURES (Revenue)
RULES (
    Revenue[FOR Year FROM 2005 TO 2010 INCREMENT 2]
        = ROUND(Revenue[2004] * (Revenue[2004]/Revenue[2003]))
)
ORDER BY Year, Dest, Model;

Output:

DEST	MODEL	YEAR	REVENUE
Bangalore	Tata Indica	2003	6500
Bangalore	Tata Sumo	2003	6300
Bangalore	Toyato Qualis	2003	6500
Mumbai	Tata Indica	2003	4500
Mumbai	Tata Sumo	2003	4500
Mumbai	Toyato Qualis	2003	4500
Shirdi	Tata Indica	2003	6500
Shirdi	Tata Sumo	2003	6900
Shirdi	Toyato Qualis	2003	8500
Bangalore	Tata Indica	2004	12500
Bangalore	Tata Sumo	2004	10500
Bangalore	Toyato Qualis	2004	10500
Mumbai	Tata Indica	2004	5500
Mumbai	Tata Sumo	2004	7500
Mumbai	Toyato Qualis	2004	9500
Shirdi	Tata Indica	2004	16500
Shirdi	Tata Sumo	2004	6500
Shirdi	Toyato Qualis	2004	12500
Bangalore	Tata Indica	2005	24038
Bangalore	Tata Sumo	2005	17500
Bangalore	Toyato Qualis	2005	16962
Mumbai	Tata Indica	2005	6722
Mumbai	Tata Sumo	2005	12500
Mumbai	Toyato Qualis	2005	20056
Shirdi	Tata Indica	2005	41885
Shirdi	Tata Sumo	2005	6123
Shirdi	Toyato Qualis	2005	18382
Bangalore	Tata Indica	2007	24038
Bangalore	Tata Sumo	2007	17500
Bangalore	Toyato Qualis	2007	16962
Mumbai	Tata Indica	2007	6722
Mumbai	Tata Sumo	2007	12500
Mumbai	Toyato Qualis	2007	20056
Shirdi	Tata Indica	2007	41885
Shirdi	Tata Sumo	2007	6123
Shirdi	Toyato Qualis	2007	18382
Bangalore	Tata Indica	2009	24038
Bangalore	Tata Sumo	2009	17500
Bangalore	Toyato Qualis	2009	16962

Output: (Continued)

DEST	MODEL	YEAR	REVENUE
Mumbai	Tata Indica	2009	6722
Mumbai	Tata Sumo	2009	12500
Mumbai	Toyato Qualis	2009	20056
Shirdi	Tata Indica	2009	41885
Shirdi	Tata Sumo	2009	6123
Shirdi	Toyato Qualis	2009	18382

45 rows selected.

Explanation:

The MODEL clause provides a FOR FROM INCREMENT construct that can be used inside rules to express computations more concisely. The FOR FROM INCREMENT construct is allowed on both sides of rules.

In the above example, a FOR FROM INCREMENT LOOP is used to specify RULES for more than one year and for every alternate year, thus avoids multiple entries for the same formulae.

This is done using the following RULE:

Revenue[FOR Year FROM 2005 TO 2010 INCREMENT 2]
= ROUND(Revenue[2004] * (Revenue[2004]/Revenue[2003]))

The above rule via the For Loop iterates through the years 2005 till 2010 but skips every next year while performing the calculations. This is because INCREMENT keyword is used with a value 2, which allows iterations to every alternate year and thereby apply calculations on the value extracted.

The FOR LOOP requires the range of values to iterate on. This is specified via the FROM keyword (i.e. **FROM 2005 TO 2010**).

Example 5:

Suppose it is desired to update the rental transactions per destination and model for the year 2004 by increasing the revenue by 10%. Use Symbolic References.

Solution:
SELECT Dest, Model, Year, Revenue
    FROM CarRevenue
MODEL
PARTITION BY (Dest, Model)
DIMENSION BY (Year)
MEASURES (Revenue)
RULES (
    Revenue[Year = 2004] = Revenue[Year = 2004] * 1.10
)
ORDER BY Year, Dest, Model;

Output:

DEST	MODEL	YEAR	REVENUE
Bangalore	Tata Indica	2003	6500
Bangalore	Tata Sumo	2003	6300
Bangalore	Toyato Qualis	2003	6500
Mumbai	Tata Indica	2003	4500
Mumbai	Tata Sumo	2003	4500
Mumbai	Toyato Qualis	2003	4500

Output:

DEST	MODEL	YEAR	REVENUE
Shirdi	Tata Indica	2003	6500
Shirdi	Tata Sumo	2003	6900
Shirdi	Toyato Qualis	2003	8500
Bangalore	Tata Indica	2004	13750
Bangalore	Tata Sumo	2004	11550
Bangalore	Toyato Qualis	2004	11550
Mumbai	Tata Indica	2004	6050
Mumbai	Tata Sumo	2004	8250
Mumbai	Toyato Qualis	2004	10450
Shirdi	Tata Indica	2004	18150
Shirdi	Tata Sumo	2004	7150
Shirdi	Toyato Qualis	2004	13750

18 rows selected.

Explanation:

Symbolic references are very powerful, but they are used solely for updating existing cells. They cannot create new cells as required in case of revenue projections for future years (Refer Example 1)

In case of a symbolic reference the value for the cell reference is matched to the appropriate dimension using Boolean conditions. All the normal operators such as <,>, IN, and BETWEEN can be used.

For Example:

> Revenue[Year > 2004] = Revenue[2003] * 1.10
> Revenue[Year < 2004] = Revenue[Year = 2004] * 1.25
> Revenue[Year BETWEEN 2001 AND 2004] = Revenue[Year = 1999] * 2

(In case of multiple cells)

> Revenue[Model = 'Tata Indica', Year < 2004] = Revenue[Model = 'Tata Indica', Year = 2004] * 1.25

In this example the query looks for the Year value equal to 2004 and increases the revenue of that year by 10%.

Example 6:

Suppose it is desired to update the rental transactions per destination for the years before 2004 by increasing the revenue by 10% only for the Tata Indica Model. Use Symbolic References and multiple dimensions.

Solution:

SELECT Dest, Model, Year, Revenue
> **FROM** CarRevenue
MODEL
PARTITION BY (Dest)
DIMENSION BY (Model, Year)
MEASURES (Revenue)
RULES (
> Revenue[Model = 'Tata Indica', Year < 2004] = Revenue[Model = 'Tata Indica', Year = 2004] * 1.10
)
ORDER BY Year, Dest, Model;

Output:

DEST	MODEL	YEAR	REVENUE
Bangalore	**Tata Indica**	**2003**	**13750**
Bangalore	Tata Sumo	2003	6300
Bangalore	Toyato Qualis	2003	6500
Mumbai	**Tata Indica**	**2003**	**6050**
Mumbai	Tata Sumo	2003	4500
Mumbai	Toyato Qualis	2003	4500
Shirdi	**Tata Indica**	**2003**	**18150**
Shirdi	Tata Sumo	2003	6900
Shirdi	Toyato Qualis	2003	8500
Bangalore	Tata Indica	2004	12500
Bangalore	Tata Sumo	2004	10500
Bangalore	Toyato Qualis	2004	10500
Mumbai	Tata Indica	2004	5500
Mumbai	Tata Sumo	2004	7500
Mumbai	Toyato Qualis	2004	9500
Shirdi	Tata Indica	2004	16500
Shirdi	Tata Sumo	2004	6500
Shirdi	Toyato Qualis	2004	12500

18 rows selected.

Explanation:
In this example the query looks for the Year value less than 2004 and increases the revenue of that year by 10% based on the revenue of the year 2004. This increase is only done for the model Tata Indica. To accomplish this a multi dimension array is used:

   DIMENSION BY (Model, Year)

The increase is done using the following RULE:

   Revenue[Model = 'Tata Indica', Year < 2004] = Revenue[Model = 'Tata Indica', Year = 2004] * 1.10

This simply indicates that the Revenue value for the years less than 2004 (in this case being 2003) will be increased by 10% of the value held in the revenue column of the year 2004. In addition the update / increase is done only for the model Tata Indica and not for the other models.

Example 7:
Suppose it is desired to forecast the revenue earned for the year 2005 for the model Toyato Qualis as 1000 more than the maximum revenue in the period 2003 to 2004. Use the BETWEEN clause.

Solution:
SELECT Dest, Model, Year, Revenue
   FROM CarRevenue
MODEL
PARTITION BY (Dest)
DIMENSION BY (Model, Year)
MEASURES (Revenue)
RULES (
   Revenue['Toyato Qualis', 2005] =
   1000 + MAX(REVENUE) ['Toyato Qualis', Year between 2003 AND 2004]
)
ORDER BY Year, Dest, Model;

Output:

DEST	MODEL	YEAR	REVENUE
Bangalore	Tata Indica	2003	6500
Bangalore	Tata Sumo	2003	6300
Bangalore	Toyato Qualis	2003	6500
Mumbai	Tata Indica	2003	4500
Mumbai	Tata Sumo	2003	4500
Mumbai	Toyato Qualis	2003	4500
Shirdi	Tata Indica	2003	6500
Shirdi	Tata Sumo	2003	6900
Shirdi	Toyato Qualis	2003	8500
Bangalore	Tata Indica	2004	12500
Bangalore	Tata Sumo	2004	10500
Bangalore	Toyato Qualis	2004	10500
Mumbai	Tata Indica	2004	5500
Mumbai	Tata Sumo	2004	7500
Mumbai	Toyato Qualis	2004	9500
Shirdi	Tata Indica	2004	16500
Shirdi	Tata Sumo	2004	6500
Shirdi	Toyato Qualis	2004	12500
Bangalore	Toyato Qualis	2005	11500
Mumbai	Toyato Qualis	2005	10500
Shirdi	Toyato Qualis	2005	13500

```
21 rows selected.
```

Explanation:

In this example, the query projects the Revenues for the Year 2005 based on the maximum Revenue earned between in the years 2003-2004 and adds up 1000 to the maximum value extracted. This RULE is applied only to the Toyato Qualis model. To accomplish this multi dimensional array is used:

> **DIMENSION BY** (Model, Year)

The projection is done using the following RULE:

> **Revenue['Toyato Qualis', 2005] =**
> **1000 + MAX(REVENUE) ['Toyato Qualis', Year between 2003 AND 2004]**

This simply indicates that the Revenue value for the year 2005 will be projected as the maximum revenue earned by the Toyato Qualis model in the years 2003 – 2004 plus 1000.

Since it's not an update but an insertion positional reference is used i.e. **Revenue['Toyato Qualis', 2005]**

Example 8:
Generate a series of dates between two dates.

Solution:
SELECT DT **FROM (SELECT TRUNC**(SYSDATE) DT **FROM** DUAL)
MODEL
DIMENSION BY (0 D)
MEASURES (DT)
RULES ITERATE(5) (
DT[ITERATION_NUMBER + 1] = **DT**[ITERATION_NUMBER] + 1
  );

Output:
```
DT
---------
03-FEB-05
04-FEB-05
05-FEB-05
06-FEB-05
07-FEB-05
08-FEB-05

6 rows selected.
```

Explanation:
In this example, the query generates a series of dates beginning from the current date. This is done using the system variable SYSDATE.

The array is dimensioned using current date, (**i.e.** value of SYSDATE given an alias as DT) as follows:
MODEL
DIMENSION BY (0 D)

Here, **0** (zero) indicates the first column extracted by the query (in this case a single column **DT** is extracted). **D** indicates that an alias has been assigned to that column.

The series is generated using the **ITERATE()** function combined with the **RULES** keyword. In this case, ITERATE(5) indicates that the specified rule should be **executed five times**.

The value of the date is generated using the following rule:
DT[ITERATION_NUMBER + 1] = **DT**[ITERATION_NUMBER] + 1

Here, DT is the name of an array and its first element holds the current date. The variable ITERATION_NUMBER is a running number maintained to generate a series of date. This is done by assigning a value, (**i.e.** current date + 1) indicated by **DT**[ITERATION_NUMBER] + 1 to the next element of the array indicated by **DT**[ITERATION_NUMBER + 1].

ORACLE SAMPLE SCHEMAS

Other then the SCOTT schema, Oracle 10g now provides many sample schemas to work with. These are:

SQL> SELECT USERNAME **FROM** DBA_USERS;

Output:
```
USERNAME
------------------------------
SYSTEM
SYS
. . .
HR
OE
SH
PM
IX
BI
SCOTT
. . .

32 rows selected.
```

By default these accounts are inactive and locked. To use them these accounts need to be unlocked and assigned a new password. This can be done as follows:

```
ALTER USER "HR" IDENTIFIED BY "<password>" ACCOUNT UNLOCK;
Output:
User altered.


ALTER USER "OE" IDENTIFIED BY "<password>" ACCOUNT UNLOCK;
Output:
User altered.


ALTER USER "SH" IDENTIFIED BY "<password>" ACCOUNT UNLOCK;
Output:
User altered.


ALTER USER "PM" IDENTIFIED BY "<password>" ACCOUNT UNLOCK;
Output:
User altered.


ALTER USER "IX" IDENTIFIED BY "<password>" ACCOUNT UNLOCK;
Output:
User altered.
```

Once these user accounts are unlocked these schemas, can be used by logging in via SQL *PLUS with their appropriate user name and password.

Assuming SQL *PLUS is open type in the following commands to connect to different user accounts and display the tables held within them.

Connecting To User Named HR.

```
SQL> CONNECT HR/<password>@<HostStringIfAny>;
SQL> SELECT * FROM TAB;
Output:
TNAME                            TABTYPE  CLUSTERID
-------------------------------- -------- ----------
REGIONS                          TABLE
COUNTRIES                        TABLE
LOCATIONS                        TABLE
DEPARTMENTS                      TABLE
JOBS                             TABLE
EMPLOYEES                        TABLE
JOB_HISTORY                      TABLE
EMP_DETAILS_VIEW                 VIEW

8 rows selected.
```

Connecting To User Named OE.

```
SQL> CONNECT OE/<password>@<HostStringIfAny>;
SQL> SELECT * FROM TAB;
```

Output:

```
TNAME                                 TABTYPE   CLUSTERID
------------------------------------- -------   ----------
CUSTOMERS                             TABLE
WAREHOUSES                            TABLE
ORDER_ITEMS                           TABLE
ORDERS                                TABLE
INVENTORIES                           TABLE
PRODUCT_INFORMATION                   TABLE
PRODUCT_DESCRIPTIONS                  TABLE
PROMOTIONS                            TABLE
COUNTRIES                             SYNONYM
LOCATIONS                             SYNONYM
DEPARTMENTS                           SYNONYM
JOBS                                  SYNONYM
EMPLOYEES                             SYNONYM
JOB_HISTORY                           SYNONYM
PRODUCTS                              VIEW
SYDNEY_INVENTORY                      VIEW
BOMBAY_INVENTORY                      VIEW
TORONTO_INVENTORY                     VIEW
PRODUCT_PRICES                        VIEW
ACCOUNT_MANAGERS                      VIEW
CUSTOMERS_VIEW                        VIEW
ORDERS_VIEW                           VIEW
DEPTVIEW                              VIEW
PURCHASEORDERS                        TABLE
STYLESHEET_TAB                        TABLE
CATEGORIES_TAB                        TABLE
PRODUCT_REF_LIST_NESTEDTAB            TABLE
SUBCATEGORY_REF_LIST_NESTEDTAB        TABLE
OC_INVENTORIES                        VIEW
OC_PRODUCT_INFORMATION                VIEW
OC_CUSTOMERS                          VIEW
OC_CORPORATE_CUSTOMERS                VIEW
OC_ORDERS                             VIEW

33 rows selected.
```

Connecting To User Named SH.

```
SQL> CONNECT SH/<password>@<HostStringIfAny>;
SQL> SELECT * FROM TAB;
```

Output:

```
TNAME                                 TABTYPE   CLUSTERID
------------------------------------- -------   ----------
SALES                                 TABLE
COSTS                                 TABLE
TIMES                                 TABLE
PRODUCTS                              TABLE
CHANNELS                              TABLE
PROMOTIONS                            TABLE
CUSTOMERS                             TABLE
COUNTRIES                             TABLE
SUPPLEMENTARY_DEMOGRAPHICS            TABLE
```

Output: (Continued)
```
TNAME                            TABTYPE   CLUSTERID
------------------------------   -------   ----------
MVIEW$_EXCEPTIONS                TABLE
CAL_MONTH_SALES_MV               TABLE
FWEEK_PSCAT_SALES_MV             TABLE
DR$SUP_TEXT_IDX$I                TABLE
DR$SUP_TEXT_IDX$K                TABLE
DR$SUP_TEXT_IDX$R                TABLE
DR$SUP_TEXT_IDX$N                TABLE
PROFITS                          VIEW
SALES_TRANSACTIONS_EXT           TABLE

18 rows selected.
```

Connecting To User Named PM.

```
SQL> CONNECT PM/<password>@<HostStringIfAny>;
SQL> SELECT * FROM TAB;
```
Output:
```
TNAME                            TABTYPE   CLUSTERID
------------------------------   -------   ----------
ONLINE_MEDIA                     TABLE
PRINT_MEDIA                      TABLE
TEXTDOCS_NESTEDTAB               TABLE
```

Connecting To User Named IX.

```
SQL> CONNECT IX/<password>@<HostStringIfAny>;
SQL> SELECT * FROM TAB;
```

Output:
```
TNAME                            TABTYPE   CLUSTERID
------------------------------   -------   ----------
ORDERS_QUEUETABLE                TABLE
AQ$_ORDERS_QUEUETABLE_S          TABLE
AQ$_ORDERS_QUEUETABLE_T          TABLE
AQ$_ORDERS_QUEUETABLE_H          TABLE
SYS_IOT_OVER_49905               TABLE
AQ$_ORDERS_QUEUETABLE_G          TABLE
AQ$_ORDERS_QUEUETABLE_I          TABLE
STREAMS_QUEUE_TABLE              TABLE
AQ$_STREAMS_QUEUE_TABLE_S        TABLE
AQ$_STREAMS_QUEUE_TABLE_T        TABLE
AQ$_STREAMS_QUEUE_TABLE_H        TABLE
SYS_IOT_OVER_49922               TABLE
AQ$_STREAMS_QUEUE_TABLE_G        TABLE
AQ$_STREAMS_QUEUE_TABLE_I        TABLE
AQ$ORDERS_QUEUETABLE_S           VIEW
AQ$ORDERS_QUEUETABLE_R           VIEW
AQ$ORDERS_QUEUETABLE             VIEW
AQ$STREAMS_QUEUE_TABLE_S         VIEW
AQ$STREAMS_QUEUE_TABLE_R         VIEW
AQ$STREAMS_QUEUE_TABLE           VIEW

20 rows selected.
```

As can be seen from the above output each schema i.e. the two letter name stands for the following:

HR	Human resources, basic topics, supports Oracle Internet Directory
OE	Order entry, intermediate topics, various datatypes
SH	Sales history, large amount of data, analytic processing
PM	Product media, used for multimedia datatypes
IX	Queued shipping, shows advanced queuing

By introducing these sample schemas, students learning Oracle and instructors teaching Oracle now have better resources at hand to use and explore when it comes to testing out different Oracle capabilities. These schemas can be used to practice SQL and PL/SQL.

HANDS ON EXERCISES

1. Extract the column details of the column **City** from the **Client_Master** table.

2. Drop the column **State** from the **Client_Master** table.

3. Rename the column named **Name** to **CustomerName** from the table **Client_Master**.

4. Retrieve all even rows from the **Product_Master** table.

5. Add a day, hour, minute and second to the date 3-Jan-1981

6. Retrieve a count of products sold per order from the **Sales_Order_Details** table

7. Retrieve only the rows ranging from 2 to 7 from the **Product_Master** table.

8. Display the Client Details in the following format:

    Customer Name: Sharanam Chaitanya Shah   ↵
    Address: Makanji Mansion   ↵
    City: Mumbai   ↵

9. Flashback the database as it was 20 minutes back.

10. Disable the database flashback system.

11. Display the tables in the Recycle Bin.

12. Recover a table named **Client_Master**, which had been accidentally deleted.

8. INTERACTIVE iSQL *PLUS

iSQL *Plus is a browser-based implementation of SQL*Plus. It can be used to connect to an Oracle database system over the Intranet / Internet to perform the same tasks as those that were performed using the SQL*Plus tool and at the SQL*Plus command line which required an Ethernet backbone to run on.

The iSQL*Plus implementation uses a Web browser, an Oracle HTTP Server with the iSQL*Plus Server and an Oracle Database.

Oracle Database 10g when installed makes available the following:
1. Oracle Database (The RDBMS Engine)
2. Oracle HTTP Server with the iSQL *PLUS Server

The Oracle HTTP Server is actually responsible to serve iSQL *Plus Environment requests from the clients. The clients (Windows or Linux based) and can interact with the HTTP server over an Intranet/Internet (i.e. a TCP/IP) backbone.

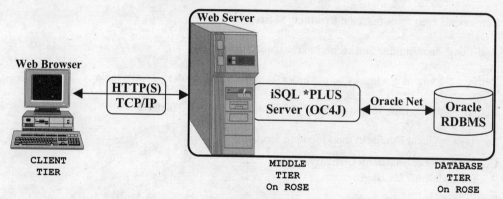

Diagram 8.1

The above framework simply depicts the following:
1. **Oracle Database 10g** is the **DATABASE TIER** installed on a Windows XP based machine named **ROSE** having an IP address 192.168.0.3
2. **iSQL *PLUS Server** is the **MIDDLE TIER** installed while Oracle Database 10g installation on the same machine i.e. **ROSE** (192.168.0.3)
3. **Windows XP** and **Linux** based Machines form the **CLIENT TIER**

THE DATABASE TIER - Oracle RDBMS

Oracle Net components provide communication between the iSQL*Plus Server and the Oracle RDBMS in a Client/Server installation manner.

THE MIDDLE TIER - iSQL*Plus Server

The iSQL*Plus Server runs as an Oracle Application Server Container for any J2EE (OC4J) application. The iSQL*Plus Server enables communication and authentication between the iSQL*Plus user interface and the RDBMS (i.e. THE DATABASE TIER). Each iSQL*Plus session is uniquely identified, which allows having multiple concurrent sessions open to the Oracle RDBMS.

THE CLIENT TIER - iSQL*Plus User Interface

The iSQL*Plus user interface runs in a Web browser. There is **no installation** or **configuration** required for the iSQL*Plus user interface.

The Database and the Middle Tiers exists on the same machine i.e. ROSE as two separate entities (i.e. the Database Engine and the HTTP Server). These entities are in the form of services that can be switched **ON/OFF** when required.

The Client tier can be the same machine or some other machine connected to the network.

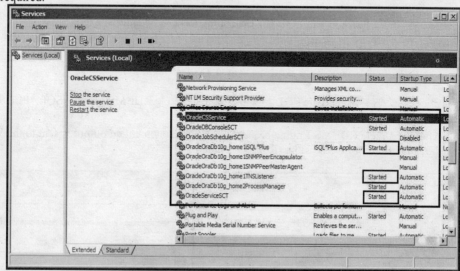

GETTING STARTED

To start using Oracle iSQL *PLUS the following services must be up and running:

Diagram 8.2.1: Verifying the Oracle services

1. Oracle Database Engine – OracleServiceSCT (In this material)
2. Listener – OracleOraDb10g_home1TNSListener (In this material)
3. iSQL *PLUS Server – OracleOraDb10g_home1iSQL*Plus (In this material)
• The iSQL *PLUS Session via a Web Browser on the client machine

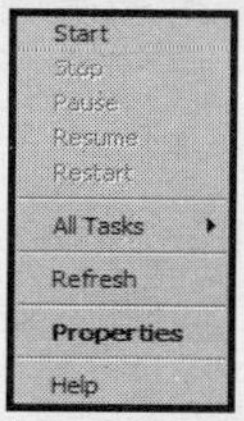

These services can be verified using the Services Console which can be activated using the following menu clicks: **Start → All Programs → Control Panel → Administrative Tools → Services**

Diagram 8.2.2

Notice the status of the above mentioned services. The status should indicate Started. If not then right click on the appropriate service and select Start. Refer diagram 8.2.2.

Starting The iSQL *PLUS Session:

❑ Invoke a web browser such as Internet Explorer / Netscape Navigator

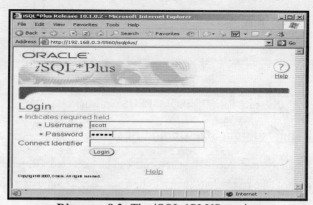

Diagram 8.3: The iSQL *PLUS session

❑ Point the browser to: **http://<Machine_Name/IP_Address>:5560/isqlplus** where the client is a machine on the network or **http://<localhost/ 127.0.0.1>:5560/isqlplus** where the same machine (i.e. The machine with Oracle Database 10g Installed) is acting as a client

Assuming the client to be a Windows XP machine over the network the browser will point to **http://192.168.0.3:5560/isqlplus**. (Refer diagram 8.3)

❑ Login by entering the **username** as **scott** and the **password** as **tiger**.

Once logged in successfully a screen as seen in diagram 8.4 appears. This screen is a workspace wherein SQL, PL/SQL and SQL *PLUS commands can be entered/executed

Using SQL Commands

❑ Enter a SQL statement in the workspace area. (Refer diagram 8.4)

❑ Click ⟨Execute⟩ to send the SQL statement to the Oracle RDBMS via the iSQL *PLUS Server (Oracle HTTP Server) for processing

After the Oracle RDBMS Engine processes the SQL statement an output is sent to the Web Browser in the same iSQL *PLUS session. (Refer diagram 8.5)

Diagram 8.4: The iSQL *PLUS workspace

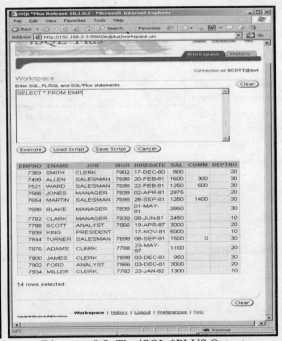

Diagram 8.5: The iSQL *PLUS Output

Using Multiple SQL Commands

Similarly, multiple SQL statements can be executed. (Refer diagram 8.6.1 and diagram 8.6.2). If the output exceeds the page limits then a button ⟨Next Page⟩ appears. Click this button to view the remaining output as seen in diagram 8.6.2.

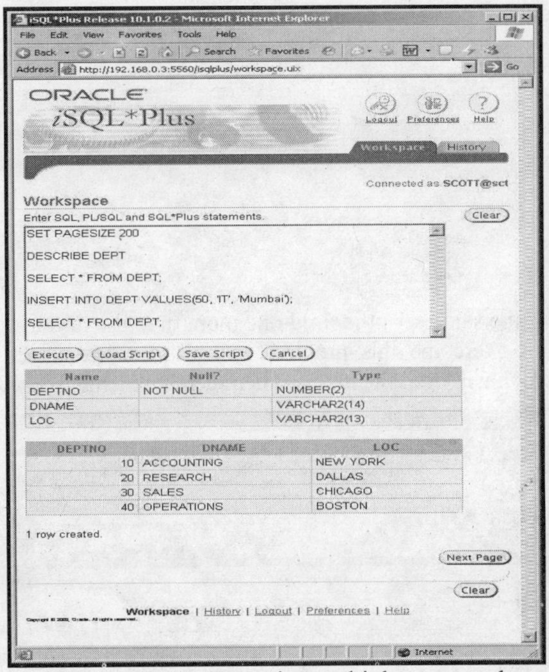

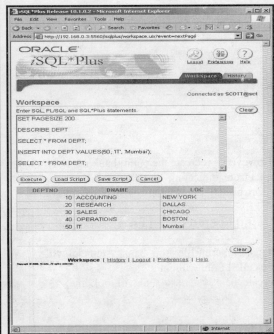

Diagram 8.6.1: Executing multiple commands

Diagram 8.6.2: Remaining Output when
Next Page is clicked

Once the results are accomplished, the workspace can be cleared by clicking on the Clear button.

Using Script Files

iSQL *PLUS also allows use of .sql files. These script files should exist under **$ORACLE_HOME/oc4j/j2ee/home/default-web-app/scripts/**. Here **script** is a directory created under: **$ORACLE_HOME/oc4j/j2ee/home/default-web-app/** to store all the script files for ease.

To run the script file named create_banksystem.sql issue the following command in the workspace.

@http://<Machine_Name/IP_Address>:5560/scripts/<ScriptFileName.sql>. In this case the command will be **@http://192.168.0.3:5560/scripts/create_banksystem.sql**. (Refer diagram 8.7.1)

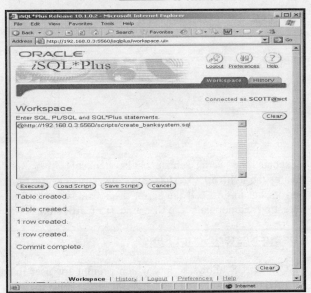

Diagram 8.7.1: Using Scripts

The script create_banksystem.sql creates a few tables, inserts some records into those tables and finally commits the entries made. This scripts looks like:

```
CREATE TABLE …

CREATE TABLE …

INSERT INTO … VALUES …

INSERT INTO … VALUES …

COMMIT
```

However to recreate the entire banking system again, if the same script is fired one more time it will throw up errors indicating that the tables already exist. To overcome this problem one more script named drop_banksystem.sql must be created (and run first) which will drop the tables. Then recreate them.

Using Nested Script Files

The new script file drop_banksystem.sql will be called from within the create_banksystem.sql and will look like:

```
DROP TABLE …

DROP TABLE …
```

The create_banksystem.sql will now look like:

@@drop_banksystem.sql

```
CREATE TABLE …

CREATE TABLE …

INSERT INTO … VALUES …

INSERT INTO … VALUES …

COMMIT
```

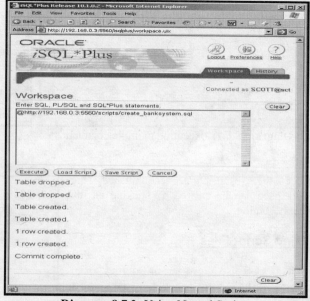

Diagram 8.7.2: Using Nested Scripts

Execute the script create_banksystem.sql using the **@http://192.168.0.3:5560/scripts/create_banksystem.sql** command. This script will not fire errors but in-turn call the script drop_banksystem.sql to drop the tables first and then proceed with the creation and population of the same. (Refer diagram 8.7.2)

Using Nested Script Files

iSQL *PLUS allows scripts which prompt for user input. This will be demonstrated via the script file named prompt.sql.

The prompt.sql holds the following code:
```
SELECT * FROM &TableName;
```

The file can be run using the following command: (Refer diagram 8.7.3 and diagram 8.7.4)
@http://192.168.0.3:5560/scripts/prompt.sql

The script will display the prompt "Enter value for tablename". Enter the table name as DEPT. Click **Continue** to send the value for processing via the script. After processing the output as seen in diagram 8.7.4 appears.

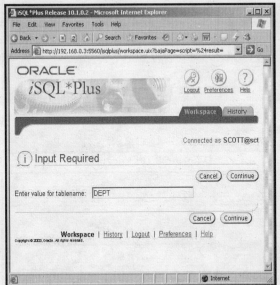 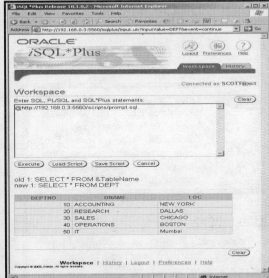

Diagram 8.7.3: Executing Script With Prompt   **Diagram 8.7.4:** Output of the script

Understanding The Environment

History

iSQL *PLUS provides a history of recently executed commands. This history can be accessed, by clicking the hyperlink **History** at the page bottom (Refer diagram 8.8) or the History TAB **Workspace History**.

Workspace | History | Logout | Preferences | Help
Copyright © 2003, Oracle. All rights reserved.

Diagram 8.8: Hyperlinks - History

Clicking the History link passes the control to the History TAB as seen in diagram 8.9.

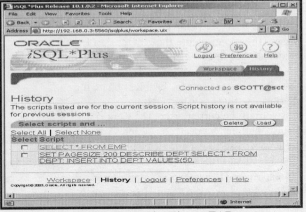

Diagram 8.9: The History TAB

A history entry is created each time a script is executed in the Workspace, **if it is not the same,** as the most recently executed script. The History screen shows the leading 80 characters of the script.

When the history limit is reached, the earliest (oldest) scripts are removed. When the session is exited history is lost. History is **not shared** between sessions.

The history TAB allows the **loading** of **all** or **selected** commands into the workspace to execute them or the **deletion** of **all** or **selected** commands from History.

Loading a command passes the control back to the workspace with the selected command loaded in the workspace's textbox.

Logout

Using the logout link simply logs out the current user and passes the control to a screen as seen in diagram 8.10. The user can logout using the logout link or the Logout button among the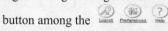

> Once the user logs-out history is also wiped clean. This means the history TAB displays only those commands, which were fired during a particular session. Once the session is closed (i.e. a user logs-out) history is deleted.

Diagram 8.10: Logout

Preferences

The iSQL *PLUS tool provides some choices to customize the iSQL *PLUS Environment. These can be accessed using the link Preferences towards the page bottom or the Preferences button among the . Clicking the preferences passes the control of the iSQL *PLUS session to the page as seen in diagram 8.11

The Preferences screen enables changing interface settings, system settings and the password of the current user. The Cancel and Apply buttons appear on each of the Preferences screens and have the same function on all Preferences screens. Click the Workspace or History tab to return to the Workspace or History screen.

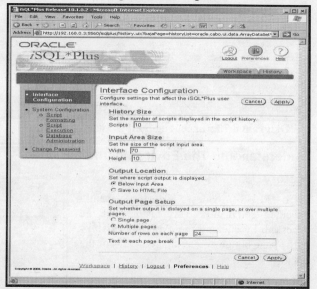

Diagram 8.11: Preferences

Help

The iSQL *PLUS provides online help. (Refer diagram 8.12)

To activate help click the link Help towards the page bottom or use the Help button from among the

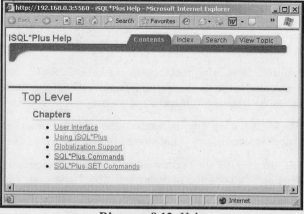

Diagram 8.12: Help

9. INTRODUCTION TO PL/SQL

Though SQL is the natural language of the DBA, it suffers from various inherent **disadvantages**, when used as a conventional programming language.

1. SQL does not have any **procedural capabilities** i.e. SQL does not provide the programming techniques of condition checking, looping and branching that is vital for data testing before its permanent storage
2. SQL statements are passed to the Oracle Engine **one** at a time. Each time an SQL statement is executed, a call is made to the engine's resources. This adds to the traffic on the network, thereby decreasing the speed of data processing, especially in a multi-user environment
3. While processing an SQL sentence if an error occurs, the Oracle engine displays its own error messages. SQL has no facility for programmed handling of errors that arise during the manipulation of data

Although SQL is a very powerful tool, its set of disadvantages prevent it from being a fully structured programming language. For a fully structured programming language, Oracle provides **PL/SQL**.

As the name suggests, PL/SQL is a **superset** of SQL. PL/SQL is a block-structured language that enables developers to combine the power of SQL with procedural statements. PL/SQL bridges the gap between database technology and procedural programming languages.

ADVANTAGES OF PL/SQL

1. PL/SQL is a development tool that not only supports SQL data manipulation but also provides facilities of conditional checking, branching and looping
2. PL/SQL sends an **entire block** of SQL statements to the Oracle engine all in one go. Communication between the program block and the Oracle engine reduces considerably, reducing network traffic. Since the Oracle engine got the SQL statements as a single block, it processes this code much faster than if it got the code one sentence at a time. There is a definite improvement in the performance time of the Oracle engine. As an entire block of SQL code is passed to the Oracle engine at one time for execution, all changes made to the data in the table are **done** or **undone**, in one go
3. PL/SQL also permits dealing with errors as required and facilitates displaying user-friendly messages, when errors are encountered
4. PL/SQL allows declaration and use of variables in blocks of code. These variables can be used to store intermediate results of a query for later processing or calculate values and insert them into an Oracle table later. PL/SQL variables can be used anywhere, either in SQL statements or in PL/SQL blocks
5. Via PL/SQL, all sorts of calculations can be done quickly and efficiently without the use of the Oracle engine. This considerably improves transaction performance
6. Applications written in PL/SQL are portable to any computer hardware and operating system, where Oracle is operational. Hence, PL/SQL code blocks written for a DOS version of Oracle will run on its Linux / UNIX version **without** any modifications at all

THE GENERIC PL/SQL BLOCK

Every programming environment allows the creation of structured, logical blocks of code that describe processes, which have to be applied to data. Once these blocks are passed to the environment, the processes described are applied to data, suitable data manipulation takes place and useful output is obtained.

PL/SQL permits the creation of structured logical blocks of code that describe processes, which have to be applied to data. A single PL/SQL code block consists of a set of SQL statements, clubbed together and passed to the Oracle engine entirely. This block has to be logically grouped together for the engine to recognize it as a singular code block. A PL/SQL block has a definite structure, which can be divided into sections. The sections of a PL/SQL block are:

❑   The Declare section
❑   The Master Begin and End section that **also** (optionally) **contains** an Exception section.

Each of these is explained below:

The Declare Section

Code blocks start with a declaration section, in which, memory variables and other Oracle objects can be declared and if required initialized. Once declared, they can be used in SQL statements for data manipulation.

The Begin Section

It consists of a set of SQL **and** PL/SQL statements, which describe processes that have to be applied to table data. Actual data manipulation, retrieval, looping and branching constructs are specified in this section.

The Exception Section

This section deals with handling of errors that arise during execution of the data manipulation statements, which make up the PL/SQL code block. Errors can arise due to syntax, logic and/or validation rule violation.

The End Section

This marks the end of a PL/SQL block.

A PL/SQL code block can be diagrammatically represented as follows:

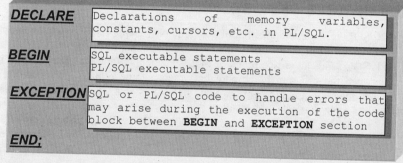

Diagram 8.1: The PL/SQL block structure.

THE PL/SQL EXECUTION ENVIRONMENT

Wherever PL/SQL technology is required (**i.e.** in the RDBMS core or in its tools), the PL/SQL engine accepts any valid PL/SQL block as input.

PL/SQL In The Oracle Engine

The PL/SQL engine resides in the Oracle engine, the Oracle engine can process not only single SQL statements but also entire PL/SQL blocks.

These blocks are sent to the PL/SQL engine, where procedural statements are executed and SQL statements are sent to the SQL executor in the Oracle engine. Since the PL/SQL engine resides in the Oracle engine, this is an efficient and swift operation.

The call to the Oracle engine needs to be made only once to execute any number of SQL statements, if these SQL sentences are bundled inside a PL/SQL block.

Diagram 8.2 gives an idea of how these statements are executed and how convenient it is to bundle SQL code within a PL/SQL block. Since the Oracle engine is called only once for each block, the speed of SQL statement execution is vastly enhanced, when compared to the Oracle engine being called once for each SQL sentence.

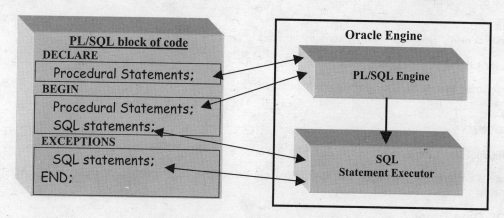

Diagram 8.2: The PL/SQL Execution Environment.

PL/SQL

The Character Set

The basic character set includes the following:

- ❑ Uppercase alphabets { **A - Z** }
- ❑ Lowercase alphabets { **a - z** }
- ❑ Numerals { **0 - 9** }
- ❑ Symbols ( ) + - * / < > = ! ; : . ' @ % , " # $ ^ & _ \ { } ? [ ]

Words used in a PL/SQL block are called **Lexical Units**. Blank spaces can be freely inserted between lexical units in a PL/SQL block. The blank spaces have no effect on the PL/SQL block.

The ordinary symbols used in PL/SQL blocks are:

( ) + - * / < > = ; % ' " [ ] :

Compound symbols used in PL/SQL blocks are:

< > != ~= ^= <= >= := ** .. || << >>

Literals

A literal is a numeric value or a character string used to represent itself.

Numeric Literal

These can be either integers or floats. If a float is being represented, then the integer part must be separated from the float part by a period.

Example:
  25, 6.34, 7g2, 25e-03, .1, 1., 1.e4, +17, -5

String Literal

These are represented by one or more legal characters and must be enclosed within single quotes. The single quote character can be represented, by **writing it twice** in a string literal. This is **definitely not** the same as a double quote.

Example:
  'Hello World', '<u>Don'</u>'t go without saving your work'

Character Literal

These are string literals consisting of single characters.

Example:
  '*', 'A', 'Y'

Logical (Boolean) Literal

These are predetermined constants. The values that can be assigned to this data type are: TRUE, FALSE, NULL

PL/SQL Data Types

Both PL/SQL and Oracle have their foundations in SQL. Most PL/SQL data types are native to Oracle's data dictionary. Hence, there is a very easy integration of PL/SQL code with the Oracle Engine.

The default data types that can be declared in PL/SQL are **number** (for storing numeric data), **char** (for storing character data), **date** (for storing date and time data), **boolean** (for storing TRUE, FALSE or NULL). **number**, **char** and **date** data types can have NULL values.

The **%TYPE** attribute provides for further integration. PL/SQL can use the **%TYPE** attribute to declare variables based on definitions of columns in a table. Hence, if a column's attributes change, the variable's attributes will change as well. This provides for data independence, reduces maintenance costs and allows programs to adapt to changes made to the table.

%TYPE declares a variable or constant to have the same data type as that of a previously defined variable or of a column in a table or in a view. When referencing a table, a user may name the table and the column or name the owner, the table and the column.

NOT NULL causes creation of a variable or a constant that **cannot** be assigned a null value. If an attempt is made to assign the value NULL to a variable or a constant that has been assigned a **NOT NULL** constraint, Oracle senses the exception condition automatically and an internal error is returned.

 Note

 As soon as a variable or constant has been declared as NOT NULL, it must be assigned a value. Hence every variable or constant declared as NOT NULL **needs** to be followed by a PL/SQL expression that loads a value into the variable or constant.

Variables

Variables in PL/SQL blocks are **named** variables. A variable name must begin with a character and can be followed by a maximum of 29 other characters.

Reserved words cannot be used as variable names **unless** enclosed within double quotes. Variables must be separated from each other by at least one space or by a punctuation mark.

Case is insignificant when declaring variable names. A space cannot be used in a variable name. A variable of any data type either native to the Oracle Engine such as number, char, date and so on or native to PL/SQL such as Boolean (i.e. logical variable content) can be declared.

Assigning Values to Variables

The assigning of a value to a variable can be done in two ways:
❑   Using the assignment operator := (i.e. a colon followed by an equal to sign).
❑   Selecting or fetching table data values into variables.

An interesting point to note here is that if PL/SQL code blocks are used for loading and calculating variables, the power of the Oracle Engine is not used. This frees up the Oracle engine for other work and considerably improves response time.

Constants

Declaring a constant is similar to declaring a variable except that the keyword **constant** must be added to the variable name **and** a value assigned immediately. Thereafter, no further assignments to the constant are possible, while the constant is **within** the scope of the PL/SQL block.

Raw

Raw types are used to store **binary** data. Character variables are automatically converted between character sets by Oracle, if necessary. These are similar to char variables, except that they are not converted between character sets. It is used to store fixed length binary data. The maximum length of a raw variable is 32,767 bytes. However, the maximum length of a database raw column is 255 bytes.

Long raw is similar to long data, except that PL/SQL will not convert between character sets. The maximum length of a long raw variable is 32,760 bytes. The maximum length of a long raw column is 2 GB.

RowId

This data type is the same as the database **ROWID** pseudo-column type. It can hold a rowid, which can be considered as a unique key for every row in the database. Rowids are stored internally as a fixed length binary quantity, whose actual fixed length varies depending on the operating system.

Various **DBMS_ROWID** functions are used to extract information about the ROWID pseudo-column. **Extended** and **Restricted** are two rowid formats. **Restricted** is used mostly to be backward compatible with previous versions of Oracle. The **Extended** format takes advantage of new Oracle features.

The **DBMS_ROWID** package has several procedures and functions to interpret the ROWIDs of records. The following table shows the **DBMS_ROWID** functions:

FUNCTION	DESCRIPTION
ROWID_VERIFY	Verifies if the ROWID can be extended; 0 = can be converted to extended format; 1 = cannot be converted to extended format
ROWID_TYPE	0 = ROWID, 1 = Extended
ROWID_BLOCK_NUMBER	The block number that contains the record; 1 = Extended ROWID
ROWID_OBJECT	The object number of the object that contains the record.
ROWID_RELATIVE_FNO	The relative file number contains the record.
ROWID_ROW_NUMBER	The row number of the record.
ROWID_TO_ABSOLUTE_FNO	The absolute file number; user need to input rowid_val, schema and object; the absolute file number is returned.
ROWID_TO_EXTENDED	Converts the ROWID from Restricted to Extended; user need to input restr_rowid, schema, object; the extended number is returned.
ROWID_TO_RESTRICTED	Converts the ROWID from Extended to Restricted.

ROWID is a pseudo-column that has a unique value associated with each record of the database.

The **DBMS_ROWID** package is created by the **ORACLE_HOME/RDBMS/ADMIN/DBMSUTIL.SQL** script.

This script is automatically run when the Oracle instance is created.

LOB Types

A company may decide that some comments about each of its vendors must be stored along with their details. This must be stored along with all the other details that they have on a particular vendor. This can be done in Oracle with the help of LOB types.

The LOB types are used to store large objects. A large object can be either a binary or a character value upto 4 GB in size. Large objects can contain unstructured data, which is accessed more efficiently than long or long raw data, with fewer restrictions. LOB types are manipulated using the **DBMS_LOB** package. There are four types of LOBs:

❑ **BLOB (Binary LOB)** – This stores unstructured binary data upto 4 GB in length. A blob could contain video or picture information.

❑ **CLOB (Character LOB)** – This stores single byte characters upto 4 GB in length. This might be used to store documents.

❑ **BFILE (Binary File)** – This stores a pointer to read only binary data stored as an external file outside the database.

Of these LOBs, **BFILE** is an **external** to the database. Internal objects store a **locator** in the Large Object column of a table. **Locator** is a pointer that specifies the actual location of LOB stored outside the database. The LOB locator for **BFILE** is a pointer to the location of the binary file stored by the operating system. The **DBMS_LOB** package is used to manipulate LOBs. Oracle supports data integrity and concurrency for all the LOBs except **BFILE** as the data is stored outside the database.

Storage for LOB data

The area required to store the LOB data can be specified at the time of creation of the table that includes the LOB column. The create table command has a storage clause that specifies the storage characteristics for the table.

Syntax:
```
CREATE TABLE <TableName> (<ColumnName> <Datatype> <Size()>,
    <ColumnName> <Datatype> <Size()>, <ColumnName> CLOB,...);
```

Logical Comparisons

PL/SQL supports the comparison between variables and constants in SQL and PL/SQL statements. These comparisons, often called **Boolean expressions**, generally consist of simple expressions separated by relational operators (<, >, =, < >, >=, <=) that can be connected by logical operators (AND, OR, NOT). A Boolean expression will always evaluate to **TRUE**, **FALSE** or **NULL**.

Displaying User Messages On The VDU Screen

Programming tools require a method through which messages can be displayed on the VDU screen.

DBMS_OUTPUT is a package that includes a number of procedures and functions that accumulate information in a buffer so that it can be retrieved later. These functions can also be used to display messages.

PUT_LINE puts a piece of information in the package buffer followed by an end-of-line marker. It can also be used to display a message. **PUT_LINE** expects a single parameter of character data type. If used to display a message, it is the **message** string.

To display messages, the **SERVEROUTPUT** should be set to **ON**. **SERVEROUTPUT** is a SQL *PLUS environment parameter that displays the information passed as a parameter to the **PUT_LINE** function.

Syntax:
```
SET SERVEROUTPUT [ON/OFF]
```

Comments

A comment can have two forms which are as follow:
- The comment line begins with a double hyphen (--). The entire line will be treated as a comment.
- The comment line begins with a slash followed by an asterisk (/*) till the occurrence of an asterisk followed by a slash (*/). All lines within are treated as comments. This form of specifying comments can be used to span across multiple lines. This technique can also be used to enclose a section of a PL/SQL block that temporarily needs to be isolated and ignored.

CONTROL STRUCTURE

The flow of control statements can be classified into the following categories:
- Conditional Control
- Iterative Control
- Sequential Control

Conditional Control

PL/SQL allows the use of an **IF** statement to control the execution of a block of code. In PL/SQL, the **IF - THEN - ELSIF - ELSE - END IF** construct in code blocks allow specifying certain conditions under which a specific block of code should be executed.

Syntax:

```
IF <Condition> THEN
    <Action>
ELSIF <Condition> THEN
    <Action>
ELSE
    <Action>
END IF;
```

Example 1:
Write a PL/SQL code block that will accept the Rental Identity, check if the customer has made an advance payment then deduct the bill amount for that customer by 10% from the Bills table. The process is fired on the Bills table.

DECLARE
```
/* Declaration of memory variables and constants to be used in the
Execution section.*/
```
    mAdvPaid number(8,2);
    mRentId number(5);
    mBillNo number(5);

BEGIN
```
/* Accept the Rental Identity */
```
    mRentId := &mRentId;
```
/* Retrieving the advance payment from the Rentals table where the
RentId in the table is equal to the mRentId entered by the user.*/
```
    SELECT AdvPaid, BillNo **INTO** mAdvPaid, mBillNo **FROM** Rentals **WHERE** RentId = mRentId;
```
/* Checking if the resultant mAdvPaid holds a value. If the condition
is satisfied a discount of 10% is provided by deducting it from the
Total column in the Bills table.*/
```
    IF mAdvPaid > 0 **THEN**
        UPDATE Bills **SET** Total = Total * 0.90
            WHERE BillNo = mBillNo;
    END IF;
END;

Output:
```
Enter value for mrentid: 1
old    9:   mRentId := &mRentId;
new    9:   mRentId := 1;

PL/SQL procedure successfully completed.
```

Iterative Control

Iterative control indicates the ability to repeat or skip sections of a code block. A **loop** marks a sequence of statements that has to be repeated. The keyword **loop** has to be placed before the first statement in the sequence of statements to be repeated, while the keyword **end loop** is placed immediately after the last statement in the sequence. Once a loop begins to execute, it will **go on forever**. Hence a conditional statement that controls the number of times a loop is executed **always accompanies** loops.

PL/SQL supports the following structures for iterative control:

Simple Loop

In simple loop, the key word **loop** should be placed before the first statement in the sequence and the keyword **end loop** should be written at the end of the sequence to end the loop.

Syntax:
```
Loop
     <Sequence of statements>
End loop;
```

Example 2:
Create a simple loop such that a message is displayed when a loop exceeds a particular value.

```
DECLARE
    i number := 0;
BEGIN
    LOOP
        i := i + 2;
        EXIT WHEN i > 10;
    END LOOP;
    dbms_output.put_line('Loop exited as the value of i has reached ' || to_char(i));
END;
```

Output:
```
Loop exited as the value of i has reached 12
PL/SQL procedure successfully completed.
```

The WHILE loop

Syntax:
```
WHILE <Condition>
LOOP
    <Action>
END LOOP;
```

Example 3:
Write a PL/SQL code block to calculate the area of a circle for a value of radius varying from 3 to 7. Store the radius and the corresponding values of calculated area in an empty table named **Areas**, consisting of two columns **Radius** and **Area**.

Table Name: Areas

RADIUS	AREA

Create the table AREAS as:
CREATE TABLE AREAS (RADIUS **NUMBER(5)**, AREA **NUMBER(14,2))**;

```
DECLARE
/* Declaration of memory variables and constants to be used in the
Execution section.*/
    pi constant number(4,2) := 3.14 ;
    radius number(5);
    area number(14,2);

BEGIN
/* Initialize the radius to 3, since calculations are required for
radius 3 to 7 */
    radius := 3;

/* Set a loop so that it fires till the radius value reaches 7 */
    WHILE RADIUS <= 7
    LOOP
    /* Area calculation for a circle */
        area := pi * power(radius,2);
    /* Insert the value for the radius and its corresponding area
    calculated in the table */
        INSERT INTO areas VALUES (radius, area);

    /* Increment the value of the variable radius by 1 */
        radius := radius + 1;
    END LOOP;
END;
```

The above PL/SQL code block initializes a variable **radius** to hold the value of 3. The area calculations are required for the radius between 3 and 7. The value for area is calculated first with radius 3 and the radius and area are inserted into the table **Areas**. Now, the variable holding the value of radius is incremented by 1, i.e. it now holds the value 4. Since the code is held within a loop structure, the code continues to fire till the radius value reaches 7. Each time the value of radius and area is inserted into the **Areas** table.

After the loop is completed the table will now hold the following:

Table Name: Areas

RADIUS	AREA
3	28.26
4	50.24
5	78.5
6	113.04
7	153.86

The FOR Loop

Syntax:

```
FOR variable IN [REVERSE] start..end
LOOP
    <Action>
END LOOP;
```

Note

The **variable** in the For Loop need not be declared. Also the increment value cannot be specified. The For Loop variable is **always incremented** by **1**.

Example 4:
Write a PL/SQL block of code for inverting a number 5639 to 9365.

DECLARE
```
/* Declaration of memory variables and constants to be used in the
Execution section.*/
    given_number varchar(5) := '5639';
    str_length number(2);
    inverted_number varchar(5);
```

BEGIN
```
/* Store the length of the given number */
    str_length := length(given_number);
/* Initialize the loop such that it repeats for the number of times
equal to the length of the given number. Also, since the number is
required to be inverted, the loop should consider the last number first
and store it i.e. in reverse order */
```
    FOR cntr **IN REVERSE 1..str_length**
```
    /* Variables used as counter in the for loop need not be declared
    i.e. cntr declaration is not required */
```
    LOOP
```
    /* The last digit of the number is obtained using the substr
    function, and stored in a variable, while retaining the previous
    digit stored in the variable*/
        inverted_number := inverted_number || substr(given_number, cntr, 1);
```
    END LOOP;
```
/* Display the initial number, as well as the inverted number, which is
stored in the variable on screen */
    dbms_output.put_line ('The Given number is ' || given_number );
    dbms_output.put_line ('The Inverted number is ' || inverted_number );
```
END;

Output:
```
The Given number is 5639
The Inverted number is 9365
```

The above PL/SQL code block stores the given number as well its length in two variables. Since the FOR loop is set to repeat till the length of the number is reached and in reverse order, the loop will fire 4 times beginning from the last digit i.e. **9**. This digit is obtained using the function **SUBSTR** and stored in a variable. The loop now fires again to fetch and store the second last digit of the given number. This is appended to the last digit stored previously. This repeats till each digit of the number is obtained and stored.

Sequential Control

The GOTO Statement

The **GOTO** statement changes the **flow of control** within a PL/SQL block. This statement allows execution of a section of code, which is not in the normal flow of control. The entry point into such a block of code is marked using the tags **<<userdefined name>>**. The **GOTO** statement can then make use of this user-defined name to jump into that block of code for execution.

Syntax:
```
GOTO <codeblock name>;
```

Example 5:
Write a PL/SQL block of code to achieve the following: If there are rental transactions which are not billed then record the rental transaction identity, the rental date and the Customer identity in the **Unbilled** table.

Table Name: Unbilled

RentId	RentDt	CustId

Create the table INACTV_ACCT_MSTR as:
CREATE TABLE Unbilled (
    RentId **NUMBER(5)**, RentDt **DATE**, CustId **NUMBER(5))**;

DECLARE
/* Declaration of memory variables and constants to be used in the Execution section.*/
    mRentId NUMBER(5);
    mANS VARCHAR2(3);
    mCustId NUMBER(5);
    mRentDt DATE;

BEGIN
/* Accept the Rental Identity */
    mRentId := &mRentId;
/* Fetch the Rental Identity into a variable */
    SELECT 'YES' **INTO** mANS **FROM** Rentals **WHERE** RentId = mRentId **AND** BillNo IS NULL;

/* If the transactions are not billed then the execution control is transferred to a user labeled section of code, labeled as notify in this example. */
    IF mANS = 'YES' **THEN**
        GOTO notify;
    ELSE
        dbms_output.put_line('Rental Identity: ' || mRentId || 'is Billed');
    END IF;

/* A labelled section of code which inserts a record in the **Unbilled** table. */

```
<<notify>>
SELECT RentDt, CustId INTO mRentDt, mCustId
    FROM Rentals WHERE RentId = mRentId AND BillNo IS NULL;
INSERT INTO Unbilled (RentId, RentDt, CustId)
        VALUES (mRentId, mRentDt, mCustId);
dbms_output.put_line('Rental Identity: '|| mRentId || ' is inserted in the Unbilled table');
EXCEPTION
/* Using the Oracle engine's named exception handler to handle the
error condition that may occur if the user enters a RentId that is not
present in the Rentals table */
WHEN NO_DATA_FOUND THEN
    DBMS_OUTPUT.PUT_LINE('Rental Identity.' || mRentId || ' is either not present in the Rentals table
                            or is already billed');
END;
```

Output:

```
SQL> SELECT * FROM Unbilled;

no rows selected

SQL>
```

Attempt 1:

```
Enter value for mrentid: 1
old  10:  mRentId := &mRentId;
new  10:  mRentId := 1;
Rental Identity.1 is either not present in the Rentals table or is
already billed

PL/SQL procedure successfully completed.
```

Attempt 2:

```
Enter value for mrentid: 41
old  10:  mRentId := &mRentId;
new  10:  mRentId := 41;
Rental Identity: 41 is inserted in the Unbilled table

PL/SQL procedure successfully completed.

SQL> SELECT * FROM Unbilled;
    RENTID RENTDT          CUSTID
---------- --------- ----------
        41 25-JAN-05             10

SQL>
```

The PL/SQL code first fetches the Rental Identity from the user into a variable **mRentId**. It then verifies using an SQL statement, whether that rental transaction is unbilled or not.

If it is, then a record is inserted in the Unbilled table and the same is indicated via a message.

But if it is not then a message stating the same is displayed.

NEW FEATURES IN ORACLE 10G PL/SQL

With every new release, Oracle Database 10g introduces some new PL/SQL language features and some new supplied PL/SQL packages.

However, the big news for PL/SQL in this release is the dramatic increase in runtime performance from transparent changes. Oracle Database 10g brings a new PL/SQL compiler and a newly tuned PL/SQL execution environment. Additionally, the system for the native compilation of PL/SQL has been substantially improved. As a result, users can expect that:
- ❑ Computationally intensive PL/SQL programs compiled under Oracle Database 10g will run, on average, twice as fast as they did under Oracle9i Database Release 2.
- ❑ They will run three times as fast as they did under Oracle8 Database.

In terms of language improvements the following features are added:
- ❑ The binary_float and binary_double datatypes (the IEEE datatypes)
- ❑ The regexp_like, regexp_instr, regexp_substr and regexp_replace builtins to support regular expression manipulation with standard POSIX syntax
- ❑ Multiset operations on nested table instances supporting operations like equals, union, intersect, except, member, and so on
- ❑ The user-defined quote character
- ❑ Indices of and values of syntax for forall
- ❑ The distinction between binary_integer and pls_integer vanishes

In terms of PL/SQL Supplied Packages the following new packages are added:
- ❑ **Utl_Mail:** This new package makes it possible for a PL/SQL programmer to send programmatically composed emails. It requires only the normal mental model of a user of a GUI email client rather than an understanding of the underlying protocol (SMTP) features. This distinguishes it from Utl_Smtp which was introduced in Oracle8i Database. Utl_Smtp requires that the programmer understands the details of the SMTP protocol. Utl_Mail is much simpler to use because it supports just a limited, but very common, subset of the functionality that Utl_Smtp provides.
- ❑ **Utl_Compress:** This new package delivers the familiar functionality of the zip and unzip utilities in a PL/SQL environment. It lets you compress and uncompress a raw or blob bytestream and guarantees return of original bytestream after a round trip.
- ❑ **Dbms_Warning:** This allows the PL/SQL programmer fine grained control over which categories of warning and which individual warnings to disable, to enable, or to treat as errors. Its expected use is at the start and end of installation scripts so that each script may run in its intended regime without affecting the regime of subsequent scripts.

SELF REVIEW QUESTIONS

FILL IN THE BLANKS

1. Each time an SQL statement is executed, a _____ is made to the engine's resources.

2. PL/SQL is a _____ language.

3. Code blocks start with a _____ section.

4. The _____ section deals with handling of errors that arise during execution of the data manipulation statements, which make up the PL/SQL code block.

5. The _____ section marks the end of a PL/SQL block.

6. Words used in a PL/SQL block are called _____ _____.

7. A _____ is a numeric value or a character string used to represent itself.

8. In a numeric literal, if a float is being represented, then the integer part must be separated from the float part by a _____.

9. _____ literals can be either integers or floats.

10. The _____ attribute is used to declare variables based on definitions of columns in a table.

11. Raw types are used to store _____ data.

12. The maximum length of a long raw column is _____.

13. _____ are stored internally as a fixed length binary quantity, whose actual fixed length varies depending on the operating system.

14. The _____ function verifies the block number that contains the record.

15. The _____ function verifies the absolute file number.

16. _____ data type stores unstructured binary data upto 4GB in length.

17. Internal objects store a _____ in the Large Object column of a table.

18. _____ is a pointer that specifies the actual location of LOB stored outside the database.

19. _____ puts a piece of information in the package buffer followed by an end-of-line marker.

20. The _____ function converts the ROWID from extended to restricted.

21. A _____ marks a sequence of statements that has to be repeated.

22. The _____ statement changes the flow of control within a PL/SQL block.

TRUE OR FALSE

23. SQL does not provide the programming techniques of conditional checking.

24. Multiple SQL statements are passed to the Oracle Engine at a time.

25. SQL has facility for programmed handling of errors that arise during manipulation of data.

26. A PL/SQL block has a definite structure which can be divided into sections.

27. Actual data manipulation, retrieval, looping and branching constructs are specified in the declare section.

28. Blank spaces can be freely inserted between lexical units in a PL/SQL block.

29. TRUE, FALSE, NULL cannot be assigned to Logical literals.

30. NOT NULL causes creation of a variable or a constant that cannot have a null value.

31. The String literals should not be enclosed within single quotes.

32. Reserved words can be used as variable names in PL/SQL.

33. The ROWID_TO_EXTENDED function converts the ROWID from restricted to extended

34. Raw is used to store ASCII data.

35. The ROWID_VERIFY function verifies if the ROWID can be extended.

36. The CLOB (Character LOB) data type stores single byte characters upto 4GB in length.

37. DBMS_PROC is a package that includes a number of procedures and functions that accumulate information in a buffer so that it can be retrieved later.

38. The DBMS_LOB package is used to manipulate LOBs.

39. The comment line begins with an asterisk followed by a slash.

40. The keyword loop has to be placed after the first statement in the sequence of statements to be repeated.

41. The variable in the FOR loop should always be declared.

10. USING REGULAR EXPRESSIONS

Regular expressions can be used to create a programming skill base that can be tapped to produce elegant, powerful SQL and PL/SQL statements, hence understanding it's nuances is pretty important for good programming.

What Is A Regular Expression?

Regular expressions are similar to the **find/replace** tools of a modern text editor. This functionality makes editing a text file a whole lot easier. Think of a regular expression as an extremely advanced, find/replace tool that saves programmers the pain of having to write custom data validation routines to check e-mail addresses, make sure phone numbers are in the correct format, and so on.

Oracle Database 10g introduces support for Regular expressions. The implementation complies with the **P**ortable **O**perating **S**ystem for UNIX (i.e. the **POSIX**) standard, controlled by the Institute of Electrical and Electronics Engineers (IEEE), for ASCII data matching semantics and syntax. Oracle's multi-lingual capabilities extend the matching capabilities of the operators **beyond** the POSIX standard.

In Oracle Database 10g Regular expressions are really simple to implement. They can be implemented in both SQL and PL/SQL. When coupled with native SQL, the use of regular expressions allows performing powerful search and manipulation operations on any data stored in an Oracle database.

Regular expressions are a method of describing both simple and complex patterns for searching and manipulating strings. String manipulation and searching contribute to a large percentage of the logic within a web-based application.

Some of the usage examples of Regular expressions are:
- Locate the word SHARANAM SHAH in a specified text
- Extraction of all URLs from a block of text
- Locate all words whose every second character is a vowel
- Validate an email address using CHECK constraints

USING REGULAR EXPRESSION

To begin using regular expressions in SQL / PLSQL the following functions could be used:

Function	Description
REGEXP_LIKE	This function is similar to the LIKE operator. It performs regular expression matching instead of simple pattern matching. It resolves to TRUE if the first argument matches a regular expression.
REGEXP_INSTR	Searches for a given string for a regular expression pattern and returns the position were the match is found.
REGEXP_REPLACE	Searches for a regular expression pattern and replaces it with a replacement string.
REGEXP_SUBSTR	Searches for a regular expression pattern within a given string and returns the matched substring.

Note

These functions support only CHAR, VARCHAR2, CLOB, NCHAR, NVARCHAR and NCLOB datatypes.

META Characters

These functions, in addition to the basic search criteria, accept META characters. META characters are special characters that have a special meaning such as a:

- Wild Card character
- Repeating character
- Non-matching character
- Range of characters

Several predefined META character symbols can be used in the pattern matching with the functions.

Symbol	Description
Anchoring Metacharacters	
^	Anchor the expression to the start of a line
$	Anchor the expression to the end of a line
Quantifiers, or Repetition Operators	
*	Matches zero or more occurrences
?	Matches zero or one occurrence
+	Matches one or more occurrences
.	Matches any character in the supported character set, except NULL
{m}	Matches exactly m times
{m, }	Matches at least m times
{m, n}	Matches at least m times but no more than n times
Alternate Matching and Grouping of Expressions	
|	Separates alternates, often used with grouping operator ()
()	Grouping expression, treated as a single subexpression
[ ]	1. Indicates a character list. Most Meta characters inside a character list are understood as literals, with the exception of character classes and the ^ and – Meta characters 2. Bracket expression to specify a list of expressions, matching any one of the expressions represented in the list
Predefined POSIX Character Classes	
[:alnum:]	All alphanumeric characters
[:alpha:]	All alphabetic characters
[:cntrl:]	All control characters (nonprinting)
[:digit:]	All numeric digits
[:lower:]	All lowercase alphabetic characters
[:print:]	All printable characters
[:punct:]	All punctuation characters
[:space:]	All space characters (nonprinting)
[:upper:]	All uppercase alphabetic characters
Others	
[^exp]	Negates the expression (If the caret is inside the brackets)
[: :]	Specifies a character class and matches any character in that class
\	Signifies: 1. Stand for itself 2. Quote the next character 3. Introduce an operator 4. Do nothing
\n	Backreference expression
[==]	Specifies equivalence classes
[..]	Specifies one collation element, such as a multicharacter element

The examples that follow demonstrate the use of regular expressions.

REGEXP_LIKE

Syntax:
REGEXP_LIKE(SRCSTR, PATTERN [,MATCH_OPTION])

In the above syntax:
- **SRCSTR** is a character expression that serves as the search value. It is commonly a character column and can be of any of the datatypes such as CHAR, VARCHAR2, NCHAR, NVARCHAR2, CLOB or NCLOB
- **PATTERN** is the regular expression. It is usually a text literal and can be of any of the datatypes such as CHAR, VARCHAR2, NCHAR or NVARCHAR2. It can contain up to 512 bytes. If the datatype of **PATTERN** is different from the datatype of **SRCSTR**, Oracle Database converts pattern to the datatype of **SRCSTR**
- **MATCH_OPTION** is the option to change default matching. This means **MATCH_OPTION** can hold one or more of the following values:

Value	Description
'c'	Use case sensitive matching (DEFAULT)
'i'	Use case insensitive matching
'n'	Allows match-any-character operator
'm'	Treats source string as multiple line

Example 1:
Locate all those cars having the Car Registration Number (CarRegNo Field in the CARS table) beginning with the following:
- MH-02
- MH-03
- MH-12
- MH-13

Solution:
SELECT CarRegNo, Model FROM Cars WHERE **REGEXP_LIKE**(CarRegNo, 'MH-[01][23]');

Output:
```
CARREGNO                 MODEL
-------------------      ------------------------
MH-02-C-5876             Omni
MH-02-Z-3840             Sumo
MH-12-A-8758             800
MH-03-X-0987             Indica
MH-03-F-3499             Santro
MH-13-P-3249             Qualis

6 rows selected.
```

Explanation:
The regular expression in the above SQL statement searches for strings in the CarRegNo Field beginning with the characters **MH-** followed by **02**, **03**, **12** or **13**. This is done using the **[ ]** (box brackets) Meta character. This Meta character allows specifying a list of expressions / characters and matching any expressions / characters represented in the list.

Example 2:
Locate all those cars having the make of the car beginning with T and ending with A (make Field in the CARS table)
Solution:
SELECT CarRegNo, Model, Make FROM Cars WHERE **REGEXP_LIKE**(Make, '^T[A-Z]*A$','i');

Output:

```
CARREGNO             MODEL                    MAKE
-------------------  --------------------     ----------------------
MH-02-Z-3840         Sumo                     Tata
MH-04-Y-4849         Safari                   Tata
MH-03-X-0987         Indica                   Tata
MH-13-P-3249         Qualis                   Toyota
MH-14-Y-4039         Indica V2                Tata
```

Explanation:
The regular expression in the above SQL statement searches for string holding T as the first character in the Make field (*This is done by using the ^ (caret) Meta character followed by the character T*). Further [A-Z]* indicates that any number of the characters in the range of A-Z can be a part of the string **following the first character T** (This is done using the * (asterix) Meta character which allows multiple characters within the range of A-Z). Finally a **$** (dollar) Meta character is followed by the character **A** which indicates that the last character in the string should be the character A. Additionally, an extra parameter **'i'** is passed to the function REGEXP_LIKE. This parameter will do a **case insensitive** match.

Example 3:
List all those customers having the 2nd last and the 4th last character as a vowel present in their First Name (FirstName Field in the CUSTOMERS table)

Solution:
SELECT FirstName, LastName FROM Customers
    WHERE **REGEXP_LIKE**(FirstName, '[AEIOU].[AEIOU].$','i');

Output:

```
FIRSTNAME            LASTNAME
-------------------  --------------------
Rahul Mohan          Sharma
John Simon           Brownie
Jennifer             Smith
Mosie                Shah
```

Explanation:
The regular expression in the above SQL statement searches for a vowel in the FirstName field (*This is done by specifying the list of characters signifying a vowel using the [AEIOU]*). Since only those records having the 2nd last and the 4th last characters as a vowel are required, a **$** (dollar) Meta character is used. This instructs to start searching for a vowel ([AEIOU]) from the last character onwards. Further a **.** (dot) Meta character is used to skip the last and the 3rd last character from the vowel test (*This means the string can hold any characters in place of the last and the 3rd last characters*). Additionally, an extra parameter **'i'** is passed to the function REGEXP_LIKE. This parameter will do a **case insensitive** match.

Example 4:
List all those customers having their addresses ending with a Punctuation Mark (Addr Field in the CUSTOMERS table)

Solution:
SELECT Custid, FirstName, Addr FROM Customers WHERE **REGEXP_LIKE**(Addr, '[[:punct:]]$');

Output:
```
    CUSTID FIRSTNAME           ADDR
---------- ------------------- -----------------------------------
         9 Ashwini             Viram Apt., M. G. Rd.,
```

Explanation:
The regular expression in the above SQL statement searches for a punctuation mark in the Addr field *(This is done using the [:punct:] character class)*. A **$** (dollar) meta character is attached towards the end of the **[:punct:]** character class. This instructs searching only those records having a punctuation mark towards the end of the string.

Example 5:
List all those customers who have mentioned their middle name along with their First Name (FirstName Field in the CUSTOMERS table)

Solution:
SELECT FirstName, LastName FROM Customers WHERE REGEXP_LIKE(FirstName, '[[:space:]].');

Output:
```
FIRSTNAME                  LASTNAME
-------------------- --------------------
Rahul Mohan                Sharma
John Simon                 Brownie
Alex Joseph                D'Mello
```

Explanation:
The regular expression in the above SQL statement searches for a space in the FirstName field *(This is done using the [:space:] character class)*. If found, it further checks if that space is followed by at least a single character *(This is done using the . (dot) meta character)*. This indicates that the field FirstName is holding a Middle Name as well.

REGEXP_INSTR

Syntax:
    REGEXP_INSTR(SRCSTR, PATTERN [, POSITION [, OCCURRENCE [, RETURN_OPTION [, MATCH_OPTION]]]])

In the above syntax:
- **SRCSTR** is a character expression that serves as the search value. It is commonly a character column and can be of any of the datatypes such as CHAR, VARCHAR2, NCHAR, NVARCHAR2, CLOB or NCLOB
- **PATTERN** is the regular expression. It is usually a text literal and can be of any of the datatypes such as CHAR, VARCHAR2, NCHAR or NVARCHAR2. It can contain up to 512 bytes. If the datatype of **PATTERN** is different from the datatype of **SRCSTR**, Oracle Database converts pattern to the datatype of **SRCSTR**
- **POSITION** is a positive integer indicating the character of **SRCSTR** where Oracle should begin the search. The default is **1**, meaning that Oracle begins the search at the first character of **SRCSTR**
- **OCCURRENCE** is a positive integer indicating which occurrence of pattern in **SRCSTR** Oracle should search for. The default is **1**, meaning that Oracle searches for the first occurrence of pattern
- **RETURN_OPTION** allows specifying what Oracle should return in relation to the occurrence:
  - If 0 is specified, then Oracle returns the position of the first character of the occurrence. This is the **default**.
  - If 1 is specified, then Oracle returns the position of the character following the occurrence

❑ **MATCH_OPTION** is the option to change default matching. This means **MATCH_OPTION** can hold one or more of the following values:

Value	Description
'c'	Use case sensitive matching (DEFAULT)
'i'	Use case insensitive matching
'n'	Allows match-any-character operator
'm'	Treats source string as multiple line

Example 1:
Locate the start position of the actual car number (CarRegNo Field in the CARS table).

Solution:
SELECT CarRegNo, **REGEXP_INSTR**(CarRegNo, '[[:digit:]]{3}') CarNo_Position FROM Cars;

Output:
```
CARREGNO                 CARNO_POSITION
--------------------     --------------
MH-01-B-2083                          9
MH-02-C-5876                          9
MMZ-888                               5
MH-02-Z-3840                          9
MH-04-Y-4849                          9
MH-12-A-8758                          9
MH-03-X-0987                          9
MH-03-F-3499                          9
MH-13-P-3249                          9
MH-14-Y-4039                          9

10 rows selected.
```

Explanation:
The regular expression in the above SQL statement searches for a string comprising of 3 or more digits in the CarRegNo Field. This is done using the **[:digit:]** character class. This class will extract all the digits from the field CarRegNo. **{3}** indicates that the search will be filtered on a criteria where 3 or more digits will be considered. Finally, when the desired string is located, the function **REGEXP_INSTR** will return the start position of that string.

Example 2:
Locate the third occurrence of one or more non-blank character in the address of the customers (Addr Field in the CUSTOMERS table).

Solution:
SELECT Addr, REGEXP_INSTR(Addr, '[^]+', 1,3) "Third_Occourance" FROM Customers;

Output:
```
ADDR                              Third_Occourance
------------------------------    ----------------
A/14, Sunray Colony               14
123/A, North Links                14
Baptisa Mansion, 37 West Links    18
A/14, Mahim Mansion               13
Krishnath Complex, 37-C           20
204, Suliman Housing Board        14
702/A, Port View                  13
```

Output: (Continued)
```
Parvati Rd., Opp. New Bazaar        14
Viram Apt., M. G. Rd.,             13
Govton Pada, Central Lane          14

10 rows selected.
```

Explanation:
The regular expression in the above SQL statement searches non-blank characters in the Addr field. This is done using the [^] Meta characters. The ^ (caret) Meta character is used to negate the condition (i.e. **not** blank (space)) by the following **blank space**. Since one or more occurrences of non-blank characters is the criteria a + (plus) Meta character is used. This is then followed by the parameters 1,3. This instructs to start the search from the first character and return the third occurrence of such non-blank character. Finally, when the desired match is located, the function **REGEXP_INSTR** will return the start position of that match.

Example 3:
Locate the 2nd occurrence of words beginning with S or I, followed by three or more alphabetic characters.

Solution:
SELECT REGEXP_INSTR('Vaishali, Sharanam, Hansel, Chhaya, Ivan', '[S|I][[:alpha:]]{3}', 1, 2) "Search_S_OR_I" FROM DUAL;

Output:
```
Search_S_OR_I
-------------
           37
```

Explanation:
The regular expression in the above SQL statement begins searching at the first character in the string and returns the position in the string of the character following the second occurrence of a three-letter word beginning with S or I. This is done using | (pipe) Meta character which alternates between **S** or **I**. This is further supported by a **[:alpha:]** character class which only extract alphabets. The parameters 1, 2 indicate the following:
1 – The search will begin from the 1 character in the string
2 – Will return the second occurrence of the match

Finally, when the desired match is located, the function **REGEXP_INSTR** will return the start position of that match.

REGEXP_SUBSTR

Syntax:
    REGEXP_SUBSTR(SRCSTR, PATTERN [, POSITION [, OCCURRENCE [, MATCH_OPTION]]])
In the above syntax:
❑ **SRCSTR** is a character expression that serves as the search value. It is commonly a character column and can be of any of the datatypes such as CHAR, VARCHAR2, NCHAR, NVARCHAR2, CLOB or NCLOB
❑ **PATTERN** is the regular expression. It is usually a text literal and can be of any of the datatypes such as CHAR, VARCHAR2, NCHAR or NVARCHAR2. It can contain up to 512 bytes. If the datatype of **PATTERN** is different from the datatype of **SRCSTR**, Oracle Database converts pattern to the datatype of **SRCSTR**
❑ **POSITION** is a positive integer indicating the character of **SRCSTR** where Oracle should begin the search. The default is **1**, meaning that Oracle begins the search at the first character of **SRCSTR**

❑ **OCCURRENCE** is a positive integer indicating which occurrence of pattern in **SRCSTR** Oracle should search for. The default is **1**, meaning that Oracle searches for the first occurrence of pattern
❑ **MATCH_OPTION** is the option to change default matching. This means **MATCH_OPTION** can hold one or more of the following values:

Value	Description
'c'	Use case sensitive matching (DEFAULT)
'i'	Use case insensitive matching
'n'	Allows match-any-character operator
'm'	Treats source string as multiple line

Example 1:
Extract the Engine No in the following format (EngineNo Field in the CARS table):
ME-03042000-A34
MODELCODE = ME
ENGINEDATE = –03042000
ENGINESERNO = –A34

Solution:
SELECT **REGEXP_SUBSTR**(EngineNo, '[^-]+') ModelCode,
     REGEXP_SUBSTR(EngineNo, '-[^-]+') EngineDate,
     REGEXP_SUBSTR(EngineNo, '-[^-]+',1,2) EngineSerNo FROM Cars;

Output:
```
MODELCODE            ENGINEDATE                  ENGINESERNO
-------------------  -------------------------   ------------------------
ME                   -03042000                   -A34
MO                   -15082000                   -B34
PP                   -30112000                   -D430
SU                   -30112000                   -T12
SA                   -17062001                   -T34
MH                   -22062001                   -H98
IN                   -20122001                   -G90
HS                   -05052002                   -T983
TQ                   -12072002                   -T53
V2                   -03012003                   -T485

10 rows selected.
```

Explanation:
The **first** regular expression in the above SQL statement searches for one or more characters (*Done using the + (plus) Meta character*) before any – (hyphen) appears (*Done using [^-] Meta characters*).

The **second** regular expression in the above SQL statement searches for first – (hyphen) (*Done using – (hyphen) Meta characters*) followed by one or more characters (*Done using the + (plus) Meta character*) after the first – (hyphen) but before encountering a second – (hyphen) (*Indicated using [^-]*).

The **third** regular expression in the above SQL statement is same as the second except for two additional parameters (**1,2**) wherein **1** indicates that the search should begin with the first character and **2** indicates that second occurrence of such match must be the criteria.

Example 2:
Extract the actual car number (digits only) from the Car Registration Number of Customers (CarRegNo Field in the CARS table).

Solution:
SELECT CarRegNo, **REGEXP_SUBSTR**(CarRegNo, **'[[:digit:]]{3,}'**) Actual_No FROM Cars;

Output:
```
CARREGNO             ACTUAL_NO
-------------------- --------------------
MH-01-B-2083         2083
MH-02-C-5876         5876
MH-02-Z-3840         3840
MH-03-F-3499         3499
MH-03-X-0987         0987
MH-04-Y-4849         4849
MH-12-A-8758         8758
MH-13-P-3249         3249
MH-14-Y-4039         4039
MMZ-888              888

10 rows selected.
```

Explanation:
The regular expression in the above SQL statement searches for all digits (*Done using [:digit:] character class*) which form at least a three digit number (*Done using {3,} Meta character*).

Example 3:
Extract the actual web address (The Domain Name) from the given URL.

Solution:
SELECT **REGEXP_SUBSTR**('http://www.ivanbayross.com/books',
                       'http://([[:alnum:]]+\.?){3,4}/?') Actual_Web_Address FROM DUAL;

Output:
```
ACTUAL_WEB_ADDRESS
--------------------------
http://www.ivanbayross.com/
```

Explanation:
The regular expression in the above SQL statement examines the given string (URL), looking for **http://** followed by a substring of one or more (*Done using + (plus) Meta character*) alphanumeric characters (*Done using [:alnum:] character class*) and optionally, a period (.) (*Done using \ (slash) i.e. a Meta character which allows alternates*). Oracle searches for a minimum of three and a maximum of four such occurrences (Done using {3,4} Meta characters) of this substring between **http://** and either a / (slash) or the end of the string (*Done using /? Meta characters where (?) indicates zero or more occurrences of (/)*).

REGEXP_REPLACE

Syntax:
REGEXP_REPLACE(SRCSTR, PATTERN [, REPLACESTR [, POSITION [, OCCURRENCE [, MATCH_OPTION]]]])

In the above syntax:
❑ **SRCSTR** is a character expression that serves as the search value. It is commonly a character column and can be of any of the datatypes such as CHAR, VARCHAR2, NCHAR, NVARCHAR2, CLOB or NCLOB

- ❑ **PATTERN** is the regular expression. It is usually a text literal and can be of any of the datatypes such as CHAR, VARCHAR2, NCHAR or NVARCHAR2. It can contain up to 512 bytes. If the datatype of **PATTERN** is different from the datatype of **SRCSTR**, Oracle Database converts pattern to the datatype of **SRCSTR**
- ❑ **REPLACESTR** can be of any of the datatypes such as CHAR, VARCHAR2, NCHAR, NVARCHAR2, CLOB or NCLOB. If **REPLACESTR** is a CLOB or NCLOB, then Oracle truncates **REPLACESTR** to **32K**. The **REPLACESTR** can contain up to 500 backreferences to subexpressions in the form \n, where n is a number from 1 to 9. If **n** is the blackslash character in **REPLACESTR**, then it must be preceded with the escape character (\\).
- ❑ **POSITION** is a positive integer indicating the character of **SRCSTR** where Oracle should begin the search. The default is **1**, meaning that Oracle begins the search at the first character of **SRCSTR**
- ❑ **OCCURRENCE** is a positive integer indicating which occurrence of pattern in **SRCSTR** Oracle should search for. The default is **1**, meaning that Oracle searches for the first occurrence of pattern
- ❑ **MATCH_OPTION** is the option to change default matching. This means **MATCH_OPTION** can hold one or more of the following values:

Value	Description
'c'	Use case sensitive matching (DEFAULT)
'i'	Use case insensitive matching
'n'	Allows match-any-character operator
'm'	Treats source string as multiple line

Example 1:
Display the city names where the Customers reside wherein each character of the city name is separated by a space (City Field in the CUSTOMERS table).

Solution:
SELECT **REGEXP_REPLACE**(City, '(.)', '\1 ') Spacer_City FROM Customers;

Output:
```
SPACER_CITY
----------------------
M u m b a i
N e w   Y o r k
N e w   Y o r k
M u m b a i
C h e n n a i
D u b a i
F u j a i r a
M u m b a i
M u m b a i
P a n j i

10 rows selected.
```

Explanation:
The regular expression in the above SQL statement examines the City Names and puts a space after each non-null character in the string. This is done by using a **.** (dot) Meta character extracts every character from the string and inserts a space after it (Done using '\1 '). The '\1 ' is a Backreference Meta character, which holds (in a Temporary Buffer) every character extracted via the first search pattern (In this case only one search pattern is used) and attaches a space following it.

Example 2:
Replace two spaces with a single space wherever applicable in the given string.

Solution 1:
SELECT **REGEXP_REPLACE**('Sharanam   Shah,   Makanji Mansion,   Mahim,   Mumbai', ' ', ' ')
Two_To_One FROM DUAL;
Solution 2:
SELECT **REGEXP_REPLACE**('Sharanam   Shah,   Makanji Mansion,   Mahim,   Mumbai', '( ){2,}', ' ')
Two_To_One FROM DUAL;

Output:
```
TWO_TO_ONE
--------------------------------------------
Sharanam Shah, Makanji Mansion, Mahim, Mumbai
```

Explanation:
In Solution 1: A simple approach is used wherein the second parameter ' ' indicates a search pattern of two spaces and the third parameter ' ' indicates that two spaces will be replaced with a single space.

In Solution 2: The regular expression in the second SQL statement examines the given string and using the ( ){2,} Meta characters searches for at least 2 spaces (*Done using {2,}*) and replaces those two spaces with a single space (Done using the third parameter ' ' which is a single blank space).

Backreferences

A useful feature of regular expressions is the ability to store sub-expressions for reuse later. This is also called **backreferencing**. It allows sophisticated replace capabilities such as swapping patterns in new positions or indicating repeated word or letter occurrences. The matched part of the sub-expression is stored in a temporary buffer. The buffer is numbered from left to right and accessed with the \digit notation, where digit is a number between 1 and 9 and matches the digit[th] sub-expression, as indicated by a set of parentheses.

Example 3: (Uses Backreferencing)
Swap the given name 'Sharanam Chaitanya Shah' as 'Shah, Sharanam Chaitanya'.

Solution:
SELECT **REGEXP_REPLACE**('Sharanam Chaitanya Shah', '(.*) (.*) (.*)', '\3, \1 \2') Swap
FROM DUAL;

Output:
```
SWAP
-----------------------
Shah, Sharanam Chaitanya
```

Explanation:
The regular expression in the above SQL statement shows three individual sub-expressions (*Done using (.*) (.*) (.*)*) enclosed within parentheses. Each individual sub-expression consists of a . (dot) (*Match any Meta character*) followed by the * (asterix) Meta character, indicating that any character (*except newline*) must be matched zero or more times. A space separates each sub-expression and must be matched with the source string as well (This is because the given name is also separated by spaces). The parentheses create sub-expressions that capture the values and can be referenced with **\digit**. The first sub-expression is assigned **\1**, the second **\2**, and so on. These backreferences are used in the last parameter of this function as **\3, \1 \2**, which effectively returns the replacement substrings and places them in the desired format (including comma and spaces).

Note

Backreferences are useful for replacing, formatting and substituting values, and can be applied to find adjacent occurrences of values.

Example 4: (Uses Backreferencing)

Convert the phone numbers of the customers residing in India in the specified format (i.e. **+91-022-(2)4404444**).

Solution:

SELECT **REGEXP_REPLACE**(Phone, '(.){1}(.*)', '+91-022-(\1)\2') Change_Format
　　　　　FROM Customers WHERE Country = 'INDIA' AND Phone IS NOT NULL;

Output:

```
CHANGE_FORMAT
------------------------
+91-022-(2)8765654
+91-022-(2)4443760
+91-022-(4)2739894
+91-022-(2)4403031
+91-022-(2)3445576
```

Explanation:

The regular expression in the above SQL statement extracts the first digit (*Done using (.){1} sub-expression wherein . (dot) Meta character indicates matching any character except null and {1} indicates extracting only the first match*). This is then followed by extraction of the remaining digits (*Done using (.*) sub-expression wherein . (dot) Meta character indicates matching any character except null and * (asterix) Meta character indicates multiple (Remaining digits) such matches*). The parentheses create two sub-expressions that capture the values and can be referenced with **\digit**. The first sub-expression is assigned **\1** and the second **\2**. The output is generated using backreferences in the last parameter of this function (as **+91-022-(\1)\2**), which help form the output by placing the strings retrieved via backreferences (i.e. **\1** and **\2**) in the desired format (including **+91-022-**).

SELF REVIEW QUESTIONS

FILL IN THE BLANKS

1. Regular expressions are similar to the _____ tools of a modern text editor

2. The implementation complies with the _____ for UNIX.

3. Regular Expressions can be implemented in both _____ and _____.

4. _____ function is similar to the LIKE operator

TRUE OR FALSE

5. REGEXP_REPLACE searches for a regular expression pattern within a given string and returns the matched substring.

6.　REGEXP_LIKE searches for a given string for a regular expression pattern and returns the position were the match is found.

7.　REGEXP_SUBSTR is similar to LIKE operator.

8.　REGEXP_INSTR searches for a given string for a regular expression pattern and returns the position were the match is found.

HANDS ON EXERCISES

1.　Locate all those products having the Product Numbers beginning with the following:
❑　P078
❑　P079

2.　Locate all those products having a description beginning with T or S and ending with S.

3.　List all those clients who have mentioned their last name along with their First Name in the Name Field of the **Client_Master** table.

4.　Locate the second occurrence of one or more non-blank character in the description of the products.

5.　Extract the actual product number (digits only) from the **ProductNo** column of **Product_Master** table

6.　Display the state names where the Clients reside wherein each character of the state name is separated by a space.

7.　Swap the names of clients to display the name as **Surname, First Name E.G.:** Shah, Sharanam.

11. TABLESPACES, DBA AND USER

TABLESPACES IN ORACLE 10g

Logical Structure Of A Database

An Oracle database comprises of a number of physical files called **data files**. These files are logically grouped together into an Oracle (logical) structure called a **Tablespace**.

Tablespaces

User data in an Oracle database is **logically** stored in tablespaces and **physically** stored in **data files**, which are bound to the corresponding tablespace.

Tablespaces are a mechanism or a means by which logical objects such as tables, indexes and views are mapped to a specific data file. Tablespaces are also used to group different types of (logical) database objects together.

A database administrator can use tablespaces to:

❑ Control hard disk or space allocation for database data
❑ Assign specific hard disk or space quotas for database users
❑ Control the availability of data by making individual tablespaces online or offline
❑ Perform partial database backup or recovery operations
❑ Allocate data storage across multiple devices to improve performance

Note

When any database is created, the Oracle engine creates a default tablespace named **System** within the database.

A database is made up of one or more tablespaces. Each tablespace is made up of one or more data files. The size of the tablespace can be determined as the sum of the sizes of all its data files. The sum of the size of all the tablespaces represents the storage capacity of the database.

The Oracle System Tablespace

When installing Oracle for the very first time **or** when creating a new database using the **CREATE DATABASE** statement a **System** tablespace is automatically created within the new database schema. The System tablespace contains the Oracle data dictionary, which holds definitions of all Oracle objects within the database.

If no other tablespace exists within the database, **user objects** (such as Tables, Views Indexes and so on) when created, will be stored in the **System** tablespace. This is because every user of an Oracle database must be bound to a tablespace so that there is a predefined place within which user objects can be stored.

Caution

When a user is created, in the absence of any other tablespace in the database, the user will be automatically bound to the System tablespace.

The storage of user objects in the **System** tablespace increases the likelihood of **space management problems,** which may destroy the tablespace and require it to be rebuilt.

Oracle **strongly recommends** that a separate tablespace be created within the database and users bound to this tablespace. This ensures that Oracle objects are kept completely isolated from user objects. A **separate tablespace** can be created (within the database) either using Oracle's GUI tools or SQL syntax.

Note

In **Oracle 7.1** and older versions, the SYSTEM tablespace could be altered or rebuilt only by recreating the Database.

This is the time, when user objects could be moved out of the SYSTEM tablespace into a separate tablespace created by the Oracle **DBA**.

Tablespace Usage

Software projects generally require a large number of tables to capture and hold user data. When these tables are placed within the System tablespace, free space can be consumed very rapidly by the growth of user tables and their associated data.

If the rapid growth of user tables and data consumes the free space within the System tablespace then the Oracle engine will not have space to save any of its vital database information to the System tablespace. This will cause the System tablespace to get corrupted. Once the System tablespace corrupts, the Oracle database cannot be mounted when invoked and is thus damaged.

To protect the Oracle database and prevent the corruption from happening Oracle Corp. strongly recommends that User tables and all other User objects are kept in another Tablespace and not within the System tablespace.

Most software development teams will have an Oracle **Data**Base **A**dministrator (DBA) as part of the team. This individual is responsible for the day-to-day, smooth running of the Oracle database. It is generally the responsibility of the Oracle DBA to create a separate tablespace within the database to hold user objects. It is very rare (definitely not recommended) that users are given permission to create their own tablespaces.

Note

In the absence of a DBA login it may be necessary to manually create one. It is imperative that such login ID's have a password to protect them and that the password is carefully preserved and changed regularly.

In the absence of a DBA login, the Sys or System logins can be used to create tablespaces. These logins are created by default when Oracle is being installed. Refer Diagram 2.4 of Chapter 2: Setting Up Oracle 10g Database.

The complete, detailed, SQL syntax for creating a tablespace along with examples follows.

The CREATE Command for TABLESPACES

All objects in Oracle database are stored in **tablespaces**, which is a unit of logical storage for an Oracle database. The **CREATE TABLESPACE** command allows creating a tablespace and one or more initial data files. It also allows specifying default storage parameters.

The **syntax for CREATE TABLESPACE** is a follows:

```
CREATE [TEMPORARY] TABLESPACE DATAFILE/TEMPFILE '<Path and Filename>'
    [AUTOEXTEND [OFF/ON NEXT <integer>[K/M]
            MAXSIZE [<integer>[K/M]/UNLIMITED] ] ]
```

```
[LOGGING/NOLOGGING] [TEMPORARY/PERMANENT] [OFFLINE/ONLINE]
DEFAULT STORAGE <storage_clause> [MINIMUM EXTENT <integer>[K/M]]
[EXTENT MANAGEMENT [DIRECTORY/LOCAL
    [AUTOALLOCATE/UNIFORM [SIZE <integer>[K/M] ] ] ] ]
[CHUNK <integer>] [NOCACHE]
```

The CREATE TABLESPACE command has the following keywords and parameters:

Attribute Name	Description		
TABLESPACE_NAME	Name of the tablespace to be created.		
DATAFILE	Specifies the data file or files used to compose the tablespace.		
MIMIMUM EXTENT	Integer clause that controls free-space fragmentation in the tablespace by ensuring that every used and/or free extent size in a tablespace is at least as large as the integer and is a multiple of a integer.		
AUTOEXTEND	Enables or disables the automatic extension of the data files:		
	Options	**Description**	
	OFF	Disables **AUTOEXTEND** if set to 'ON'. **NEXT** and **MAXSIZE** are set to zero. To re-enable the feature after **AUTOEXTEND** is disabled, specify the values again for **NEXT** and **MAXSIZE** via the **ALTER TABLESPACE AUTOEXTEND** commands.	
	ON	Enables **AUTOEXTEND**.	
	NEXT	Specifies disk space to allocate to the data file when more extents are required.	
	MAXSIZE	Specifies the maximum disk space allowed for allocation to the data file.	
	UNLIMITED	Allows the data file to have no limit on allocation of disk space	

Caution

Be careful with **AUTOEXTEND** on all versions of Oracle 8 and Oracle 8i, because in versions of Oracle up to 8.1.7.1, the maximum block allocation for Oracle is 4,194,303 Oracle blocks. This limit on the number of blocks leads to a hard limit on the maximum size of an Oracle data file, which can be **silently** exceeded by **AUTOEXTEND**, causing data dictionary corruption.

Attribute Name	Description
LOGGING/ NOLOGGING	Specifies the default logging attributes of all tables, indexes and partitions within the tablespace. **LOGGING** is the default. If **NOLOGGING** is specified, no undo and redo logs are generated for operations that support the **NOLOGGING** option on the tables, indexes and partitions within the tablespace. The tablespace-level, logging attribute can be overridden by logging specifications at the table, index and partition level.
DEFAULT STORAGE	Specifies the default storage parameters for all objects created in the tablespace.
ONLINE	Makes the tablespace available immediately after creation to users who have been granted access to the tablespace.
OFFLINE	Makes the tablespace unavailable immediately after creation.

Note

By default, the tablespace is set to **ONLINE** and **LOGGING**.

Attribute Name	Description
PERMANENT	Specifies that the tablespace will be used to hold permanent objects. This is default.
TEMPORARY	Specifies that the tablespace will be used only to hold temporary objects. For example, Segments used by implicit sorts to handle ORDER BY clause.
EXTENT MANAGEMENT	Can be either **DICTIONARY** (the default) or **LOCAL**. If **LOCAL** management is specified, a bitmap located in the tablespace itself is used to manage extends reducing the load on the **FET$** and **UET$** data dictionary extent management tables and recursive SQL. **LOCAL** managed extents can either be **AUTOALLOCATED** or **UNIFORM**. If **UNIFORM**, the **SIZE** for each extent in **K** or **M** can be specified.
CHUNK	Specifies a multiple of the database block size up to **32K**. Used for specifying **LOB** storage area.
NOCACHE	Specifies that the objects within the tablespace should not be cached.

Caution

The concept of the **CREATE TEMPORARY TABLESPACE** command was introduced in **Oracle 9i**. This differs for a **CREATE TABLESPACE ... TEMPORARY'** command. As the former uses a **TEMPFILE**, while the latter uses a **DATAFILE**.

The **CREATE TABLESPACE ... TEMPORARY** type tablespace **can be** altered to hold **PERMANENT** objects, whereas a **CREATE TEMPORARY TABLESPACE** type tablespace **cannot** be altered.

The STORAGE clause and its options are as follows:

```
... STORAGE( [INITIAL <integer>[K/M]] [NEXT <integer>[K/M]]
    [MINEXTENTS <integer>] [MAXEXTENTS <integer>/UNLIMITED]
    [PCTINCREASE <integer>]
    [FREELISTS <integer>] [FREELIST GROUPS <integer>]
    [OPTIMAL <integer>[K/M]/NULL ]
    [BUFFER_POOL '<pool_name>' [DEFAULT] / [KEEP/RECYCLE] ]
) ...
```

The STORAGE clause has the following parameters:

Attribute Name	Description
INITIAL	Size in bytes of the initial extent of the object segment. The default value is the size of **5 data blocks**. The minimum value is the size of **2 data blocks** for **non-bitmapped segments** or **3 data blocks** for **bitmapped segments**, plus **one data block** for each **free list group** specified. The maximum value depends on the operation system. Oracle rounds values up to the next multiple of the data block size for values less than 5 data blocks and it rounds up to the next multiple of 5 data blocks for values greater than 5 data blocks.
NEXT	Size for the next extent after **INITIAL** is used. The default is **5 blocks**, the minimum is **1 block** and the maximum is **4,095 MB**. This is the value that will be used for each new extent, if **PCTINCREASE** is set to '**0**'.

Attribute Name	Description
MINEXTENTS	Number of initial extents for the objects. Generally, except for rollback segments, it's set to '**1**'. If a large amount of space is required and if there's not enough contiguous space for the table sitting, using a smaller extent size and specifying several extents may solve the problem.
MAXEXTENTS	Largest number of extents allowed for object. This defaults to the maximum allowed for the block size, as of **version 7.3**. However, it is possible to set **MAXEXTENTS** to unlimited after **version 8**, allowing over **2 billion extents**. However, Oracle suggests **not** going over **4,000 extents** for a single object.
OPTIMAL	Used only for rollback segments. Specifies the value to which a rollback segment will shrink after extending.
FREELISTS GROUPS	Parameter that specifies the number of freelist groups to maintain for a table or index. This parameter is generally meaningful for only parallel server database and can't be specified unless a database is altered into parallel or share mode.
PCTINCREASE	Specifies how much to grow each extent after the **INITIAL** and **NEXT** extents are used. A specification of **50** will grow each extent after **NEXT** by **50%** for each subsequent extent. This means that for a table created with one **INITIAL** and a **NEXT** extent, any further extents will increase in size by **50%** over the predecessors. In **Oracle 7.2** and later versions, this parameter is applied only against the size of the previous extent. Increase this value if it is not known how much the table will grow, though significantly. The value of **PCTINCREASE** indicates a growth rate for subsequent extents. A tablespace with a default storage setting for **PCTINCREASE** of **0** will not be automatically coalesced by the SMON process.
FREELISTS	For objects other than tablespaces, specifies the number of freelists for each of the freelist groups for the table, index or cluster. The minimum value is **1** and the maximum is block-size dependent. Before **version 8.1.6**, this could not be reset without re-creating the table. In **8.1.6** and greater, it can be reset dynamically if the **COMPATIBLE** initialization parameter is set to **8.1.6** at a minimum.
BUFFER_POOL <pool_name>	Specifies the area of the buffer pool where the object will be cached. The **<pool_name>** parameter corresponds to: <table><tr><td>**DEFAULT**</td><td>The value assigned if no **BUFFER_POOL** parameter is specified</td></tr><tr><td>**KEEP**</td><td>For objects that should not be rapidly aged out of the buffer pool.</td></tr><tr><td>**RECYCLE**</td><td>For objects that should be rapidly aged out of the buffer pool.</td></tr></table> The **KEEP** and **RECYCLE** pools are sub-sections of the **DEFAULT** pools and must be configured in the initialization parameters **BUFFER_POOL_KEEP** and **BUFFER_POOL_RECYCLE** before being used.

Note

Once any tablespace is created it must be **Online** to be useable. The create tablespace syntax, by default, ensures that the Tablespace is placed online. Only when the tablespace is online can users bound to the tablespace use it for storing their objects.

Creating A Tablespace Using SQL *Plus

Start a session of **SQL Plus** by clicking on the **Start** button on the taskbar. Then select **All Programs** →
Oracle - OraDb10g_home1 → **Application Development** → **SQL Plus**. Refer to diagram 11.1.

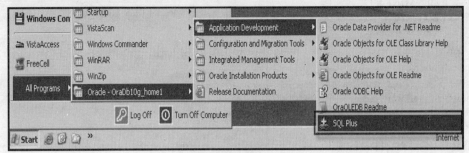

Diagram 11.1

Enter the **User Name** as **SYSTEM** and the **Password** as the one defined while Oracle 10g Database
Installation earlier in the fields appearing on the **Oracle Log On** dialog box. Refer to diagram 11.2. Click
on [OK] to connect to Oracle database server.

After a successful SQL Login the **Oracle SQL * Plus** window will be visible as shown in diagram 11.3.

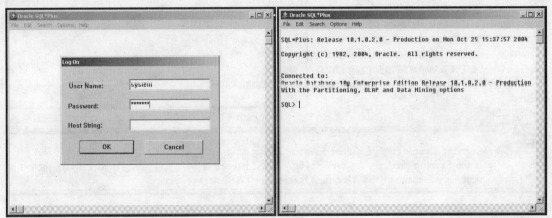

Diagram 11.2: Login dialog box for SQL *Plus.   **Diagram 11.3:** Successful Login of Oracle SQL *Plus.

Example:
To create a tablespace named **SCT_Admin** connected to data file **sct_admin.dat** with a size of **10 MB**.

CREATE TABLESPACE SCT_Admin
    DATAFILE 'sct_admin.dat' **SIZE** 10M **ONLINE;**

Create a tablespace named **SCT_Data**. The name of the data file is **SCT_Data.dat** and the size is **20 MB**.
The specification for the tablespace's storage parameters is as follows:
    INITIAL EXTENT SIZE 10k
    NEXT EXTENT SIZE 50k
    MINEXTENTS 1 **MAXEXTENTS** 999
    PCTINCREASE 10

Using SQL statement:
CREATE TABLESPACE SCT_DATA
   DATAFILE 'SCT_Data.dat' **SIZE** 20M
   DEFAULT STORAGE(INITIAL 10K
    NEXT 50K **MINEXTENTS** 1
    MAXEXTENTS 999
    PCTINCREASE 10
) ONLINE;

When the above SQL commands are typed into Oracle SQL *Plus window the results are as shown in diagram 11.4.

CREATING TABLESPACE THROUGH ENTERPRISE MANAGER

The **Oracle Enterprise Manager 10g**, the HTML based utility, has been designed to assist Oracle DBA's in managing the Oracle 10g database. It is user-friendly due to its GUI and multiple features.

One of it's many features is its ability to create tablespaces. This reduces the need to remember the actual syntax to create a tablespace. This part of the material will deal with the creation of a tablespace through this tool available in **Oracle 10g - Enterprise Edition**.

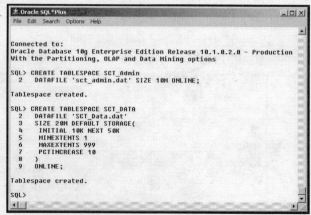

Diagram 11.4: Output of Tablespace created.

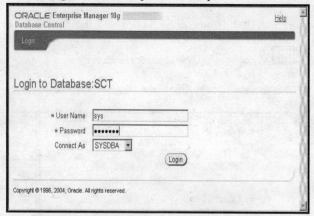

Diagram 11.5: Oracle Enterprise Manager Login.

Starting Oracle 10g's Listener Service
If the **Startup** property for **Oracle10g - TNSListener** service has been set to manual, then it is necessary to manually **START** the **Oracle10g - TNSListener** service.

Creating A Tablespace

Open the **Oracle Enterprise Manager 10g** by pointing the default Web Browser to:
http://<IP_ADDRESS>:5500/em/

This will open a page as shown in diagram 11.5.

Login using **SYS** as the **User Name**, provide the **Password** specified earlier and select **SYSDBA** in the **Connect As** dropdown List-box, screens as seen in diagram 11.6.1 (if invoked for the first time) and diagram 11.6.2 appears. In the first screen: The Oracle 10g Licensing Information (i.e. diagram 11.6.1) click **I Agree**.

When the **Oracle Enterprise Manager 10g – Database: <SID> – Home** page appears click on the **Administration** link. Refer to diagram 11.6.2.

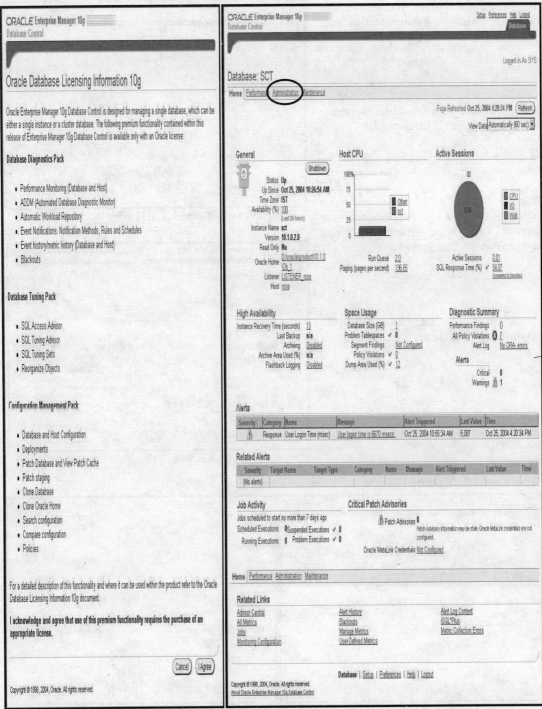

Diagram 11.6.1: Oracle Enterprise Manager Licensing Information

Diagram 11.6.2: Oracle Enterprise Manager

The **Oracle Enterprise Manager 10g –
Database: <SID> – Administration** page
appears as shown in diagram 11.7.

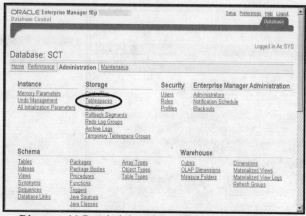

Click the **Tablespaces** link under **Storage** to
get a page as shown in diagram 11.8.

Click the (Create) option to get the **Create
Tablespace** page (General tab) as shown in
diagram 11.9.1. Enter a **Name** for the new
tablespace in the field provided.

Diagram 11.7: Administration tab for Oracle Enterprise
Manager 10g.

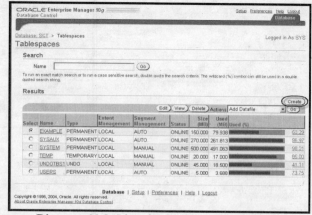

As shown in diagram 11.9.2, scroll to
Datafiles section and click (Add).

Diagram 11.8: List of Tablespace under Oracle.

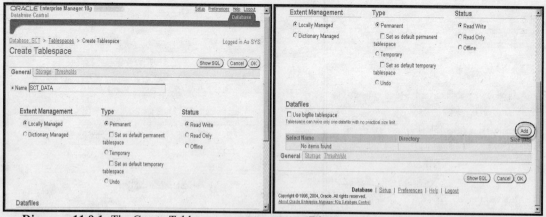

Diagram 11.9.1: The Create Tablespace page   **Diagram 11.9.2:** The Datafiles section

The **Create Tablespace: Add Datafile** page appears as shown in diagram 11.10.1. Fill in the details such as the filename, path and size of a datafile.

The default values for a datafile, set in this page are:

File Name	- -
File Directory	<Oracle Home>\ **ORADATA**\<SID>
Size	**100 MB**

Diagram 11.10.1: The Create Tablespace: Add Datafile

Enter appropriate values in File Name, File Directory and File Size. This will be passed as values to parameters required by the **CREATE TABLESPACE** command executed while creating a tablespace. Refer diagram 11.10.2.

In the **Storage** section, select the option that activates the datafile's **AUTOEXTEND** parameter. Specify the values for the fields **Increment** and **Maximum File Size**. Refer diagram 11.10.2.

Having entered the above information click (Continue) to return to the **Create Tablespace** page. (Refer diagram 11.11)

Diagram 11.10.2: The Create Tablespace: Add Datafile

The **Datafiles** section will now display details of the datafile just created. Refer diagram 11.11.

Note

Multiple **Datafiles** can be added to a tablespace by clicking (Add) in the **Datafiles** section. On being clicked, the **Create Tablespace: Add Datafile** page will reappear with default values.

Diagram 11.11: The Create Tablespace dialog box

In the Create Tablespace page click the Storage tab to get page as shown in diagram 11.12.

This tab accepts values for the following attributes:

❑ Extent Allocation

❑ Segment Space Management

❑ Enable Logging

It also provides the Block Size of the tablespace.

Clicking the Threshold tab will display a page as shown in diagram 11.13.

The options available on these two tabs can be kept at their default values.

Finally, click OK to create the tablespace and return to the **Tablespaces** page. Refer to diagram 11.14.

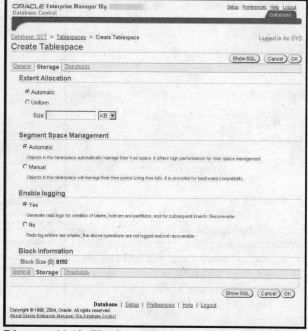

Diagram 11.12: The Create Tablespace's Storage tab page.

At the beginning of the page a message indicates that the new tablespace was created successfully.

Additionally, the new tablespace will be listed with the ones already existing within the database.

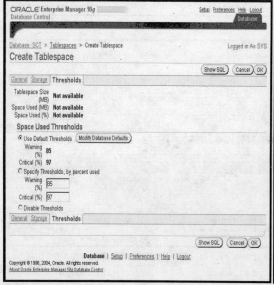

Diagram 11.13: The Create Tablespace's Threshold tab page.

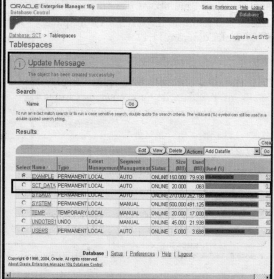

Diagram 11.14: The details of the Tablespace created.

CREATING A DBA LOGIN ID

If a DBA login ID does not exist then it has to be created manually. The following steps indicate how a DBA login ID is created and appropriate privileges given to the DBA login ID with a special focus on creating tablespaces.

Note

Starting Oracle 10g's Listener Service
If the **Startup** property for **Oracle10g - TNSListener** service has been set to manual, then it is necessary to manually START the **Oracle10g - TNSListener** service.

Creating A DBA Login ID

Open the **Oracle Enterprise Manager 10g** by pointing the default Web Browser to: **http://<IP_ADDRESS>:5500/em/**

This will open a page as shown in diagram 11.5.

Login using **SYS** as the **User Name**, provide the **Password** specified earlier and select **SYSDBA** in the **Connect As** dropdown List box, screens as seen in diagram 11.5 (if invoked for the first time) and diagram 11.6.1 and 11.6.2 appears. In the first screen: The Oracle 10g Licensing Information (i.e. diagram 11.6.1) click **I Agree**.

When the **Oracle Enterprise Manager 10g – Database: <SID> – Home** page appears click on the **Administration** link. Refer diagram 11.6.2.

The **Oracle Enterprise Manager 10g – Database: <SID> – Administration** page appears as shown in diagram 11.15.

Click the **Users** link under **Security** to get a page as shown in diagram 11.16.

Click on ⟨Create⟩ option to get the **Create User** page (General tab) as shown in diagram 11.17.

Enter **DBA_BANKSYS** as the value of the **Name** field.

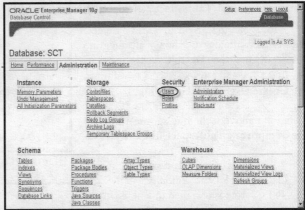
Diagram 11.15: The User link on the Administration tab for Oracle Enterprise Manager 10g.

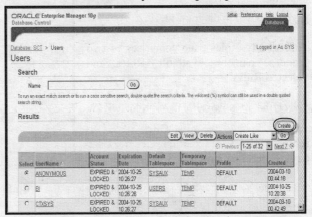
Diagram 11.16: List of existing Oracle users.

Diagram 11.17: The Create User page.

Make appropriate entries for the **Enter Password** and the **Confirm Password** fields.

For the **Default Tablespaces** field, click to get the **Search and Select: Tablespace** dialog as shown in diagram 11.18. Select the Default Tablespace as **SCT_DATA** and click Select to return to the **Create User** page (General tab).

Using the above technique set the value for the **Temporary Tablespace** to **TEMP**.

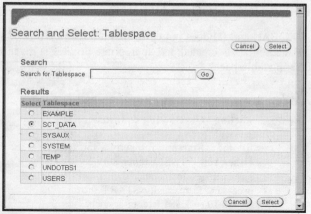

Diagram 11.18: The Search and Select: Tablespace page.

Click the **Roles** tab to get a page as shown in diagram 11.19.1. Initially, only the CONNECT role is assigned to a new Oracle user.

For additional roles click Modify to get a page as shown in diagram 11.19.2.

The **Modify Roles** page comprises of two sections, namely **Available Roles** and **Selected Roles**.

Select the role named **DBA** and click on Move to add the role. Click OK to return to the **Roles** tab for **Create User** page. Refer diagram 11.19.3.

Diagram 11.19.1: The Roles tab for Create User page.

When the new list of Roles comes up, select the **Admin Option** checkbox for **DBA**. Refer diagram 11.19.3.

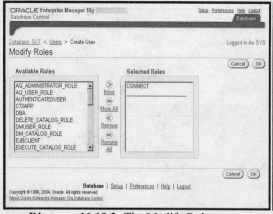

Diagram 11.19.2: The Modify Roles page.

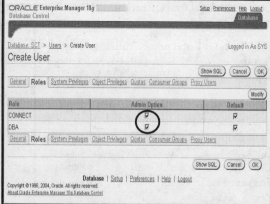

Diagram 11.19.3: New list of Roles.

Click (OK) to create the User with DBA rights and return to the **Users** page. Refer to diagram 11.20.1.

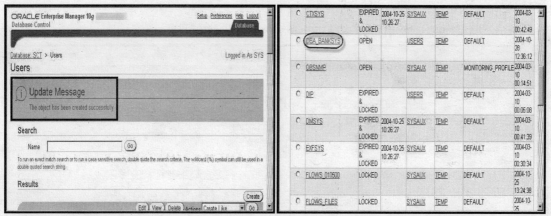

Diagram 11.20.1: Message for new Oracle User.   **Diagram 11.20.2:** The new list for Oracle Users.

At the beginning of the page a message indicates that the new user was created successfully.

Additionally, the new user will be listed with the ones already existing within the database as shown in diagram 11.20.2.

CREATING A USER

The Database Administrator (DBA) can, use the **Enterprise Manager Console** utility to create new users who will use Oracle 10g resources. Users created by the DBA will have limited privileges, being restricted to creating and managing tables or views within a single tablespace.

The technique of creating a **User**, under Oracle 10g, is similar to creating the DBA. The difference is in the set of privileges assigned to a user.

Note

Starting Oracle 10g's Listener Service
If the **Startup** property for **Oracle10g - TNSListener** service has been set to manual, then it is necessary to manually START the **Oracle10g - TNSListener** service.

Creating A User For Oracle 10g

Open the **Oracle Enterprise Manager 10g** by pointing the default Web Browser to:
http://<IP_ADDRESS>:5500/em/

This will open a page as shown in diagram 11.5.

Login using **SYS** as the **User Name**, provide the **Password** specified earlier and select **SYSDBA** in the **Connect As** dropdown List-box, screens as seen in diagram 11.5 (if invoked for the first time) and diagram 11.6.1 and 11.6.2 appears. In the first screen: The Oracle 10g Licensing Information (i.e. diagram 11.6.1) click **I Agree**.

When the **Oracle Enterprise Manager 10g – Database: <SID> – Home** page appears click on the **Administration** link. Refer to diagram 11.6.2.

The **Oracle Enterprise Manager 10g – Database: <SID> – Administration** page appears as shown in diagram 11.21.

Click the **Users** link under **Security** to get a page as shown in diagram 11.22.

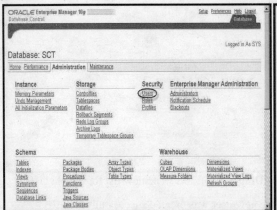

Diagram 11.21: The User link on the Administration tab for Oracle Enterprise Manager 10g.

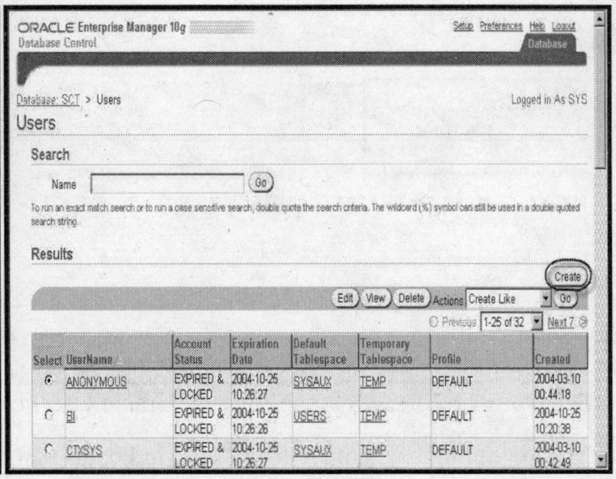

Diagram 11.22: List of existing Oracle users.

Click on Create option to get the **Create User** page (General tab) as shown in diagram 11.23.

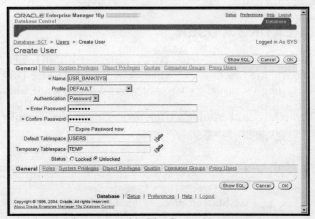

Enter an appropriate user name as the value of the **Name** field. Refer diagram 11.23.

Make appropriate entries for the **Enter Password** and the **Confirm Password** fields. Refer diagram 11.23.

Diagram 11.23: The Create User page.

For the **Default Tablespaces** field, click to get the **Search and Select: Tablespace** dialog as shown in diagram 11.24. Select the Default Tablespace as **SCT_DATA** and click Select to return to the **Create User** page (General tab). Refer diagram 11.23.

Using the above technique set the value for the **Temporary Tablespace** to **TEMP**. Refer diagram 11.23.

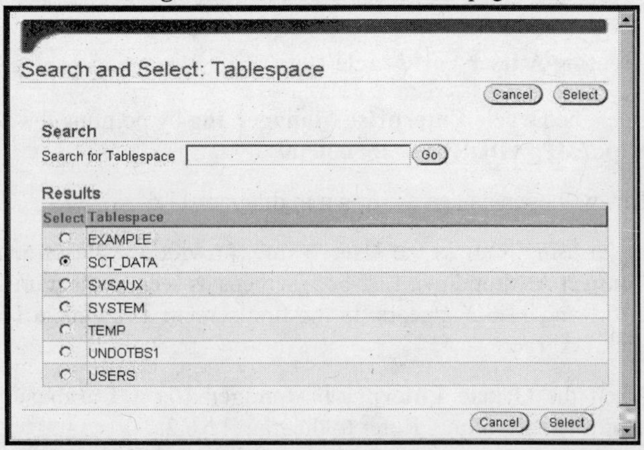

Diagram 11.24: The Search and Select: Tablespace page.

Click the **Roles** tab to get a page as shown in diagram 11.25. Initially, only the CONNECT role is assigned to a new Oracle user. Select the **Admin Option** checkbox for **CONNECT**.

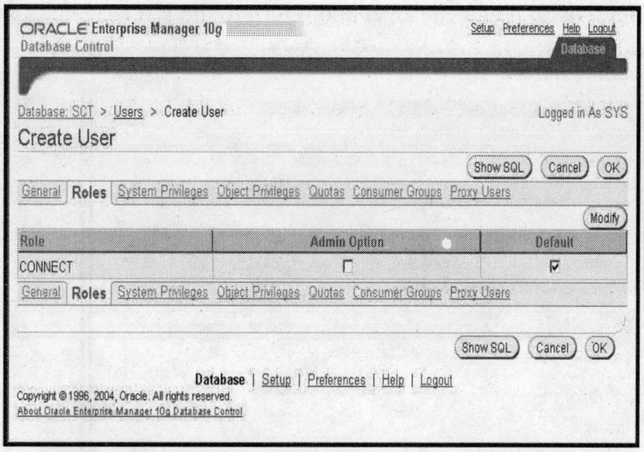

Click the **System Privileges** tab to get a page as shown in diagram 11.26.1. Initially, no privileges are assigned to a new Oracle user.

To add privileges, click ⬭Modify⬭ to get a page as shown in diagram 11.26.2.

Diagram 11.25: The Roles tab for Create User page.

Diagram 11.26.1: The System Privileges tab for Create User page.

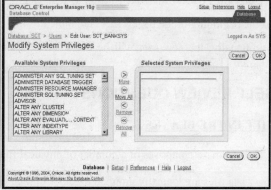

Diagram 11.26.2: The Modify System Privileges page.

Select the desired privileges from the list of **Available System Privileges** and click ⬭Move⬭ to add them.

Include privileges required by a user to performing basic SQL operations like**:**
❑ Creating, modifying and deleting tables or views
❑ Inserting, modifying and deleting data within self created tables
❑ Commit or Rollback SQL operations

Click ⬭OK⬭ to return to the **System Privileges** tab for **Create User** page. Refer diagram 11.26.3.

The new list of System Privileges comes up as shown in diagram 11.26.3.

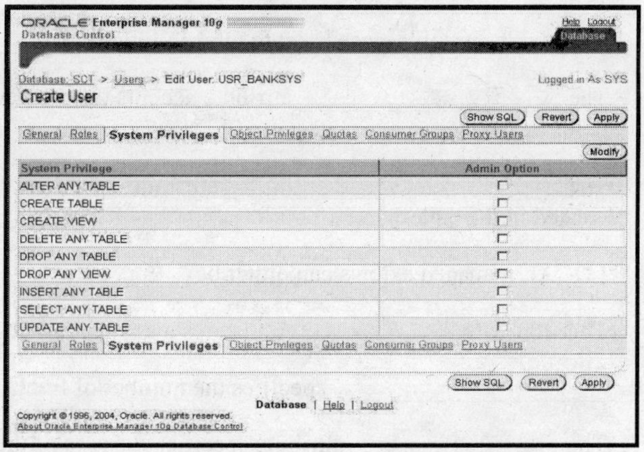

Diagram 11.26.3: New list of System Privileges.

Click **OK** to create the User and return to the **Users** page. Refer to diagram 11.27.1.

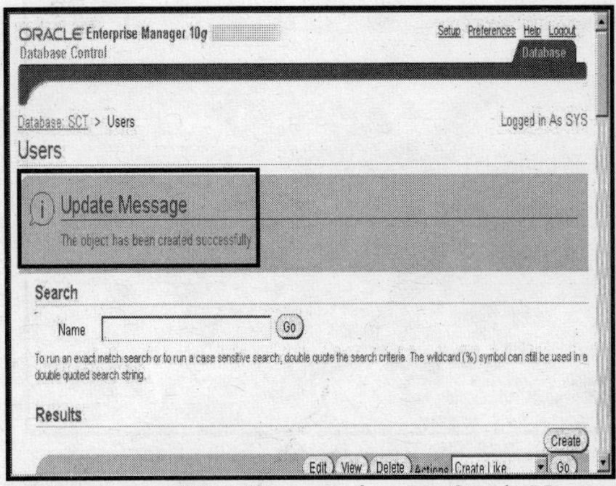

Diagram 11.27.1: Message for new Oracle User. 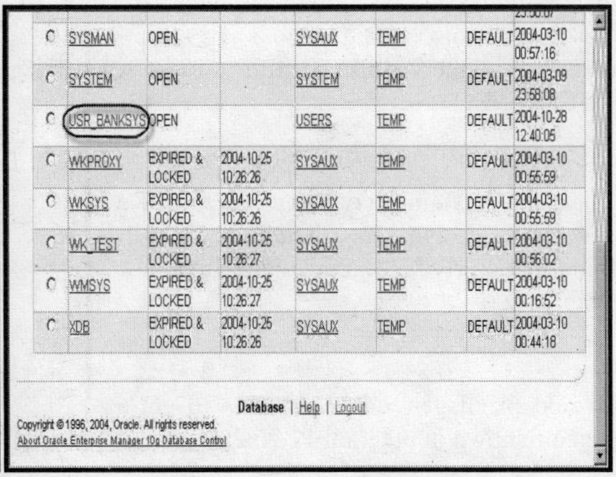   **Diagram 11.27.2:** The new list for Oracle Users.

At the beginning of the page a message indicates that the new user was created successfully.

Additionally, the new user will be listed with the ones already existing within the database as shown in diagram 11.27.2.

SELF REVIEW QUESTIONS

FILL IN THE BLANKS

1. A database comprises of a number of physical files called _____ _____.

2. Data files are logically grouped together into an Oracle (logical) structure called a _____.

3. The size of the tablespace can be determined as the _____ of the sizes of all its data files.

4. When any database is created, the Oracle engine creates a default tablespace named _____ within the database.

5. By default, the tablespace is set to ONLINE and _____.

6. The _____ attribute accepts the integer clause that controls free-space fragmentation in the tablespace.

7. The _____ _____ attribute specifies the default storage parameters for all objects created in the tablespace.

8. LOCAL managed extents can either be _____ or _____.

9. The value of _____ indicates a growth rate for subsequent extents.

10. _____ specifies the number of freelist groups to maintain for a table or index.

11. The _____ attribute specifies the area of the buffer pool where the object will be cached.

TRUE OR FALSE

12. User data in an Oracle database is logically stored in data files.

13. A database is made up of one or more tablespaces.

14. User objects when created are stored in the System tablespace.

15. All objects in Oracle database are stored in tables, which is a unit of logical storage for an Oracle database.

16. The AUTOEXTEND attribute enables or disables the automatic extension of the data files.

17. The OFFLINE attribute makes the tablespace available immediately after creation to users who have been granted access to the tablespace.

18. The TEMPORARY attribute specifies that the tablespace will be used only to hold temporary objects.

19. The NOCACHE attribute is used for specifying LOB storage area.

20. The OPTIMAL attribute specifies the value to which a rollback segment will shrink after extending.

21. FREELISTS specifies the number of freelists for each of the freelist groups for the table, index or cluster including tablespaces.

22. Multiple Datafiles can be added to the table by typing the filename in the blank row provided within the table.

HANDS ON EXERCISES

1. Using the SQL*PLUS tool, create a tablespace named **SCT_INVT**. The name of the data file will be **SCT_Invt.dat** and the size will be **25 MB**. The specification for the tablespace's storage parameters is as follows:
   INITIAL EXTENT SIZE 10k **NEXT EXTENT SIZE** 50k
   MINEXTENTS 1 **MAXEXTENTS** 499 **PCTINCREASE** 10

2. Using the SQL*PLUS tool, create a user bound to the **SCT_INVT** tablespace. The name of the Oracle user will be **DBA_INVTSYS** and will have a password of choice.

3. Using the SQL*PLUS tool, convert the user named **DBA_INVTSYS** into a super admin (Oracle DBA) for the SCT_INVT tablespace.

ANSWERS TO SELF REVIEW QUESTIONS

5. INTERACTIVE SQL PART - I

FILL IN THE BLANKS

1. table
2. Create Table
3. single
4. Where Clause
5. SELECT DISTINCT
6. Target, Source
7. ALTER TABLE
8. UPDATE
9. single record
10. Constraints
11. NULLABLE
12. mandatory
13. NOT NULL
14. NULL
15. Simple
16. UNIQUE
17. Foreign
18. Detail
19. ON DELETE CASCADE
20. CHECK
21. Boolean
22. Integrity
23. indexes

TRUE OR FALSE

24. False
25. False
26. True
27. False
28. True
29. False
30. True
31. True
32. False
33. True
34. True
35. False
36. False
37. True
38. False
39. True
40. False
41. True
42. True
43. False
44. True
45. False
46. True
47. True

6. INTERACTIVE SQL PART - II

FILL IN THE BLANKS

1. OR
2. LIKE
3. percent
4. Dual
5. Group Functions
6. arguments
7. INITCAP
8. LTRIM
9. RPAD
10. TO_NUMBER
11. TO_CHAR (date conversion)
12. MONTHS_BETWEEN
13. Uid
14. GROUP BY
15. HAVING

TRUE OR FALSE

21. True
22. False
23. False
24. True
25. False
26. True
27. True
28. False
29. True
30. False
31. True
32. False
33. True
34. False
35. True

FILL IN THE BLANKS		**TRUE OR FALSE**	
16.	subquery	36.	True
17.	nested	37.	False
18.	Equi Joins	38.	True
19.	Union	39.	False
20.	intersect	40.	True
		41.	False
		42.	False
		43.	True
		44.	False

10. USING REGULAR EXPRESSIONS

FILL IN THE BLANKS		**TRUE OR FALSE**	
1.	find/replace	5.	False
2.	POSIX	6.	False
3.	SQL, PL/SQL	7.	False
4.	REGEXP_LIKE	8.	True

11. TABLESPACES, DBA AND USER

FILL IN THE BLANKS		**TRUE OR FALSE**	
1.	data files	12.	False
2.	Tablespace	13.	True
3.	sum	14.	True
4.	System	15.	False
5.	LOGGING	16.	True
6.	MIMIMUM EXTENT	17.	False
7.	DEFAULT STORAGE	18.	True
8.	AUTOALLOCATED or UNIFORM	19.	False
9.	PCTINCREASE	20.	True
10.	FREELISTS GROUPS	21.	False
11.	BUFFER_POOL	22.	True

SOLUTIONS TO HANDS ON EXERCISES

5. INTERACTIVE SQL PART - I

1. **SQL Statement for creating the tables:**

a) **Table Name:** CLIENT_MASTER
   CREATE TABLE CLIENT_MASTER(CLIENTNO varchar2(6) PRIMARY KEY,
       NAME varchar2(20) NOT NULL, ADDRESS1 varchar2(30), ADDRESS2 varchar2(30),
       CITY varchar2(15), PINCODE number(8), STATE varchar2(15), BALDUE number(10,2),
       CONSTRAINT ck_client CHECK (CLIENTNO like 'C%'));

b) **Table Name:** PRODUCT_MASTER
   CREATE TABLE PRODUCT_MASTER(PRODUCTNO varchar2(6) PRIMARY KEY,
       DESCRIPTION varchar2(15) NOT NULL, PROFITPERCENT number(4,2) NOT NULL,
       UNITMEASURE varchar2(10) NOT NULL, QTYONHAND number(8) NOT NULL,
       REORDERLVL number(8) NOT NULL, SELLPRICE number(8,2) NOT NULL,
       COSTPRICE number(8,2) NOT NULL,
       CONSTRAINT ck_product CHECK (PRODUCTNO like 'P%'),
       CONSTRAINT ck_sell CHECK (SELLPRICE <> 0),
       CONSTRAINT ck_cost CHECK (COSTPRICE <> 0));

c) **Table Name:** SALESMAN_MASTER
   CREATE TABLE SALESMAN_MASTER(SALESMANNO varchar2(6) PRIMARY KEY,
       SALESMANNAME varchar2(20) NOT NULL, ADDRESS1 varchar2(30) NOT NULL,
       Address2 varchar2(30), CITY varchar2(20), PINCODE number(8), State varchar2(20),
       SALAMT number(8,2) NOT NULL, TGTTOGET number(6,2) NOT NULL,
       YTDSALES number(6,2) NOT NULL, REMARKS varchar2(60),
       CONSTRAINT ck_salesman CHECK (SALESMANNO like 'S%'),
       CONSTRAINT ck_sal CHECK (SALAMT <> 0),
       CONSTRAINT ck_target CHECK (TGTTOGET <> 0));

d) **Table Name:** SALES_ORDER
   CREATE TABLE SALES_ORDER(ORDERNO varchar2(6) PRIMARY KEY,
     CLIENTNO varchar2(6) REFERENCES CLIENT_MASTER, ORDERDATE date,
     DELYADDR varchar2(25), SALESMANNO varchar2(6) REFERENCES SALESMAN_MASTER,
     DELYTYPE char(1) DEFAULT 'F', BILLEDYN char(1), DELYDATE date,
     ORDERSTATUS varchar2(10), CONSTRAINT ck_order CHECK (ORDERNO like 'O%'),
     CONSTRAINT ck_dely_type CHECK (DELYTYPE IN ('P', 'F')),
     CONSTRAINT ck_ord_status
        CHECK(ORDERSTATUS IN ('In Process', 'Fulfilled', 'Backorder', 'Cancelled')));

e) **Table Name:** SALES_ORDER_DETAILS
   CREATE TABLE SALES_ORDER_DETAILS(
       ORDERNO varchar2(6) REFERENCES SALES_ORDER,
       PRODUCTNO varchar2(6) REFERENCES PRODUCT_MASTER,
       QTYORDERED number(8), QTYDISP number(8), PRODUCTRATE number(10,2),
       PRIMARY KEY (ORDERNO, PRODUCTNO));

2. **SQL Statement for inserting into their respective tables:**

a) Data for **CLIENT_MASTER** table:
INSERT INTO Client_Master (ClientNo, Name, City, PinCode, State, BalDue)
    VALUES ('C00001', 'Ivan Bayross', 'Mumbai', 400054, 'Maharashtra', 15000);
INSERT INTO Client_Master (ClientNo, Name, City, PinCode, State, BalDue)
    VALUES ('C00002', 'Mamta Muzumdar', 'Madras'', 780001, 'Tamil Nadu', 0);
INSERT INTO Client_Master (ClientNo, Name, City, Pincode, State, BalDue)
    VALUES ('C00003', 'Chhaya Bankar', 'Mumbai', 400057, 'Maharashtra', 5000);
INSERT INTO Client_Master (ClientNo, Name, City, PinCode, State, BalDue)
    VALUES ('C00004', 'Ashwini Joshi', 'Bangalore', 560001, 'Karnataka', 0);
INSERT INTO Client_Master (ClientNo, Name, City, PinCode, State, BalDue)
    VALUES ('C00005', 'Hansel Colaco', 'Mumbai', 400060, 'Maharashtra', 2000);
INSERT INTO Client_Master (ClientNo, Name, City, PinCode, State, BalDue)
    VALUES ('C00006', 'Deepak Sharma', 'Mangalore', 560050, 'Karnataka', 0);

b) Data for **PRODUCT_MASTER** table
INSERT INTO Product_Master VALUES ('P00001', 'T-Shirts', 5, 'Piece', 200, 50, 350, 250);
INSERT INTO Product_Master VALUES ('P03453', 'Shirts', 6, 'Piece', 150, 50, 500, 350);
INSERT INTO Product_Master VALUES ('P06734', 'Cotton Jeans', 5, 'Piece', 100, 20, 600, 450);
INSERT INTO Product_Master VALUES ('P07865', 'Jeans', 5, 'Piece', 100, 20, 750, 500);
INSERT INTO Product_Master VALUES ('P07868', 'Trousers', 2, 'Piece', 150, 50, 850, 550);
INSERT INTO Product_Master VALUES ('P07885', 'Pull Overs', 2.5, 'Piece', 80, 30, 700, 450);
INSERT INTO Product_Master VALUES ('P07965', 'Denim Shirts', 4, 'Piece', 100, 40, 350, 250);
INSERT INTO Product_Master VALUES ('P07975', 'Lycra Tops', 5, 'Piece', 70, 30, 300, 175);
INSERT INTO Product_Master VALUES ('P08865', 'Skirts', 5, 'Piece', 75, 30, 450, 300);

c) Data for **SALESMAN_MASTER** table
INSERT INTO Salesman_Master VALUES ('S00001', 'Aman', 'A/14', 'Worli', 'Mumbai', 400002,
                          'Maharashtra', 3000, 100, 50, 'Good');
INSERT INTO Salesman_Master VALUES ('S00002', 'Omkar', '65', 'Nariman', 'Mumbai', 400001,
                          'Maharashtra', 3000, 200, 100, 'Good');
INSERT INTO Salesman_Master VALUES ('S00003', 'Raj', 'P-7', 'Bandra', 'Mumbai', 400032,
                          'Maharashtra', 3000, 200, 100, 'Good');
INSERT INTO Salesman_Master VALUES ('S00004', 'Ashish', 'A/5', 'Juhu', 'Bombay', 400044,
                          'Maharashtra', 3500, 200, 150, 'Good');

d) Data for **SALES_ORDER** table
INSERT INTO Sales_Order (OrderNo, OrderDate, ClientNo, DelyType, BilledYn, SalesmanNo, DelyDate,
    OrderStatus) VALUES('O19001', '12-june-02', 'C00001', 'F', ' N', 'S00001', '20-july-02', 'In Process');
INSERT INTO Sales_Order (OrderNo, OrderDate, ClientNo, DelyType, BilledYn, SalesmanNo, DelyDate,
    OrderStatus) VALUES('O19002', '25-june-02', 'C00002', 'P', ' N', 'S00002', '27-july-02', 'Cancelled');
INSERT INTO Sales_Order (OrderNo, OrderDate, ClientNo, DelyType, BilledYn, SalesmanNo, DelyDate,
    OrderStatus) VALUES('O19003', '18-feb-02', 'C00003', 'F', ' Y', 'S00003', '20-feb-02', 'Fulfilled');
INSERT INTO Sales_Order (OrderNo, OrderDate, ClientNo, DelyType, BilledYn, SalesmanNo, DelyDate,
    OrderStatus) VALUES('O19003', '03-apr-02', 'C00001', 'F', 'Y', 'S00001', '07-apr-02', 'Fulfilled');
INSERT INTO Sales_Order (OrderNo, OrderDate, ClientNo, DelyType, BilledYn, SalesmanNo, DelyDate,
    OrderStatus) VALUES('O46866', '20-may-02', 'C00004', 'P', 'N', 'S00002', '22-may-02', 'Cancelled');
INSERT INTO Sales_Order (OrderNo, OrderDate, ClientNo, DelyType, BilledYn, SalesmanNo, DelyDate,
    OrderStatus) VALUES('O19008', '24-may-02', 'C00005', 'F', 'N', 'S00004', '26-july-96', 'In Process');

e)   Data for **SALES_ORDER_DETAILS** table
INSERT INTO Sales_Order_Details (OrderNo, ProductNo, QtyOrdered, QtyDisp, ProductRate)
       VALUES('O19001', 'P00001', 4, 4, 525);
INSERT INTO Sales_Order_Details (OrderNo, ProductNo, QtyOrdered, QtyDisp, ProductRate)
       VALUES('O19001', 'P07965', 2, 1, 8400);
INSERT INTO Sales_Order_Details (OrderNo, ProductNo, QtyOrdered, QtyDisp, ProductRate)
       VALUES('O19001', 'P07885', 2, 1, 5250);
INSERT INTO Sales_Order_Details (OrderNo, ProductNo, QtyOrdered, QtyDisp, ProductRate)
       VALUES('O19002', 'P00001', 10, 0, 525);
INSERT INTO Sales_Order_Details (OrderNo, ProductNo, QtyOrdered, QtyDisp, ProductRate)
       VALUES('O46865', 'P07868', 3, 3, 3150);
INSERT INTO Sales_Order_Details (OrderNo, ProductNo, QtyOrdered, QtyDisp, ProductRate)
       VALUES('O46865', 'P07885', 3, 1, 5250);
INSERT INTO Sales_Order_Details (OrderNo, ProductNo, QtyOrdered, QtyDisp, ProductRate)
       VALUES('O46865', 'P00001', 10, 10, 525);
INSERT INTO Sales_Order_Details (OrderNo, ProductNo, QtyOrdered, QtyDisp, ProductRate)
       VALUES('O46865', 'P03453', 4, 4, 1050);
INSERT INTO Sales_Order_Details (OrderNo, ProductNo, QtyOrdered, QtyDisp, ProductRate)
       VALUES('O19003', 'P03453', 2, 2, 1050);
INSERT INTO Sales_Order_Details (OrderNo, ProductNo, QtyOrdered, QtyDisp, ProductRate)
       VALUES('O19003', 'P06734', 1, 1, 12000);
INSERT INTO Sales_Order_Details (OrderNo, ProductNo, QtyOrdered, QtyDisp, ProductRate)
       VALUES('O46866', 'P07965', 1, 0, 8400);
INSERT INTO Sales_Order_Details (OrderNo, ProductNo, QtyOrdered, QtyDisp, ProductRate)
       VALUES('O46866', 'P07975', 1, 0, 1050);
INSERT INTO Sales_Order_Details (OrderNo, ProductNo, QtyOrdered, QtyDisp, ProductRate)
       VALUES('O19008', 'P00001', 10, 5, 525);
INSERT INTO Sales_Order_Details (OrderNo, ProductNo, QtyOrdered, QtyDisp, ProductRate)
       VALUES('O19008', 'P07975', 5, 3, 1050);

3.   **SQL Statement for retrieving records from a table:**

a)   Find out the names of all the clients.
     SELECT Name FROM Client_Master;
b)   Retrieve the entire contents of the Client_Master table.
     SELECT * FROM Client_Master;
c)   Retrieve the list of names, city and the sate of all the clients.
     SELECT Name, City, State FROM Client_Master;
d)   List the various products available from the Product_Master table.
     SELECT Description FROM Product_Master;
e)   List all the clients who are located in Mumbai.
     SELECT * FROM Client_Master WHERE City = 'Mumbai';
f)   Find the names of salesmen who have a salary equal to Rs.3000.
     SELECT Salesman_name FROM Salesman_Master WHERE SalAmt = 3000;

4.   **SQL Statement for updating records in a table:**

a)   Change the city of ClientNo 'C00005' to 'Bangalore'.
     UPDATE Client_Master SET City = 'Bangalore' WHERE ClientNo = 'C00005';
b)   Change the BalDue of ClientNo 'C00001' to Rs. 1000.
     UPDATE Client_Master SET BalDue = 1000 WHERE Client_no = 'C00001';

c) Change the cost price of 'Trousers' to Rs. 950.00.
UPDATE Product_Master SET CostPrice = 950.00 WHERE Description = 'Trousers';

d) Change the city of the salesman to Pune.
UPDATE Client_Master SET City = 'Pune';

5. SQL Statement for deleting records in a table:

a) Delete all salesmen from the Salesman_Master whose salaries are equal to Rs. 3500.
DELETE FROM Salesman_Master WHERE SalAmt = 3500;

b) Delete all products from Product_Master where the quantity on hand is equal to 100.
DELETE FROM Product_Master WHERE QtyOnHand = 100;

c) Delete from Client_Master where the column state holds the value 'Tamil Nadu'.
DELETE FROM Client_Master WHERE State = 'Tamil Nadu';

6. SQL Statement for altering the table structure:

a) Add a column called 'Telephone' of data type 'number' and size ='10' to the Client_Master table.
ALTER TABLE Client_Master ADD (Telephone number(10));

b) Change the size of SellPrice column in Product_Master to 10,2.
ALTER TABLE Product_Master MODIFY (SellPrice number(10,2));

7. SQL Statement for deleting the table structure along with the data:

a) Destroy the table Client_Master along with its data.
DROP TABLE Client_Master;

8. SQL Statement for renaming the table:

a) Change the name of the Salesman_Master table to sman_mast.
RENAME Salesman_Master TO sman_mast;

6. INTERACTIVE SQL PART - II

1. Generate SQL Statements to perform the following computations on table data:

a. Listing of the names of all clients having 'a' as the second letter in their names.
SELECT Name FROM Client_Master WHERE Name like '_a%';

b. Listing of clients who stay in a city whose first letter is 'M'.
SELECT ClientNo, Name FROM Client_Master WHERE City LIKE 'M%';

c. List all clients who stay in 'Bangalore' or 'Mangalore'
SELECT ClientNo, Name FROM Client_Master WHERE City IN('Bangalore', 'Mangalore');

d. List all clients whose BalDue is greater than value 10000.
SELECT ClientNo, Name FROM Client_Master WHERE Baldue > 10000;

e. Print the information from Sales_Order table for orders placed in the month of June.
SELECT * FROM Sales_Order WHERE TO_CHAR(OrderDate,'MON') = 'JUN';

f. Displaying the order information of ClientNo 'C00001' and 'C00002'.
SELECT * FROM Sales_Order WHERE ClientNo IN('C00001', 'C00002');

g. List products whose selling price is greater than 500 and less than or equal to 750.
SELECT ProductNo, Description FROM Product_Master
    WHERE SellPrice > 500 AND SellPrice < 750;

h. Listing of products whose selling price is more than 500 with the new selling price calculated as original selling price plus 15%.
   SELECT ProductNo, Description, SellPrice, SellPrice*15 new_price FROM Product_Master
       WHERE SellPrice > 500;

i. Listing of names, city and state of clients who are not in the state of 'Maharashtra'.
   SELECT Name, City, State FROM Client_Master WHERE State NOT IN('Maharashtra');

j. Count the total number of orders.
   SELECT COUNT(OrderNo) 'No. Of Order' FROM Sales_Order;

k. Calculating the average price of all the products.
   SELECT AVG(SellPrice) FROM Product_Master;

l. Determining the maximum and minimum price for the product prices.
   SELECT MAX(SellPrice) max_price, MIN(SellPrice) min_price FROM Product_Master;

m. Count the number of products having price greater than or equal to 500.
   SELECT COUNT(ProductNo) FROM Product_Master WHERE SellPrice <= 1500;

n. Find all the products whose QtyOnHand is less than reorder level.
   SELECT ProductNo, Description FROM Product_Master WHERE QtyOnHand < ReorderLvl;

2. SQL Statements for Date Manipulation:

a. Display the order number and day on which clients placed their order.
   SELECT OrderNo, TO_CHAR(OrderDate, 'day') FROM Sales_Order;

b. Display the month (in alphabets) and date when the order must be delivered.
   SELECT TO_CHAR(DelyDate, 'month'), DelyDate FROM Sales_Order
       ORDER BY TO_CHAR(DelyDate, 'month');

c. List the OrderDate in the format 'DD-Month-YY'. e.g. 12-February-02.
   SELECT TO_CHAR(Orderdate, 'DD-Month-YY') FROM Sales_Order;

d. Find the date, 15 days after today's date.
   SELECT SYSDATE + 15 FROM DUAL;

3. SQL statements for using Having and Group By Clauses:

a. Printing the description and total quantity sold for each product.
   SELECT description, SUM(QtyDisp) FROM Product_Master, Sales_Order_Details
       WHERE Product_Master.ProductNo = Sales_Order_Details.ProductNo
       GROUP BY Description;

b. Finding the value of each product sold.
   SELECT Sales_Order_Details.ProductNo, Product_Master.Description,
       SUM(Sales_Order_Details.QtyDisp * Sales_Order_Details.ProductRate) 'Sales Per Product'
       FROM Sales_Order_Details, Product_Master
           WHERE Product_Master.ProductNo = Sales_Order_Details.ProductNo
           GROUP BY Sales_Order_Details.ProductNo, Product_Master.Description;

c. Calculating the average quantity sold for each client that has a maximum order value of 15000.00.
   SELECT CM.ClientNo, CM.Name, AVG(SOD.QtyDisp) 'Avg. Sales'
       FROM Sales_Order_Details **SOD**, Sales_Order **SO**, Client_Master **CM**
           WHERE CM.ClientNo = SO.ClientNo AND SO.OrderNo = SOD.OrderNo
           GROUP BY CM.ClientNo, Name
               HAVING MAX(SOD.QtyOrdered * SOD.ProductRate) > 15000;

d. Finding out the total of all the billed orders for the month of June.
   SELECT SO.OrderNo, SO.OrderDate, SUM(SOD.QtyOrdered * SOD.ProductRate) 'Order Billed'
       FROM Sales_Order SO, Sales_Order_Details SOD WHERE SOD.OrderNo = SO.OrderNo
       AND SO.Billed = 'Y' AND to_char(OrderDate, 'MON') = 'Jun' GROUP BY SO.OrderNo;

4. Exercises on Joins and Correlation:

a. Find out the products, which have been sold to 'Ivan Bayross'.
   SELECT SOD.ProductNo, PM.Description
      FROM Sales_Order_Details SOD, Sales_Order SO, Product_Master PM, Client_Master CM
       WHERE PM.ProductNo = SOD.ProductNo AND SO.OrderNo = SOD.OrderNo
        AND CM.ClientNo = SO.ClientNo AND CM.Name = 'Ivan Bayross';

b. Finding out the products and their quantities that will have to be delivered in the current month.
   SELECT SOD.ProductNo, PM.Description, SUM(SOD.QtyOrdered)
      FROM Sales_Order_Details SOD, Sales_Order SO, Product_Master PM
       WHERE PM.ProductNo = SOD.ProductNo AND SO.OrderNo = SOD.OrderNo
        AND TO_CHAR(DelyDate, 'MON-YY') = TO_CHAR(SYSDATE, 'MON-YY')
       GROUP BY SOD.ProductNo, PM.Description;

c. Listing the ProductNo and description of constantly sold (i.e. rapidly moving) products.
   SELECT DISTINCT Product_Master.ProductNo, Description
      FROM Sales_Order_Details, Product_Master
       WHERE Product_Master.ProductNo =Sales_Order_Details.ProductNo;

d. Finding the names of clients who have purchased 'Trousers'.
   SELECT DISTINCT Sales_Order.ClientNo, Client_Master.Name
      FROM Sales_Order_Details, Sales_Order, Product_Master, Client_Master
       WHERE Product_Master.ProductNo = Sales_Order_Details.ProductNo
        AND Sales_Order.OrderNo = Sales_Order_Details.OrderNo
        AND Client_Master.ClientNo = Sales_Order.ClientNo
        AND Description = 'Trousers';

e. Listing the products and orders from customers who have ordered less than 5 units of 'Pull Overs'.
   SELECT Sales_Order_Details.ProductNo, Sales_Order_Details.OrderNo
      FROM Sales_Order_Details, Sales_Order, Product_Master
       WHERE Sales_Order.OrderNo = Sales_Order_Details.OrderNo
       AND Product_Master.ProductNo = Sales_Order_Details.ProductNo
       AND Sales_Order_Details.QtyOrdered < 5
       AND Product_Master.Description = 'Pull Overs';

f. Finding the products and their quantities for the orders placed by 'Ivan Bayross' and 'Mamta Muzumdar'.
   SELECT SOD.ProductNo, PM.Description, SUM(QtyOrdered) 'Units Ordered'
      FROM Sales_Order_Details SOD, Sales_Order SO, Product_Master PM, Client_Master CM
       WHERE SO.OrderNo = SOD.OrderNo AND PM.ProductNo = SOD.ProductNo
        AND CM.ClientNo = SO.ClientNo
        AND (CM.Name = 'Ivan Bayross' OR CM.Name = 'Mamta Muzumdar')
       GROUP BY SOD.ProductNo, PM.Description;

g. Finding the products and their quantities for the orders placed by ClientNo 'C00001' and 'C00002'.
   SELECT SO.ClientNo, SOD.ProductNo, PM.Description, SUM(QtyOrdered) 'Units Ordered'
      FROM Sales_Order SO, Sales_Order_Details SOD, Product_Master PM, Client_Master CM
       WHERE SO.OrderNo = SOD.OrderNo AND SOD.ProductNo = PM.ProductNo
        AND SO.ClientNo = CM.ClientNo
       GROUP BY SO.ClientNo, SOD.ProductNo, PM.Description
        HAVING SO.ClientNo = 'C00001' OR SO.ClientNo='C00002';

2. SQL statements for exercises on Sub-queries:

a. Finding the non-moving products i.e. products not being sold.
   SELECT ProductNo, Description FROM Product_Master
      WHERE ProductNo NOT IN(SELECT ProductNo FROM Sales_Order_Details);

b. Finding the name and complete address for the customer who has placed Order number 'O19001'.
    SELECT Name ,Address1, Address2, City, State, PinCode FROM Client_Master
        WHERE ClientNo IN(SELECT ClientNo FROM Sales_Order
            WHERE OrderNo = 'O19001');
c. Finding the clients who have placed orders before the month of May'02.
    SELECT ClientNo, Name FROM Client_Master WHERE ClientNo IN(SELECT ClientNo
        FROM Sales_Order WHERE TO_CHAR(OrderDate, 'MON,YY') < 'MAY,02');
d. Find out if the product 'Lycra Tops' has been ordered by any client and print the ClientNo, Name to
    whom it was sold.
    SELECT ClientNo, Name FROM Client_Master WHERE ClientNo
        IN(SELECT ClientNo FROM Sales_Order WHERE OrderNo IN(SELECT OrderNo
            FROM Sales_Order_Details WHERE ProductNo IN(SELECT ProductNo
                FROM Product_Master WHERE Description = 'Lycra Tops')));
e. Find the names of clients who have placed orders worth Rs. 10000 or more.
    SELECT Name FROM Client_Master WHERE ClientNo IN(SELECT ClientNo
        FROM Sales_Order
            WHERE OrderNo IN(SELECT OrderNo FROM Sales_Order_Details
                WHERE (QtyOrdered * ProductRate) >= 10000));

7. INTERACTIVE SQL PART - III

1. Extracting column details of the column **City** from the **Client_Master** table.
    SELECT DUMP(City) FROM Client_Master;

2. Dropping the column **State** from the **Client_Master** table.
    ALTER TABLE Client_Master DROP COLUMN City;

3. Renaming the column named **Name** to **CustomerName** from the table **Client_Master**.
    ALTER TABLE Client_Master ADD (CustomerName VARCHAR2(25));
    UPDATE Client_Master SET CustomerName = Name;
    ALTER TABLE Client_Master DROP COLUMN Name;

4. Retrieving all even rows from the **Product_Master** table.
    SELECT ROWNUM, ProductNo, Description, QtyOnHand FROM Product_Master
        GROUP BY ROWNUM, ProductNo, Description, QtyOnHand
            HAVING MOD(ROWNUM,2)=0 OR ROWNUM = 2-0;

5. Adding a day, hour, minute and second to the date 3-Jan-1981
    SELECT TO_CHAR(TO_DATE('3-Jan-1981'), 'DD-MON-YYYY HH:MI:SS') "Date",
        TO_CHAR(TO_DATE('3-Jan-1981')+1, 'DD-MON-YYYY HH:MI:SS') "By 1 Day",
        TO_CHAR(TO_DATE('3-Jan-1981')+1/24, 'DD-MON-YYYY HH:MI:SS') "By 1 Hour",
        TO_CHAR(TO_DATE('3-Jan-1981')+1/1440, 'DD-MON-YYYY HH:MI:SS') "By 1 Minute",
        TO_CHAR(TO_DATE('3-Jan-1981')+ 1/86400, 'DD-MON-YYYY HH:MI:SS') "By 1 Second"
        FROM DUAL;

6. Retrieving a count of products sold per order from the **Sales_Order_Details** table.
    SELECT OrderNo, COUNT(*) "Products Sold" FROM Sales_Order_Details GROUP BY OrderNo;

7. Retrieving only the rows ranging from 2 to 7 from the **Product_Master** table.
    SELECT * FROM (SELECT ROWNUM RN, ProductNo, Description FROM Product_Master
        WHERE ROWNUM < 8) WHERE RN BETWEEN 2 and 7;

8. Displaying the Client Details in specific format.
    SELECT 'Customer Name: ' || Name || CHR(10) || 'Address: ' || Address1 || CHR(10) ||
        'City: ' || City "Customer Details" FROM Client_Master;

9. Using Flashback to reset the database, as it was 20 minutes earlier.
    EXECUTE DBMS_FLASHBACK.ENABLE_AT_TIME(SYSDATE - 20 / 1440);

10. Disabling the database flashback system.
    EXECUTE DBMS_FLASHBACK.DISABLE();

11. Displaying the tables in the Recycle Bin.
    SHOW RECYCLEBIN;

12. Recovering a table named **Client_Master**, which had been accidentally deleted.
    FLASHBACK TABLE Client_Master TO BEFORE DROP;

10. USING REGULAR EXPRESSIONS

1. Locating products having the Product Numbers beginning with 'P078' and 'P079'.
    SELECT ProductNo, Description FROM Product_Master
        WHERE REGEXP_LIKE(ProductNo, 'P0[7][8/9]');

2. Locating products having a description beginning with 'T' or 'S' and ending with 'S'.
    SELECT ProductNo, Description FROM Product_Master
        WHERE REGEXP_LIKE(Description, '^[T/S][A-Z]*S$','i');

3. Listing all clients who have mentioned their last name along with their First Name in the Name Field
    of the **Client_Master** table.
    SELECT Name FROM Client_Master WHERE REGEXP_LIKE(Name, '[[:space:]].');

4. Locating the second occurrence of one or more non-blank character in the description of the products.
    SELECT Description, REGEXP_INSTR(Description, '[^]+', 1,2) "Second_Occourance"
        FROM Product_Master;

5. Extracting the actual product number (digits only) from the **ProductNo** column of **Product_Master**
    table.
    SELECT ProductNo, REGEXP_SUBSTR(ProductNo, '[[:digit:]]{1,}') Actual_No
        FROM Product_Master;

6. Displaying the state names in which Clients reside wherein each character of the state name is
    separated by a space.
    SELECT REGEXP_REPLACE(State, '(.)', '\1 ') Spacer_State FROM Client_Master;

7. Swapping the names of clients to display the name as **Surname, First Name E.G.:** Shah, Sharanam.
    SELECT REGEXP_REPLACE(Name, '(.*) (.*)', '\2, \1') Swap FROM Client_Master;

11. TABLESPACES, DBA AND USER

1. SQL Statement for creating the Tablespace:
    CREATE TABLESPACE SCT_INVT DATAFILE 'SCT_Invt.dat' SIZE 25M DEFAULT STORAGE(
        INITIAL 10K NEXT 50K MINEXTENTS 1 MAXEXTENTS 499 PCTINCREASE 10)
    ONLINE;

2. SQL Statement for creating the User:
    CREATE USER "DBA_INVTSYS" PROFILE "DEFAULT" IDENTIFIED BY "sct2306"
    DEFAULT TABLESPACE "SCT_INVT" TEMPORARY TABLESPACE "TEMP"
    ACCOUNT UNLOCK;

3. SQL Statement for granting the user permission of an Oracle DBA:
    GRANT "DBA" TO "DBA_INVTSYS" WITH ADMIN OPTION;

12. OVERVIEW AND GETTING STARTED

OVERVIEW

HTML DB provides a declarative development framework for creating database-centric web applications. Development is done using an online service. Deployment is done by downloading a runtime module and an application and running it within the enterprise.

HTML DB is the new **rapid application development** tool for the Oracle database, delivered as part of Oracle Database 10g or as a separate download for Oracle 9i 9.2.0.3 or higher. HTML DB helps generating PL/SQL web applications, with the Oracle Portal **look and feel**, using a declarative GUI environment that is aimed at developers and power users with a basic understanding of SQL and PL/SQL. HTML DB is a browser-based development environment, with no client downloads or tools to install.

Applications built using HTML DB are positioned somewhere between Oracle Portal applications (built using the forms and chart wizards within Portal) and full-blown J2EE applications, built using JDeveloper, UIX, BC4J and so on.

Features Of HTMLDB

Basically, it's a web applications development environment that's particularly suited to PL/SQL developers.

HTML DB looks very east to use. It's aimed at all the Microsoft Access developers, and consequently the building process is iterative and encourages experimentation and trying things out. Each form and report that is build has an **edit** link at the bottom, allowing administrators to change things around and rerun the form without the need to recompile, relink and rebuild the application.

Data from spreadsheets and text files can be easily uploaded to the database, with HTML DB creating tables and auto-incrementing primary key columns behind the scenes.

Everything is done graphically and this makes it easy to add functionality to an application as one goes along.

HTML DB applications can authenticate against Oracle OID and Single Sign-On, other LDAP servers, external authentication methods or use Oracle database security.

Because HTML DB is pure PL/SQL, and runs directly on top of the Oracle database, it's got a smaller footprint and appears to run faster than a java web application, and would be easier for a PL/SQL developer to design and debug than a n-tier java application.

What components make up HTML DB?

HTML DB contains three main components, namely:

Application Builder	The Application Builder allows building database-centric interactive web applications.
SQL Workshop	The SQL Workshop allows running SQL statements and SQL scripts.
Data Workshop	The Data Workshop helps loading data into and extracting data from the database.

Terminology

The following concepts are important to know when working with HTML DB:

Application	An Application is a collection of pages with branches that connect them. Its attributes include the authentication method, default UI templates, and authorization rules.
Page	A page is defined by how it is rendered or displayed and by how it is processed. Processing refers to the events and logic that occur when the page is submitted. Each page is rendered dynamically at runtime from meta data defined by the Application developer. Page templates control how a page looks.
Region	Content is displayed in regions, which are logical subsections of a page. Each page can have any number of regions of several different types. These types include: HTML text, SQL Queries, PL/SQL generated HTML and charts. Each region is rendered using a region template. Regions are positioned on the page using display points defined in the page template.
Item	Application items are used to generate HTML form elements. The Applications engine manages the generation of the HTML, the developer simply chooses the item type. Applications support over 50 such types including date pickers, popup lists of values, text areas with spell checking, etc. The value of an item is automatically stored into session state, which can be referenced at any point within the user's session.

Architecture

All applications are rendered in real time from data stored in database tables. When an application is created or extended, no code is generated, metadata is created or modified and stored in database tables. The applications rendering engine reads the metadata and displays the page accordingly.

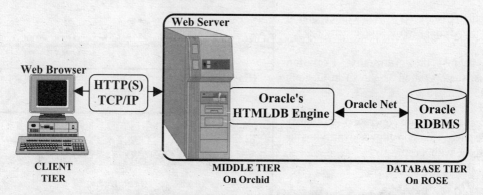

Diagram 12.1: Architecture for HTMLDB.

All session state is also stored in the database. Each page view results in a new database session, so when the applications engine is not processing a page, no database resources are consumed (except for storage space used by table rows). The unique session identifier used to manage the application's session state as the user runs the application from start to finish is unrelated to the many individual database sessions created and run by the runtime engine for each page view.

Applications that execute SQL or PL/SQL are parsed as the "owner" of the application. When a workspace is provisioned, the right to parse as a specific schema is given. Thus all of the Oracle database rights and privileges (for that workspace) are in accordance to the schema chosen to parse as.

CREATING A WORKSPACE

Before beginning development in Oracle HTML DB it is necessary to create a workspace. A workspace is a similar to a directory under which all the project details are stored.

The following steps are performed to create a Workspace.

Enter the following URL to login to HTML DB:

http://<hostname>:7777/pls/htmldb/htmldb

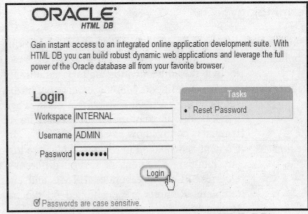

Diagram 12.2: Login screen for HTML DB.

Enter the system workspace as INTERNAL, username as ADMIN and password (as the one specified while installing HTMLDB). Click Login . (Refer diagram 12.2)

After authentication of the Admin login, the **Administration Home** page appears as shown in diagram 12.3.

Select the **Create New Workspace** option under the **Manage Workspace** section.

This begins the **Manually Provision Workspace** operation as shown in diagram 12.4.1.

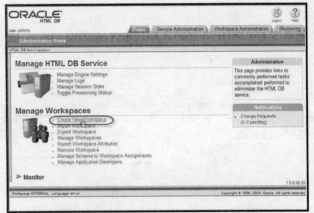

Diagram 12.3: Selecting the Create New Workspace option.

The first step is in this operation is **Identify Workspace**. This step allows identifying the workspace with a name.

 Caution

The name assigned to the new workspace should be a unique.

Additionally, a description for the workspace can be given along with its **Security Group Id**, which is optional.

Click Next> to proceed to the next step.

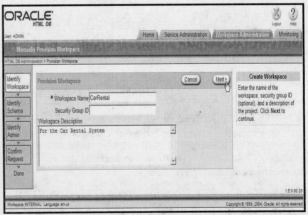

Diagram 12.4.1: Identify Workspace step in the Manually Provision Workspace page.

The second step is **Identify Schema**. Refer diagram 12.4.2.1. This step accepts the schema name that will operate the new workspace.

To select a schema from the database click on 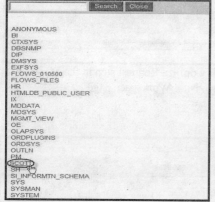 (List option) to get a Search Dialog box as shown in diagram 12.4.2.2.

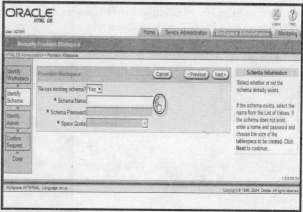

Diagram 12.4.2.1: Identify Schema step in the Manually Provision Workspace page.

Diagram 12.4.2.2: The Search Dialog box for selecting a Schema for the Workspace.

Select an appropriate schema, (in this case, the **SCOTT** schema is selected to develop the Car Rental system), to close the **Search Dialog** box.

On returning to the **Identify Schema** page, the **Schema Name** field will display the schema selected via the Search Dialog box. Refer diagram 12.4.2.3.

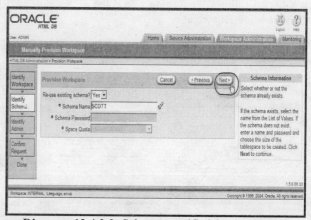

Diagram 12.4.2.3: Schema specified for the Identify Schema step in the Manually Provision Workspace page.

Click ⟨Next >⟩ to proceed to the **Identity Admin** step. Refer diagram 12.4.3.

Enter the Administrator's Username and Password along with an E-mail address. The username specified will be used at the time of login, (accessing the new workspace).

The First Name and Last Name fields are optional fields.

Click ⟨Next >⟩ to proceed.

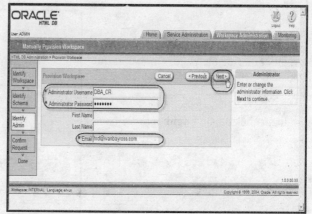

Diagram 12.4.3: Identify Admin step in the Manually Provision Workspace page.

The fourth step in the **Manually Provision Workspace** operation is **Confirm Request**.

This step provides a summary of the new workspace to be created. Refer diagram 12.4.4.

Click **Provision** to complete the creation of the workspace.

This displays a page with **Workspace successfully provisioned** message. Refer diagram 12.4.5.

The **Return to Internal Administration** button on this page, allows returning to the **Administration Home** page.

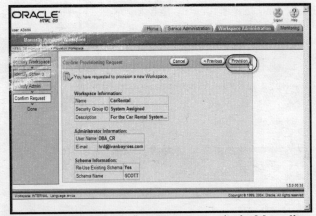

Diagram 12.4.4: Confirm Request step in the Manually Provision Workspace page.

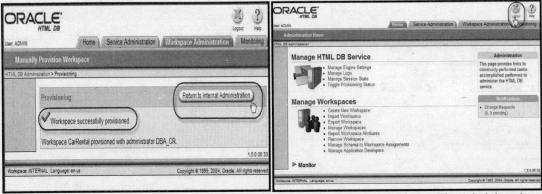

Diagram 12.4.5: Message on successful provision of the new workspace.

Diagram 12.5.1: Returning to The Administration Home page and clicking Logout.

Click on the **Logout** option available at the top right corner of the page. On successful logout the screen as shown in diagram 12.5.2 appears.

To re-login click on the **Login** option.

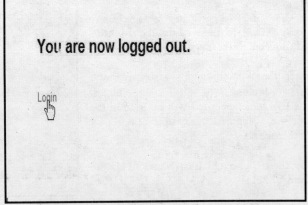

Diagram 12.5.2: Message on successful logout.

CREATING A TABLE FROM A SPREADSHEET

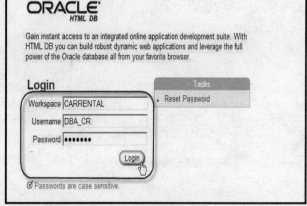

Diagram 12.6: Login page for HTMLDB.

To load data from a spreadsheet perform the following:

Enter the following URL to login to HTML DB:
http://<hostname>:7777/pls/htmldb/htmldb

Enter the name of the workspace (just created), username and password. Click **Login**. (Refer diagram 12.6.)

To create the table on which the application will be based on, click **Data Workshop**. (Refer diagram 12.7.)

Diagram 12.7: Selecting the Data Workshop option.

To import data into a table from a spreadsheet, click **Import Spreadsheet Data**. (Refer diagram 12.8.)

A page as seen in diagram 12.9.1 appears.

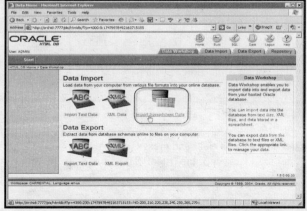

Diagram 12.8: Selecting the Import Spreadsheet Data option.

Ensure that **Import To** is set to **New table** and **Import From** is set to **Copy and paste (up to 30KB)** and click Next> . (Refer diagram 12.9.1.)

This is the first step of the **Import Data** process and is called **Target and Method**.

Open any spreadsheet (in this case Customers.**xls**) in MS Excel. Select all the data in the spreadsheet and press **Ctrl + C** to copy the data to the clipboard. Refer diagram 12.9.2.1.

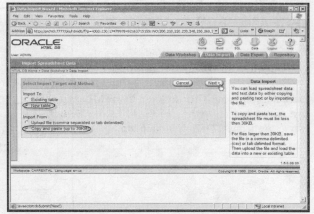

Diagram 12.9.1: Selection in the Target Import and Method step for the Import Data process.

Diagram 12.9.2.1: Copying data from the Excel spreadsheet.

Switch back to the browser where a session of HTML DB is active (i.e. the second step in the Import Data process, namely **Data**). Refer diagram 12.9.2.2.

Click in the **Data** field and press **Ctrl + V** to paste the data into the field. Then click Next>.

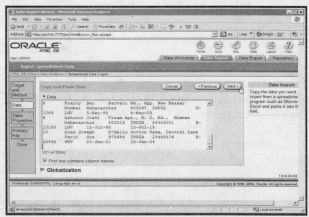

Diagram 12.9.2.2: Pasting data into the Data step for the Import Data process.

Table Properties is the third step in the **Import Data** process, as shown in diagram 12.9.3.

The Table Properties window will appear which shows the columns in the table and their format, as well as the data that will be inserted into the table once the table is created. Enter the table name (in this case Customers) and click Next >.

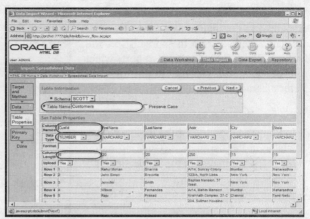

Diagram 12.9.3: The Table Properties step in the Import Data process.

Caution

An error is encountered if the table name specified in the above step **already exists** under the current schema.

The fourth step of the Import Data process is named Primary Key. Refer diagram 12.9.4.1.

Note

If the column(s) in the table does not support a primary key field, the Create new column option can be used. This option adds a new column row in the table and assigns it a unique value.

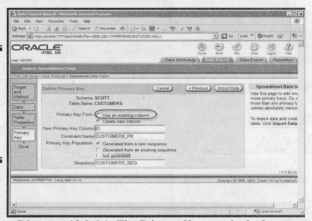

Diagram 12.9.4.1: The Primary Key step in the Import Data process.

For the **Primary Key Form** field, select the option **Use an existing column**. The page appears as shown in diagram 12.9.4.2.

Select an appropriate field from the table and enter the name of the constraint.

Click Import Data to continue.

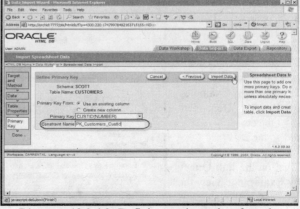

Diagram 12.9.4.2: Defining a primary key from the existing fields in the table.

The Import Data process performs the actual creation and population of a table based on the data received from the spreadsheet file. On completion it generates a report, which can be accessed via the Repository tab. Refer diagram 12.10.

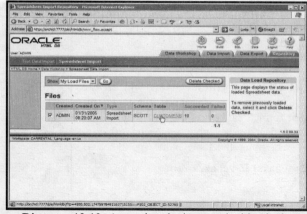

A link to the properties of the import table is available in the list of files. Clicking on the value (i.e. Customers) in the Table field will display the table properties.

The Table Summary appears as shown in diagram 12.11.

Diagram 12.10: Accessing the imported table via the Repository tab.

It provides table details such as name, schema, tablespace, indexes, triggers and constraints.

It also provides information related to the columns in the table.

The right hand section of the window provides links to frequent tasks such as row count, insert rows, view data and so on. It also provides links to perform following operations:
- ❑ Create Lookup Table
- ❑ Drop the table
- ❑ Generate Create Table Script
- ❑ Query By Example
- ❑ Report Dependent Objects

and so on.

Click on the link **Query By Example** to view the data held in the table.

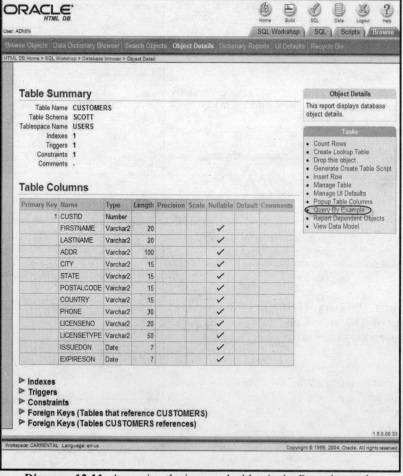

Diagram 12.11: Accessing the imported table via the Repository tab.

The link **Query By Example** displays the **Identify Query Attributes** page as shown in diagram 12.12.

Click the **Check All** checkbox and click **Query**.

The output of the query is displayed in the Query Result page as shown in diagram 12.13.

To return to the home page click on the link **SQL Workspace**. A page as shown in diagram 12.14 is displayed.

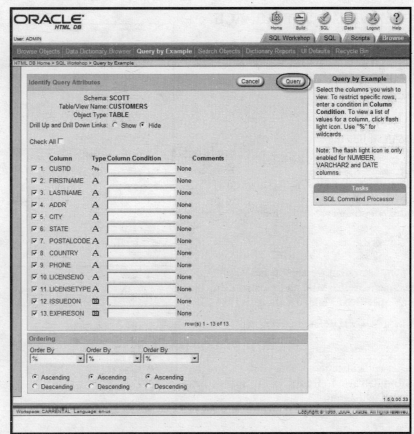

Diagram 12.12: Identifying Query Attributes.

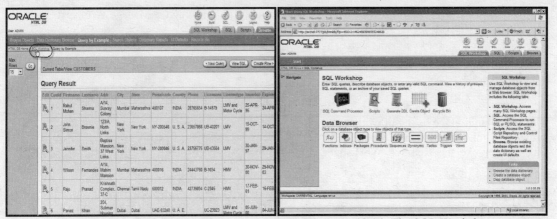

Diagram 12.13: Query Result.   **Diagram 12.14:** The SQL Workshop page.

REMOVING A WORKSPACE

Some times during development in Oracle HTML DB it may be necessary to re-create or drop a workspace, (i.e. the workspace needs to be deleted).

Do the following to delete a Workspace.

Enter the following URL to login to HTML DB:
http://<hostname>:7777/pls/htmldb/htmldb

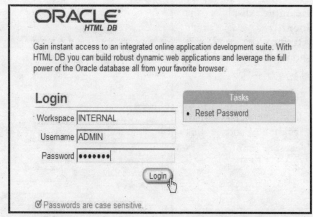

Diagram 12.15: Login screen for HTML DB.

Enter the system workspace as INTERNAL, username as ADMIN and password (as the one specified while installing HTMLDB). Click **Login**. (Refer diagram 12.15)

After authentication of the Admin login, the **Administration Home** page appears as shown in diagram 12.16.

Select the **Manage Workspace** option under the **Manage Workspace** sub head.

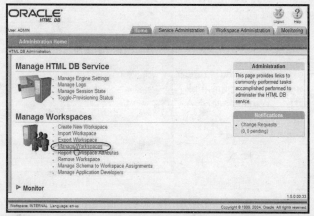

Diagram 12.16: Selecting the Manage Workspace option.

The **Manage Workspace** page will appear as shown in diagram 12.17. This page lists all existing workspaces under the Oracle 10g HTML DB service.

The last column in the listing of workspaces provides a link labeled **Delete**. Clicking the link will invoke the **Remove Workspace** wizard

 Caution

 If a workspace is deleted, it contents are lost permanently .

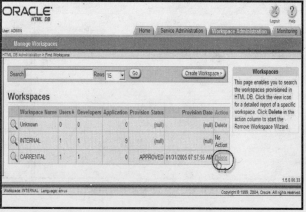

Diagram 12.17: The Manage Workspace page.

The **Remove Workspace** wizard begins as shown in diagram 12.18.1.

The first step is in this operation is **Identify Workspace**. This step allows identifying the workspace with a name.

Click **Next >** to proceed to the next step.

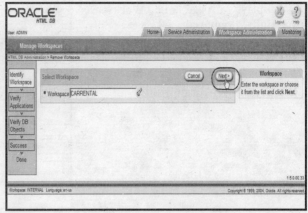

Diagram 12.18.1: Identify Workspace page in the Remove Workspace wizard.

The **Verify Applications** step is the second step in the **Remove Workspace** wizard. Refer to diagram 12.18.2.

The page provides options to:
❑ Confirm the removal of the workspace
❑ Confirm the removal of all request for the workspace (i.e. cancel access to users currently logged into the workspace)

Additionally, the page displays the number of user(s) and application(s) currently active within the workspace.

Select the two confirmation options and click **Next >** to proceed.

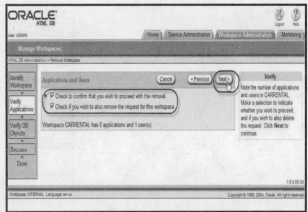

Diagram 12.18.2: Verify Application page in the Remove Workspace wizard.

The third step is the **Verify DB Objects** page, as shown in diagram 12.18.3.

This step gives a summary-cum-warning above the deletion operation of a workspace.

 Note

     The deletion of a workspace does not delete the database tablespace in which the workspace is stored.

Click **Remove Workspace** to remove the workspace.

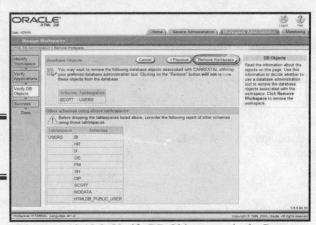

Diagram 12.18.3: Verify DB Object page in the Remove Workspace wizard.

This displays a page with **Workspace successfully removed** message. Refer diagram 12.18.4.

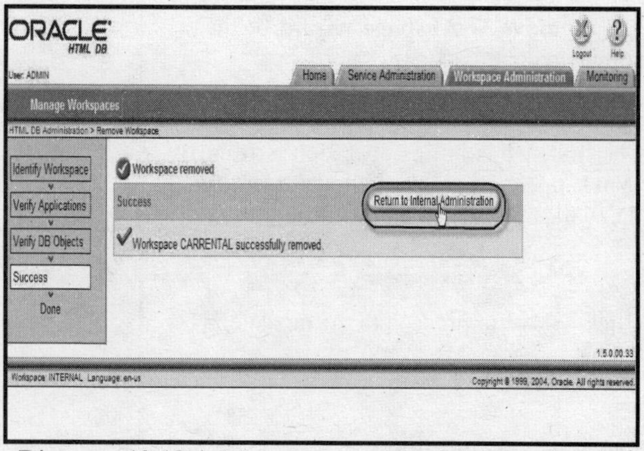

Diagram 12.18.4: Message on successful removal of the workspace.

The Return to Internal Administration button on this page, allows returning to the **Administration Home** page.

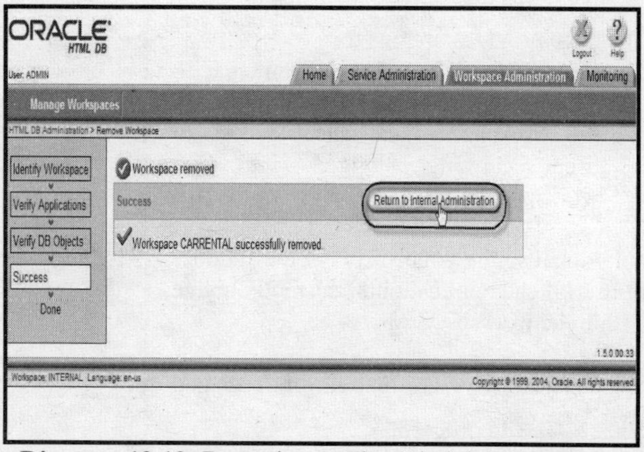

Diagram 12.19: Returning to The Administration Home page and clicking Logout.

Click on the Logout option available at the top right corner of the page. On successful logout the screen as shown in diagram 12.20.2 appears.

Diagram 12.20: Message on successful logout.

To re-login click on the **Login** option when required.

13. WORKING WITH FORMS (THE AUTOMATIC WAY)

CREATING AN APPLICATION

The objective is to create a Car Rental Application based on the following tables:

- Customers
- Cars
- Rentals
- Bills
- Receipts

The codespec containing the create and insert statements for the Car Rental System is available in the book's accompanying CD-ROM under:
CDROM:\Book_Codes\Chap13_Codes \Chap13_TblStr_Cnstr.txt

The username and workspace used will be: (Refer Diagram 13.1.)

- Username – DBA_CR
- Workspace – CARRENTAL

Application Creation via HTMLDB involves the following steps: (Refer diagram 13.0.)

- Creation Method
- Table / View Owner
- Table / View Name
- Application Options
- Confirm

To begin the creation of an application via the HTML DB interface perform the following:

Enter the following URL to login to HTML DB:
http://<hostname>:7777/pls/htmldb/htmldb

Enter the name of the workspace, username and password. Click **Login**. (Refer diagram 13.1.)

After authentication of the login for the **CARRENTAL** workspace, the **Start** page appears as shown in diagram 13.2.

Click the **Application Builder** option as shown in diagram 13.2.

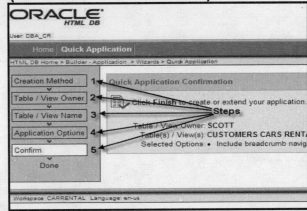

Diagram 13.0: Steps in Automatic application creation.

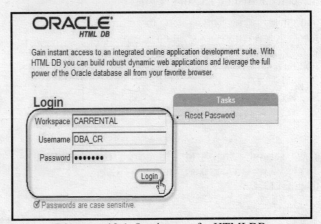

Diagram 13.1: Login page for HTMLDB.

Diagram 13.2: Selecting the Application Builder option.

To create the application based on a table held within the Oracle database, click **Create Application**. (Refer diagram 13.3.)

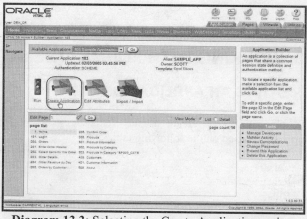

Diagram 13.3: Selecting the Create Application option.

The **Select Creation Method** page is displayed as shown in diagram 13.4.1.

This is the **first step** in the Create Application process.

Select the **Based on Existing Tables** option and click [Next >]. This is done to automate the forms/reports creation process. However, manual creation of forms/reports will be handled later.

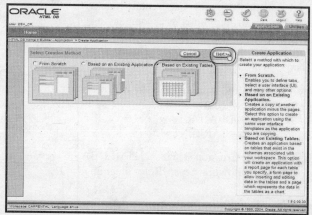

Diagram 13.4.1: Selecting the creation method for the application.

The **second step**, to **Identify the Table/View Owner** page, follows. Refer diagram 13.4.2.

Select an appropriate schema that will be authenticated to operate the application, (in this case, SCOTT).

Click [Next >] to continue.

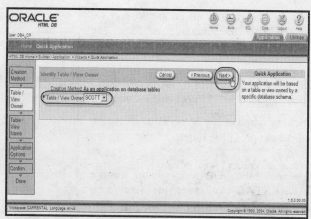

Diagram 13.4.2: Specifying the parsing schema.

The **third step** is the **Identify Table / View Name** page. Refer diagram 13.4.3.1.

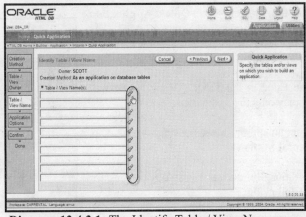

Specify the table(s), which will be accessed by the application.

Diagram 13.4.3.1: The Identify Table / View Name page.

To select a table from the database click on (List option) to get a Search Dialog box as shown in diagram 13.4.3.2.

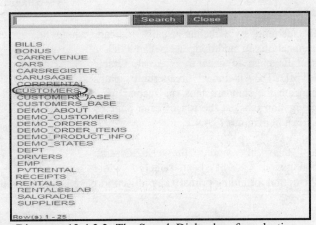

Select an appropriate table, (in this case, the **CUSTOMERS** table), to close the **Search Dialog** box.

Select the additional/remaining tables by specifying them in the other empty fields. Refer diagram 13.4.3.3.

Diagram 13.4.3.2: The Search Dialog box for selecting a Table for the Application.

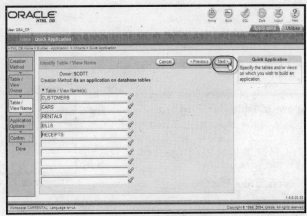

The number forms / reports created (automatically) will be based on the number of tables selected in this step. Since the system being built is the Car Rental System, all five tables belonging to it are selected.

Click **Next >** to continue.

Diagram 13.4.3.3: Specifying the tables associated with the application.

The **fourth step** – the **Quick Application** page, is as shown in diagram 13.4.4.1. The Application Option step accepts a name for the application.

The value in the **Table / View Name** will display only the first table selected.

Enter an appropriate name (in this case, **Car Rental System**).

Additionally, the page provides options for the following:

❑   Including Breadcrumb Navigation Aids
❑   Hiding Primary Key in Report Page

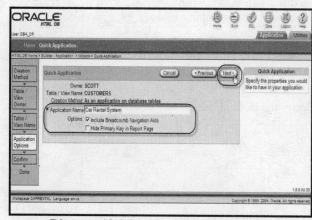

Diagram 13.4.4.1: Naming the application.

Breadcrumb style menus usually indicate where the current page is relative to other pages in the application. In addition, users can click a specific page to instantly view it. Oracle HTML DB includes breadcrumb paths beneath the standard tabs (or second level navigation tabs) at the top of each page as shown in diagram 13.4.4.2.

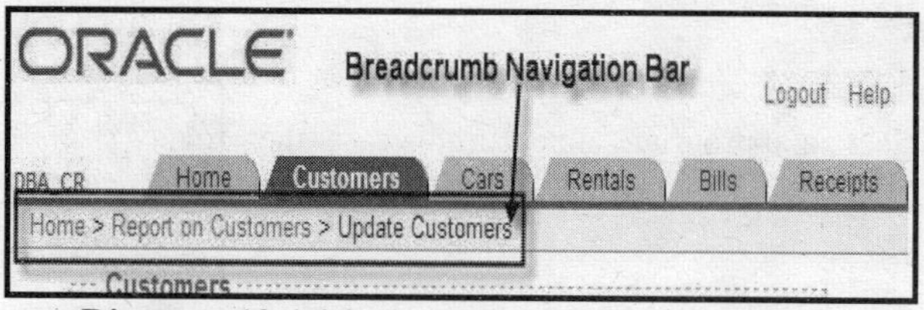

In this illustration the Breadcrumb Navigation Aids has been **selected**, while the option for hiding primary key in Report page is **de-selected**.

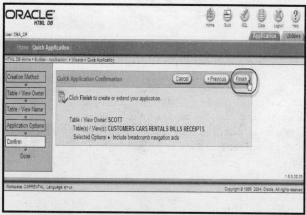

Diagram 13.4.4.2: A sample for the Breadcrumb.

Click Next > to proceed to the next step.

The **fifth step** is the **Quick Application Confirmation** page, as shown in diagram 13.4.5.

A summary of the options selected such as the owner, tables involved and so on for the creation of the application is displayed.

To confirm the creation of the application, click Finish .

Diagram 13.4.5: The Confirmation page for creating the application.

Finally, the application is created and it is confirmed via a message, refer diagram 13.5.

This page provides a link to run the application created, Refer diagram 13.5.

Click on the **Run Application** link to execute the application.

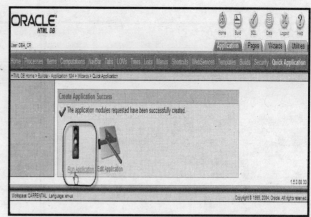

Diagram 13.5: Application created confirmation.

When the application begins a Login screen appears to authenticate the access. Refer diagram 13.6.

Enter the correct login information and click Login to continue.

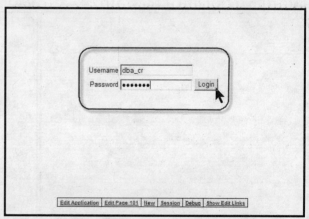

Diagram 13.6: Application Login page.

The **Home** page for the application appears as shown in diagram 13.7.

The page provides links to the various reports, forms and analysis contained within the application.

Navigate across the forms / reports created using these links.

The screenshots of forms / reports follow auto created for the Car Rental System: (Refer diagrams 13.8.1 to 13.8.10.)

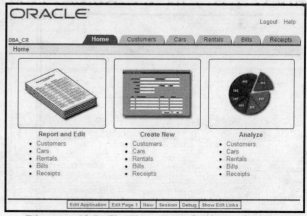

Diagram 13.7: The Home page for the application.

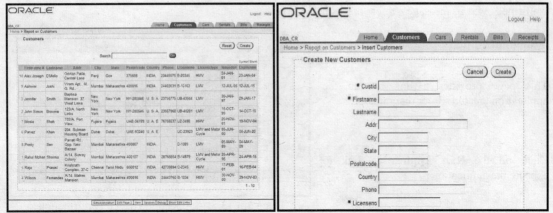

Diagram 13.8.1: Report For Customers table.   **Diagram 13.8.2:** Form For Customers table.

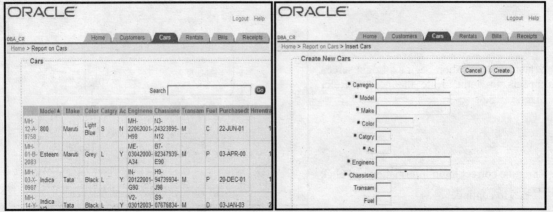

Diagram 13.8.3: Report For Cars table.   **Diagram 13.8.4:** Form For Cars table.

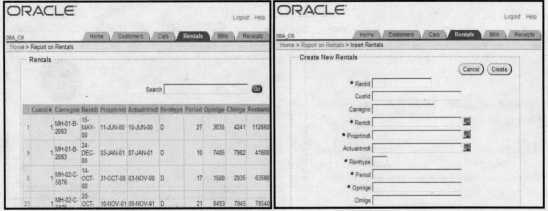

Diagram 13.8.5: Report For Rentals table.   **Diagram 13.8.6:** Form For Rentals table.

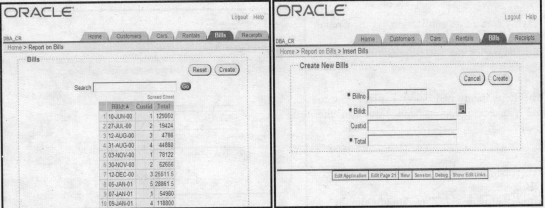

Diagram 13.8.7: Report For Bills table.   **Diagram 13.8.8:** Form For Bills table.

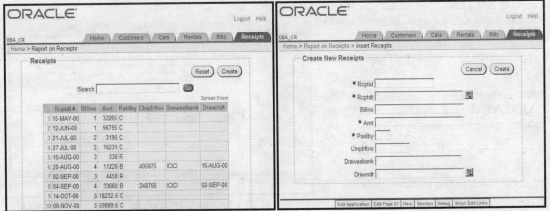

Diagram 13.8.9: Report For Receipts table.   **Diagram 13.8.10:** Form For Receipts table.

Applying Constraints To Data Entry Forms

The **Create Application** wizard within HTMLDB, is capable of identifying constraints attached to database tables. Since the tables in the Car Rental System have been designed with constraints, the wizard applies these constraints automatically to the data entry form as well.

For example, columns with the NOT NULL constraints are marked with ✳ (i.e. mandatory fields). Refer diagram 13.11.

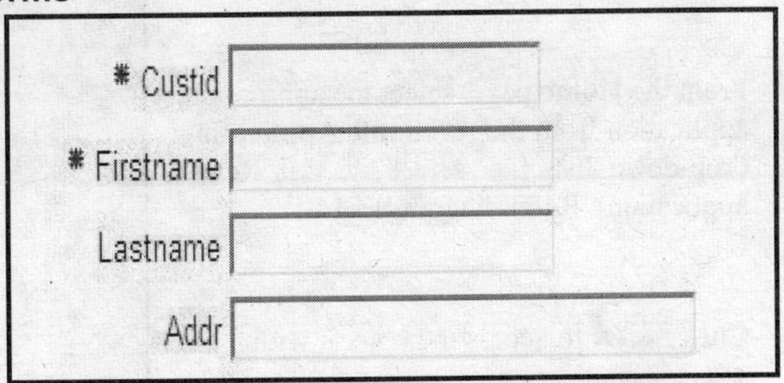

Diagram 13.11: The Home page for the application.

WORKING WITH AN APPLICATION

Having created an application via the Create Application wizard, understanding the functioning of the form operations is fairly simple.

The steps mentioned below explain how to use / execute reports and forms in the application.

Enter the following URL to login to HTML DB:
http://<hostname>:7777/pls/htmldb/htmldb

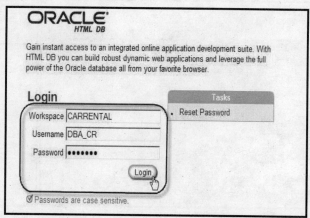

Diagram 13.12: Login page for HTMLDB.

Enter the name of the workspace, username and password. Click **Login**. (Refer diagram 13.12.)

After authentication of the login for the **CARRENTAL** workspace, the **Start** page appears as shown in diagram 13.13.

Click the **Application Builder** option.

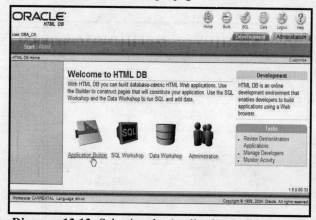

Diagram 13.13: Selecting the Application Builder option.

From the **Home** page, select the appropriate application from the **Available Application** drop-down list, (i.e. select the Car Rental application). Refer diagram 13.14.

Click **Go** to access the objects within the selected application.

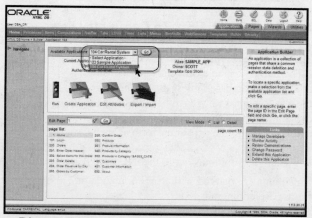

Diagram 13.14: Selecting the Car Rental application.

The Home page for the required application (i.e. the Car Rental System) appears as shown in diagram 13.15.

The center of the Home page consists of a listing of various pages created in the application.

Click on the **Run** link to execute the application.

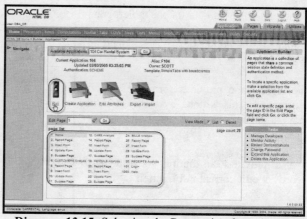

Diagram 13.15: Selecting the Run option from the Car Rental application's Home page.

When the application begins a Login screen appears to authenticate user access. Refer diagram 13.16.

Enter the correct login information and click Login to continue.

The **Home** page for the application appears as shown in diagram 13.17.

The page provides links to various reports, forms and analysis contained within the application.

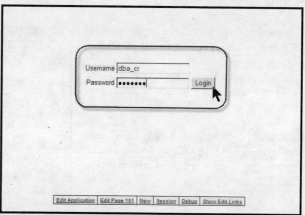

Diagram 13.16: Application Login page.

Viewing Reports

A report provides a method to view data held within database table(s).

Click any one of the link below the **Report and Edit** section of the **Home** page, (in this case, **Customers**) to view a report. Refer diagram 13.17.

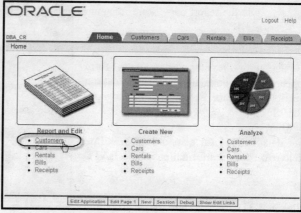

Diagram 13.17: The Home page for the application.

The report retrieves data for the table(s) and displays it in a presentable manner (i.e. the template of the application). Refer diagram 13.18.

The report page provides sorting of report information. This is done by a mouse click on a particular column on which the sorting is required.

It also provides an option to **add** new records or **edit** current information.

·Click ⟨Create⟩ to add a new record. Refer diagram 13.18.

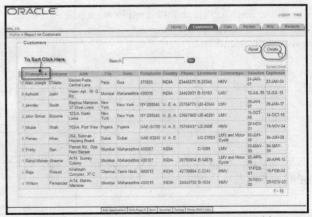

Diagram 13.18: Report for the Customers table.

Adding New Records

A data entry form provides a method to add and edit data held within database table(s).

The application's Home page (refer diagram 13.17) provides links to run a data entry form.

Click any one of the links below the **Create New** section of the **Home** page, (refer diagram 13.17) (in this case, **Customers**) to access a data entry form.

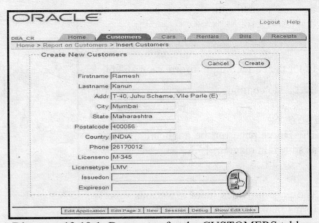

Diagram 13.19.1: Data entry for the CUSTOMERS table.

Note

 Click ⟨Create⟩ to add a new record via the report page. Refer diagram 13.18.

A page with the empty data entry form appears. When populated with information, the form appears as shown in diagram 13.19.1.

The data entry form also provides a **date picker** to capture information of the **DATE** type.

Clicking 📅 causes a Date Picker to popup on the screen in a separate window. Refer diagram 13.19.2.

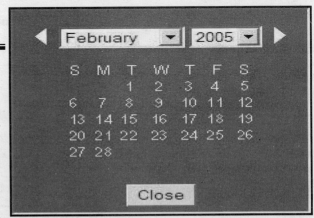

Diagram 13.19.2: A Date popup box.

Having entered information click (Create), which is placed on the top-right corner of the data entry page. This creates a new record in the database table. Refer diagram 13.20.

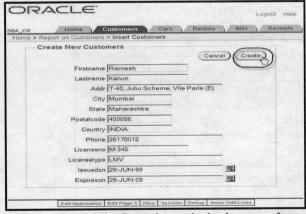

This is immediately followed by a confirmation. Refer diagram 13.21.

Additionally, the confirmation page provides an option to either insert another record or to view a report on the table recently appended.

Diagram 13.20: The Create button in the data entry form.

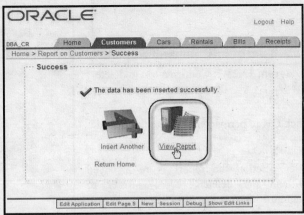

The newly inserted record, held within the table, can be listed along with previous information be clicking the **View Report** option.

The report page appears in a tabular format, with the new record, as shown in diagram 13.22.

Diagram 13.21: A confirmation page for data inserted successful.

Deleting Existing Records

To delete a particular record from the table it is necessary to first view the report for that table.

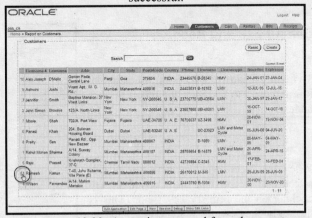

When the records in the table are listed, select the record to be deleted by clicking on the primary key field. (This is the only key with a hyperlink.) Refer diagram 13.22.

Diagram 13.22: Accessing a record from the report.

The record is transferred to the data entry form in the **Edit** mode (i.e. the top-right corner of the data entry form provides options to delete or update information rather than create). Refer diagram 13.23.1.

Click (Delete) to delete the record currently displayed on the page with the data entry form in the **Edit** mode.

A confirmation to delete the record is popup of the screen as shown in diagram 13.23.2.

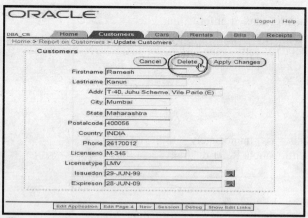

Diagram 13.23.1: Option to delete currently visible record.

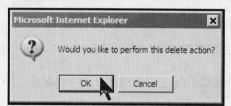

Diagram 13.23.2: Confirmation to delete the record.

Click **OK** to permanently delete the record.

After deletion the report is re-displayed (without the deleted record). Refer to diagram 13.24.

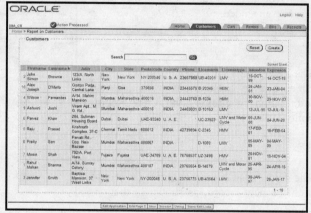

Diagram 13.24: Customers Report after deletion.

Editing Existing Records

To modify a particular record from the table, it is necessary to first view the report for that table.

When the records in the table are listed, select the record that will be edited by clicking on the primary key field. (This is the only key with a hyperlink.) Refer diagram 13.25.

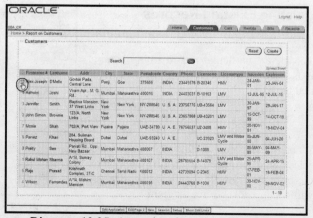

Diagram 13.25: Accessing the record for edition.

The record is transferred to the data entry form in the **Edit** mode. Refer diagram 13.23.1.

Perform the modification by changing the information held within the fields of the data entry form.

Click (Apply Changes) to update the record in the database with the changes made on the page with the data entry form in the **Edit** mode. Refer diagram 13.26.

A confirmation of the update is displayed by re-displaying the report. Refer diagram 13.27.

Validations Based On Database Table Constraints

The **Create Application** wizard is capable of adding data validation code to form fields. Validation is based on information retrieved while scanning table(s) specified in the **third step** (i.e. the **Identify Table / View Name** page) of the wizard. Refer diagram 13.4.3.1.

The automatically created validation is of the following type:

❑ **Empty Field Validation** – It is applied to fields bound to table columns having the NOT NULL constraints attached to them.

❑ **Numeric Field Validation** – It is applied to fields bound to table columns having a numeric datatype.

Since the data-entry form for creating new customer information is based on the Customers table held in the database, the column-level constraints attached to the Customers table are used to generate form field validations. This can be verified by attempting to insert an empty record in the Customers table, via the Customer's data-entry form. Refer diagram 13.28.

The form displays data validation messages, indicated in red text.

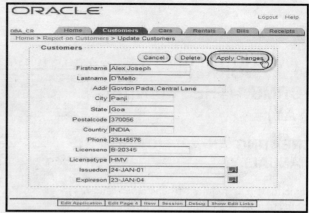

Diagram 13.26: Applying the changes make to a record.

Diagram 13.27: Customers Report after applying the changes make to a record.

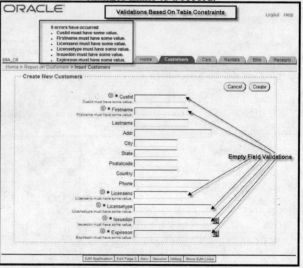

Diagram 13.28: Form field validations based on Customers table constraints.

14. WORKING WITH FORMS (THE MANUAL WAY)

CREATING AN APPLICATION MANUALLY

Sometimes it is required to customize an application as per customer requirements such as additional forms / reports, master detail forms and so on. This is easily done with a manually created application. Initially empty, and then appropriately populated, as desired with components such as forms, reports, graphs and so on.

The focus here is to manually create forms and reports for the Car Rental Application from scratch. The manual application creation via HTMLDB involves the following steps: (Refer to diagram 14.0.)
- ❑ Creation Method
- ❑ Name and Authentication
- ❑ Pages, Tabs, Other Attributes
- ❑ Page Names
- ❑ Tabs
- ❑ UI Theme
- ❑ Confirm

To create an application via the HTML DB interface do the following:

Enter the following URL to login to HTML DB:
http://<hostname>:7777/pls/htmld/htmldb

Enter the name of the workspace, username and password. Click Login. (Refer diagram 14.1.)

After authentication of the login for the **CARRENTAL** workspace, the **Start** page appears as shown in diagram 14.2.

To create an application, click the **Application Builder** option. (Refer diagram 14.2.)

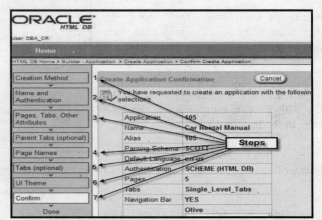

Diagram 14.0: Steps in Manual application creation.

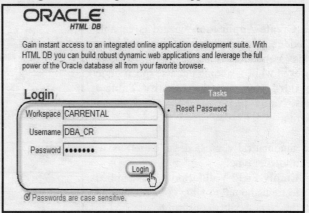

Diagram 14.1: Login page for HTMLDB.

Diagram 14.2: Selecting the Application Builder option.

To create the form based on a table held within the Oracle database, click **Create Application**. (Refer diagram 14.3.)

The **Select Creation Method** page is displayed as shown in diagram 14.4.1.

This is the **first step** in the Create Application process.

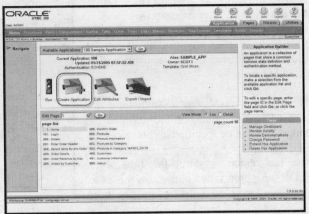

Diagram 14.3: Selecting the Create Application option.

Select the **From Scratch** option and click Next >. This manually creates the application, (i.e. forms and reports are **not created** at this time). However, the manual creation of forms/reports will be handled later.

The **Name and Authentication** page, the **second step**, follows. Refer diagram 14.4.2.

Specify an application name and number.

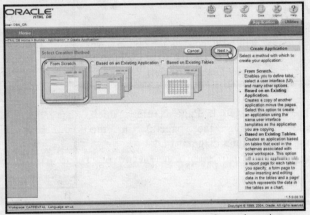

Diagram 14.4.1: Selecting the From Scratch option.

Select an appropriate schema that will be authenticated to operate the application, (in this case, SCOTT).

To know the language settings for the application expand the Globalization Options by clicking ▶. Refer diagram 14.4.2.

Click Next > to continue.

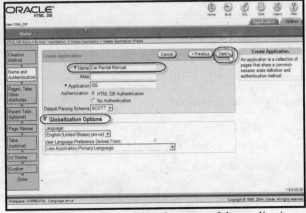

Diagram 14.4.2: Specifying the name of the application.

The **third step** is the **Pages, Tabs, Other Attributes** page, refer diagram 14.4.3.

Specify the number of pages that should be allotted and created for the application. The default being **5**.

The option of displaying a Navigation Bar (Refer Diagram 14.4.3) on the pages in the application can be specified in this step.

The last option is select the **tabs** style. Select an appropriation option, (in this case, the **One Level of Tabs** option has been selected). Click Next> to continue.

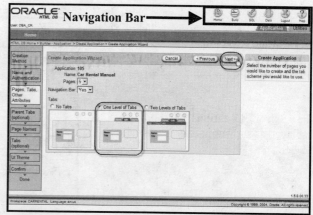

Diagram 14.4.3: Specifying the number of tab levels.

 Note

The **Parent Tabs (optional)** step will be skipped as the option **Two Levels of Tabs** was not selected. (Refer Diagram 14.4.4)

The **fourth step** is **Page Names**, which allows naming the page(s) in the application. Refer diagram 14.4.4.

After naming the page(s), click Next> to continue.

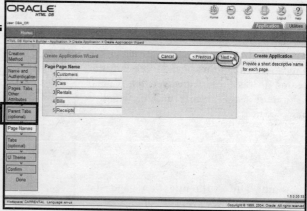

Diagram 14.4.4: Specifying the name for the pages in the application.

Creating the **Tabs** follows as the **fifth step**. Refer diagram 14.4.5.

This is skipped, if the option **No Tabs** was selected in the **third step**.

This allows specifying the name of the second or inner level tab(s).

Specify the name or label that should appear on the tab(s) and click Next> .

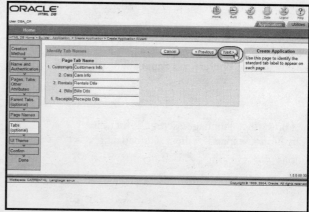

Diagram 14.4.5: Specifying the name for the tabs in the application.

The **sixth step** is the **UI Theme** page, refer diagram 14.4.6.

Use this page to select a default template for the application's pages. Select an appropriate template and click 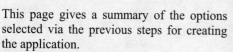 to continue.

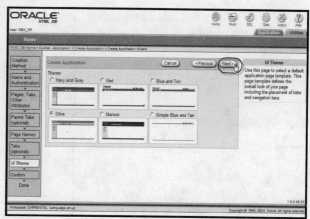

Diagram 14.4.6: Specifying the default template for the application.

The **seventh step** is the **Confirm** page as shown in diagram 14.4.7.

This page gives a summary of the options selected via the previous steps for creating the application.

Use the **‹ Previous** button to make changes to the attributes of the application selected earlier if required.

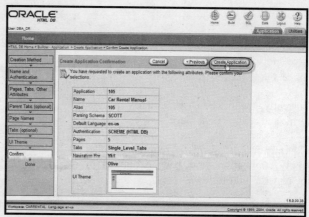

Diagram 14.4.7: Summary of the options selected for creating the application manually.

To confirm the creation of the application click **Create Application**.

Finally, the application is created and its confirmation appears on the Application Builder's **Home** page, Refer diagram 14.5.

Click on the **Run** link to execute the application.

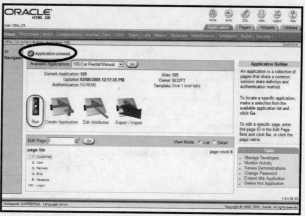

Diagram 14.5: Running the application.

When the application begins a Login screen appears to authenticate the access appears. Refer diagram 14.6.

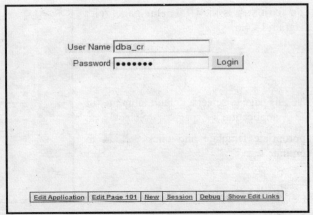

Enter the correct login information and click Login to continue.

Diagram 14.6: Login page for the application created manually.

The **Home** page for the application appears as shown in diagram 14.7.

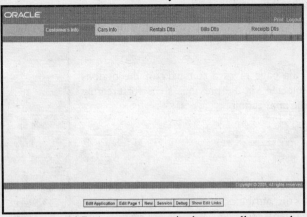

Since the form or reports for the application have not been created, an empty page appears in the template selected.

Currently, the Framework, which will hold forms and reports is in place.

The creation of forms / reports for this empty application have been explained in the material that follows.

Diagram 14.7: An empty page in the manually created application.

CREATING FORMS / REPORTS MANUALLY

The manual creation of forms and reports via HTMLDB involves the following steps: (Refer diagram 14.8.)

❑   Table / View Owner
❑   Table / View Name
❑   Report Page and Region Attributes
❑   Report Columns
❑   Report Edit Link
❑   Form Page and Region Attributes
❑   Form Tab
❑   Primary Key
❑   Form Columns
❑   Process Options
❑   Confirm

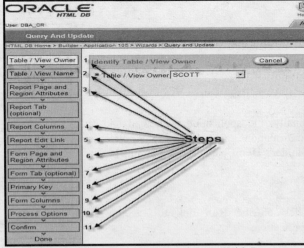

Diagram 14.8: Steps in Manual Form With Report creation.

Return to the empty template page of the application.

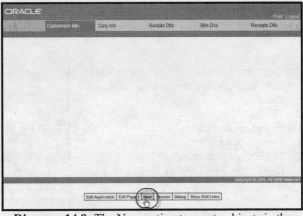

To create a **form** on the Customers Info Tab of the application, click the **New** option on the footer bar. Refer diagram 14.9.

Diagram 14.9: The New option to create objects in the application created manually.

The **Create New** page appears as shown in diagram 14.10.

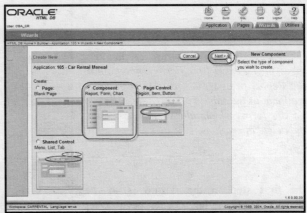

Select the **Component** option. This allows adding Forms, Reports and Charts to the application.

Click **Next >** to continue.

Diagram 14.10: Selecting the option to create a new component for the application.

The **Select Component Type** page appears, as shown in diagram 14.11.

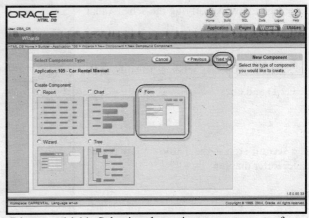

Select the **Form** radio button to create a new data entry form for the application.

Click **Next >** to continue.

Diagram 14.11: Selecting the option to create a new form for the application.

The **New Form Wizards** page appears, as shown in diagram 14.12.

This page provides six options via which a form can be created. These options are:

❑ Table
❑ Tabular Form
❑ Procedure Arguments
❑ Form with Report
❑ SQL Query (fetch row)
❑ Display Only on Existing Items

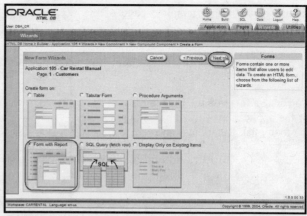

Diagram 14.12: Selecting the option to create a form with a report.

Select the **Form with Report** option and click Next> to invoke the **Query and Update** wizard.

The Query and Update wizard creates two pages in a Report and Form combination. The Report provides a view of the records available in the table and provides a link to the d/e form, which allows insert, update and delete operations.

The **first step** in the wizard is to the **Identify Table / View Owner** page. Refer diagram 14.13.1.

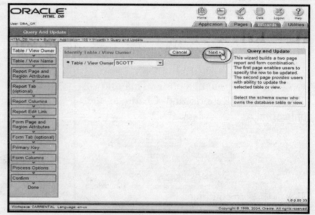

Diagram 14.13.1: Specifying the owner of the database object, used for creating the new form.

This page allows specifying the schema that owns the database table or view.

Select an appropriate schema, (in this case, SCOTT) and click Next>.

The **second step** is the **Table / View Name** page. Refer diagram 14.13.2.1.

Specify the table or view on which the report and form will be based.

Diagram 14.13.2.1: Specifying the database table to be bound to the new form.

To select a table from the database click on (List option) to get a **Search Dialog** box as shown in diagram 14.13.2.2.

Select an appropriate table, (in this case, the **CUSTOMERS** table), to close the **Search Dialog** box.

Click [Next >] to continue.

The **Identify Page and Region Attributes for Report** is the **third step** in the wizard. Refer diagram 14.13.3.

The Report page is used to view the rows in the table. It also includes a link to create a new record. If the **page** specified does not exist, the wizard will create it.

Additionally, specify the name of the page and the title for the region in which the report will be displayed.

The last required attribute is the region template.

After providing the values for the attributes of the report's page and region, click [Next >] to continue.

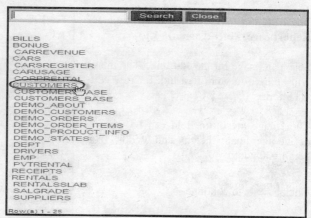

Diagram 14.13.2.2: The Search **Dialog** box for selecting a Table for the **Application**.

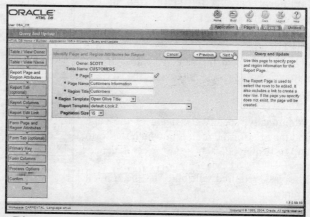

Diagram 14.13.3: Specifying attributes belonging to the report page created along with the new form.

Note

The wizard's next step is the **Report Tab** page. However, this page is not displayed while creating a Form with report.

The **fourth step** is the **Identify Columns for Report** page. Refer diagram 14.13.4.

Select the columns to be included in the report page.

Optionally, a condition can be specified to restrict the result set from which the report is generated.

To allow the report to display all information held within the previously selected table / view, have all the columns selected and do not specify any WHERE clause. Continue by clicking [Next >].

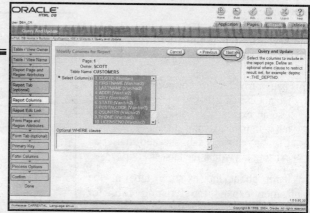

Diagram 14.13.4: Specifying the table column(s), whose data will be displayed on the report page.

The **fifth step** is the **Edit Link Image for Report** page. Refer diagram 14.13.5.

Select an image for the edit link. The image will be used to point to a link for row edits via a form.

The **Image attribute** field can be used to define the image height and width, (e.g. height=30 width=40).

Click Next> to continue.

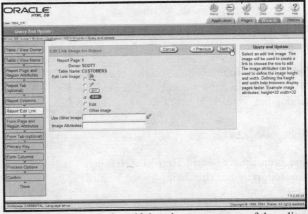

Diagram 14.13.5: Specifying the appearance of the edit link on the report page.

The **Identify Page and Region Attributes for Form** page is the **sixth step** in the wizard. Refer diagram 14.13.6.

The Form page is used to insert, update and delete rows from the selected table. If the **page** specified does not exist, the wizard will create it

Additionally, specify the name of the page and the title for the region in which the form will be displayed.

The last required attribute is the region template.

After providing the values for the attributes of the form's page and region, click Next> to continue.

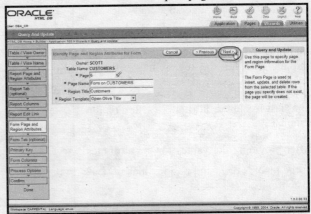

Diagram 14.13.6: Specifying the attributes of the new form.

The **seventh step** is the **Identify Tab for Form** page as shown in diagram 14.13.7.

This page provides three options:
❑ Do not use tabs.
❑ Use an existing tab set and create a new tab within the existing tab set.
❑ Use an existing tab set and reuse an existing tab within the tab set.

To learn about the existing tabs in the application expand the Existing Tabs for Application by clicking ▶. Refer diagram 14.13.7.

Select the **Do not use tabs** option and click Next> to continue.

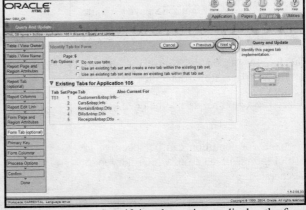

Diagram 14.13.7: Specifying the option to display the form on a page without tabs.

The **Identify Primary Key** page is the **eighth step** in the wizard. Refer diagram 14.13.8.

Select the primary key column of the table.

Optionally, a second primary column can be identified, (only for tables with composite, primary keys).

Click [Next>] to continue.

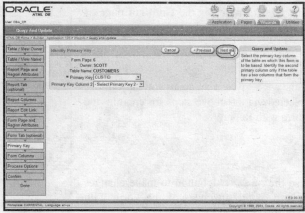

Diagram 14.13.8: Specifying the Primary key field(s) on the new form.

The **ninth step** is the **Identify Columns for Form** page as shown in diagram 14.13.9.

Select the columns to be included in the form page, (i.e. columns to be represented by a data capture field on the form).

Click [Next>].

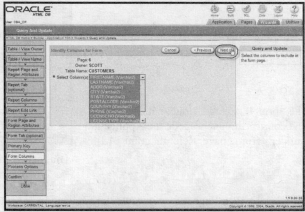

Diagram 14.13.9: Specifying the columns, which will have a data entry field on the new form.

The **tenth step** is the **Identity Process Options** page as shown in diagram 14.13.10.

This page identifies the processes the form allows a user. The processes include operations like Insert, Update and Delete. (Select **Yes** for all three processes.)

Click [Next>] to continue.

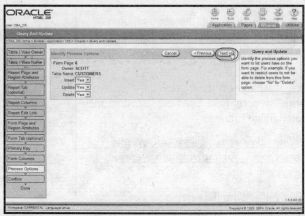

Diagram 14.13.10: Specifying the processes, which will be available on the new form.

The **eleventh step** is the **Confirm** page as shown in diagram 14.13.11.

This page gives a summary of the options selected via the above steps for creating the Form with Report.

Use the < Previous button to make changes to any of the attributes of the Form with Report if required.

To confirm the creation of the Form with Report click Finish .

The form is created along with its report. The confirmation appears on the Application Builder's **Home** page, Refer diagram 14.14.

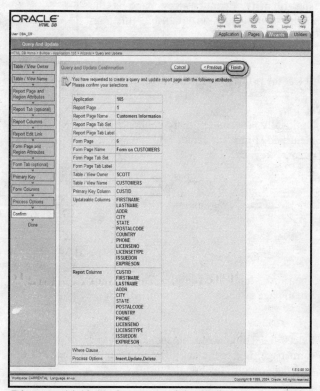

Diagram 14.13.11: Summary of the attributes selected for the creation of the new form with report.

Click on the **Run Page** link to execute the application.

The **Home** page for the application now displays a report as shown in diagram 14.15.1.

The working of these manually created forms / reports have been explained in the material that follows.

Follow the same steps to create the forms/reports for the remaining entities in the system.

What follows are the screenshots of forms / reports manually created for the Car Rental System: (Refer diagrams 14.15.1 to 14.15.10.)

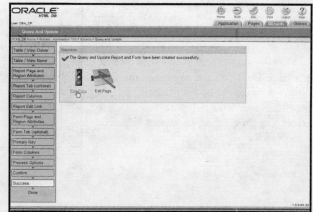

Diagram 14.14: Selecting the option to run the new form with the manually created application.

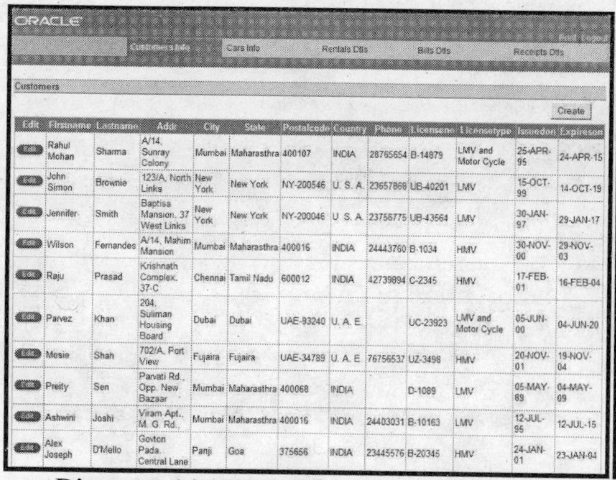

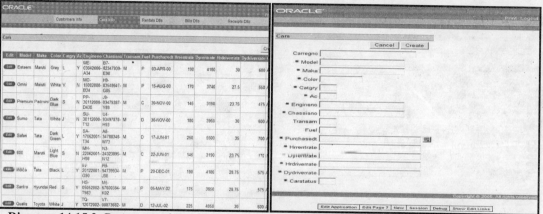

Diagram 14.15.1: Report page bound to the Customers table.

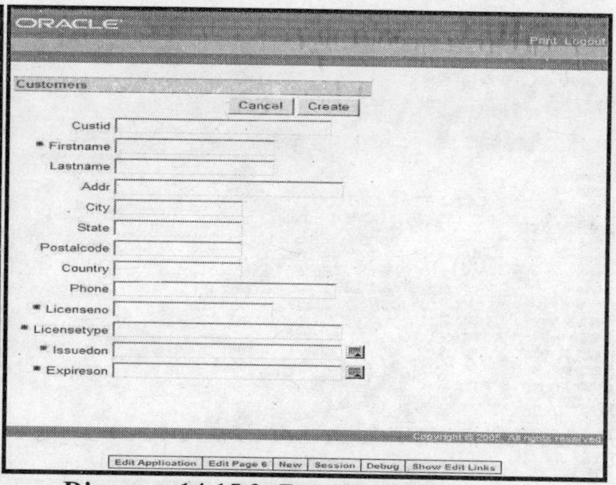

Diagram 14.15.2: Form page bound to the Customers table.

Diagram 14.15.3: Report page bound to the Cars table.

Diagram 14.15.4: Form page bound to the Cars table.

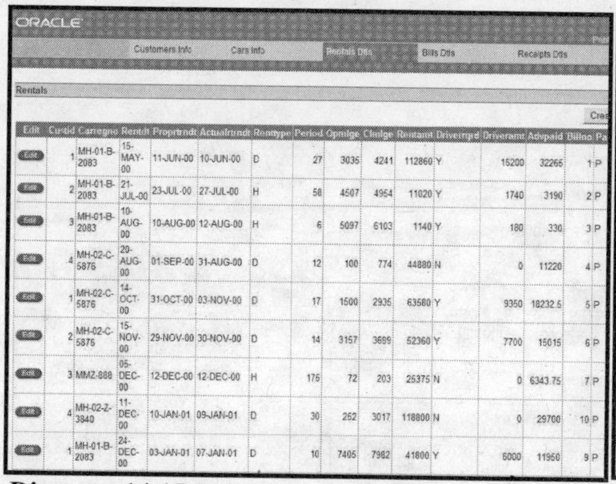

Diagram 14.15.5: Report page bound to the Rentals table.

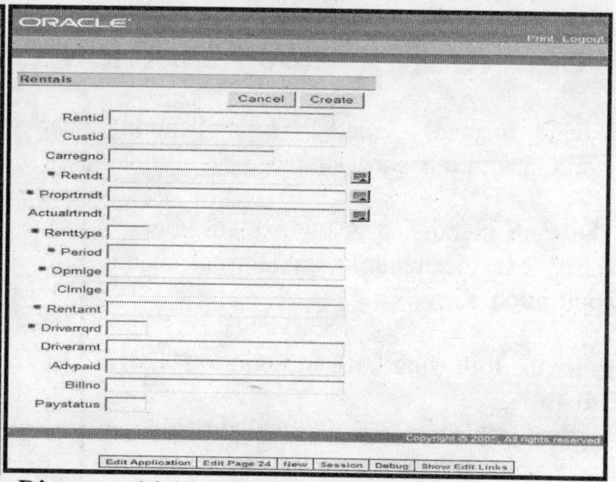

Diagram 14.15.6: Form page bound to the Rentals table.

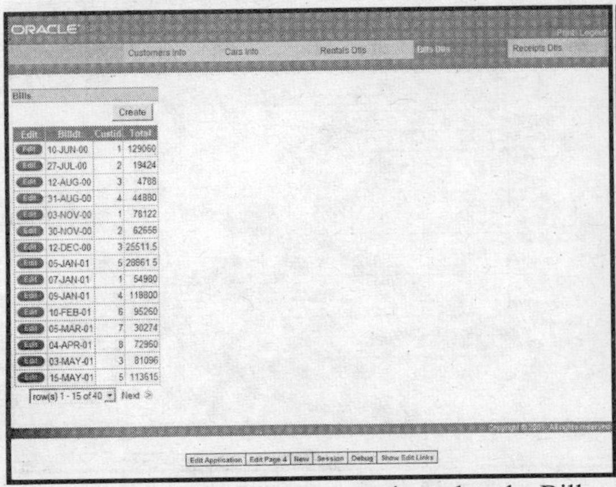

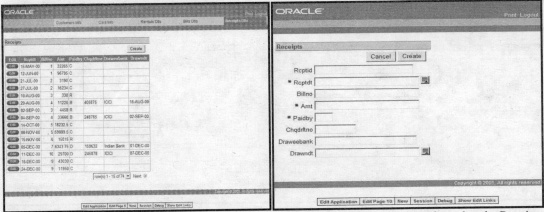

Diagram 14.15.7: Report page bound to the Bills table.

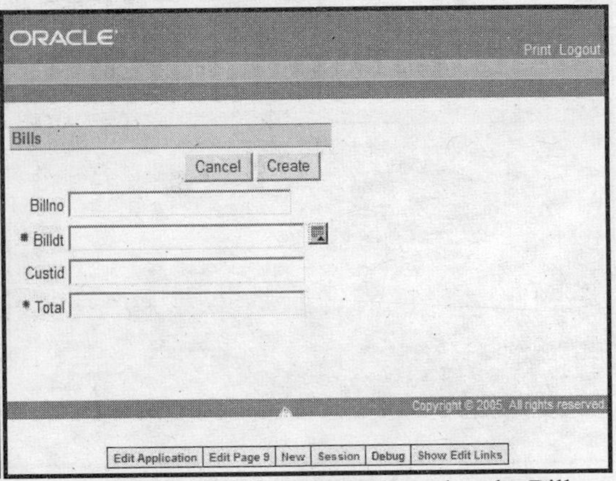

Diagram 14.15.8: Form page bound to the Bills table.

Diagram 14.15.9: Report page bound to the Receipts table.

Diagram 14.15.10: Form page bound to the Receipts table.

WORKING WITH AN APPLICATION

Having manually created an application, working with it is fairly simple.

The steps mentioned below explain how to use / execute reports and forms in an application.

Enter the following URL to login to HTML DB:
http://<hostname>:7777/pls/htmldb/htmldb

Enter the name of the workspace, username and password. Click Login . (Refer diagram 14.16.)

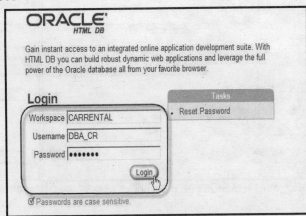

Diagram 14.16: Login page for HTMLDB.

After authentication of the login for the **CARRENTAL** workspace, the **Start** page appears as shown in diagram 14.17. Click the **Application Builder** option.

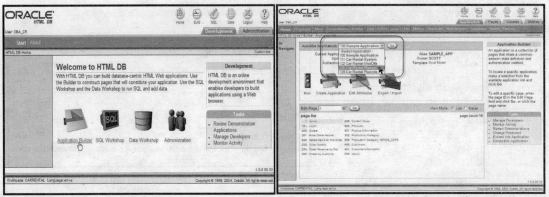

Diagram 14.17: Selecting the Application Builder option.

Diagram 14.18: Selecting the Car Rental application.

From the **Home** page, select the appropriate application from the **Available Application** drop-down list, (i.e. select Car Rental Manual). Refer diagram 14.18.

Click **Go** to access the objects within the selected application.

The Home page for the required application (i.e. the Car Rental System) appears as shown in diagram 14.19.

The center of the Home page consists of a listing of various pages created in the application.

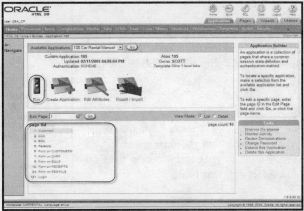

Diagram 14.19: Selecting the Run option from the Car Rental application's Home page.

Click on the **Run** link to execute the application.

When the application begins a Login screen appears to authenticate the access. Refer diagram 14.20.

Enter the correct login information and click **Login** to continue.

Since the application has no **Home** page, the first tab (i.e. A Report on Customers table) is the displayed.

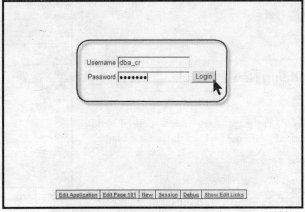

Diagram 14.20: Application Login page.

Editing Existing Records

To modify a particular **record from** the table, it is necessary to first **view the report** for that table.

When the **records in the table** are listed, select the **record that will** be edited by clicking **Edit**. Refer diagram 14.21.1.

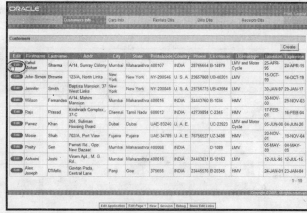

Diagram 14.21.1: Selecting the Edit link in the report page of the application.

The record is transferred to the data entry form in the **Edit** mode, (i.e. the top-right corner of the data entry form provides options to delete or update information). Refer diagram 14.21.2.

Perform the modification by changing the information held within the fields of the data entry form.

Click **Apply Changes** to update the record in the database with the changes made on the page with the data entry form in the **Edit** mode. Refer diagram 14.21.2.

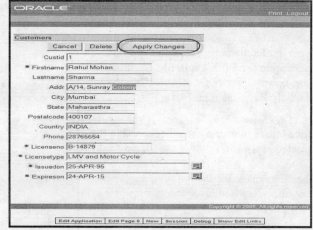

Diagram 14.21.2: Applying the changes made in the data entry form.

A confirmation for the update is displayed by re-displaying the report with the updated data.

Adding New Records

A data entry form provides a method to add and edit data held within database table(s).

Click **Create** option in the report page to add a new record. Refer diagram 14.22.1.

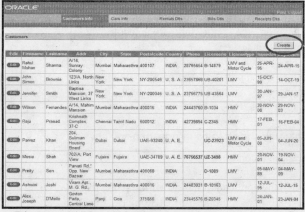

Diagram 14.22.1: Selecting the option to create a new record.

A page with an empty data entry form appears.

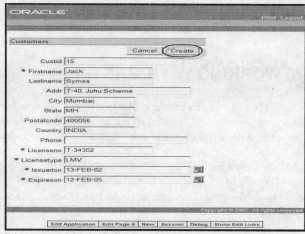

Having entered information click `Create`, which is placed on the top-right corner of the data entry form. This creates a new record in the database table. Refer diagram 14.22.2.

The insertion of the new record is confirmed by listing it along with the information previously held in the table.

Diagram 14.22.2: Selecting the Create option from the data entry form.

The report page appears in a tabular format, with the new record, as shown in diagram 14.23.1.

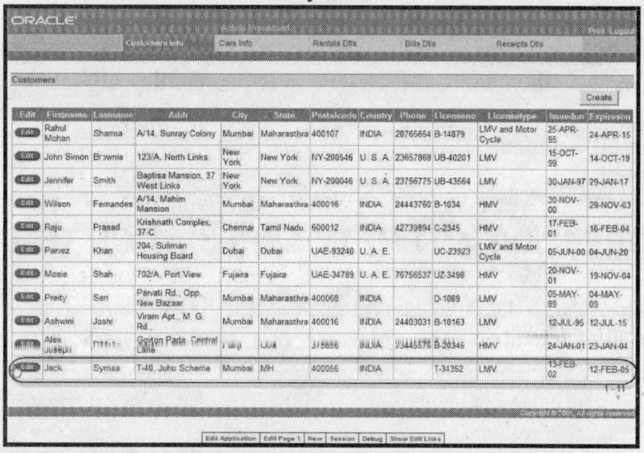

Deleting Existing Records

To delete a particular record from the table it is necessary to first view the report for that table.

When the records in the table are listed, select the record to be deleted by clicking `Edit`. Refer diagram 14.23.1.

Diagram 14.23.1: Selecting the Edit link for the new record displayed on the report page.

The record is transferred to the data entry form in the **Edit** mode (i.e. the top-right corner of the data entry form provides options to delete or update information). Refer diagram 13.23.1.

Click `Delete` to delete the record currently displayed on the page with the data entry form in the **Edit** mode.

After deletion the report is re-displayed (without the deleted record).

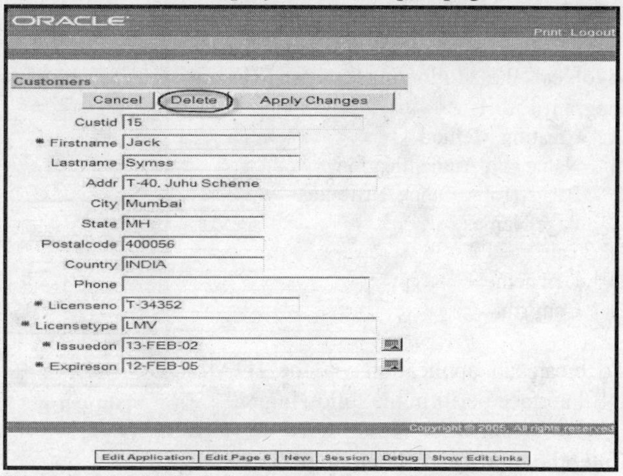

Diagram 14.33.2: Selecting the Delete option from the data entry form.

15. WORKING WITH MASTER DETAILS USER INTERFACES

Information is said to be having a Master-Details relationship, when a set of one-time (Master) information has one or more set(s) of related (Details) information. For example, the master set of information contains a person's name, while each and every contact number for that person forms a details entry.

A Master-Detail form is capable of handling the relationship between the two sets of information, (i.e. it should be able to allow access to master information as well as to the details belonging to that master. The layout for a Master-Details user interface comprises of two sections, namely:
❑ The Master Information section
❑ The Details Information section

In general, the Master section handles only one set of master information. It is made up of data objects like textboxes, radio buttons, list boxes, check boxes and so on.

On the other hand, the Details section handles all sets of details (belong to the master only). Data is managed by arranging them in a form of a grid. Each row in the grid represents a single set of details information.

CREATING AN EMPTY APPLICATION TEMPLATE MANUALLY

The Master-Details user interface can be created in an empty application. Following possibilities are available while creating Master-Detail forms for the Car Rental System:
❑ Customer-wise Transactions
❑ Bill-wise Payments

The focus here is to manually create the Master Details user interface for the Car Rental application from scratch. The manual application creation via HTMLDB involves the following steps: (Refer diagram 15.0.)
❑ Creation Method
❑ Name and Authentication
❑ Pages, Tabs, Other Attributes
❑ Page Names
❑ Tabs
❑ UI Theme
❑ Confirm

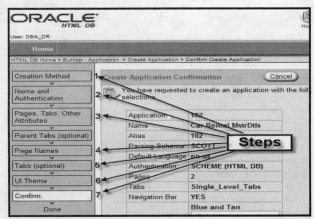

Diagram 15.0: Steps in Manual application creation.

To create an application via the HTML DB interface perform the following:

Enter the following URL to login to HTML DB:
http://<hostname>:7777/pls/htmld/htmldb

Enter the name of the workspace, username and password. Click Login . (Refer diagram 15.1.)

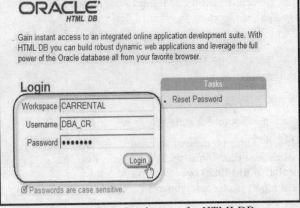

Diagram 15.1: Login page for HTMLDB.

After authentication of the login for the **CARRENTAL** workspace, the **Start** page appears as shown in diagram 15.2.

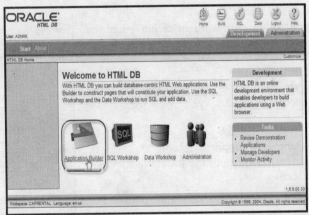

Diagram 15.2: Selecting the Application Builder option.

To create an application, click the **Application Builder** option. (Refer diagram 15.2.)

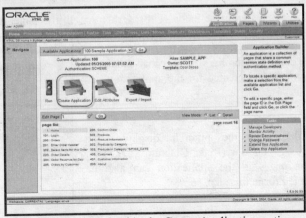

To create the form, click **Create Application**. (Refer diagram 15.3.)

Diagram 15.3: Selecting the Create Application option.

The **Select Creation Method** page is displayed as shown in diagram 15.4.1.

This is the **first step** in the Create Application process.

Select the **From Scratch** option and click Next >. This is manual creation of the application, (i.e. forms and reports are **not created** at this time) only the page to hold a form/report is created. However, the manual creation of forms/reports will be handled later.

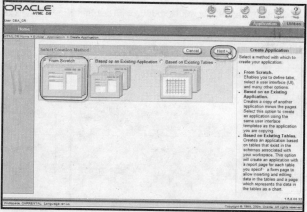

Diagram 15.4.1: Selecting the From Scratch option.

The **Name and Authentication** page, the **second step**, follows. Refer diagram 15.4.2.

Specify an application name and number (appears automatically).

Select an appropriate schema that will be authenticated to operate the application, (in this case, SCOTT).

Click Next > to continue.

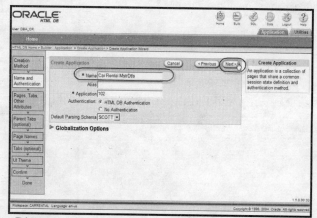

Diagram 15.4.2: Specifying the name of the application.

The **third step** is the **Pages, Tabs, Other Attributes** page, refer diagram 15.4.3.

Specify the number of pages that should be allotted and created for the application, (in this case 2 pages).

Additionally, the option for displaying the Navigation Bar (Refer Diagram 15.4.3) on the pages in the application can also be opted for in this step.

The last option is select the tabs style. Select an appropriation option, (in this case the **One Level of Tabs** option has been selected). Click Next > to continue.

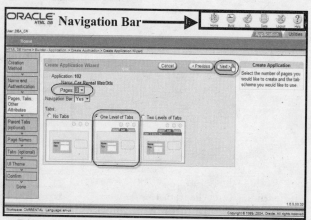

Diagram 15.4.3: Specifying the number of tab levels.

Note

The **Parent Tabs (optional)** step will be skipped as the option **Two Levels of Tabs** was not selected. (Refer Diagram 15.4.4)

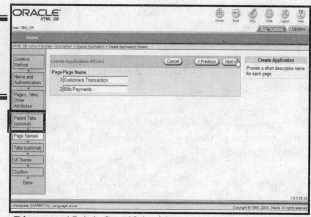

Diagram 15.4.4: Specifying the name for the pages in the application.

The **fourth step** is **Page Name**, which allows naming the page(s) in the application. Refer diagram 15.4.4.

After naming the page(s), click Next > to continue.

The **Tabs** step follows as the **fifth step**. Refer diagram 15.4.5.

This is skipped, if the option **No Tabs** is selected in the **third step**.

It allows specifying the name of the second or inner level tab(s).

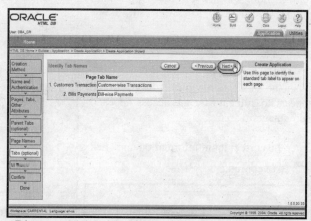

Diagram 15.4.5: Specifying the name for the tabs in the application.

Specify the name or label that should appear on the tab(s) and click Next >.

The **sixth step** is the **UI Theme** page, refer diagram 15.4.6.

Use this page to select a default template for the application's pages. Select an appropriate template and click Next > to continue.

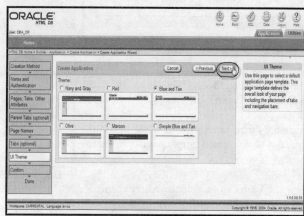

Diagram 15.4.6: Specifying the default template for the application.

The **seventh step** is the **Confirm** page as shown in diagram 15.4.7.

This page gives a summary of the options selected via the steps for creating the application.

Use the 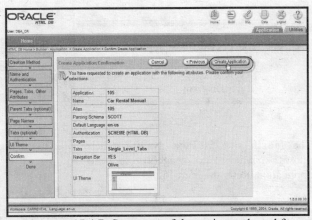 button to make changes to the attributes of the application selected earlier if required.

To confirm the creation of the application click [Create Application].

Diagram 15.4.7: Summary of the options selected for creating the application manually.

Finally, the application is created and its confirmation appears on the Application Builder's **Home** page, Refer diagram 15.5.

Click on the **Run** link to execute the application.

When the application begins, a Login screen appears to authenticate the access appears. Refer diagram 15.6.

Enter the correct login information and click [Login] to continue.

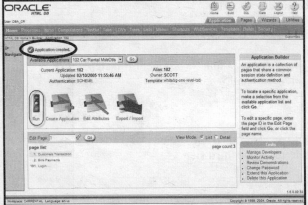

Diagram 15.5: Running the application.

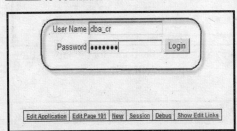

Diagram 15.6: Login page for the Master Details application created manually.

The **Home** page for the application appears as shown in diagram 15.7.

Since the forms or reports for the application have not been created empty page appears in the template selected.

Now the Framework, which will hold forms and reports, is in place.

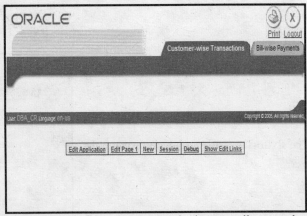

Diagram 15.7: An empty page in the manually created application.

The steps to create a master details application have been explained in the material to follow.

CREATING A MASTER DETAILS USERS INTERFACE MANUALLY

The creation of the user interface for a Master Details form is a two-phase process:

❑ Building the Master section
❑ Building the Details section
❑ Binding the Details section to the Master section

Diagram 15.8.1: The report page for the Master section.

Building The Master Section

In this phase of the Master Details user interface creation, the report and data entry form for the master section is designed.

The report and form are placed on difference pages (preferably, the form is rendered on a tab-less page). Refer diagrams 15.8.1 and 15.8.2.

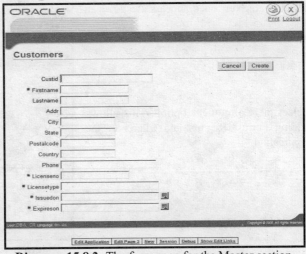

Diagram 15.8.2: The form page for the Master section.

The manual creation (report and form) for the Master Section, via HTMLDB involves the following steps: (Refer diagram 15.9.)

❑ Table / View Owner
❑ Table / View Name
❑ Report Page and Region Attributes
❑ Report Columns
❑ Report Edit Link
❑ Form Page and Region Attributes
❑ Form Tab
❑ Primary Key
❑ Form Columns
❑ Process Options
❑ Confirm

Diagram 15.9: Steps in building the Master section manually.

Return to the empty template page of the application.

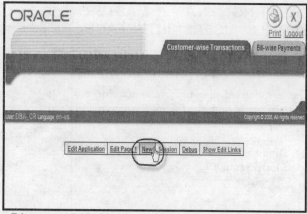

To create a report on the **Customer-wise Transactions** tab of the application, click the **New** option on the footer bar. Refer diagram 15.10.

Diagram 15.10: The New option to create objects in the application created manually.

The **Create New** page appears as shown in diagram 15.11.1.

Select the **Component** option. This allows adding Forms, Reports and Charts to the application.

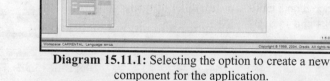

Click  to continue.

Diagram 15.11.1: Selecting the option to create a new component for the application.

The **Select Component Type** page appears, as shown in diagram 15.11.2.

Select the **Report** radio button to create a new report for the Master section in the application.

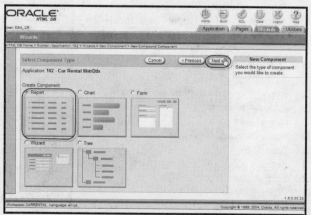

Click ~~Next >~~ to continue.

Diagram 15.11.2: Selecting the option to create a new report for the application.

The **New Form Wizards** page appears, as shown in diagram 15.12.

This page provides three options via which a report can be created. These options are:
- ❑ Easy Report
- ❑ SQL Report
- ❑ Report with Form

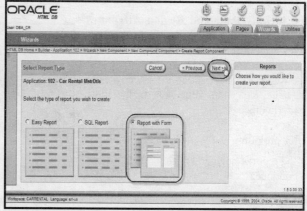

Select the **Report with Form** option and click Next > to invoke the **Query and Update** wizard.

Diagram 15.12: Selecting the option to create a report with a form.

The Query and Update wizard creates two pages in a Report and Form combination. The Report provides a view of the records available in the table and provides a link to the d/e form, which allows insert, update and delete operations.

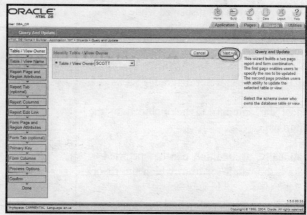

The **first step** in the wizard is the **Identify Table / View Owner** page. Refer diagram 15.13.1.

Diagram 15.13.1: Specifying the owner of the database object, used for creating the new report with a form.

This page allows specifying the schema that owns the database table or view.

Select an appropriate schema, (in this case, SCOTT) and click Next >.

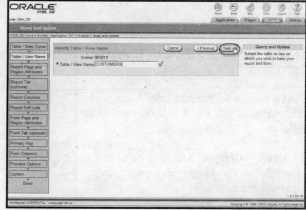

The **second step** is the **Table / View Name** page. Refer diagram 15.13.2.

Specify the table or view on which the report and form will be based. (In this case, the **Customers** table)

Click Next > to continue.

Diagram 15.13.2: Specifying the database table to be bound to the new report with a form.

The **Identify Page and Region Attributes for Report** is the **third step** in the wizard. Refer diagram 15.13.3.

The Report page is used to view the rows in the table. Keep the value held in the **Page** field, (in this case **1**).

After providing the values for the attributes of the report's page and region, click Next> to continue.

Note

> The wizard's next step is the **Report Tab** page. However, this page is not displayed while creating a Form with report.

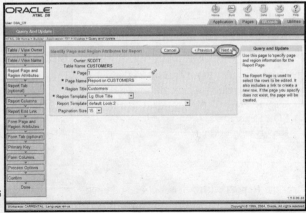

Diagram 15.13.3: Specifying attributes belonging to the report page created along with the new report with a form.

The **fourth step** is the **Identify Columns for Report** page. Refer diagram 15.13.4.

Select the columns to be included in the report page.

Optionally, a condition can be specified to restrict the result set from which the report is generated.

To allow the report to display all information held within the previously selected table / view, have all the columns selected and do not specify the WHERE clause. Continue by clicking Next>.

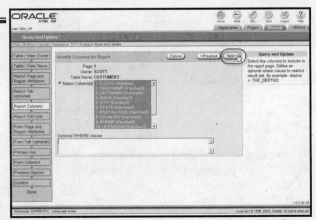

Diagram 15.13.4: Specifying the table column(s), whose data will be displayed on the report page.

The **fifth step** is the **Edit Link Image for Report** page. Refer diagram 15.13.5.

Select an image for the edit link. The image will be used to point to a link for row edits via a form.

The **Image attribute** field can be used to define the image height and width, (e.g. height=30 width=40).

Click Next> to continue.

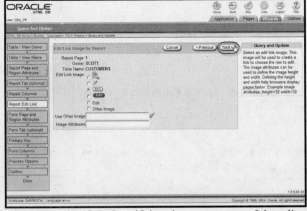

Diagram 15.13.5: Specifying the appearance of the edit link on the report page.

The **Identify Page and Region Attributes for Form** page is the **sixth step** in the wizard. Refer diagram 15.13.6.

Specify a non-existing page number for the **Page** field, (in this case **3**). As the **page** specified does not exist, the wizard will create it.

After providing the values for the attributes of the form's page and region, click **Next >** to continue.

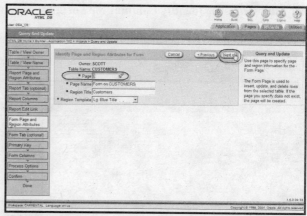

Diagram 15.13.6: Specifying the attributes of the new form.

The **seventh step** is the **Identify Tab for Form** page as shown in diagram 15.13.7.

This page provides three options:

❑ Do not use tabs.
❑ Use an existing tab set and create a new tab within the existing tab set.
❑ Use an existing tab set and reuse an existing tab within the tab set.

Select the **Do not use tabs** option and click **Next >** to continue.

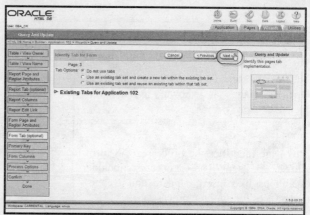

Diagram 15.13.7: Specifying the option to display the form on a page without tabs.

The **Identify Primary Key** page is the **eighth step** in the wizard. Refer diagram 15.13.8.

Select the primary key column of the table.

Optionally, the second primary column can be identified, (only for tables with two columns forming the primary key).

Click **Next >** to continue.

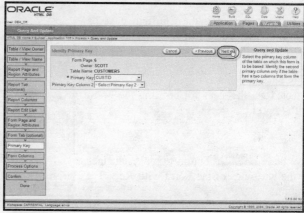

Diagram 15.13.8: Specifying the Primary key field(s) on the new form.

The **ninth step** is the **Identify Columns for Form** page as shown in diagram 15.13.9.

Select the columns to be included in the form page, (i.e. columns to be represented by a data capture field on the form). Click Next >.

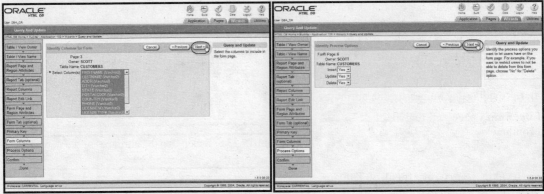

Diagram 15.13.9: Specifying the columns, which will have a data entry field on the new form.   **Diagram 15.13.10:** Specifying the processes, which will be available on the new form.

The **tenth step** is the **Identity Process Options** page as shown in diagram 15.13.10.

This page identifies the processes the form allows a user. The processes include operations like Insert, Update and Delete. (Select **Yes** for all three processes.)

Click Next > to continue.

The **eleventh step** is the **Confirm** page as shown in diagram 15.13.11.

This page gives a summary of the options selected via the steps for creating the Form with Report.

Use the < Previous button to make changes to the attributes of the Form with Report if required.

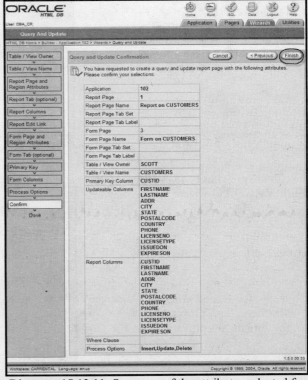

Diagram 15.13.11: Summary of the attributes selected for the creation of the new report with a form.

To confirm the creation of the Form with Report click Finish.

The report is created along with its form. The confirmation appears on the Application Builder's **Home** page, Refer diagram 15.14.

Click on the **Run Page** link to execute the application.

The **Home** page for the application now displays a report as shown in diagram 15.15.1.

Click Create to get the data entry form, in a tab-less page. Refer diagram 15.15.2

Diagram 15.14: Selecting the option to run the new report with a form within the manually created application.

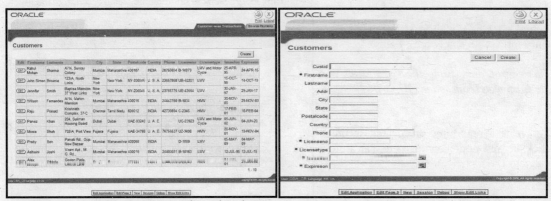

Diagram 15.15.1: Report page bound to the Customers table.

Diagram 15.15.2: Form page bound to the Customers table – Master section.

Building The Detail Section

The second phase in the creation of the Master Details User Interface is the report forming the Details section.

The phase includes placing the report and the form on difference pages **with the exception** that the report for the Details section is placed exactly below the data entry form of the Master section. Refer diagrams 15.16.

The form for the Details section will be placed on a separate tab-less page.

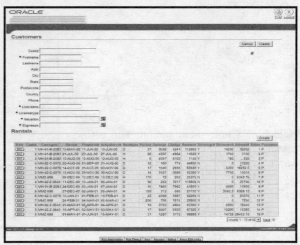

Diagram 15.16: Details section's report placed under the Master section's form.

As in the case of the Master section, the manual creation (report and form) for the Details Section, via HTMLDB involves the following steps: (Refer diagram 15.17.)

❑ Table / View Owner
❑ Table / View Name
❑ Report Page and Region Attributes
❑ Report Columns
❑ Report Edit Link
❑ Form Page and Region Attributes
❑ Form Tab
❑ Primary Key
❑ Form Columns
❑ Process Options
❑ Confirm

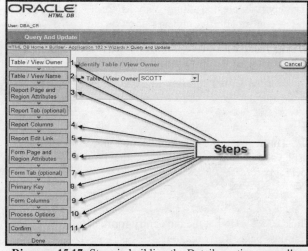

Diagram 15.17: Steps in building the Details section manually.

Return to the page with Master section's data entry form (with empty form fields).

This can be done using the Create link on the Customer Transactions Report.

To create a report for the details section, click the **New** option on the footer bar. Refer diagram 15.18.

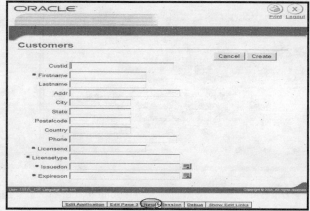

Diagram 15.18: The New option to create the Details section.

The **Create New** page appears as shown in diagram 15.19.1.

Select the **Component** option. This allows adding Forms, Reports and Charts to the application.

Click Next> to continue.

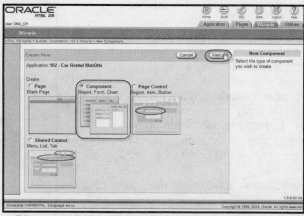

Diagram 15.19.1: Selecting the option to create a new component for the application.

The **Select Component Type** page appears, as shown in diagram 15.19.2.

Select the **Report** radio button to create a new report for the Master section in the application.

Click [Next>] to continue.

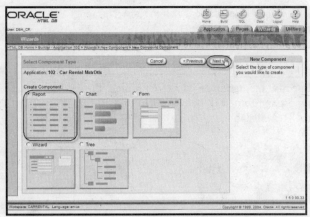

Diagram 15.19.2: Selecting the option to create a new report for the application.

The **Select Report Type** page appears, as shown in diagram 15.20.

Select the **Report with Form** option and click [Next>] to invoke the **Query and Update** wizard.

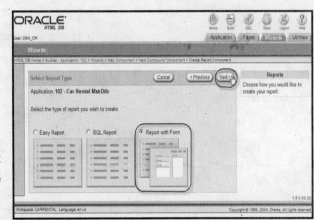

Diagram 15.20: Selecting the option to create a report with a form.

The **first step** in the wizard is the **Identify Table / View Owner** page. Refer diagram 15.21.1.

This page allows specifying the schema that owns the database table or view.

Select an appropriate schema, (in this case, SCOTT) and click [Next>].

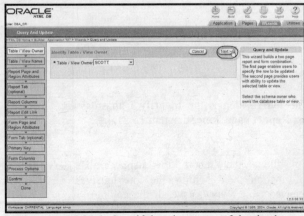

Diagram 15.21.1: Specifying the owner of the database object, used for creating the new report with a form.

The **second step** is the **Table / View Name** page. Refer diagram 15.21.2.

Specify the table or view on which the report and form will be based. (In this case, the **Rentals** table)

Click to continue.

Diagram 15.21.2: Specifying the database table to be bound to the Details section's report with a form.

The **Identify Page and Region Attributes for Report** is the **third step** in the wizard. Refer diagram 15.21.3.

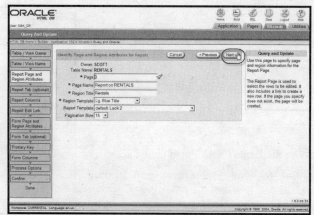

The Report page is used to view the rows in the table. Keep the value held in the **Page** field, (in this case **3**).

After providing the values for the attributes of the report's page and region, click [Next >] to continue.

Diagram 15.21.3: Specifying attributes belonging to the report page created for the Details section.

Note

The wizard's next step is the **Report Tab** page. However, this page is not displayed while creating a Form with report.

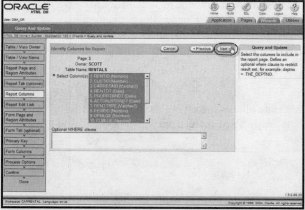

The **fourth step** is the **Identify Columns for Report** page. Refer diagram 15.21.4.

To allow the report to display all information held within the previously selected table / view, have all the columns selected and do not specify the WHERE clause. Continue by clicking [Next >].

Diagram 15.21.4: Specifying the table column(s), whose data will be displayed on the Details section's report page.

The **fifth step** is the **Edit Link Image for Report** page. Refer diagram 15.21.5.

Select an image for the edit link. The image will be used to point to a link for row edits via a form.

Click Next> to continue.

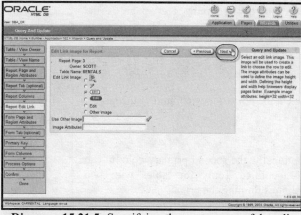

Diagram 15.21.5: Specifying the appearance of the edit link on the Details section's report page.

The **Identify Page and Region Attributes for Form** page is the **sixth step** in the wizard. Refer diagram 15.21.6.

Specify a non-existing page number for the **Page** field, (in this case **4**). As the **page** specified does not exist, the wizard will create it

After providing the values for the attributes of the form's page and region, click Next> to continue.

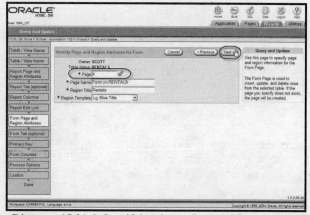

Diagram 15.21.6: Specifying the attributes of the new form.

The **seventh step** is the **Identify Tab for Form** page as shown in diagram 15.21.7.

This page provides three options:
- ❏ Do not use tabs.
- ❏ Use an existing tab set and create a new tab within the existing tab set.
- ❏ Use an existing tab set and reuse an existing tab within the tab set.

Select the **Do not use tabs** option and click Next> to continue.

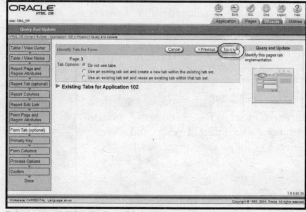

Diagram 15.21.7: Specifying the option to display the form on a page without tabs.

The **Identify Primary Key** page is the **eighth step** in the wizard. Refer diagram 15.21.8.

Select the primary key column of the table.

Optionally, the second primary column can be identified, (only for tables with two columns forming the primary key).

Click 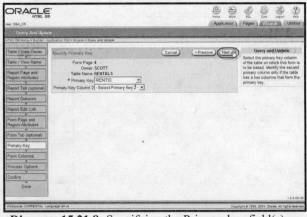 to continue.

Diagram 15.21.8: Specifying the Primary key field(s) on the Details section's form.

The **ninth step** is the **Identify Columns for Form** page as shown in diagram 15.21.9.

Select the columns to be included in the form page, (i.e. columns to be represented by a data capture field on the form). Click Next >

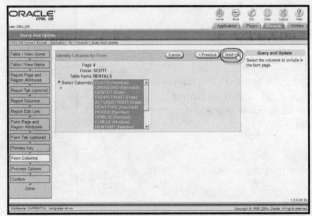

Diagram 15.21.9: Specifying the columns, which have a data entry field on the Details section's form.

The **tenth step** is the **Identity Process Options** page as shown in diagram 15.21.10.

This page identifies the processes the form allows a user. The processes include operations like Insert, Update and Delete. (Select **Yes** for all three processes.)

Click Next > to continue.

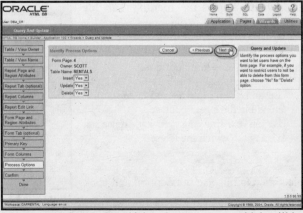

Diagram 15.21.10: Specifying the processes, which will be available on the Details section's form.

The **eleventh step** is the **Confirm** page as shown in diagram 15.21.11.

This page gives a summary of the options selected via the steps for creating the Form with Report.

Use the `< Previous` button to make changes to the attributes of the Form with Report if required.

To confirm the creation of the Form with Report click `Finish`.

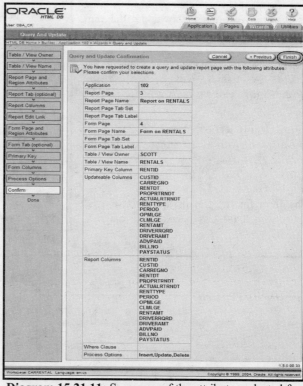

Diagram 15.21.11: Summary of the attributes selected for the creation of the Details section's report with a form.

The report is created along with its form. The confirmation appears on the Application Builder's **Home** page, Refer diagram 15.22.

Click on the **Run Page** link to execute the application.

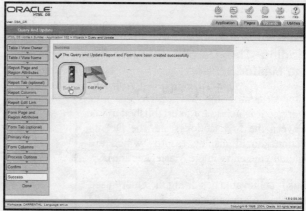

Diagram 15.22: Selecting the option to run the Details section's report with a form.

The **Home** page for the application now displays a report as shown in diagram 15.23.1.

The detail section report now displays all the records by default. *This is because the master-detail relationship is yet to be set.*

In the Details section, click Create to get the data entry form as shown in diagram 15.23.2.

The form for the Details section (Rentals) appears in a tab-less page. Refer diagram 15.23.3.

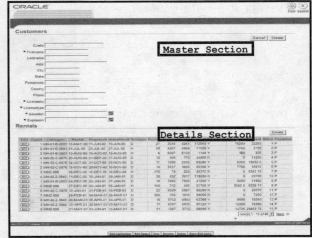

Diagram 15.23.1: The Master Details User Interface.

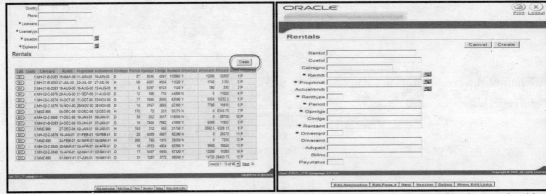

Diagram 15.23.2: Details section's Create option selected.   **Diagram 15.23.3:** Form page bound to the Rentals table.

Binding The Details Section To The Master Section

After designing the Master Details user interface it is necessary to established a link between the two sections, (i.e. the Details section should display records which are bound to the entry in the Master section).

This is achievable be editing the Query used to retrieve information for the Details section.

To bind the two sections the steps are as follows:
Return to the Master Details user interface. Click the **Edit Page 3** link placed on the page's Footer bar. Refer diagram 15.24.

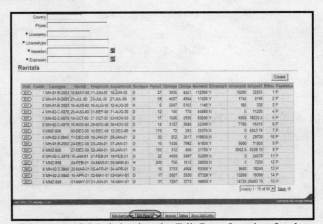

Diagram 15.24: Selecting the Edit Page 3 option for the Footer bar on the Master Details user interface.

The Page Definition page for the Master Details user interface page appears as shown in diagram 15.25.

This page displays the property for the Master Details user interface page. The properties of the page is divided into three main categories, namely:

❏ Page Rendering – Contains sub-section such as Page, Regions, Buttons, Items, Computations and Processes
❏ Page Processing – Contains sub-section such as Computations, Validations, Processes and Branching
❏ Shared Components – Contains sub-section such as Parent Tabs, Standard Tabs, Lists of Values, Templates and Navigation Bar

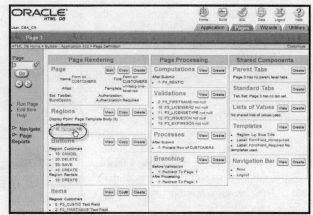

Diagram 15.25: The Page Definition for the Master Details user interface page.

The **Regions** sub-section (found under the Page Rendering division) displays various regions present on the page. Click the region for the details section, (i.e. the option labeled **Q Rentals**) to get the property page of the report displayed on the Master Details user interface.

The **Edit Page Region** page appears as shown in diagram 15.26.1. The page provided access to the settings of the Report on the Master Details user interface.

Click the internal page hyperlink labeled **Source**, (refer diagram 15.26.1).

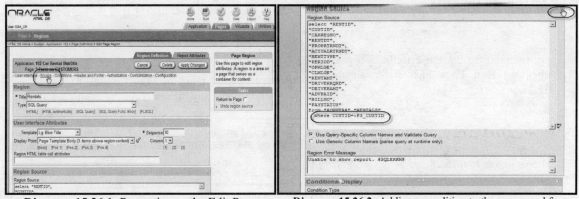

Diagram 15.26.1: Properties on the Edit Page Region page for the Details section's report.

Diagram 15.26.2: Adding a condition to the query used for retrieving details information.

The internal link scrolls the Edit Page Region to the Region Source section. Refer diagram 15.26.2. The section displays the query used for retrieving rows for the details section's report in the Master Details user interface.

Append the condition to the query to restrict the rows retrieved to the master section. The condition will be structured as:

　　　WHERE <Details Table Column>=<Master Form Field>

In the illustration used for explaining the Master Details user interface, the where clause will appear as shown below:

where CUSTID=:P3_CUSTID

Refer diagram 15.26.2.

Here, P3_CUSTID is the field within the Master section's form, (bound to the **CustId** column in the **Customers** table). The colon (**:**) is used to distinguish between a variable / field name and a column in the database table. *P3 is the page number and CUSTID is the column name.*

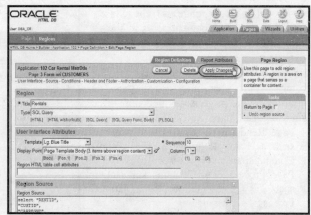

Diagram 15.26.3: Applying changes made via the Edit Page Region for the Master Details user interface page.

After appending the query click 🔝 to return to the top of the current page.

When returned to top of the **Edit Page Region** page, click **Apply Changes** to confirm and apply the changes made on the page. Refer diagram 15.26.3.

On returning to the **Page Definition** page, click the **Run Page** link. Refer diagram 15.27.

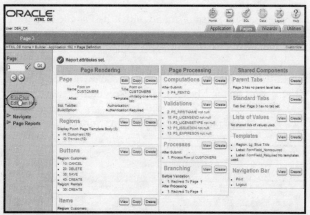

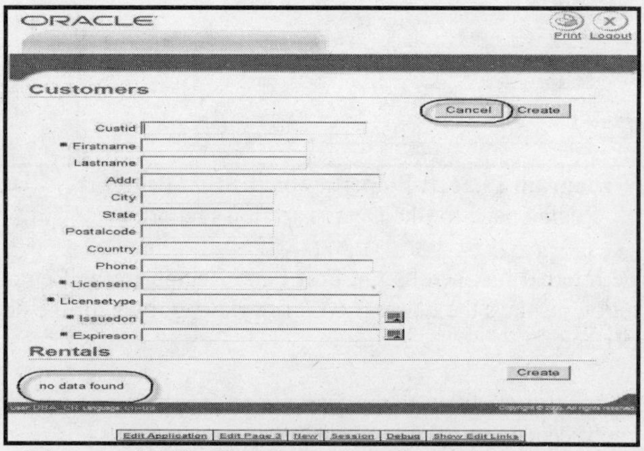

Diagram 15.27: Running the Master Details user interface page after modifying the query for the details section.

The Master Details user interface appears as shown in diagram 15.28.

The Details section is now bound to the Master section and no rows are retrieved for the report. This is because the master section is empty and hence the details section cannot fulfill the condition specified.

Click **Cancel** to return to the report of the Master section.

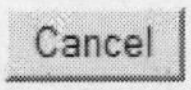

Diagram 15.28: The Master Details user interface page with no information for the details section.

When the report page for Master section appears (i.e. Customers report), click on the **Edit** option besides any one record in the report. Refer diagram 15.29.1.

The Master Details user interface appears as shown in diagram 15.29.2.

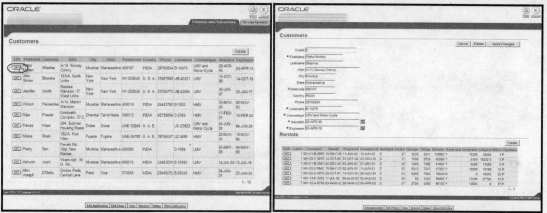

Diagram 15.29.1: Selecting the Edit link on the report page bound to the Customers table.

Diagram 15.29.2: Master Details user interface page for Customer-wise Transactions in the edit mode.

To edit a record in the details section click on the **Edit** option besides any one record in the report section, (i.e. Rentals report). Refer diagram 15.30.1.

The form page for the Details section appears as shown in diagram 15.30.2.

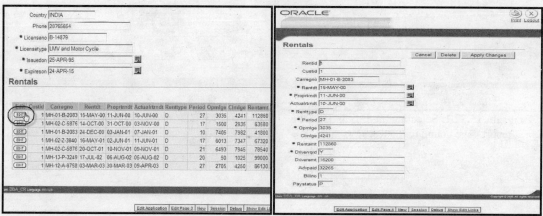

Diagram 15.30.1: Selecting the Edit link on the report page bound to the Rentals table.

Diagram 15.30.2: Form page bound to the Details table Rentals.

Follow the same steps to create the Master Details User Interface for the Bill-wise Payments tab in the system.

Following are the screenshots of Master Details user interface manually created for the Bill-wise Payments tab: (Refer diagrams 15.31.1 to 15.32.2.)

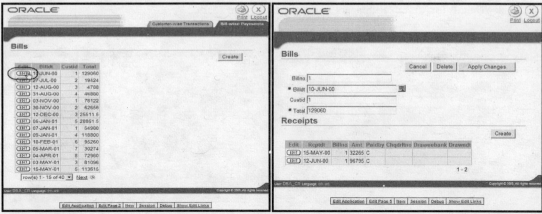

Diagram 15.31.2: Selecting the Edit link on the report page bound to the Bills table.

Diagram 15.31.2: Master Details user interface page for Bill-wise Payments in the edit mode.

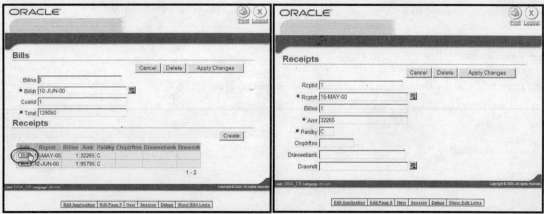

Diagram 15.32.1: Selecting the Edit link on the report page bound to the Receipts table.

Diagram 15.32.2: Form page bound to the Details table Receipts.

16. REPORTS AND CHARTS

CREATING REPORTS

After valid data is stored in Oracle tables, it is necessary to extract this data from the table, process this raw data as required and finally display it on a VDU or obtain hard copy from a printer. The simplest processing done to raw table data is **formatting** it as required by business managers before its display on a VDU or taking a printout. A more sophisticated way of processing raw table data would be converting it to graphs, which displays statistical data in the form of a picture.

Business managers then use this output to make informed business decisions based on their interpretation of the data displayed either on VDU or via a print out on paper.

The process of data extraction, processing it appropriately and finally displaying it is called **Report creation**. For creating reports, Oracle HTMLDB provides a **Report Component**, which can be placed on a page. This component accepts an SQL Query as input and provides the output in HTML format.

To begin creating reports an application needs to be created which will hold all the required reports. However, adding an **extra page** to the existing application will also do.

The focus here is to create three reports displaying the following:
1. Customer-Wise Transactions
2. Car-Wise Transactions
3. Customer-Wise Payments

The SQL Queries for the above said reports will be as follows:
1. **Customer-Wise Transactions**
SQL:
SELECT FirstName, LastName, **SUM(ADVPAID) AS** "Advance Recd.",
    SUM(RentAmt) AS "Amount Earned **AS** Rent", **Sum(ClMlge-OpMlge) AS** "Kms. Runned"
    FROM CUSTOMERS, RENTALS
       WHERE CUSTOMERS.CUSTID = RENTALS.CUSTID
          GROUP BY FirstName, LastName;

When the above query is fired in SQL *PLUS:

```
FIRSTNAME       LASTNAME        Advance Recd. Amount Earned AS Rent Kms. Runned
-------------   -------------   ------------- --------------------- -----------
Raju            Prasad             138181.88                631040        8769
Mosie           Shah                   22650                 90600        2000
Parvez          Khan                   37670                141680        3743
Preity          Sen                    80665                313060        4421
Wilson          Fernandes              40920                163680        3439
Ashwini         Joshi                  15500                139150        2485
Jennifer        Smith               49043.75                284795        4615
John Simon      Brownie                63150                331010        4047
Alex Joseph     D'Mello                92080                463870        6704
Rahul Mohan     Sharma              129212.5                549230        8524

10 rows selected.
```

The above query displays all those customers involved in rental transactions along with the following details:

- **Advance Received**
- **Amount Earned As Rent**
- **Kms. Runned**

These details are calculated on the rental transactions performed and displayed on a per customer basis.

2. Car-Wise Transactions

SQL:
SELECT MODEL, MAKE, **SUM**(RentAmt) **AS** "Amount Earned As Rent",
    Sum(ClMlge-OpMlge) **AS** "Kms. Runned"
    FROM CARS, RENTALS
        WHERE CARS.CARREGNO = RENTALS.CARREGNO
           GROUP BY MODEL,MAKE;

When the above query is fired in SQL *PLUS:

MODEL	MAKE	Amount Earned As Rent	Kms. Runned
800	Maruti	181830	3394
Omni	Maruti	452540	7393
Sumo	Tata	578160	10798
Esteem	Maruti	430160	6454
Indica	Tata	259160	3502
Qualis	Toyota	430650	5830
Safari	Tata	137500	1623
Santro	Hyundai	157850	2830
Premium	Padmini	286665	5042
Indica V2	Tata	193600	1881

10 rows selected.

The above query displays all those cars (Model and the Make) involved in rental transactions along with the following details:

- **Amount Earned As Rent**
- **Kms. Runned**

These details are calculated on the rental transactions performed and displayed on a per car (Model →
Make) basis.

3. Customer-Wise Payments

SQL:
SELECT FIRSTNAME, LASTNAME, RENTID, RENTALS.BILLNO, BILLDT, TOTAL,
    RCPTID, RCPTDT, AMT
    FROM CUSTOMERS, RENTALS, BILLS, RECEIPTS
        WHERE CUSTOMERS.CUSTID = RENTALS.CUSTID
           AND RENTALS.BILLNO = BILLS.BILLNO
           AND BILLS.BILLNO = RECEIPTS.BILLNO;

When the above query is fired in SQL *PLUS:

FIRSTNAME	LASTNAME	RENTID	BILLNO	BILLDT	TOTAL	RCPTID	RCPTDT	AMT
Rahul Mohan	Sharma	1	1	10-JUN-00	129060	1	15-MAY-00	32265
Rahul Mohan	Sharma	1	1	10-JUN-00	129060	2	12-JUN-00	96795
John Simon	Brownie	2	2	27-JUL-00	19424	3	21-JUL-00	3190
John Simon	Brownie	2	2	27-JUL-00	19424	4	27-JUL-00	16234
Jennifer	Smith	3	3	12-AUG-00	4788	5	10-AUG-00	330
Wilson	Fernandes	4	4	31-AUG-00	44880	6	20-AUG-00	11220
Jennifer	Smith	3	3	12-AUG-00	4788	7	02-SEP-00	4458
Wilson	Fernandes	4	4	31-AUG-00	44880	8	04-SEP-00	33660
Rahul Mohan	Sharma	5	5	03-NOV-00	78122	9	14-OCT-00	18232.5
Rahul Mohan	Sharma	5	5	03-NOV-00	78122	10	08-NOV-00	59889.5
John Simon	Brownie	6	6	30-NOV-00	62656	11	15-NOV-00	15015
Jennifer	Smith	7	7	12-DEC-00	25511.5	12	05-DEC-00	6343.75
Wilson	Fernandes	8	10	09-JAN-01	118800	13	11-DEC-00	29700
Rahul Mohan	Sharma	9	9	07-JAN-01	54980	14	16-DEC-00	43030
Rahul Mohan	Sharma	9	9	07-JAN-01	54980	15	24-DEC-00	11950
Raju	Prasad	10	8	05-JAN-01	28861.5	16	27-DEC-00	6328.13
Raju	Prasad	10	8	05-JAN-01	28861.5	17	07-JAN-01	22533.38
. . .								
Jennifer	Smith	24	24	21-JAN-02	103448	47	23-DEC-01	22990
Preity	Sen	25	25	10-FEB-02	167200	48	02-JAN-02	41800
Jennifer	Smith	24	24	21-JAN-02	103448	49	21-JAN-02	80458
Preity	Sen	25	25	10-FEB-02	167200	50	12-MAR-02	125400
Alex Joseph	D'Mello	26	26	17-APR-02	95200	51	25-MAR-02	22990
Raju	Prasad	27	27	05-JUN-02	137390	52	27-APR-02	32725
Alex Joseph	D'Mello	26	26	17-APR-02	95200	53	02-MAY-02	72210
Mosie	Shah	28	28	05-JUN-02	70825	54	15-MAY-02	15400
Parvez	Khan	29	29	01-JUL-02	68400	55	17-JUN-02	17100
Raju	Prasad	27	27	05-JUN-02	137390	56	25-JUN-02	104665
Mosie	Shah	28	28	05-JUN-02	70825	57	30-JUN-02	55425
Preity	Sen	30	30	24-JUL-02	82500	58	10-JUL-02	20625
Rahul Mohan	Sharma	31	31	05-AUG-02	111000	59	17-JUL-02	27750
Parvez	Khan	29	29	01-JUL-02	68400	60	02-AUG-02	51300
Rahul Mohan	Sharma	31	31	05-AUG-02	111000	61	23-AUG-02	83250
Preity	Sen	30	30	24-JUL-02	82500	62	17-AUG-02	61875
Raju	Prasad	33	33	14-NOV-02	83250	63	31-OCT-02	20812.5
Raju	Prasad	33	33	14-NOV-02	83250	64	28-NOV-02	62437.5

64 rows selected.

The above query displays the following details:
- **Customer's First And Last Name**
- **Rental Identity via which the transaction was performed**
- **Billing Details such as:**
  - **Bill Number**
  - **Bill Date**
  - **Total Amount Of Bill**
- **Receipt Details such as:**
  - **Receipt Number**
  - **Receipt Date**
  - **Amount Of Receipt**

This report thus shows the total amount a customer has to pay (i.e. The Bill Amount) and the amount a customer has paid (i.e. The Receipt Amount against the Bill Amount).

To begin creating the above reports it is assumed that an application with three blank pages on three new tabs is already created. *(The application can be created by following the steps as shown in Chapter 14.)*

The application looks like the one seen in diagram 16.1

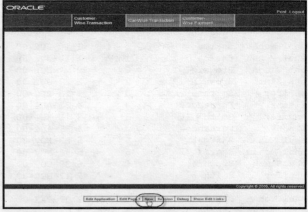

Diagram 16.1: An Empty Application For Reports.

Select the **Customer-Wise Transaction** tab and click **New**, Refer diagram 16.1.

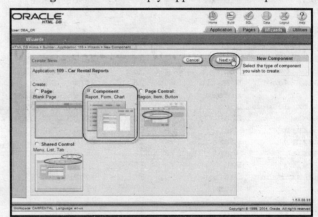

The **Create New** page appears as seen in diagram 16.2, Select **Component** and click Next >.

Diagram 16.2: The Create New page.

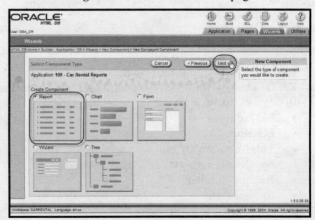

The **Select Component Type** page appears as seen in diagram 16.3, Select **Report** among the types of components displayed and click Next >.

Diagram 16.3: The Component Type page.

The **Select Report Type** page appears as seen in diagram 16.4, Select **SQL Report** among the types of reports displayed and click Next >.

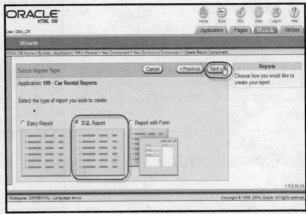

Diagram 16.4: The Report Type page.

The **Identify Page Attributes** page appears as seen in diagram 16.5.1. This page will accept the Page Number and the Page Name. Enter an appropriate page name and keep the page number unchanged. This means that the report component will be added on an already existing page numbered 1. No new page will be created.

Click Next > to continue.

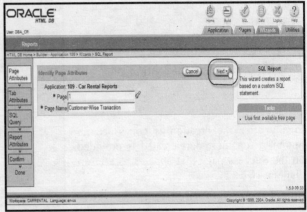

Diagram 16.5.1: The Identity Page Attributes page.

The **Tab attributes** page will be skipped as the page number while specifying the page attributes was unchanged. This means no new tab will be created.

The **SQL Query** page appears as seen in diagram 16.5.2. Enter the SQL Query responsible to generate the actual report. This is because SQL Query type of report was selected while the report creation process.

Click Next > to continue.

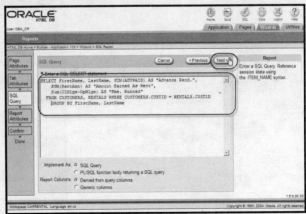

Diagram 16.5.2: The SQL Query page.

The Report Attributes page appears as seen in diagram 16.5.3.

This page will allow selection of a template to suit the report needs. It also accepts the maximum rows to be displayed per page, the region name and so on.

Click 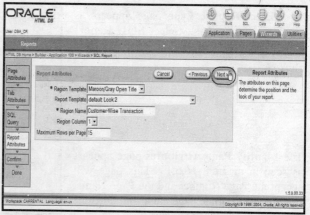 to continue.

This completes the steps involved in report creation. The completion is confirmed with a SQL Report Confirmation page as seen in diagram 16.5.4.

Click **Finish** to accept the confirmation.

Diagram 16.5.3: The Reports Attributes page.

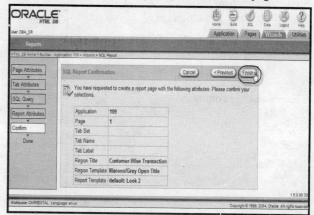

Finally after the creation is confirmed an option to run the report created is provided on the **Success** page that appears as seen in diagram 16.6.

Click **Run Page** link to run the report created.

Diagram 16.5.4: The SQL Report Confirmation page.

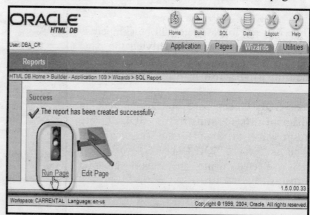

Diagram 16.6: The Success page.

The **Customer-Wise Transaction** report runs as seen in diagram 16.7.1.

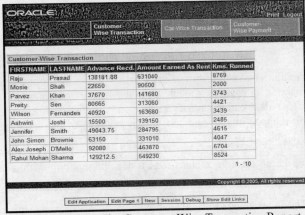

Diagram 16.7.1: The Customer-Wise Transaction Report.

Similarly, following the steps as seen earlier while creating the **Customer-Wise Transaction**, create the **Car-Wise Transaction** and **Customer-Wise Payment** reports.

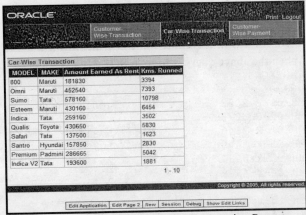

Diagram 16.7.2: The Car-Wise Transaction Report.

After creation the reports will look like the ones seen in diagrams 16.7.2 and 16.7.3.

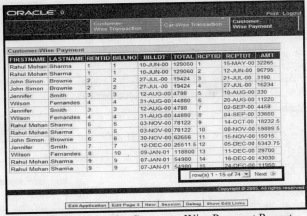

Diagram 16.7.3: The Customer-Wise Payment Report.

If the number of rows to be displayed exceed 10 then a combo box as seen diagram 16.7.3 appears allowing traversing through next 10 rows.

CREATING CHARTS

Corporations today are flooded with valuable information. The challenge is to transform this flood of information in a format, which is easily understood by business managers.

A chart is a visual form of information representation, which can display a lot of information in a compact manner. A chart is a mechanism that allows organization staff to visually analyze business information. Chart data can be retrieved from a variety of sources and displayed, using pie charts, line drawing, bit-mapped images and so on. An example of the use of a chart in a Car–Wise Revenue is shown in the diagram 16.14.

To begin creating a chart, add a new page along with a tab to the Car Rental Reports Application just created for Reports.

The focus here is to create a simple vertical bar chart displaying the following:
1.   Car–Wise Revenue

The SQL-Queries for the above said reports will be as follows:
SELECT CarRegNo, **SUM**(RentAmt)
    FROM Rentals **GROUP BY** CarRegNo;

When the above query is fired in SQL *PLUS:

```
CARREGNO                 SUM(RENTAMT)
-------------------      ------------
MH-01-B-2083                   430160
MH-02-C-5876                   452540
MH-02-Z-3840                   578160
MH-03-F-3499                   157850
MH-03-X-0987                   259160
MH-04-Y-4849                   137500
MH-12-A-8758                   181830
MH-13-P-3249                   430650
MH-14-Y-4039                   193600
MMZ-888                        286665

10 rows selected.
```

The above query displays all cars along with:
❑ **Sum of Revenue Earned**

These details are calculated on the rental transactions performed and displayed per car basis.

To begin creating the above charts run the application having the three reports generated earlier.

The application looks like the one seen in diagram 16.8.

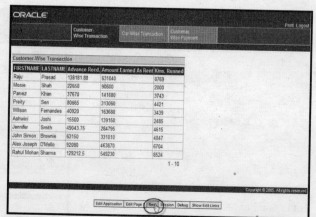

Diagram 16.8: New option clicked from the Footer bar.

In the **Customer-Wise Transaction** tab, click **New** option from the footer bar. Refer diagram 16.8.

The **Create New** page appears as seen in diagram 16.9.

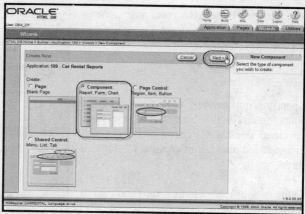

Select **Component** option and click Next >.

Diagram 16.9: Selecting the Component option from the Create New page.

The **Select Component Type** page appears as seen in diagram 16.10.

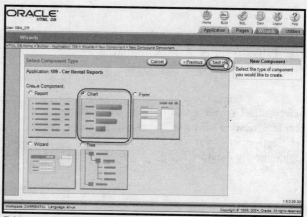

Select the **Chart** option from the types of components displayed and click Next >.

Diagram 16.10: Selecting the Chart option from the Select Component Type page.

The **Select Type of Chart** page appears as seen in diagram 16.11.

This page provides the following options for selecting the Chart type:
❑ SVG
❑ HTML

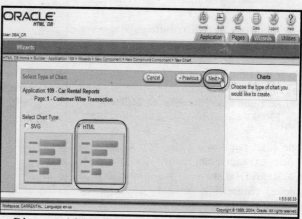

Select **HTML** option and click Next >.

Diagram 16.11: Selecting the HTML option from the Select Type of Chart page.

The **Identify Page Attributes** page appears as seen in diagram 16.12.1. This page will accept the Page Number and the Page Name.

Specify a non-existing page number in the **Page** field, (in this case **4**). As the **page** specified does not exist, the wizard will create it and also ask to create a tab for that page.

Enter an appropriate **page name** and **region name**.

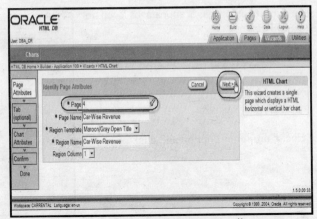

Diagram 16.12.1: The Identity Page Attributes page.

Click Next> to continue.

The **Tab attributes** page is displayed as shown in diagram 16.12.2.

Select the **Use an existing tab set and create a new tab within the existing tab set** option to get addition field as highlighted in diagram 16.12.2.

Select the existing tab and specify a label for the new tab.

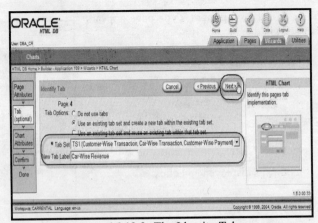

Diagram 16.12.2: The Identity Tab page.

Click Next> to continue.

The **Identity Chart Attribute** page appears as seen in diagram 16.12.3.

Enter the following SQL Query responsible to generate the actual chart:
SELECT null link, CarRegNo, **SUM**(RentAmt)
    FROM Rentals **GROUP BY** CarRegNo;

The chart requires a Link/URL to point to when an individual entity (in this case **CarRegNo**) displayed via the query is clicked. Since just a chart needs to be created, no link is specified, but the link i.e. the first column in the query being a parameter a **null link** is passed. Click Next> to continue.

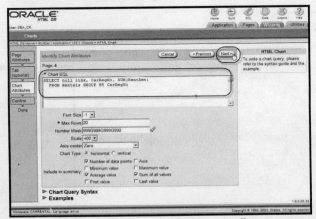

Diagram 16.12.3: The Identify Chart Attribute page.

The **HTML Chart Confirmation** page appears as seen in diagram 16.12.4.

This page gives a summary of the options selected via the steps for creating the Chart.

Click Finish to accept the confirmation.

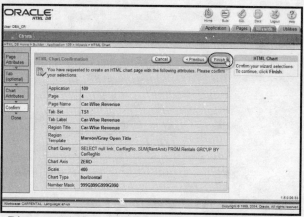

Diagram 16.12.4: The HTML Chart Confirmation page.

Finally after the creation is confirmed an option to run the report created is provided on the **Success** page that appears as seen in diagram 16.13.

Click **Run Page** link to run the report created.

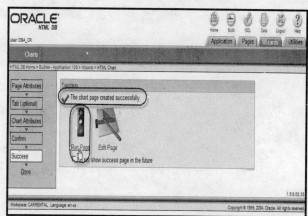

Diagram 16.13: The Run Page option clicked in the Success page.

The **Car-Wise Revenue** chart runs as seen in diagram 16.14.

The chart is displayed on the newly created page, which in turn is placed within the newly created tab. Refer diagram 16.14.

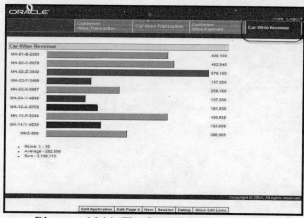

Diagram 16.14: The Car-Wise Revenue Chart.

INDEX